EXSIOR, MN

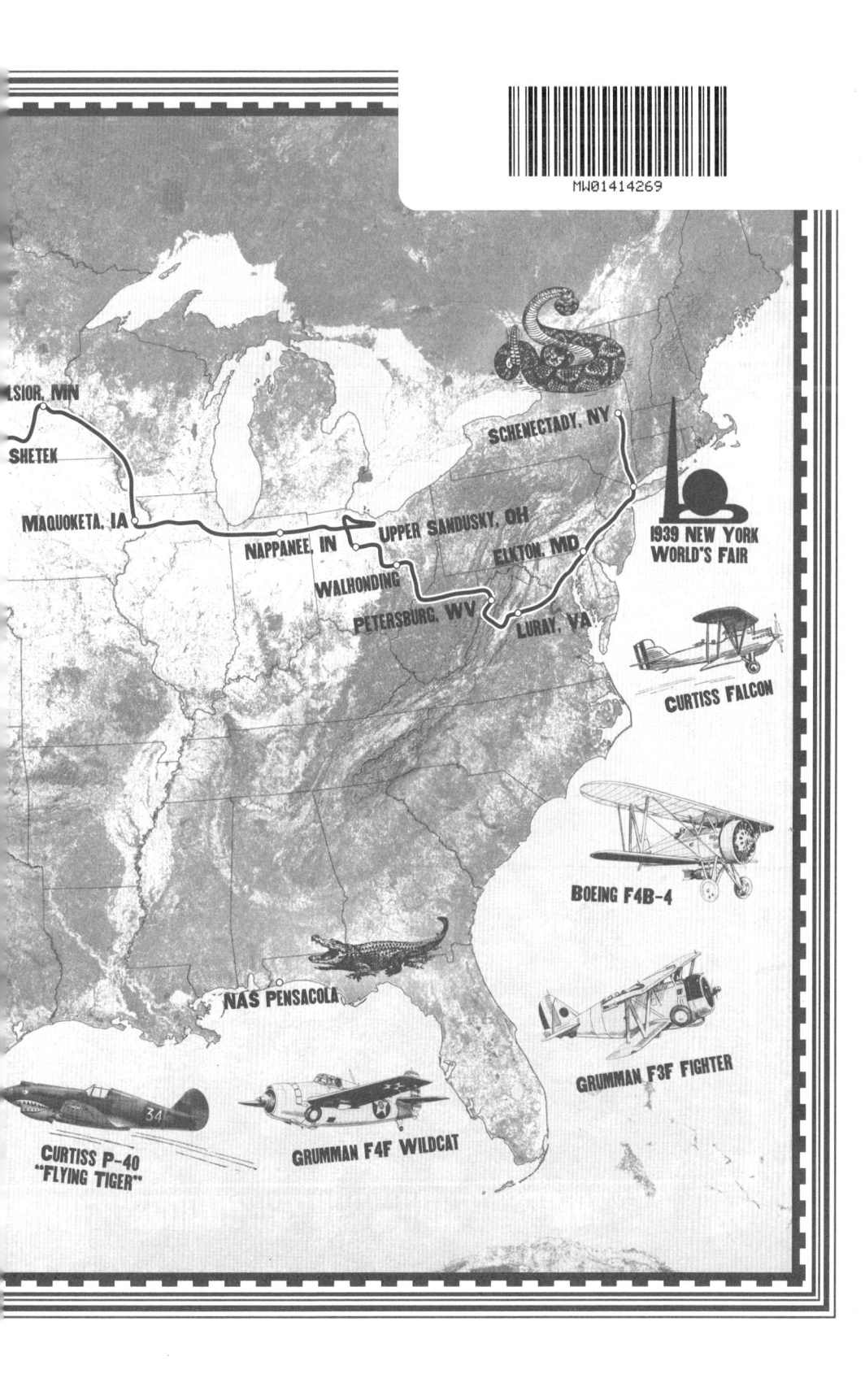

SHETEK

MAQUOKETA, IA

NAPPANEE, IN

UPPER SANDUSKY, OH

WALHONDING

PETERSBURG, WV

SCHENECTADY, NY

ELKTON, MD

LURAY, VA

1939 NEW YORK WORLD'S FAIR

CURTISS FALCON

BOEING F4B-4

NAS PENSACOLA

GRUMMAN F3F FIGHTER

CURTISS P-40 "FLYING TIGER"

GRUMMAN F4F WILDCAT

# THE OLD MAN
★ ★ ★ AND THE ★ ★ ★
# HARLEY

# THE OLD MAN
★ ★ ★ AND THE ★ ★ ★
# HARLEY

*A Last Ride Through Our* **FATHERS' AMERICA**

## JOHN J. NEWKIRK

**Thomas Nelson**
*Since 1798*

NASHVILLE   DALLAS   MEXICO CITY   RIO DE JANEIRO   BEIJING

© 2008 by John J. Newkirk

All rights reserved. No portion of this book may be reproduced, stored in a retrieval system, or transmitted in any form or by any means—electronic, mechanical, photocopy, recording, scanning, or other—except for brief quotations in critical reviews or articles, without the prior written permission of the publisher.

Published in Nashville, Tennessee. Thomas Nelson is a registered trademark of Thomas Nelson, Inc.

Published in association with the literary agency of WordServe Literary Group, Ltd., 10152 S. Knoll Circle, Highlands Ranch, Colorado, 80130.

The flying Bengal tiger logo is a registered trademark of the Flying Tigers Association and is reprinted with their permission.

The following story is true. While every effort has been made to ensure accuracy, in some cases the author's sources conflicted with each other. In such circumstances, the license granted historical novelists was used to reconstruct the most plausible scenario. Various names, dates, and places have been altered to protect individual privacy.

Certain language, idioms, or period phrases within the narrative may be offensive to some, but are included to accurately depict the prevailing cultural milieu.

The audiobook derivative of *The Old Man and the Harley* contains historic recordings from 1939 as well as live audio recorded during the modern retracing. It is read by the author and set to the music of Aaron Copland, Glenn Miller, William Grant Still, and others. For a gallery of photos and audio clips, please visit www.theoldmanandtheharley.com.

Thomas Nelson, Inc., titles may be purchased in bulk for educational, business, fund-raising, or sales promotional use. For information, please e-mail SpecialMarkets@ThomasNelson.com.

ISBN: 978-1-59555-180-1

*Printed in the United States of America*

08 09 10 11 12 QW 6 5 4 3 2 1

To the memory of
Allen B. Christman
Flight Leader
American Volunteer Group
and
Major Alton G. Miller
U.S. Army Air Corps

★ ★ ★

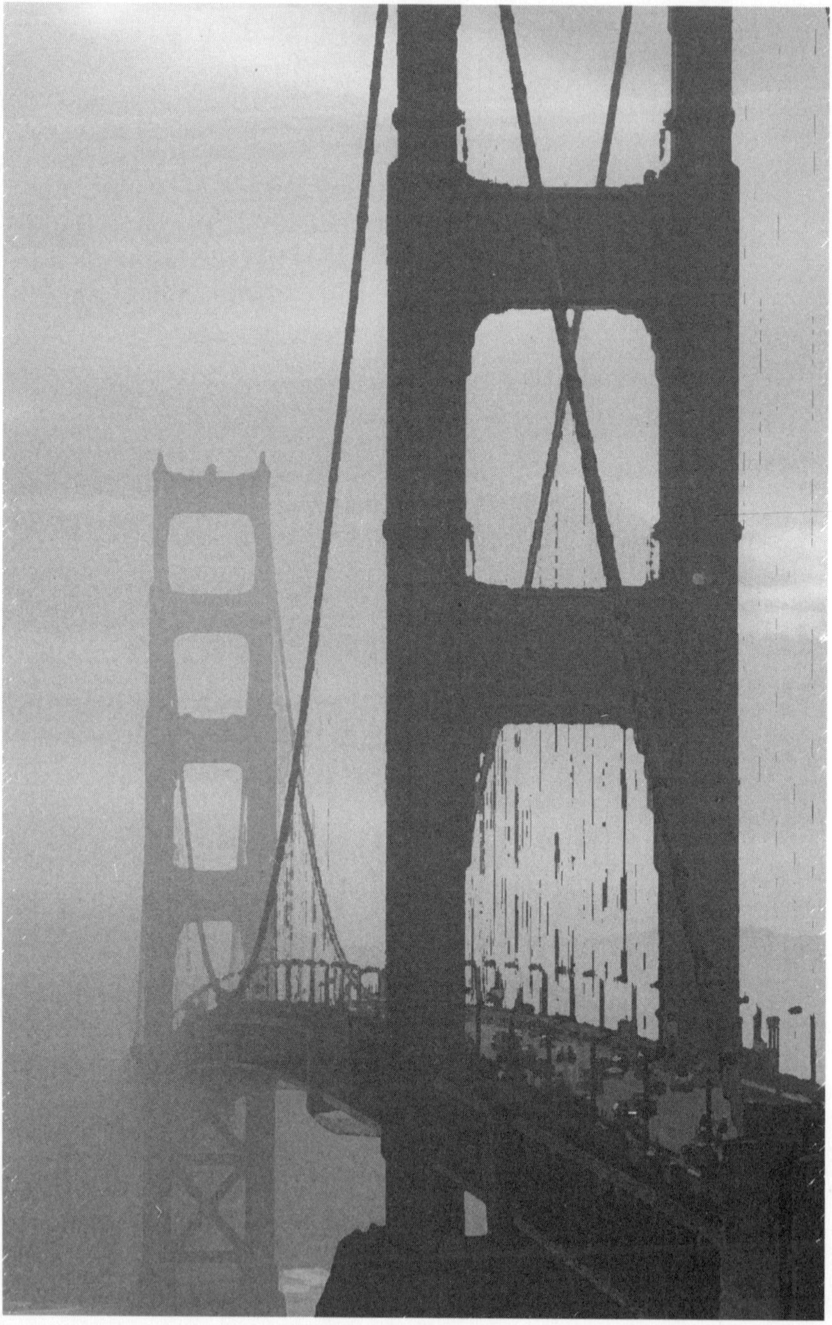

*O wad some Power the giftie gie us*
*To see oursels as others see us!*
—Robert Burns

IT'S SUNRISE ON a Sunday and San Francisco is a quiet city. I sit at the crest of the Golden Gate Bridge and watch the sun creep over Mount Diablo as it burns off the fog blanketing the bay. My Harley waits patiently as a squad car rolls by, and the cop inside gives me a wary eye. Maybe he thinks I'm a jumper. Or maybe he just doesn't like the looks of me.

From head to toe, I'm covered in leather: boots, chaps, and a leather jacket festooned with patches. On my back there's an embroidered outline of the Golden Gate and a white, three-sided dagger points skyward next to what looks like a baseball. On my right shoulder a Bengal tiger pounces on an unseen enemy. On my left a panda bear sits beside the number thirty-four.

The cop slows down and asks if everything's all right.

I nod. But the fact is, I see ghosts.

To the north, three ghost riders on Harleys roar out of the mist. Their leader is a skinny kid, pumping both fists in the air and laughing out loud.

He kind of looks like me.

A foghorn blasts from a spectral ship below, and I can just make out the letters on her hull: *Jagersfontein*. She's Dutch. A dark-haired rogue peers upward from the deck with his right hand raised and fingers stretched up to the sky. A stunning blond appears at the bridge rail in high heels and a silky dress; a string of pearls dangles from her neck as she leans over the water and hurls something over the side. As the ship disappears, another takes its place: the *Bloemfontein*. The ships leave full of young men. They come back empty.

In a biker's world it's all about respect. And I certainly have some respects to pay as I stand here on this bridge. This place draws me to it—

and its ghosts call out names that, until now, meant very little to me: Jack, Pete, and June; Scarsdale and Janie; Bert, Pappy, Tex, Buster, Charlie.

To the cop it looks as if I ride alone. But from now on, I know I never will.

★ ★ ★

**EARLIER—10,371 MILES EARLIER**—I'd flipped down my kickstand beside the San Francisco waterfront. My leathers squeaked as I stretched my road-weary limbs. Then, slowly and deliberately, I walked down the sidewalk toward the imposing stone archway of San Francisco's Pier 33.

I had looked forward to this moment most of my life.

Through this portal, my father—and thousands of other young Americans—shipped out to the South Pacific during World War II. My uncle Horace served at the naval shipyard down the street. And it was here that my father's cousin—my namesake—John "Scarsdale Jack" Newkirk set sail for China on July 10, 1941.

In the early days of the war, Scarsdale Jack was one of the most written-about fighter pilots in the nation. As squadron leader of Chennault's legendary Flying Tigers, Jack inspired millions during the dark days that followed Pearl Harbor by leading what historians now consider the first American offensive mission of World War II. He was one of the nation's top aces until a Japanese machine gunner shot down his shark-toothed P-40 fighter plane on March 24, 1942.

Now—more than six decades later—I stood at the arch of Pier 33 in the shadow of my forefathers.

We'd come full circle.

Young, strong, alive, and free—I embodied what they fought for. I wanted them to be proud, and I hoped the departed would rest in peace knowing the torch had been passed to a grateful generation, ready and willing to take on all enemies.

I thrust a fist into the air and walked resolutely back to the Harley, ready to begin the journey. I would ride from San Francisco to New York, retracing my father's solo motorcycle trip between the 1939 New York World's Fair and San Francisco's Golden Gate Exposition, those two epic events of that last, gilded summer before the war changed the world—and my family—forever.

A lump of resentment began to rise in my throat.

My father—untimely ripped from his boyhood and thrust into a war in the South Pacific. Scarsdale Jack—a man whose name I carried but whom I would never meet. And the thousands of men who went on to die from Japanese bullets, torpedoes, or kamikazes.

*But we showed them*, I gloated. *By God, we showed them.*

Coral Sea. Midway. Guadalcanal. Iwo Jima. Okinawa. Hiroshima. Nagasaki.

Feeling almost godlike, I swung my leg over the saddle, fired up the V-twin, and pointed the Harley toward the Golden Gate Bridge.

But I hadn't gone a block before I saw a crowd gathering in the plaza west of the pier.

Although I had many miles to go that day, a voice inside told me to stop right then and there. As if guided by unseen hands, I popped the Harley onto the sidewalk, rumbled slowly over the concrete squares of Embarcadero Plaza, and parked between two limos.

An official waved me close to the stage. Apparently my leather vest and long-lensed Nikon camera made him think I was press. What was going on here?

A magnificent, white sailing ship was docked at the pier. Her four masts stretched a hundred feet into the sky and towered over the small group of Japanese monks gathered onstage.

I strained to read the calligraphy swirling around their broad straw hats.

It said, "Full Circle."

A few feet to my right, a commanding figure with black hair and a ponytail sat beside an old Japanese man. The dark-haired man looked vaguely familiar. He glanced my way, nodded politely, and then turned his eyes toward the woman at the microphone. The crowd fell silent as she spoke: "Today, July 16, marks sixty years since world war led us to create the atomic bomb. The first detonation took place on this date in 1945 at the Trinity test site near Los Alamos, New Mexico."

I was stunned at the coincidence. I'd unknowingly arrived on the anniversary of the world's first atomic bomb detonation—the same day the doomed USS *Indianapolis* departed from this harbor for the island of Tinian, not far from where my father was stationed. The ship carried the bomb that *Enola Gay* would drop over Hiroshima.

The woman continued:

> Behind me is the tall ship *Nippon Maru*, an international symbol of peace, friendship, and cultural exchange. Being escorted to the podium by actor Steven Seagal is Mr. Takashi Tanemori, who was playing hide-and-seek in his schoolyard when the first atomic bomb exploded over Hiroshima. He is carrying a lantern with the actual atomic flame that was kindled from the embers of his city. He will hand this flame to Daijo Ohta of the Zen Sotoshu in Nagasaki, who, together with monks from Nipponzan-Myohoji and Jodo Shinshu, will begin a twenty-five-day, sixteen-hundred-mile journey over mountains and across deserts to close the circle by returning the atomic flame to the exact place of its inception, where it will be extinguished in silence.

*I don't believe this*, I fumed. *These people slaughtered thousands in Nanking, Kunming—all over China! They bombed Pearl Harbor, marched my countrymen to death at Bataan, packed them into the Hell Ships, torpedoed the* Indianapolis*—and killed Scarsdale Jack! So now it's supposed to be "Hands Across America" for these guys? Give me a break!*

My jaws clenched and my brow furrowed in anger. I was ready to head back to the Harley and roar off in disgust when Steven Seagal stood up beside me and gingerly escorted the old Japanese man to the podium. The old man began to speak:

> This is my own story, to share with your children, and with your children's children. For me, it is the process—the journey—that made me who I am today. I have become a peacemaker.
>
> I had a wonderful family, with my father at the helm, and under his leadership I felt secure, protected, and guided by his strong hand. He taught me many things. It was these principles that kept me from self-destruction after I lost my family to the atomic bomb in 1945.

My life turned like a kite without a string. I was like a migrant bird unable to find a tree to rest my weary wings. Without my father's guidance, I was like a blind man groping in a cave.

The monks stared at the ground as they struggled to maintain their composure. The old man looked straight at me and began to cry.

Through my journey, I came to realize that the anger in my heart continued burning, fed by a flame I was unable to control—and that anger and revenge will continue to bring more revenge. It is never-ending!

Why can't we have peace? I ask, how can we establish global peace, if you and I cannot first have our own peace in our hearts? I believe that all human conflict and suffering is not just caused by nuclear weapons or the wars going on today—it's the wars within our own hearts.

Tears rolled down my weatherworn cheeks as the old man feebly lifted the atomic flame high into the air for all to see. The bitterness I'd nurtured for years began to melt, and at that moment I felt I was the only man standing in the Embarcadero.

I had expected him to condemn my country for its use of the atomic bomb, but he had only condemned the evil that compels men to hate each other. I realized then that these men were not the enemy. The true enemy comes in many disguises: Anger, Hatred, Misconception, Defeatism, Apathy, and Fear. All of them injure the spirit.

I smiled broadly and gave these strangers a leather-clad American Biker's Salute: *From my heart to yours, today you and I have become brothers of the open road. Go in peace, my brothers.*

The old Japanese man smiled back at me and lowered the flame. Both of us understood that we travel the same roads, and we are both on a similar journey.

★ ★ ★

## XII ★ THE OLD MAN AND THE HARLEY

"DAD!" I SHOUTED into my cell phone. "Can you hear me? I'm in San Francisco. I'm standing on the Golden Gate Bridge."

"Johnny!" he said. "I can hear you fine. Everything on schedule?"

"Yes," I replied, "I just came from Pier 33."

The Old Man paused.

"You visited the pier?" he asked.

"Yes," I answered, "and something happened there. Something I want to tell you about."

He paused again.

"I've been meaning to tell you a few things myself," he sighed. "We'll talk on the road."

"Well," I said, "I'm ready to begin the journey. See you in Montana."

"See you there," he replied.

"But Johnny," the Old Man added, "this really isn't the beginning."

"What do you mean?" I asked.

"We'll talk on the road," he repeated. "But for us, this journey really began three hundred and fifty years ago. You and I are just continuing it."

And it would be 10,371 miles later before I finally understood what the Old Man had been talking about.

# PART I

## *The World of Tomorrow*

*What you can do, or dream you can do, begin it;*
*Boldness has genius, power and magic in it.*
—Attributed to J. W. von Goethe

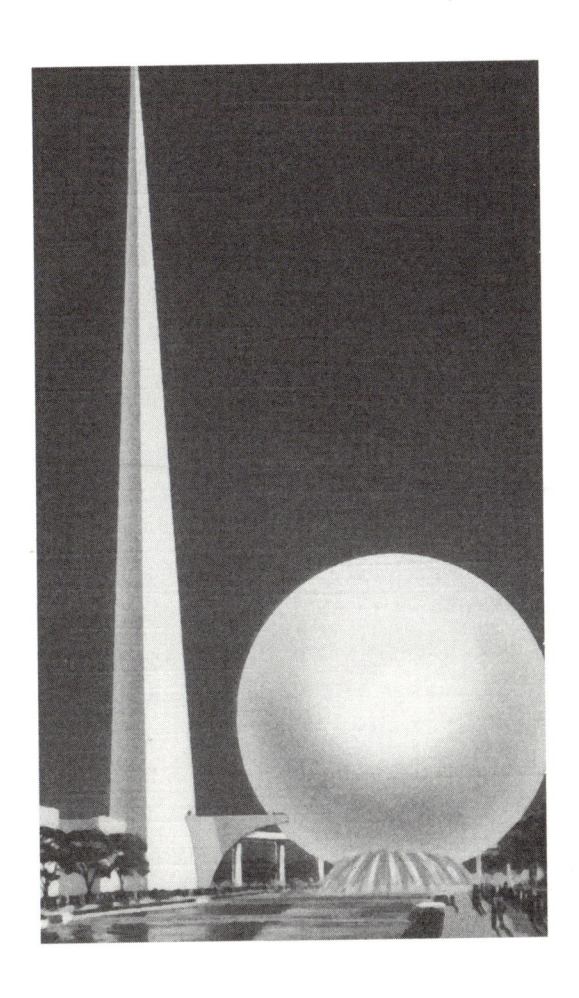

# The Promise of Living

ON THE TWENTY-FIFTH of April 1659, the Dutch ship *Moesman* sailed from Amsterdam for the Americas. For reasons unknown, perhaps to avoid the southern hurricane season, the ship took the less common northern crossing to Newfoundland and followed the Labrador stream south along the Atlantic coast. After nearly three months at sea, the *Moesman* sailed past the island of Nantucket, and Captain Jacob Janszen Staets had a decision to make.

His destination port was normally reached by skirting the southern coast of Long Island and then turning north into a narrow passage discovered 135 years earlier by Italian explorer Giovanni Verrazano.

But Captain Staets was frowning as he studied the horizon.

He didn't like the looks of the weather, and considered steering his ship into the protected waters of Long Island Sound. This route, however, meant the *Moesman* would have to navigate the Hellegat—the Hell Gate—a notorious tidal passage constricting the East River. While ships had done this for decades, it posed an additional risk to the cargo, passengers, and crew.

Atlantic storms, however, brought serious dangers of their own, and a small ship overloaded with immigrants and trade goods could easily be lost at sea.

After pacing the deck a half-dozen times, Captain Staets reluctantly ordered his helmsman west toward Block Island, and during the next few days the *Moesman* wended its way through Long Island Sound as ocean-weary passengers gazed upon the tender land with a mixture of anticipation, trepidation, and relief. As the weather improved, the emigrants were treated to spectacular views of the New World, where their Dutch compatriots had already settled such towns as Vlissingen and Breuckelen.

On the ninth of August, after successfully passing through the Hellegat, the *Moesman* dropped anchor where the East River meets the Hudson, at a large island purchased forty years earlier from local Indians. This settlement, known as New Amsterdam, sat on the southern tip of an island the natives called *Manna-hata*.

The Europeans called it "Manhattan."

Among the disembarking passengers were twenty-two-year-old Gerrit Cornelius van Nieuwkerk, his wife, and their infant son. Van Nieuwkerk, a Christian name, literally meant "of the New Church." Gerrit and his family hoped to escape the oppression of their Old World, and New Amsterdam offered the freedom to work, worship, and prosper as they saw fit. While the Dutch were among the first to colonize the region, they had ample company from their European neighbors, as reflected in the ever-changing town names. Vlissingen would become Flushing, part of the borough of Queens. Breuckelen became Brooklyn, and in 1665—under an increasingly British influence—New Amsterdam was reincorporated under a new name: New York City.

The van Nieuwkerks anglicized their name to Newkirk and moved north throughout the state of New York, marrying mostly among fellow Dutch and British colonists. By the late 1800s, the family had spread out like ivy on a wall, but the lives of four of them would become intertwined in ways that Gerrit Cornelius van Nieuwkerk never could have imagined.

★ ★ ★

TWO HUNDRED MILES north of Manhattan, the Adirondack Mountains form the drainage divide between the Hudson and St. Lawrence watersheds of upstate New York. The Laurentian Glacier covered much of this region until 8,000 BC. When the ice sheet finally retreated, it left behind a recessional moraine of boulders, sand, and stone that created a natural dam. This dam formed the "queen of American lakes"—Lake George.

Fourteen miles north of the dam, Lake George is split by the prominent Tongue Mountain range, with Northwest Bay on one side and a group of islands called "The Narrows" on the other. The Tongue Mountain range became noted not only for its scenic views of the lake, but also for its large concentration of *crotalus horridus*—the eastern timber rattlesnake—which inhabits the many rocks, crevasses, and burrows in the area.

*Crotalus horridus* developed such an intimidating reputation that the snake became a de facto symbol of the American Revolution. A variety of revolutionary flags—including the first U.S. Navy Jack—were fabricated depicting *crotalus* poised to strike any aggressor with the stern warning, "Don't Tread on Me."

By the summer of 1929, the New York Central Railroad's famous "Millionaire's Line" was carrying ten thousand visitors into the Adirondack region each season, as Wall Street lived large in an unprecedented—and unsustainable—economic boom. Against this backdrop, cousins Louis Hasbrouck Newkirk and Burt Leroy Newkirk—both descendants of Gerrit Cornelius van Nieuwkerk—busily raised their boys during America's Roaring Twenties.

# 1

SOME NINE HUNDRED MILES west of Lake George, a black and white metal sign hung over the entryway of an imposing redbrick building in Milwaukee, Wisconsin:

OFFICE<br>
HARLEY-DAVIDSON<br>
MOTOR CO.

There was little activity outside the building, but the inside buzzed with anticipation. A new line of motorcycles was in the works, to be introduced in August 1929 for the 1930 model year: the Harley-Davidson VL Big Twin.

Harley-Davidson considered the VL to be revolutionary with its new frame, drop-forged steel I-beam fork, larger clutch, removable cylinder heads, downdraft manifold, and magnesium alloy pistons. It also featured smaller flywheels, interchangeable and quickly demountable wheels, a two-inch-lower saddle height, a steering head lock, drop center rims with straight side balloon tires, improved brakes, an oil drain tap, and an upgraded battery. The VL would be the first Harley to be powered by the seventy-four-cubic inch, side-valve V-twin engine, which could deliver a whopping twenty-eight horsepower.

This engine had a total-loss lubrication system designed to dribble oil over the chain during operation. Touted as the "automatic chain oiler," it required the operator to periodically replenish the bike's seven-quart oil tank with SAE 70 weight motor oil. Thus, the engine never needed an oil change—one quart of oil was simply added to the left tank every 250 miles.

The motorcycle also featured dual side-by-side headlights, with the idea that this would not only provide brighter light but also a degree of redundancy should either bulb burn out on the road. A bell-shaped Klaxon 11 vibrator horn sat between the headlights with a round toolbox underneath. Considered by many to be the first modern Harley, the VL was an entirely new motorcycle compared to the 1929 J-series.

The VL's factory base price was $340.

Optimism was high in the fall of 1929 as Harley-Davidson projected strong demand for its new Big Twin. Most of the bike's components were manufactured right inside the Harley-Davidson building, where quality control was top priority. A stripped thread, oversized hole, or small casing crack would be reason to toss the offending part onto the junk heap near the Highland Avenue viaduct—much to the delight of the young boys who regularly raided the pile after hours in an attempt to slap together a mishmash motorcycle of their own.

Walter Davidson, the company's president and general manager, was a skilled mechanic and machinist who'd learned his trade from the Milwaukee railroad shops. Famous for random visits to the assembly line, Walter developed a stern reputation but was arguably more interested in the reputation of his company. Shortly after the Big Twin's official release, Davidson walked to the area of his building where engines were assembled and stopped next to a partially built motor casing that had just been stamped with the serial number: 30V8229C.

The worker swallowed hard and stood at attention as Davidson examined the metal assembly.

"Looks good," Davidson snapped as he stared the employee in the eye. "Just remember, someday someone's going to count on your work to get them home at night."

"Yes, sir," came the relieved reply.

Several weeks later, as the finishing touches were put onto the raw frame and engine of what would become Harley-Davidson VL Big Twin Serial No. 30V8229C, Willam Harley called the Davidson brothers into his office.

It was the last week of October.

"I take it you've seen the papers, gentlemen," Harley said grimly.

"Yes," answered Art Davidson, "but maybe this will just blow over. I mean, the whole country's overreacting, don't you think?"

"It doesn't matter," said Harley. "The last thing we needed was a stock market crash. Motorcycles will be seen as luxury items. This could really hurt us, boys."

"All right," Walter sighed. "Let's just keep delivering the best products we can. Nothing changes. We'll cross those bridges when we get there."

★ ★ ★

**VL NO. 30V8229C** was painted a drab, olive green and accented with broad vermillion stripes and maroon edging around her fuel and oil tanks. The rear chain guard was unembellished, but the tool and battery boxes sported outlines similar to the tanks.

After a test ride, 30V8229C was drained of gas, crated, and loaded onto a boxcar bound for Chicago. There the crate sat two days before it was transferred to the New York Central line.

The last of the autumn leaves had fallen as the train chugged eastward over the cold steel rails paralleling U.S. Highway 6. The caravan slowed as it approached numerous Indiana towns such as Southbend, Goshen, and Waterloo. At Toledo, Ohio, the train stopped to take on additional cargo and off-load freight bound for Columbus. The boxcars hugged the south side of Lake Erie as they clattered toward Buffalo over the historic Erie Canal route to Albany where the motorcycle was finally transferred to a southbound train that followed the west bank of the Hudson down to Jersey City.

The next day a truck appeared at the loading dock and four burly men with thick, New Jersey accents hefted the crate onto its cargo bed. The truck drove south through Bayonne and crossed the toll bridge across Kill Van Kull to Staten Island. It motored east toward the northwestern shore of the Narrows and finally creaked to a stop at a small motorcycle shop on Bay Street.

During the next few months, VL No. 30V8229C sat stoically in the showroom as the gloom of the Great Depression continued to gel. A few young men occasionally dropped in, bounced on the VL's seat, twisted the throttle, and made mock revving sounds.

"So, you fellas interested, or what?" asked the owner, a slender Italian by the name of Lombardi.

"I'm interested, sir," admitted one of them, a Columbia student named Elliot Mills. "I just don't have the money now. Gee, who does?"

"Yeah, *che macello!*" the owner lamented. "But my friend, things always get better, *capisce*? Three hundred forty dollars is a lot of money now, I know. But you come back in spring; maybe I let you ride this one. Then maybe you see—maybe you fall in love with her. Then you say the money not so bad, no? You don't have to pay at once. You put down money, I put her away. No one else touch her."

In true Italian style, the man gesticulated as he spoke, moving his hands passionately over the motorcycle's frame, tanks, and headlights as if conducting an orchestra. He rolled the bike outside and started the motor, which required him to speak even louder as he vibrantly described the merits of Harley-Davidson's new V-series and the overall thrill of motorcycling.

Elliot Mills hadn't been serious about buying a bike when he first walked in, but the man's movements were beginning to mesmerize him, and Mills was captivated by the concept of unbridled freedom on the road. By the time he shook the owner's hand and left the shop, his imagination was running wild.

Three months later a light rain fell over the Upper Bay as Elliot Mills made his way down to Battery Park in lower Manhattan—alone this time. He fished a nickel out of his pocket and stepped aboard the Staten Island Ferry. Thirty-five minutes later Mills got off at St. George and caught the bus that ran up and down Bay Street.

To his relief the motorcycle was still standing in the elevated bay window to the right of the door. Her dual headlights protruded from the handlebars toward the far shore of the Verrazano Narrows like the eyes of a doe gazing out from her cage, and Mills could see his distorted reflection in the chrome. The tan leather saddle looked firm and inviting, and he remembered the deep, throaty roar her engine had made when he advanced the throttle.

"I can give you two hundred dollars now," he told the Italian, "and I'll get the rest to you by the end of the month."

★ ★ ★

Two hundred and thirty miles to the north, a female *crotalus horridus* slowly slithered toward a rocky outcropping near the summit of Tongue Mountain. Within the snake's banded body were ten eggs that were soon to hatch inside of her. She settled into a recessed area under a rock and within a week gave birth to ten squirming, foot-long neonates—each immediately capable of delivering a dangerous, venomous bite.

One of the young was a large male—two inches longer than the others.

A foraging raccoon once ventured too close to the rock and the mother snake produced a loud and definitive burst from her rattle. This caused the raccoon to instantly jump sideways, and both animals escaped the encounter without injury. By reflex the young male had also attempted to rattle, but the end of his tail contained only a small pre-button that would not generate noise until his first shed. Thereafter each annual shedding of skin would produce a new rattle segment, just as it had for his mother—who now carried thirteen of them.

# 2

THE RUBBER-TIPPED MISSILE swished through the air and bounced off the man's elbow with a *thock*. The bushes rustled as three boys giggled and tried to make their getaway, but they were no match for the older man—who just happened to be the county sheriff.

The sheriff soon caught up with them and grabbed one of the boys by the scruff of the neck.

"Now which one of you shot that arrow?" he barked.

"I did, sir," whimpered the boy in the sheriff's grip. "The others dared me to shoot at whoever came by next—and I couldn't go back on my word."

"What's your name?" the sheriff growled.

"Jack Newkirk," he sniffed, "but my daddy calls me Johnny."

"And who's this?"

"I'm Horace, sir. Horace Newkirk."

"Well, Horace, you're old enough to know better."

The sheriff released his grip and knelt in front of the youngest of the group, a six-year-old boy with a Jackie Coogan pageboy haircut.

"And who are you, son?"

"I'm Jack Newkirk," he replied.

"I thought that was his name," said the perplexed sheriff.

"It is," said the archer. "He's my little cousin. We're both Jack Newkirk."

"All right," the sheriff said, "I know all your names now. Don't let me catch you in any more trouble—or it's off to reform school for the lot of you, understand?"

"Yes, sir," they answered in unison.

The elder Jack had been born in 1913 and lived in Scarsdale, New York, where his father, Louis, was an attorney. The younger boy, born in 1920, lived up the Hudson in Schenectady, where his father, Burt, worked for General Electric.

Two Jack Newkirks in the same extended family was the source of some confusion, so the elder Jack simply became known as "Scarsdale Jack"—or "Scarsdale" for short.

Scarsdale Jack joined the Boy Scouts shortly before the Wall Street crash and could think of little else but obtaining the rank of Eagle Scout. He toiled away at his merit badges and spent much of 1930 as a *coeur du bois*—a sixteen-year-old man of the woods. He became proficient in building campfires and shooting his bow and arrow. One day Scarsdale impressed his cousins by taking aim at a sparrow and knocking the bird off of its branch, killing it instantly.

"My father says it's a sin to kill an animal if you don't eat it!" chided cousin Horace, whereupon Scarsdale promptly kindled a fire and then plucked, roasted, and ate his meager fare.

After this episode the boys nicknamed him "he-man Newkirk," and Scarsdale Jack became the undisputed alpha male of the clan.

★ ★ ★

**AS SCARSDALE WORKED** diligently toward his Eagle Scout medal, the younger Jack Newkirk swam and cavorted among the Lake George Narrows, where his parents had set up camp for the summer. One day young Jack was daydreaming on the shore of Sarah Island when he suddenly jumped up with a start.

"Horace! Horace!" yelled Jack as he hopped up and down, barely able to contain himself.

"So where's the fire?" asked his brother, breathless from racing across the island.

"There's an empty canoe out there!" Jack shouted. "By all means let's go out and fetch it!"

Horace and Jack swam out to the bright red canoe and within minutes their prize was pulled onto the island for inspection. She was manufactured by the Morris Canoe Company and bore the cryptic initials "SBYMCA" on her bow.

Upon his return to the lake, Burt looked at the boat and slowly shook his head.

"Son, this looks like it belongs to the YMCA at Silver Bay. It probably came untied from the dock and the wind caught it. We'll have to take it back. You understand?"

"Yes, Father," Jack whimpered.

After returning the boat to its rightful owner, Jack sat brooding on the shore of Sarah Island. Tears ran down his cheeks as wavelets gently struck the rocks, but across the island his parents were discussing something over the campfire. Each took turns speaking, and after nodding in agreement they got up and prepared their family for bed.

The next Saturday, Burt and Jack motored south to Dunham's Bay on the lake's southeastern shore. There, to Jack's delight, his father told him he could pick out any canoe he wanted as long as it was twenty dollars or less. This instantly ended Jack's gloom, and he scoured the boathouse for a vessel similar to the red canoe. He finally found one near the oversized door leading to the water's edge.

This one was painted blue.

"That'd be a swell choice, son," said the owner. "Morris doesn't make those anymore. The factory closed down."

Young Jack ran his hands longingly over the keel.

"How much, sir?" he asked reluctantly.

"Twenty dollars," the man answered with a wink and a nod.

★ ★ ★

**FRANK LOMBARDI MOVED** the Harley-Davidson VL Big Twin No. 30V8229C from his display window to a storage shed west of Bay Street. On June 2, 1930, Elliot Mills paid off the balance of $140 and added several factory options before riding away: a jiffy stand, crash bar, luggage carrier, and a Corbin speedometer driven by a spur gear off the rear-wheel-drive sprocket.

The motorcycle's maiden voyage began with a northbound ride on the Staten Island Ferry to Battery Park, where Mills proudly rode the bike off the ferry ramp and weaved his way through lower Manhattan and west toward the Hudson River. At Fifty-seventh Street, Mills turned east and headed toward Columbus Circle, then took Central Park West to

Cathedral Parkway, past the Cathedral Church of St. John the Divine, and on to Columbia University.

His sudden appearance on campus produced the effect he'd hoped for.

"Hey Mills, how'd you score the vampy scoot?" shouted a friend.

"Boy, you got moxie if you just rode *that* through Manhattan!" quipped another.

"Are you going to give us a ride?" asked a visiting girl.

"I would," Elliot replied, "but this is a single-saddled affair. It's just the two of us."

★ ★ ★

**ON FEBRUARY 14, 1931,** seventeen-year-old Scarsdale Jack Newkirk of Boy Scout Troop No. 3 was personally awarded the rank of Eagle Scout by Rear Admiral Richard E. Byrd, one of the most famous aviators of the day. As part of the ceremony, Byrd gave a thrilling account of his recent exploits in Antarctica:

> I'm often asked about the difference between military aviators. I am biased of course, but I shall leave any of you aspiring pilots with this: It is the navy man who—after completing his mission—must return to his carrier, attempt to land on a spot that looks like a postage stamp in a vast ocean and catch the arrest wire, while his engine is at full power as the carrier races through the ocean at twenty knots, night or day, rain, snow, or shine, equipment failures, fatigue or even shot up—and it must be done 100 percent correctly.

Admiral Byrd shook Scarsdale's hand and presented him with the Eagle Scout medal—a sterling silver pendant of a bald eagle with outstretched wings attached to a ribbon of red, white, and blue, supported by a small silver scroll that simply read "Be Prepared." Byrd also gave him a brand new, eight-by-ten, illustrated hardback entitled *Flying High: A Book of Aviation Stories and Model Airplanes for Boys*, which he autographed alongside the text:

*As there have been golden days of sailing ships, of steam, and of electricity—today beckons the adventurous and the pioneer into the air.*
*Rear-Admiral Richard E. Byrd*

From that day forward, any hope Scarsdale's father may have had for his son to follow a career in law or medicine was gone forever.

*I will be a pilot someday,* Scarsdale promised himself.

As the ceremony continued, he fixated on a medal pinned to the admiral's chest. It was a bronze cross, overlaid with a four-bladed propeller on rays of light emanating from the center, all suspended by a rectangular bar and a red, white, and blue ribbon.

It was the Distinguished Flying Cross—the first ever awarded to a naval aviator.

*Not only will I be a pilot,* vowed Jack, *someday I will earn that medal.*

As an Eagle Scout, Jack memorized "The Knight's Code" from his *Handbook for Boys*:

*NEVER break your promise.*
*BE PREPARED to fight in the defense of your country.*
*MAINTAIN the HONOR of your country with your life.*
*DEFEND the poor, and help them that cannot defend themselves.*

Scarsdale's slender frame did not lend itself well to fist fighting, so he began to develop social skills that would allow him to avert a conflict before it escalated to physical blows. What he could not endure, however, was to watch larger boys harass smaller ones—and on more than one occasion he came home from school with his nose bloodied or his lip fattened because he'd intervened on behalf of a junior student, a Jewish kid, or some other bullied classmate.

Both Scarsdale and young Jack excelled in sprinting, high jumping, and other activities that required strong aerobic abilities. Horace, on the other hand—the eldest of the three—was a member of his high school gymnastics team. Within a few years, however, Horace developed a muscular and balanced body, and the bullies picked on him much less.

One summer at the lake, Horace astounded the others by climbing into his canoe, placing his hands amidships on the starboard and port gunwales, and gracefully arching into a handstand. Then—as if this weren't enough—Horace began to perform handstand pushups as his tricep and deltoid muscles rippled in the sun. This feat, from the unstable platform of his notoriously tippy canoe, required an extraordinary degree of strength and balance, and the Newkirk cousins talked about it for years to come.

★ ★ ★

**IN HARTFORD, CONNECTICUT,** Harley-Davidson No. 30V8229C had become the primary mode of transportation for Elliot Mills. At church one day, he met a pretty young girl named Marjorie Hart who, to his delight, expressed interest in the motorcycle.

Coincidentally, Harley-Davidson had just announced a new option for the V-series called the buddy seat—an oversized leather saddle that could accommodate two riders in an intimate arrangement where the passenger had the option of holding on to a set of seat handles—or wrapping both arms around the driver's waist, as the case may be. There had also been reports that the bike's two headlights were placed so close together it caused the Harley VL to be mistaken for a distant car, which resulted in several nighttime riding accidents. Some states actually banned the dual headlights altogether, so Harley-Davidson altered the design to accommodate a single light.

Mills removed his solo saddle and replaced it with a buddy seat. He then removed the two Solar Cycle headlights from the fork and replaced them with a flat-lensed, John Brown Motolamp that contained a 6-volt, 15-watt General Electric lightbulb.

# 3

**R**ENSSELAER POLYTECHNIC INSTITUTE sits on a hill overlooking the Hudson River in Troy, New York. Founded in 1824, it was the first technological university in the English-speaking world. As Rensselaer began to produce some of the nation's preeminent leaders, a group of investors and inventors in nearby Schenectady formed the General Electric Company—and the resulting confluence of education, innovation, and industry turned New York's Capital District into the Silicon Valley of its day.

Young Jack's father, Burt Newkirk, was a respected scientist at General Electric, but—like countless others—lost his job during the Great Depression. After several years of discouraging rejections, Burt was hired as a professor at Rensselaer.

Scarsdale Jack's father, Louis, strongly encouraged his son to go to college. While Scarsdale didn't oppose the idea, it was no secret that he really wanted to fly airplanes for a living. His mother was dead-set against this, as she simply considered flying too dangerous. His father was more supportive and said if he wanted to be a pilot, he'd have a distinct advantage with a college diploma, preferably in a technical field. The best place to get such a degree, Louis opined, was 150 miles up the Hudson at Rensselaer.

"Remember, you've got family up there," said Louis. "It's close enough that you could come home on weekends—and there's talk of a new department dedicated entirely to aeronautical engineering. That ought to interest you!"

As Scarsdale warmed up to the idea, Louis quietly worried about how to pay for it.

Thus, the fall of 1932 saw Scarsdale Jack Newkirk begin his freshman year at Rensselaer. His father, mother, and sister Janet helped move his belongings into White Hall where he would spend the next year on campus. Once his family had left, however, Scarsdale wasted no time. He visited an airfield near Troy and made friends with the owner of a Curtiss Falcon—an open cockpit biplane used primarily as an aerial observation platform.

One sunny October morning, Scarsdale gingerly climbed into the Falcon's passenger seat as his instructor fired up the Liberty engine. The aircraft bounced and bumped its way over the field as they taxied toward the end of the runway.

As the plane slowly began to pick up speed, Scarsdale's senses were bombarded with unfamiliar stimuli—the smell of exhaust and hot oil, the rush of warm air, the roar of the twelve-cylinder engine at full throttle, and an uneasy feeling of instability as the aircraft lifted off terra firma. The ground dropped away faster than Jack had expected, and before long they were flying north at nearly a hundred miles per hour with the Hudson River rolling beneath their right wing. They crossed the Mohawk near the town of Halfmoon and the instructor gave Scarsdale control of the aircraft over Saratoga Battlefield Historic Park.

"Just keep it steady," he said. "Don't try to counteract every little bump. Follow the river."

Jack felt the aircraft banking to the left, so he moved the stick in the opposite direction. The Falcon responded by banking right in an adverse yaw.

The instructor patiently allowed Jack to slosh around as he got the feel of the airplane, then took the controls back and demonstrated proper use of the stick. As they approached Glens Falls, the Hudson bent sharply to the west and Jack was instructed to circle the town and follow the river back home. He pushed down clumsily on the left rudder pedal; this kicked the tail to the right and the airplane skidded through the air.

"Left aileron!" shouted the instructor. "And pull back just a little."

Jack gently moved the stick to the left and applied slight backpressure. This caused the airplane to bank into a natural turn that pushed him down gently into his seat.

"That's it!" came the response. "You're getting it, son."

By the time they landed back in Troy, Jack felt lightheaded and woozy. The flight had taken less than an hour, but the bumpy air and unfamiliar environment had put his senses on overload. He was rethinking all this flying business. Jack sat down on the grass beside the Falcon and thought he was going to throw up.

"A swell pilot I'll make," Jack muttered, "I can't even stand a little motion."

"Son, you did just fine," the instructor chuckled. "Nearly everyone turns green the first time around. You were a different pilot on the way back—a fast learner. Just stick with it and you'll see."

★ ★ ★

**BACK IN CONNECTICUT,** Elliot Mills had just invited his girlfriend for a ride in the country on that sunny October afternoon. She saw the eagerness in his eyes and in her resourcefulness figured out how to tuck her skirt inside a long duster jacket to protect it from the motorcycle's greasy frame and still preserve her modesty. With a picnic basket lashed to the VL's luggage carrier, the motorcycle rumbled northwest out of Hartford on Route 44, then passed through Winsted and turned north on Road 49 past the small town of Norfolk. With Bald Mountain looming to their left, Mills pulled into Campbell Falls State Park south of the Massachusetts border and kicked down the jiffy stand.

He fumbled his way through lunch and made awkward conversation with his pretty young date, who sat on a checkered blanket still wearing her outfit from church—a gored skirt, puffed sleeves, and tailored bodice. Bright red lipstick augmented her skin, and her cheeks had just a hint of pink rouge. This all made for an unlikely motorcycle passenger, but that was one of the things he loved about her.

"Marjorie . . ." he demurred, "if I asked you, uh—"

She sensed his anxiety and countered it.

"Yes, Elliot. My answer would be yes."

And in the shadow of Bald Mountain, within a sunlit grove of oak, maple, and ash trees, Harley-Davidson VL No. 30V8229C bore silent witness as Elliot Mills got down on one knee and asked Marjorie Hart to be his bride.

★ ★ ★

**SCARSDALE JACK NEWKIRK** earned a 3.1 grade point average at Rensselaer, which was sufficient to place him within the top half of his class. While his grades didn't necessarily suffer from his extracurricular flying activities, his finances did. All of Jack's spare cash—and most of his tuition for the next year—went toward flying lessons.

One spring day Jack and his instructor followed the Hudson to Glens Falls and flew over Fort William Henry at the southern end of Lake George.

"Big massacre down there before the Revolution," remarked the instructor. "You wouldn't want to be anywhere around here in 1757. Ever read *Last of the Mohicans*?"

They continued north over the lake as Scarsdale gazed at the spring leaves greening the shore of Northwest Bay, Tongue Mountain, and the Lake George Narrows. He felt like one of the luckiest nineteen-year-olds on earth.

"Lots of rattlesnakes down there," said his instructor, snapping Scarsdale out of his reverie.

A few weeks later, Scarsdale Jack sheepishly told his parents he didn't have enough money to return to Rensselaer that fall. Surprisingly, his father understood. With the Depression at its worst, there simply wasn't enough money to educate the children. Sister Janet was working, brother Bobby was still in high school, and Louis Jr. had been the only one to finish college.

Louis suggested that Scarsdale try to get a job. Perhaps he could return to Rensselaer that following year. Scarsdale's mother, Edna, was less enthusiastic, and asked him to promise he wouldn't try to make a living flying airplanes. Jack nodded grudgingly—but his mother could see it was like trying to change the course of a river.

★ ★ ★

**IN THE SPRING OF 1934,** a classified ad appeared in *The Hartford Courant*:

FOR SALE
1930 H-D MOTORCYCLE
RUNS SWELL. LOW MILES.
SW CORNER OF FAIRFIELD & LINNMORE

Five days later, a young man got off the bus at Fairfield Avenue and White Street and walked one block south. He was pleased to see that the bike for sale was a powerful Harley-Davidson VL Big Twin, with a John Brown Motolamp, luggage carrier, buddy seat, and front safety guard. He looked the motorcycle over with a keen eye. The Corbin odometer displayed just 14811. The left crankcase below the cylinder barrels had been stamped with the number 30V8229C.

He walked up to the house and knocked.

"My name's Eustace Hetzel," said the young man. "Is that your cycle for sale?"

"Elliot Mills," replied the elder. "And yes, that's my baby. Well she was, that is, until my wife announced we'll be having a real one."

"Understood," Hetzel laughed. "She's a nice bike. How much do you want for her?"

"I need two hundred dollars," said Mills. "And she's worth every nickel. I hate to see her go, but with the little one on the way I won't be doing much riding."

Eustace Hetzel shook hands with Elliot Mills and made arrangements to pay for the bike.

As Hetzel rode off, a blossoming Marjorie Mills stepped out of the house, walked down the porch stairs, and wrapped her arms around her husband's waist as she'd done so often from the back of their Harley. As the rhapsodic rumble of the 74-cubic-inch flathead faded into the distance, Marjorie noticed Elliot's eyes were brimming with tears.

★ ★ ★

**WHEN NEW YORK MAYOR** Fiorello LaGuardia took office in 1934, New York City was the most populous city in the United States during the nation's worst economic depression.

LaGuardia's New York was not only the epicenter of world finance, it was also the cultural hub of the country, offering such diverse venues as Carnegie Hall, the Apollo Theater, Broadway, and the Metropolitan Museum of Art. Performing arts groups included the American Ballet Company, the New York Philharmonic, and the Metropolitan Opera. The city was large enough to support three Major League baseball teams: the New York Giants, the Brooklyn Dodgers, and the New York Yankees—a team that produced many of the game's legends, including Babe Ruth, Joe DiMaggio, and Lou Gehrig.

Mayor LaGuardia began his term during the Golden Age of Radio—and was the first mayor many New Yorkers heard speak on the air. By 1935, twenty million radio sets were spread throughout the country and occupied two out of three American homes. Radio became the central medium of the Great Depression, and both Mayor LaGuardia and President Roosevelt exploited this new technology to project themselves into the living rooms of millions.

★ ★ ★

**AS THE NEWKIRK BOYS** plowed into their college studies, construction workers in Queens began to move earth in a marshy New York dump known as Flushing Meadows. Three thousand miles to the west, dredges and barges gathered hundreds of thousands of tons of dirt and rock and unloaded them onto a shoal in San Francisco Bay.

Elsewhere in the country, a horse named Seabiscuit had just won the Continental Handicap, gaining the top spot in the 1937 winnings race by upsetting the legendary War Admiral. A brash young pilot named Howard Hughes broke his own speed record by flying from California to New York City in seven hours and twenty-eight minutes. The New York Yankees prevailed over the Giants in a World Series rematch as Lou Gehrig slammed in a magnificent home run during game four. San Francisco celebrated her new Golden Gate suspension bridge—the longest in the world—and Walt Disney released the world's first full-length, animated, Technicolor movie: *Snow White and the Seven Dwarves*.

Despite these inspirational diversions, America was in desperate need of an economic stimulus and a boost to national morale. To this end, New York City and San Francisco were preparing for what would become the most monumental societal events of the twentieth century.

# 4

EUSTACE HETZEL AND his friend Pete Milton hatched an ambitious plan to ride Harley-Davidson No. 30V8229C from Hartford, Connecticut, to Kansas City, Kansas. In the spring of 1937, they loaded the luggage carrier with as much as they dared and headed west. Milton found the buddy seat uncomfortable at first, but they stopped regularly to stretch their legs and fill up the bike's gas and oil tanks. They crossed the Ohio River at Wheeling and took Highway 40 through Indianapolis and Springfield, Illinois. At St. Louis they crossed Route 66 and rumbled toward Kansas. They watched with fascination as they passed rag-tag caravans of jalopies overloaded with migrant workers headed to what they hoped would be better lives.

In Kansas City, Hetzel made the mistake of riding parallel over a set of trolley tracks, which pulled his front wheel into the track groove and upset the bike. The boys escaped injury, but the accident smashed the exhaust pipe and the bike sustained a few dents and scratches—along with some structural weakening that wouldn't become apparent until a few years down the road. Upon Hetzel's return, more than three thousand miles had been added to the Corbin odometer.

★ ★ ★

BACK IN NEW YORK CITY, Scarsdale Jack Newkirk was getting discouraged. Unable to afford Rensselaer's tuition, he'd taken a year off to work but found employment extremely hard to come by. A job opportunity arose at a large chemical firm, but they wanted him to take a few more chemistry courses. Scarsdale promptly had his transcript sent from Rensselaer to Columbia and worked the chemist job during the day as he took night classes in the city.

One year turned into two, and then three.

Scarsdale joined the National Guard and immediately felt more in his element. He won a marksmanship competition at the regiment's annual two-week training camp, but when he returned to New York City someone else had taken his chemist job. Undaunted, he got a position as a reservations clerk for United Airlines. While this was a step down professionally, Scarsdale was delighted to be associated with airplanes and flying again. He made it a point to speak with the pilots whenever possible.

One morning a secretary approached him with a grim look.

"Phone call for you, Jack."

It was his father, who broke the news that Jack's mother, Edna, had just died at their home.

Jack left work and took a tearful walk around Central Park in hopes his thoughts would settle. He was twenty-three years old and in a holding pattern. And while he enjoyed his job, it was clearly not what he wanted to do for the rest of his life.

Scarsdale had fulfilled his promise to his mother, but she was gone now and he could no longer hold back his burning desire to be a pilot—and not just any pilot. He wanted to be a naval aviator—an Eagle Scout of the air, just like his idol Richard Byrd.

After the funeral, Scarsdale took a bus to Floyd Bennett Field in Brooklyn and met with a navy recruiter. When Scarsdale dropped Admiral Byrd's name, it evoked an immediate stare of reverence. The navy was eager to have Jack on board, but the recruiter explained that they required at least two years of college. Scarsdale had only one.

This put a kink in Jack's plan, but he suddenly remembered that his father's cousin Burt was now a professor at Rensselaer. Perhaps he could ask for his help. Excited by the possibility, Scarsdale boarded a train, headed up the Hudson, and bounded up the massive granite staircase of the Approach to Rensselaer Polytechnic Institute.

Scarsdale found Burt sitting in his ground-level office in the new Palmer C. Ricketts Building.

"Jack!" Burt enthused. "Good to see you. I was sorry to hear about your mother. How are your father and the rest of the family?"

"We're swell, sir," Scarsdale replied as he shook hands with the silver-haired professor. "But our belts are pretty tight in this lousy depression."

"We've all got that in common, I'm afraid," lamented Burt. "So tell me what you're up to."

Scarsdale Jack explained his situation. He spoke with confidence and clarity, articulating exactly what he intended to accomplish. *This young man has clearly grown into a leader,* thought Burt, as Scarsdale and he ate a late lunch at the campus dining hall.

"Jack will be here in the fall, you know—my Jack," Burt remarked. "He'll be studying metallurgy right here in the Ricketts Building."

"Little Jackie?" Scarsdale exclaimed. "When did that kid grow into a college man?"

"He's not so little anymore," said Burt. "And you should think twice before challenging him to a footrace. He can run like a deer."

By the end of the meeting, Burt had no qualms about recommending Scarsdale Jack to be reinstated at Rensselaer's Department of Aeronautical Engineering, with the understanding that he'd remain just one year as required by the navy.

★ ★ ★

**ONE OF PROFESSOR NEWKIRK'S** senior students was Eustace Hetzel, who was often seen sputtering around campus on his noisy old Harley-Davidson VL motorcycle. After nearly eight years of continuous service, the bike was beginning to show its age. One afternoon, while riding back from Hartford, Hetzel feel asleep, ran off the road, and crashed into a billboard advertising Lucky Strike cigarettes. Hetzel suffered a bruised arm and a headache. The Harley, however, sustained a broken left handlebar, a large dent to the gas tank, and a bent fender.

Professor Newkirk and his family moved to their Lake George cabin that summer and regularly entertained guests from the city. One afternoon, Eustace Hetzel rode his old Harley-Davidson VL to Bolton Landing, where young Jack met him at Bell Point with his blue canoe. Together they paddled two miles to camp beneath the cliffs of Tongue Mountain.

"That's some cycle you've got there, Hetz," remarked Jack between paddle strokes.

"She's seen better days," said Hetzel. "But boy, the stories she can tell! Saved me a bundle on gas—goes about forty-five miles for each gallon."

"What will you do with her after you graduate?" Jack inquired.

"Don't know," said Hetzel.

★ ★ ★

*High on Tongue Mountain,* Crotalus horridus *lay in ambush for a red squirrel that was busy collecting spruce cones. The snake first located the animal by taking an air sample with his tongue, and then honed in on it using the two heat—sensitive pits between his eyes and nostrils. The snake struck with lightning rapidity. Five minutes later he swallowed his prey headfirst and slithered back underneath his rock.*

# 5

**T**WO HUNDRED THIRTY miles south of Tongue Mountain, a throng of reporters, photographers, and dignitaries were gathered at the former Flushing Meadows dumpsite in Queens, New York. Among them were Borough President George Harvey, Parks Commissioner Robert Moses, Mayor LaGuardia, and New York's official greeter, the congenial Grover Whalen.

The time had come to set the cornerstone for the New York City Building, the first major structure to be built for the 1939 New York World's Fair—the "World of Tomorrow."

Its organizers promised it would be the greatest exhibition the world had ever known.

On the west coast, San Francisco was in a heated race with New York City. Workers had spent the last few years dumping fill material from the Sacramento River Delta onto a shoal north of Yerba Buena Island. Legend said this dirt was laden with gold washed down from the Sierra Nevadas. The resulting landmass was aptly called "Treasure Island," and its 1939 Golden Gate International Exposition would celebrate two of the city's newly built bridges: the Bay Bridge connecting San Francisco to Oakland, and the Golden Gate Bridge spanning the channel between San Francisco and Marin County.

The nation's leaders hoped that two world's fairs, at the same time, on both sides of the country, might bolster the economy. Americans and foreigners alike were encouraged to crisscross the country by automobile, bus, train, airplane, or any other means—and of course spend money all along the way. The Shell Oil Company's 1939 Road Maps trumpeted:

> KEEP IN MIND THE DATES OF
> **1939's TWO WORLD FAIRS**
> • Golden Gate International Exposition on San Francisco Bay — February 18 to December 2, 1939.
> • New York World's Fair — Opens April 30, 1939.

Both world's fairs were eager to upstage the other. On February 22, 1939, comedian Fred Allen poked fun at the upcoming New York Fair from his radio show, *Town Hall Tonight:*

> **ALLEN:** San Francisco's Golden Gate Fair opened on Saturday last! Gala crowd of one hundred thousand votes California pageant "a glittering spectacle." Town Hall News shows word of Golden Gate Fair's opening being received here in New York City. The scene? Grover Whelan's office.
> **SECRETARY:** Mr. Whelan, the San Francisco Fair is open!
> **WHELAN:** Arrrgh! *(rips out hair and gnashes teeth)*

The epicenter of the 1939 New York World's Fair was a solid 610-foot triangular tower called the Trylon, which stood beside a 180-foot-diameter globe dubbed the Perisphere. Trylon and Perisphere were painted flat white, and neither name would generally be spoken without the other.

The hallmark of San Francisco's Golden Gate International Exposition—the "Pageant of the Pacific"—was the magnificent Tower of the Sun, a sleek four hundred-foot bell tower with a carillon that rang out some of the fairgoers' favorite melodies.

Both fairs attracted millions of dollars in investment capital and resulted in an unprecedented mobilization of artists, architects, designers, composers, construction workers, landscapers, planners, performers, sponsors, exhibitors, and maintenance staff—and millions of Americans began to make plans to visit New York City or San Francisco.

★ ★ ★

**SCARSDALE JACK SPENT** a month at the Floyd Bennett Field and easily passed his preliminary flight tests. In the fall of 1938, he was transferred to Naval Air Station Pensacola in Florida to begin flight training in earnest. His first aircraft was an N3N Canary, a two-seat, open cockpit, radial-engine biplane from the Naval Aircraft Factory in Philadelphia. While the fundamentals of flight had not changed since his days as a nineteen-year-old student, the techniques demonstrated by his instructor made his head spin. He learned the chandelle, barrel roll, Immelmann turn, stalls, spins, Split-S, and dozens more aerobatic maneuvers. He also practiced short-field landings in preparation for carrier ops.

In the spring of 1939, Scarsdale flew the Grumman F3F, the navy's biplane fighter aircraft. The F3F was powered by a Wright R-1820 radial engine with a General Electric turbocharger, which allowed Scarsdale to climb to more than thirty thousand feet and fly at two hundred fifty miles per hour—numbers unheard of in normally aspirated airplanes such as the Curtiss Falcon.

The F3F was also the first airplane he flew with armament: two Browning M2 machine guns, capable of firing more than a thousand rounds per minute, and one Mk IV bomb under each wing. While his primary emphasis was on flying, Scarsdale was eager to start weapons training, and silently wondered if he would be as good a marksman in the air as he had been on the ground.

★ ★ ★

**BY ALL RESPECTS,** Harley-Davidson VL No. 30V8229C had seen a long and productive life. In nearly a decade of operation, she had logged thirty-five thousand miles, traveled halfway across the country, and carried her passengers loyally—all while enduring a wide variety of weather conditions, road surfaces, and wear and tear. But her fenders were rusty and her gas tank was dented. The fuel petcocks leaked and the chain needed to be replaced. The frame had some hairline cracks, the exhaust was falling apart, and the cylinder heads were beginning to rust.

The bike's useful life seemed just about over.

Her current owner, Eustace Hetzel, had been elected Grand Marshal of Rensselaer's Class of 1939—the highest student office on campus—and Professor Newkirk helped Hetzel line up a few job prospects. Young Jack, now a sophomore, was also looking to establish contacts that might lead to future employment. At Burt's suggestion, Hetzel and Jack made plans to take the motorcycle to visit some of the large industrial firms in the northeast. Toward this end, Burt gave his eager son a hundred dollars that was to last him all summer.

Shortly before graduation, Hetzel received a job offer from the California Institute of Technology and was forced to scuttle the motorcycle trip. Hetzel had one last cup of coffee at the Troy Rail Station with roommate John Mattern before leaving for Pasadena.

"You know, John, about that Harley I'm dumping on you," said Hetzel.

"Yeah, I really don't know what I'm going to do with her," Mattern responded. "What do you think she's worth?"

"In the shape she's in?" Hetzel laughed. "Probably sixty—tops. You might get a hundred if you fix her up, but that'd be a big job. I'm thinking maybe we should talk to Jack Newkirk."

"Which one?" asked Mattern. "Scarsdale Jack or the younger?"

"I'm talking about the younger one. He was pretty blue when I told him we weren't taking our trip. He doesn't know how to ride, but you could teach him, couldn't you?"

"Sure, he's bright enough," said Mattern.

"Poor kid," lamented Hetzel. "His family hardly has two nickels to rub together. His dad got laid off from GE a few years back and couldn't find a job in this lousy depression. The only reason those Newkirk boys can afford college is because Burt's a professor here."

"Really?" said Mattern.

"Yup," said Hetzel, "Rensselaer gave their family some tuition breaks in exchange for Professor Newkirk teaching the likes of you and me."

"So what about the Harley?" Mattern asked.

"Well, I've caught Jack checking her out a few times. She may seem like a junker to you and me, but he stares at her like she's Helen of Troy."

"So you think he might be interested?"

"Why don't you teach him to ride and he can try her out for a few weeks? If he gets the hang of it, tell him he can have her for forty bucks. If Newkirk doesn't want her, then she's probably headed to the junk heap."

"OK, Hetz. Can do."

★ ★ ★

**YOUNG JACK NEWKIRK** walked deflated and crestfallen down the granite steps of the Approach from Rensselaer Polytechnic Institute to downtown Troy. Proctor's Theater on Fourth Street was replaying a dime matinee of *Love Finds Andy Hardy* with Mickey Rooney and Judy Garland. This would distract him for a few hours.

As the theater darkened, Jack prepared himself to sit through the obligatory newsreel that always preceded the feature. To his delight it began with Judy Garland and Mickey Rooney ad libbing for the camera along with Mayor LaGuardia:

> ROONEY: Mr. Mayor, um, I'd like to ask you a few questions.
> 
> LAGUARDIA: Go ahead, Mickey.
> 
> ROONEY: Well, I have a lot of friends around, uh, out where I live out on the Coast, and they'd like to come and visit the world's fair but I want to ask you if there's any place that they can stay other than the Park Avenue hotels!
> 
> LAGUARDIA: Why sure, Mickey. New York City's like every other town in this country—except that we can give you better accommodation and better food for less money!
> 
> ROONEY: *laughs*
> 
> LAGUARDIA: Now they can come here and, uh—Judy, you have friends, too, haven't you?
> 
> GARLAND: Yes, I have.
> 
> LAGUARDIA: Now you can tell the boys and girls, the high school students, that they can come to New York and get accommodations—safe, sanitary, cheerful, inspected rooms—all the way from fifty to seventy-five cents a night. And if they come in groups we can give it to them as cheap as fifty cents a night!
> 
> GARLAND: That's wonderful!
> 
> ROONEY: Oh, Mr. Mayor, that looks like we're going to move in!
> 
> LAGUARDIA: You bet the lot! You move in—you tell the kids. Hey, what do you think of this fair?
> 
> GARLAND: Oh, it's wonderful!

For the first time, Jack realized that two world's fairs were being staged on opposite sides of the country. Maybe he could take a train to New York City, but there was no way on God's green earth he could ever get to San Francisco.

After the movie, Jack made his solitary way up the Approach and suddenly heard someone shouting his name.

"Hey, Jack! Jack Newkirk! We were just talking about you."

He looked down to see John Mattern running up the steps.

"Hetz says maybe you'd be interested in his old Harley," said Mattern. "What do you say?"

Time seemed to stop. A few hours earlier, he wouldn't have even considered it. But the seed had been planted, taken root, and was growing furiously inside his mind.

*No*—said an insidious voice within—*no! You don't even know how to ride a motorcycle, much less take one clear across the country. Just go home and forget about it!*

Dusk was settling over the Hudson as empty barges lined up for the downstream run to New York City. The drawbridge at the end of Congress Street slowly ratcheted up, and an occasional foghorn blast could be heard in the distance.

"So, what do you think, Jack?" persisted Mattern. "Hetz says she's yours for forty dollars."

"Well, heck yeah," Jack finally blurted out. "But who'll teach me how to ride?"

"I will," replied Mattern, "but we'd have to start right away. I have to be on a train for Bellmore tomorrow morning."

"OK! Let's meet at the corner of Tibbits and Burdett at nine tomorrow!"

Jack could hardly sleep that night as he pondered what he'd done. Money would be the major constraint. The hundred dollars his father gave him would go fast, so every nickel had to count. He knew the bike needed repairs, but had no idea as to the extent of them. Then there was the matter of his parents. They'd agreed to let Jack go with Hetzel because it was career reconnaissance. A solo trip to both world's fairs would be seen as pure leisure.

Still, Jack's excitement outweighed his fear when he recalled how he'd salvaged a canoe ten years earlier as it drifted down the middle of Lake George. The canoe had opened up the lake to him. This motorcycle would open up the country.

At nine o'clock the next morning, Jack walked to the southern end of Burdett Avenue: a mile long, relatively flat, and straight as an arrow. Nervous to begin with, Jack became even more agitated as ten minutes ticked by, then twenty, and at nine twenty-five he was still waiting. Finally, he heard the rumble of the Harley coming down the road as a flustered John Mattern pulled up, did a U-turn, and shut off the motorcycle.

"Sorry I'm late Jack," Mattern apologized. "I've had a heck of a time getting packed and out of here."

"It's OK," said Jack.

"Now, I've got to be down at the train station in half an hour, but I can show you the basics—and I did manage to find the manual."

Mattern thrust a five-by-seven-inch booklet with a dirty, yellowish cover into Jack's hand. It was nearly blackened over from a decade's worth of greasy thumbprints.

"You know how to ride a bicycle, don't you?" Mattern asked.

"Sure," Jack nodded.

"Well, this isn't much different. This bike's just heavier and you go faster. Uh, here's the brake by your right foot, clutch on your left, and the gear shifter is on the gas tank. Three speeds. Here's neutral—you know what neutral is, right? OK, you start it by switching on the ignition—just watch me—and kicking down on the kick-start pedal. Oh yeah, you should move the spark control to fully advanced, then open the throttle a little bit. Probably doesn't need the choke now. Make sure the clutch is engaged. Then push down on the kick-starter until you feel compression. Let it ratchet back and you're ready to kick, you see?"

Jack's head was spinning. Mattern put his entire body weight on the kick-starter and the VL roared to life.

"OK," Mattern yelled over the idling V-twin, "now I'll disengage the clutch with my left foot and put her into first gear."

Mattern stamped his heel down on the rear clutch pedal. With his left hand, he moved the gearshift lever out of the neutral detent and pushed it forward into low. He revved the engine and pushed the ball of his left foot on the front clutch pedal, and the Harley took off gracefully down the road. After a hundred yards Mattern turned back and stopped in front of Jack.

"OK, now you climb on the back and watch what I do!" shouted Mattern.

Jack swung his leg over the bike and Mattern repeated the takeoff. At twenty miles an hour he stepped on the clutch, took his left hand off the handgrip, and moved the shift lever to second. They cruised along at thirty miles an hour past Sage and Peoples Avenue, then Mattern reversed course back toward Tibbits.

"Any questions?" asked Mattern, as they rolled to a stop.

Jack didn't know where to start. As he opened his mouth to speak, a loud *ah-OO-gah* bellowed from a Model A Ford bouncing up the road. One of the passengers leaned out the window.

"Hey Mattern, come on! We'll be late for the train."

"Sorry Jack, I've got to go," said Mattern.

The Ford creaked to a stop and Mattern climbed inside.

"Don't worry," he shouted, "you'll get the hang of it! Just start slowly—and read the manual. Watch out for cars. Some of them like to turn left in front of you, so I ride with the headlamp on, even in the daytime. And don't worry about paying for the bike. Just ride her for a few weeks. You can send the forty dollars later."

Jack sat down on the grass next to the 390-pound iron horse. A sense of awkwardness, like a teenager on his first date, hung in the air and the engine pinged expectantly as its cylinder heads cooled in the morning air. Jack opened the *Harley-Davidson Rider's Handbook* and began to read about gasoline, oil, and spark plugs. He familiarized himself with the location of the bike's controls, knobs, filler caps, switches, levers, and pedals. He pressed the horn button and the bike responded with an eager *beep*.

With a deep breath, Jack put his left hand on the grip, swung his right leg over the frame, and planted himself firmly in the saddle. For a while he just sat there gazing at the world from this new vantage point. He imagined the ground whizzing by at thirty-five miles per hour with wind rushing through his hair. Ever since his sixteenth birthday he'd wondered if he'd be able to afford motorized transportation.

*This is the day*, he thought, *and this motorcycle is the one.*

Jack turned to the "Starting Motor" section and traced down the checklist with his index finger:

**2. STARTING A WARM MOTOR:** (This applies to a motor halfway between hot and cold.) Lift choke lever to ⅓ closed position (1st upward position) and with throttle closed, kick the starter down once or twice. Then, set throttle about ¼ to ⅓ open, turn ignition switch ON, and kick the starter down quickly. Soon after the motor starts, the choke lever should be moved back to full open position. *Remember, this starting procedure calls for having the throttle partway open during the starting strokes after the switch has been turned ON.*

After meticulously setting the choke and throttle, Jack snapped out the starter pedal with his right heel and gave it his full weight. His thigh crashed down painfully on the leather seat as the starter offered no resistance.

*The clutch*, he remembered, *I forgot to engage the clutch.*

He pushed down the clutch pedal and turned the engine over a few times with the kick-starter, slowly ratcheting it back after each kick. Then he cautiously turned the ignition switch to the ON position.

After a swift kick, the motorcycle roared to life, but Jack had the throttle too far open and the high rpm frightened him. Overcompensating, he rolled back the throttle and the engine died.

He tried again—ready on the throttle this time. The engine fired, but then quit as it became starved for fuel. Trying for the third time, Jack was finally able to sustain the motor at a steady idle. Turning back to the *Rider's Handbook*, Jack turned the page and nervously read how "To Start and Stop Motorcycle on the Road":

1. Release clutch and set gear shifter lever in forward position marked LOW; then, with spark fully advanced, engage clutch very slowly and at the same time open the throttle slightly.

He twisted the throttle back. The bike perked up.

Jack's mouth felt like dry cotton as he pressed down on the clutch lever. The bike surged forward and died with a *blumph*.

He tried again with the same result, then took an embarrassed look around to see if anyone had been watching and carefully re-read the procedure: "... engage clutch *very slowly* ..."

On his third try, Jack successfully launched the motorcycle off the shoulder and down the middle of the road. For the first hundred yards, he swerved and swayed like a drunken sailor, but by the time he reached Sage Avenue his stability had dramatically improved. When he stopped at Hoosick Street he actually remembered to disengage the clutch. To his delight, the motor continued to purr, and he slowly turned around and motored back to Tibbits.

After forty-five minutes of starting, stopping, shifting, accelerating, braking—and a couple of waves and horn honks to passing pedestrians—Jack felt ready to take the next big step.

Turning left onto Hoosick, he soared down the hill to Eighth Street, where he rode south and paralleled the Hudson River until he hit Congress Street. He did his best to blend with traffic as he lined up to cross the drawbridge onto the Troy-Schenectady Road. The V-twin began to labor as he rode up the hill from Watervliet toward home. He twisted the throttle toward him. The motor responded in kind, and the Harley pulled him effortlessly up the hill like a locomotive.

For the first time in his life, Jack had tasted the freedom of the road.

He could go anywhere he wanted—and to twist that throttle and have it respond!

There are precious few moments in life when a boy feels such exhilaration, and for young Jack Newkirk—penniless but proud—this moment was one of them.

# 6

THE 1920s AND '30s were arguably the most contrasting consecutive decades in American history. Those born early in the century came of age during the grandiloquent boom of the Roaring Twenties—only to be hit head-on with the Great Depression as they attempted to enter the workforce. Few professions were spared, as legions of bankers, lawyers, engineers, and other workers were reduced to rags. Musicians in particular found employment hard to come by, yet it was this arduous era that produced two of America's most enduring musical icons.

Alton Miller had taken up the trombone as a teenager. He played by ear until his high school band teacher him taught to read music. This mentor—whom Miller simply called Boss—hired him to sit in with his weekend dance band.

"Boss," Miller confided shortly before graduation, "I have this dream. Someday I want to have a band of my own—a band so good it will sound like just one musician."

"That's swell, Glenn," he replied, knowing Miller preferred to go by his middle name. "You know, dreams are the building blocks of life, but persistence is how you make them come true. When your dreams fall apart—and they will—just pick up the pieces and start over. It shows the timber in a man to face a broken dream."

By the early 1930s Glenn Miller had flunked his first college music class, blown his first audition, and found himself in New York City playing for a meager sixty-two dollars per week. As Miller struggled to make ends meet, Boss's advice never seemed more fitting—while a few miles away in Brooklyn another young musician was eking out a living in pursuit of his own passion.

Aaron Copland was the son of Jewish immigrants. When Copland announced he wanted to be a composer, it came as a blow to his father, who immediately asked where he got such a strange idea. But like Glenn

Miller, Copland had an encouraging mentor—an influential French composer by the name of Nadia Boulanger. Copland studied with Boulanger for three years in Paris, only to return to America and face the same hardships as Miller.

The struggling Copland often had to rely on financial assistance from a close-knit group of friends and patrons. He took a summer job at a Poconos resort playing piano, but had to compete with noisy construction workers who made it difficult to concentrate on his music. Upon returning to New York City, Copland sent cards to potential students with the idea of teaching music theory and composition out of his small Manhattan studio. Not one student came forward.

In 1939, after gaining recognition from compositions *El Salón México* and *Billy the Kid*, Aaron Copland was commissioned to write music for the 1939 New York World's Fair.

That same year, Glenn Miller received an invitation to play at the famed Glen Island Casino in New Rochelle, New York. While the pay wasn't great, Miller knew NBC would be broadcasting these shows over their coast-to-coast radio network and would give his band exposure that other musicians could only dream of.

On May 17, 1939—as the lights of Fort Slocum reflected over Long Island Sound—the new Glenn Miller Orchestra, with singers Marion Hutton and Ray Eberle, took the stage of the Glen Island Casino's second-floor dining room and awaited their cue. The radio engineer held up his index finger and silently mouthed the words *three-two-one*.

The "On The Air" sign came to life, and the host offered a flattering introduction that would launch the career of a legend:

> Amid spotlights and celebrities, the Glen Island Casino opens its 1939 season. Let's listen to Glenn Miller's music.
> *(Cue orchestra to begin Moonlight Serenade)*
>     Good evening ladies and gentlemen. Tonight there comes music from beside the waters of Long Island Sound. NBC's microphones are present at Glenn Miller's smart opening in the Glen Island Casino, Mecca of music for moderns, just off the shore road at New Rochelle, New York.

Now may we proffer our invitation to dance to the music of one of America's foremost swing trombonists and ace arrangers, Glenn Miller and his orchestra.

After twenty years of ups, downs, bad checks, worse audiences, loose playing, and tight budgets, Glenn Miller's high school dream had finally come to fruition. As the radio waves carried Miller's *Moonlight Serenade* across the nation, he hoped that somewhere out there, Boss might be listening.

★ ★ ★

**ONE HUNDRED FIFTY MILES** up the Hudson, young Jack Newkirk had to admit his old Harley needed major repairs before she'd be ready for a trip across the country and back. The front fender was about to rattle off its mount from cracks near the fork bolts. The dents in the starboard gas tank reduced fuel capacity by more than a quart and needed to be pounded out. The bracket holding the rear fender to the frame had cracked from years of fatigue and was in danger of lodging in the spokes of the rear wheel. The carburetor needed de-varnishing, the fuel screen was dirty, and each of the motorcycle's two-dozen-odd Alemite fittings needed grease.

Nevertheless, Jack proudly pulled his prize into the driveway as his parents watched with mouths agape. Burt couldn't help but think of the scene on Lake George when Jack had hauled that decrepit canoe out of the water and called it his own. Neither parent had the heart to tell him he couldn't take the trip, though they silently wondered how this ramshackle bike could take their boy all the way to San Francisco.

Jack sensed their anxiety and reminded his parents that he had three relatives along the way—all within hitchhiking distance of each other. His mother's family, the Leavenworths, lived near Minneapolis. His brother, Horace, was going to college in Idaho, and his cousin Walter Smith lived in Portland, Oregon. If Jack got into trouble, he could probably get to one of them and find a way home. Furthermore, Jack's boyhood chum Stuart Crossman had always wanted to see Washington, D.C. and Virginia, and offered to share travel expenses. For at least the first few days, Jack wouldn't be riding alone.

He bought an oversized, light blue *1939 State Farm Road Atlas* at a used bookstore for twenty-five cents and began to do some arithmetic. He'd have sixty dollars left after paying for the Harley. Gasoline, on average, cost eighteen cents per gallon, and San Francisco—according to the State Farm atlas—was some four thousand miles away by his preferred route. At forty miles per gallon, he calculated he'd go through one hundred gallons of gas and four gallons of SAE 70 oil to get to California. This would cost about twenty dollars.

He'd buy bread, cheese, salami, and chocolate for lunch and get his breakfast at grocery stores. In the evenings he would treat himself to supper from one of the many roadside diners trying to make ends meet during the Depression years. A three-course dinner cost about a quarter, and he figured he'd leave a nickel tip. If he budgeted fifty cents a day, he could be gone six weeks and spend only twenty dollars on food. Admission to the New York World's Fair was seventy-five cents and the Golden Gate Exposition was half a dollar. His direct route home—only three thousand miles—would only cost fifteen dollars in fuel and oil. This left about five dollars for unplanned expenses, but he already had twelve in the bank from his business selling groceries out of his canoe to Lake George campers.

Motels were out of the question. He simply couldn't afford to stay inside, so he'd camp every night beside the motorcycle. From his Boy Scout days he retrieved two woolen army blankets that measured five-by-seven feet, then went to a fabric store and spent a dollar on a nine-by-nine-foot piece of twelve-ounce canvas. His mother helped him fashion this into a ground cloth by folding over the edges, sewing them shut, and swagging grommets into each corner. Jack spent ten cents on a block of paraffin wax that he dissolved into two pints of gasoline and then saturated the canvas with the resulting compound. After the whole thing was allowed to dry, he had a first-class, waterproof, nine-by-nine shelter cloth that cost just a dollar and a half.

His mother looked at the buddy seat and couldn't imagine her boy riding thousands of miles on top of that hard leather. She took a thick, white sheepskin off their fainting couch and placed it over the bike's saddle. With a china marker, she traced the outlines of the seat on the smooth leather underside like a butcher's diagram. Leaving plenty of room for the saddle lip, she cut away the excess material with thick garden shears and sewed three black elastic bands onto the leather.

Jack took the Harley to a local metal shop where he was quoted a price of $7.50 to weld the cracks in the frame, fenders, and various mounting brackets. It would be an extra $2.50 to take out the dent in the right fuel tank. He left the shop discouraged—unable to afford the $10.00 for metal work.

It was then that he thought of Dr. Hess.

Dr. Wendell Hess ran Rensselaer Polytechnic Institute's welding lab and was considered an expert in metallurgy and welding techniques. Jack had spent a considerable amount of time with Professor Hess in the metal shop on the upper floor of the Ricketts Building and had impressed him with his enthusiasm and thoroughness.

On Monday, June 12, 1939, Jack rode his motorcycle back to Troy. He parked on Sage Avenue in front of the Ricketts Building, then walked up the stairs to Hess's office and innocently asked if he'd come down and look at his Harley.

"I bet I could fix these fender cracks with the arc welder," Jack opined. "But I might need to use oxyacetylene on the frame here. What do you think?"

*I think this bike ought to be taken straight to the junkyard*, thought Hess.

"She needs some work, all right," Hess replied. "What were you going to use for a welder?"

"Well," Jack hesitated, "I was wondering—since classes are over—I was wondering if I could use the welding lab. The shop in Schenectady was going to charge me ten dollars and I don't have it. I also need the practice, Dr. Hess. These cracks right here are great examples of the stress fractures you spoke of in class."

Hess looked at this fresh-faced, enthusiastic boy so eager to see the world.

"Well, we're really not supposed to use the school's equipment for personal projects," he hesitated. "But tell you what. You come back on Wednesday, load her into the freight elevator, and we'll take a look."

"Gee, Dr. Hess, that's swell!" Jack shouted. "Thanks a million!"

"Now be sure to drain the fuel and remove the tanks and carburetor first," cautioned Hess. "We don't want gasoline vapor anywhere near those welders."

"Sure thing."

"Now, you'll probably want to spot weld it right here, then take the arc and make a pass on this side. Of course, you'll have to paint over it later or it's liable to rust."

Two days later, Jack rumbled back to the Ricketts Building. As he began to disassemble the fuel tanks, his friend Dick Hill came walking up the sidewalk.

"Hey Jack, whatcha got there?"

"It's a 1930 Harley-Davidson VL Big Twin. Seventy-four cubic inches. I'm taking her from New York City to San Francisco to see both world's fairs."

"You gotta be kidding!" Hill laughed. "I wouldn't go around the block on that raspberry, much less try to ride across the country!"

"Just what do you mean by 'raspberry'?" Jack shot back.

"That's what she sounds like—a big ol' raspberry. You know, the 'Bronx cheer.' I could hear you coming all the way up Fifteenth Street."

Hill's jab only strengthened Jack's resolve.

*All right,* Jack thought defiantly. *I'll call her the Raspberry. But when we get to San Francisco, I'm going to send a note to Dick Hill and rub it in his face!*

Under the guidance of Wendell Hess, Jack completed the Raspberry's metal repairs in three days. She now had a sound frame, tank, and fenders, and next needed a fresh coat of paint. Jack bought a quart of navy blue enamel and another of cherry red—the same red used for Rensselaer's colors. To show his appreciation for use of the school's welding equipment, Jack affixed a large, white Rensselaer surveyor's logo to the starboard gas tank.

He polished the Raspberry as well as he could with a light-blue chamois cloth, then rode out into the country and parked the bike beside a cornfield. Jack took a Kodak Bantam camera out of his coat pocket and carefully snapped a picture of his new pride and joy.

Crotalus horridus *concealed himself among the blueberry bushes along the path leading to Tongue Mountain's summit and waited for a chipmunk, mouse, or ground squirrel to pass by as a smattering of wooden boats covered the lake below. A young fawn poked its nose into the brush and accidentally stepped on* Crotalus *with its hoof, and after a perfunctory rattle the snake lurched forward and sank his fangs deep into the deer's muzzle. The fawn stumbled back and ran to its mother. Within five minutes it was dead—not from cardiac arrest, but from suffocation as its air passages swelled shut from the snake's venom.*

*Over the past decade,* Crotalus *had grown to five feet in length and was by far the largest snake on Tongue Mountain. And while hikers did visit this area from time to time, in all his ten years* Crotalus *had yet to encounter a human being.*

# 7

**S**IXTY FOREIGN COUNTRIES set up exhibits at the 1939 New York World's Fair. The nation of Germany, however, was conspicuously absent.

Mayor LaGuardia, highly critical of the Nazi regime, scornfully suggested a special pavilion be created as "a chamber of horrors" to expose Reich Chancellor Adolf Hitler, whom LaGuardia unblushingly labeled a "brown shirted fanatic." In response, Germany's government-controlled press called LaGuardia a "whoremonger" and a "dirty Talmud Jew." Compounding this ill will, fate had subjected Germany to annual embarrassments during the past few years as the Third Reich attempted to assert the superiority of its Aryan *übermensch*.

In 1936, two African-Americans named Jesse Owens and Cornelius Johnson won five gold medals at the Summer Olympics in Berlin, soundly beating the "racially superior" Nazis. Hitler snubbed Johnson by refusing to shake his hand.

In 1937, the German airship *Hindenburg*—the largest aircraft ever built—exploded in a spectacular crash over Lakehurst, New Jersey. What should have been a striking display of German might turned into a public relations nightmare as the huge Nazi swastikas on the blimp's tail plummeted to the ground in flames.

In 1938, a twenty-four-year-old black boxer named Joe Louis stepped into New York's Yankee Stadium to face Germany's Max Schmeling—the former heavyweight champion of the world. The press characterized this match as traditional good versus evil, with Louis representing American ideals and Schmeling as a symbol of Nazi tyranny. As seventy million Americans listened to their radios, Joe Louis proceeded to knock out Max Schmeling in one round.

By 1939, Germany was in no mood to participate in the New York World's Fair.

* * *

**MEANWHILE, SCARSDALE JACK** Newkirk had built up several hundred hours in a variety of naval aircraft, including the N3N Canary, the North American SNJ, the Grumman F3F fighter, and the Boeing F4B-4. He was now ready to try out the Brewster F2A Buffalo, the navy's first carrier-based monoplane fighter. The Buffalo carried two .50-caliber M2 Browning machine guns and two 100-pound bombs. Its supercharged Wright Cyclone engine could take it to thirty-three thousand feet and speeds of more than three hundred miles per hour.

Within a week, Scarsdale felt comfortable with the airplane, though he knew he hadn't scratched the surface of the fighter's potential. The ever-increasing airspeeds were a concern, as the faster an airplane flew, the less time he had to pull out of a dive. Even so, he was looking forward to the coming weeks when his fellow cadets and he would finally start training in advanced aerial combat.

* * *

**ON THE MORNING** of June 22, 1939, young Jack Newkirk walked out the front door and swung his leg over his Harley-Davidson VL 30V8229C. He wore an L.L. Bean wool jacket over a thin, long-sleeved shirt on top of a cotton undershirt next to his skin. His khaki denim pantaloons flared at the hip and tapered down to his ankles where a pair of lace-up leather boots came up to his calf muscles. He also wore a thin pair of leather gloves, goggles, and a cloth helmet that could be rolled up and put in a pocket.

His two canvas saddlebags, straight from a World War I army horse, contained a long-sleeved cotton shirt, extra socks and underwear, his State Farm atlas, pencil and paper, two bandanas, a canteen, a Barlow knife with a can opener, a waterproof match safe, toothbrush, soap, washcloth, and a toolkit. He left room in one saddlebag for food, and his two woolen blankets were safely wrapped inside the shelter cloth, which was lashed to the luggage carrier with cotton rope.

"Are you going to stop and see Scarsdale on the way down?" asked his mother.

"I'd like to, Mom," Jack replied, "but he's not there. He's down in Florida."

As his parents looked on, Jack clacked the Raspberry's shift lever into the neutral detent, engaged the clutch, and closed the choke lever. He turned on the right fuel petcock, then folded out the starter pedal and kicked it down twice to prime the cylinders. He moved the choke to the one-third position, turned on the ignition, and with a firm kick the V-twin fired up. He let it run for a full half minute before moving the choke to full open.

At ages sixty-three and fifty-four, Burt and Louise Newkirk were not overly emotional parents. Yet the sight of their youngest boy about to ride off into the early morning mist caught them off guard. To Louise, this moment seemed the end of an era that had passed all too quickly— the day the last of their children would leave the nest. The Newkirk boys had spread out like leaves in the wind: Horace in Idaho; Scarsdale in Florida; his brother Bobby in Texas; and now Jack off to California.

Jack turned to wave goodbye. From a distance he saw his father slowly raise his right hand into the air. If this action had been performed with swiftness and rigidity—fingers held together—it could be mistaken for the Nazi salute. But Burt's hand remained motionless, outstretched and open, as if part of a Michelangelo painting. It was the "Newkirk salute"—a traditional family gesture seldom used except at reunions—or when a family member begins a journey that will take them far away from the others.

Jack returned the salute, and his eyes began to well up with tears.

Shortly before noon, Jack was groping through a maze of streets in Upper Manhattan looking for Stuart Crossman's apartment. After a few false turns, Jack found Crossman sitting on the front steps of the building.

"Hey, Happy!" said Jack, calling Crossman by his nickname. "Been waiting long?"

Jack removed the blankets and tarp from the luggage carrier, unloaded his saddlebags, and placed the contents on the bed inside. Happy and he climbed aboard the Raspberry and rode to 125th Street, where they took the Triborough Bridge over Hell Gate and onto the Grand Central Parkway. They could see Trylon and Perisphere towering in the distance, and the sight filled Jack with anticipation. Up to now, he'd only seen them in the newspaper.

A uniformed parking attendant motioned them to the east side of the City Parking Lot where they pushed the bike onto a grassy berm. Jack could hardly grasp the immensity of the fairgrounds. He'd seen a few fairs in Schenectady, but they'd only occupied five to ten acres. The New York World's Fair took up more than twelve hundred.

The fair wasn't crowded that Thursday afternoon, so they had little trouble meeting up with Crossman's cousin Jim at the north side of the Trylon for lunch. The three boys walked to the central Food Zone, bought some hamburgers, and then began to explore the fair in earnest.

The first stop was the General Motors Building, which they reached by riding a four-car tractor train across the Bridge of Wheels—one of two bridges that crossed the Grand Central Parkway to the fair's Transportation Zone. Here, General Motors had built an astonishing thirty-six-thousand-square-foot diorama called *Futurama*.

*Futurama* was the largest and most realistic scale model ever constructed—a "vast miniature cross-section of America" as it might appear in the far-off year of 1960. Fairgoers sat in moving chairs equipped with speakers narrating a "flyover" of the artificial landscape below. It was one of the fair's most popular attractions. Jack, Happy, and Jim took their seats and were instantly enthralled. Upon leaving they were given a blue and white button that read "I Have Seen the Future."

They walked to the Ford Building and stared at its half-mile, helical "Road of Tomorrow." Next they decided to split up and meet at Trylon and Perisphere in a couple of hours. Happy and Jim wanted to see the Aviation building while Jack wanted to visit U.S. Steel. He walked back across the Bridge of Wings to the main fairgrounds and turned right toward the Westinghouse building. He went inside and saw a demonstration of Electro—an eight-foot robot who walked, talked, counted on his fingers, and was master of a metallic dog named Sparko.

Jack's family history compelled him to visit the General Electric building, which was marked by an imposing stainless steel lightning bolt. The main auditorium had been named after his father's former colleague Dr. Charles Steinmetz.

The U.S. Steel building looked like a huge metal helmet that Buck Rogers might wear in space. An animated diorama went through the fundamental steps of producing industrial-grade steel from open-pit mine to blast furnace to rolling mill. As a metallurgy student, Jack was intensely interested in the exhibit and dreamed one day he might even work for this company.

After nearly an hour at U.S. Steel, Jack walked across the Plaza of Light, stepped inside the Hall of Pharmacy, and sat down in the Medicine Chest Theater where a recorded host announced that a twelve-foot-high puppet show called *From Sorcery to Science*—the "Drug Store of Tomorrow"—was about to begin. A huge medicine cabinet served as a stage and an oddly translucent mirror was its "curtain." Popular radio personality Lowell Thomas narrated over an orchestra that played music written and conducted by a young composer named Aaron Copland.

After the puppet show, Jack walked northwest past Trylon and Perisphere until he came to the Science and Education Building. A documentary called *The City* was playing in the auditorium, and once again Jack took a seat. The movie portrayed the typical American city as an ominous, dirty, almost hopeless place to grow up. It offered a utopian alternative in the form of a modern suburbia with affordable housing, quasi-communal living, and structured "motor-parkways [that] weave together city and countryside." As the credits rolled Jack noticed that the same composer he'd seen at the Hall of Pharmacy—Aaron Copland—had written the score.

At six o'clock the boys regrouped at the Theme Center on the northern side of the Perisphere to take advantage of the light dinnertime lines. They rode up the "world's longest escalator" and into the interior of the Trylon. From there they walked inside the Perisphere and stood on one of two rotating rings that hovered over *Democracity*, a futuristic urban diorama. A narrator described the merits of this brave new metropolis while William Grant Still's *Rising Tide*, a "symphonic poem of a thousand voices," played continuously in the background. After the show they walked down the Helicline ramp toward the food zone again, where they discussed how to best spend their remaining hours.

"We haven't even hit the Government Zone," said Jim. "And then there's the Amusement Area. They had a Miss Nude 1939 Pageant over there and boy did that make the mayor sore!"

"Jack, what do you think?" asked Happy. "We could see as much as we can tonight and come back tomorrow. Or we could go to a dance club and hear some swing. Glenn Miller's playing at the Glen Island Casino—it's only a half hour from here, across the Whitestone Bridge."

Jack thought hard about the seventy-five cents it cost to get into the fair. He couldn't really afford another day—or the Glen Island Casino, for that matter. Much as he'd love to hear Glenn Miller, he was too embarrassed to ask Happy for money.

"Well, fellows," said Jack. "If it's OK by you I'd like to spend the rest of the evening looking around the fair. Then Happy and I could start off in the morning and beat the weekend traffic into Virginia."

"Good idea," said Crossman. "It'd be better if we didn't take that ride on a Friday afternoon."

"Hey," Jack suddenly remembered, "is there a postbox anywhere? I want to mail a card to my folks."

"Postbox? Jack, they've got an entire post office here! It's by the Communications Building."

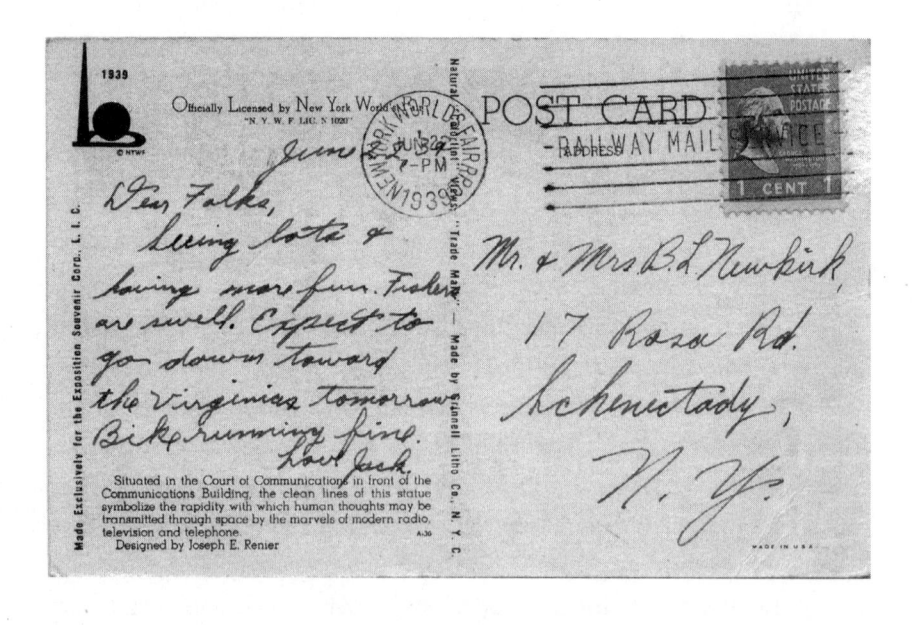

# 8

THE NEXT MORNING, Jack pulled on his cloth helmet, placed his goggles snugly over his eyes, and fired up the Harley. Stuart Crossman would ride with him for three days to the Shenandoah Valley and then make his way home by bus from Harrisonburg, Virginia. Both boys were eager to start their adventure.

They'd ridden just a hundred yards when the engine started to cough and wheeze.

"What's up?" shouted Stuart.

"Don't know," replied Jack as the Raspberry bucked and sputtered down the street.

"Oh, cuss!" said Jack. "I forgot to turn on the fuel petcock."

Jack reached down with his right hand and fumbled for the lever. A jolt of electricity shot through his body and for a split second he could feel his hair stand on end.

"Criminy!" Jack cried as they lurched to a stop. "Something just shocked the dickens out of me."

Jack looked down and realized his right hand had brushed against the Raspberry's rear spark plug, which was connected to its ignition wire by an uninsulated, knurled brass ring. It was a mistake he wouldn't make again. He sheepishly had Crossman get off the bike as he opened the fuel petcock, primed the engine, and started it up again.

During his ride down the Hudson, Jack had noticed the Raspberry seemed to settle into her comfort zone at about forty-three miles per hour. At slower speeds, the engine labored. At higher speeds, the entire bike shook. For whatever reason, forty-three was the Raspberry's sweet spot, where she would run smoothly and sip only a gallon of gasoline per hour.

As Jack and Happy puttered along the Pennsylvania countryside, the Raspberry abruptly began to cough and sputter again. Jack pulled off the road a mile outside of Goshenville and scratched his head as Happy looked on.

"Do you think she's out of gas?" Crossman asked.

"Doesn't sound like it."

Jack got out his tools and *Rider's Handbook*. He could smell the pungent odor of burnt SAE 70 oil that had splattered from the chain oiler onto the Raspberry's exhaust pipe. He made sure both fuel petcocks were off, then used a crescent wrench to remove the metal fuel lines from the bottom of each tank. They were welded as a Y-assembly, which allowed either tank to feed the carburetor, and Jack thought something might be clogging the line. He covered one end with his thumb and blew through the other, then did the same thing with the opposite end. Air flowed freely through both lines, so he knew there was no obstruction. Next he held a rag underneath each fuel petcock, opened them briefly, and noted that gas poured out freely each time.

"Well, it's not the fuel system," Jack announced. "I suppose it could be the ignition."

"Oh boy," said Happy, who at eighteen was only a few months younger than Jack. "I don't know anything about that stuff. Does it say anything about it in the manual?"

The shoulder of the road was dotted with small colonies of ants that had taken advantage of pavement cracks to build their nests. Stuart Crossman stared down at the anthills as Jack sat sidesaddle on the Raspberry with his back toward the road and his face buried in the *Rider's Handbook*.

"Say, do you fellows need any help?"

Jack looked up to see a Chrysler Imperial convertible slowing to a stop.

"Uh, yes sir, maybe," he replied. "My motorcycle started cutting out a few miles ago and now she's misfiring like crazy."

The man got out of his car and walked over to the Raspberry.

"Harley-Davidson VL Big Twin. They stopped making those a few years back."

"Yes, sir. She's a 1930 model."

"Well," the man said as he stared at the engine, "a misfire usually means an ignition issue—or something with your carburetor. Did you check the fuel lines?"

"Sure did—they're both clear."

"Then let's take a look at those breaker points."

The man squatted down and looked intently at where Jack had just been staring a few minutes earlier.

"Hmmm... points look clean enough. Are you getting a good spark?"

"I can attest to that," said Jack, recalling the jolt he'd received that morning.

"OK, then let's check the breaker gap. What do they call for, .022 inches?"

"Yes, that's right," said Jack, as he handed the man his gap tool.

"Let's make sure it's... well, what the heck? Here's your problem, son. Both lock screws are loose. Your point gap is jumping all over the place. Those adjustment screws need to be cinched down tight."

They measured the proper breaker point gap, tightened the adjustment lock screws, and reassembled the case. After priming the cylinders, Jack kicked over the starter and the Raspberry came to life as though nothing had ever happened.

"We owe you one, mister," said Stuart. "Thanks a lot!"

"You're welcome," he responded. "I've had some experience with these bikes—and I know what it's like to be stuck. I've found you can usually fix 'em as long you have the right tools, an understanding of your bike, and a little imagination and persistence."

"Yes, thanks," added Jack. "I wish we could return the favor."

"You can," the man said as he got back into his Chrysler. "I don't know where you're headed, but someday, somewhere, you'll come across someone who needs your help. You do them a favor and the world will be a better place. Just help the next fellow on down the road."

"I'll do that," Jack promised.

"Have a safe ride, boys!"

And with that, the stranger drove off toward Philadelphia.

When they stopped for gas at West Chester, Jack dropped a penny postcard into the mail:

June 23, 1939
Chester, PA

Dear Folks:
 Got off rather late this morning. Received your special with Horace's letter within. Sent it back after reading it. Expect to be in the Shenendoa(?) Valley (Luray) by & all tomorrow afternoon. Stuart will leave me the next morning.
 Love, Jack

The next morning, they hit the outskirts of the city and bought a simple breakfast of bread and apples. They filled the main tank, topped off the oil, and continued on to Washington, D.C.

Both boys had seen pictures of the District of Columbia in their schoolbooks, but the sight of the Washington Monument towering in the distance gave them goose bumps. As they motored down toward Washington Circle, Jack noticed the Raspberry was starting to hesitate slightly whenever he opened the throttle. By the time they got to Pennsylvania Avenue, the engine was coughing and the exhaust pipe began to pop and spurt.

"Oh, brother!" shouted Happy. "Now what?"

The Raspberry gasped and backfired loudly as Jack rolled to a stop beside the White House. The boys climbed off and Jack dug through the saddlebags for his toolkit. Their cacophonous arrival attracted the attention of a mounted Capitol police officer, who thought the Raspberry's backfires sounded like multiple gunshots.

"What's going on here, boys?" asked the policeman sternly.

The horse gave a loud snort and sneered down his nose at the Raspberry.

"I don't know, officer," Jack replied. "My motorcycle started acting up a few blocks back and I was going to try to fix it."

"Well, you need to do that," the officer affirmed. "We can't have that kind of racket going on around here."

"Oh—is President Roosevelt in there?" Crossman inquired.

"I can't tell you that, son," explained the officer, "but if you use common sense, you'll understand why it's not good business to have explosions outside the White House."

"Yes, sir," answered both boys simultaneously.

The officer began to soften as he looked down at these young men in their abject state of affairs. They looked like a two-wheeled version of the countless overloaded jalopies he'd seen headed for California during the past decade.

"Where are you boys from?"

"New York."

"Where are you headed?"

"I'm going to California," Jack announced proudly. "I'm going to see the fair."

"That's pretty ambitious," remarked the officer. "All right, I'll tell you what. I need to ride my beat down to Constitution. If you haven't fixed it by the time I come back, I'll have to ask you to push the bike over to the YMCA on G Street. You can work on it there. Even stay the night if you have to."

"Thanks, mister," said Happy.

"Yeah, thanks," echoed Jack. "We'll get on it right now."

"OK, then," said the officer, "now it sounded to me like a fuel problem. Your engine was coughing as though it wasn't getting enough gas. You might check your carburetor."

Jack shut off the fuel petcock and loosened the nut underneath the carburetor's float bowl. Clean gasoline dribbled out, and there didn't seem to be any sign of dirt or water. As he tightened the float bowl lock nut, Jack noticed looseness in the carburetor assembly that hadn't been there before. He grabbed the carburetor and wiggled it. He traced the carburetor to the right side of the bike where it attached to the engine's intake manifold with three hexagonal screws. The screws were loose, which allowed the carburetor to float on the manifold.

"I may have found something here," said Jack. "If the carb isn't tight on the manifold, the fuel-air mixture will be all out of whack—no wonder it's acting up. Boy, the screws on this bike sure have a way of shaking loose."

Jack turned each of the three manifold screws down tight and once again followed the starting procedure in the *Rider's Handbook*. The

Raspberry growled its approval, then purred at an idle as Jack turned the handgrip forward.

"Hot dog!" shouted Happy. "That was it."

Jack smiled with satisfaction as he looked up at the Oval Office.

As they puttered past the Department of State, they saw the same Capitol policeman riding back north. Both boys waved and the officer nodded in approval. The horse gave the Raspberry a quick glance and lifted its nose high into the air.

They stopped at the Lincoln Memorial and had a light lunch of bread, cheese, and salami purchased earlier that morning. At Arlington Memorial Bridge, they took U.S. Highway 50 west until they hit Route 211 and followed it for the rest of the day over the Blue Ridge Mountains, across Skyline Drive, and down to Luray, Virginia.

As they rolled into town, they saw a gas station with a large sign that read "7-4-1."

"What's that mean," Jack asked the attendant, "seven-four-one?"

"Oh, that's seven-for-one. Seven gallons for a dollar."

"Wish I could hold seven gallons," said Jack. "This bike only carries half that."

"Well that's fourteen cents per gallon then. You want to fill 'er up?"

"You bet."

Jack and Happy parked the bike near the entrance of Luray Caverns and set up camp. That evening Jack got out a piece of paper and wrote a letter to his parents:

June 24, 1939
Luray, West Virginia

Dear Folks:
    Started early outside Wilmington. Went through Washington, D.C. Saw the Capitol, Wash. Monument, etc. Gas Cheap. Continued south over <u>beautiful</u> Blue Ridge Mountains of VA and a little west to Luray, where we went through the caverns. It cost more than expected but I went anyway. Had fine weather making the ride most enjoyable. Stuart is a good companion and I'll be sorry to leave him

tomorrow. I expect to start west tomorrow taking it easy and enjoying it just as I'm doing now.

Love, JBN

They awoke to the sound of a scarlet tanager flitting around the Raspberry and occasionally landing on the branches above their shelter cloth. After breaking camp they mounted the Raspberry and headed toward Harrisonburg.

Jack noticed the weather was getting noticeably hotter the farther south he went and he was rethinking his route across the country. He'd originally planned to ride to St. Louis and then take Route 66 through Oklahoma City, Albuquerque, Arizona, and into Los Angeles, where he'd visit Eustace Hetzel before heading up the coast to the Golden Gate International Exposition.

But Jack found he didn't like the hot wind against his bare face; it chapped his lips and gave him a windburn. He tried a bandana around his neck, but it flapped in the wind, chaffed his skin, and made him look like a masked bandit. *Maybe a northern route would be cooler*, he thought, *and then maybe I wouldn't have to—*

POWSHhhhhh!

The Raspberry shook violently. Jack snapped to attention. Happy reflexively grabbed on to the handles of the buddy seat and screamed. Jack did everything he could to keep the motorcycle upright as they wobbled to the side of the road two miles outside of Luray.

"Great Caesar's ghost!" said Crossman. "What happened?"

"Blowout," said Jack as he looked over the rear wheel. "Good thing we were going slowly. It was all I could do to keep her upright."

Stuart Crossman sat down on the grass, put both elbows on his knees, and cradled his head.

"Oh for Pete's sake!" Jack cried. "Now we've got a tire to fix. Why did this have to happen now? It's Sunday morning and everyone's in church."

"I should probably be there myself," said Stuart, who was a devout Catholic.

Jack examined the rear tire and found the metal valve stem had split. His rubber tire repair kit was useless. He'd probably have to replace the entire tube.

"Hey, Happy," said Jack, sensing Crossman's anxiety, "there's no way we'll make it to Roanoke in time for you to start back today. Why don't we hitch back to Luray—you can go to mass while I look for a garage."

"Sounds swell, Jack," said a relieved Crossman. "I'll cross the road and start thumbing."

"OK—I'll get this tube out of the tire."

Jack removed the rear wheel and set it flat on the grass. Next he used two tire irons to pry the casing over the rim—ever careful not to damage the bead or pinch the inner tube.

"This fellow is stopping, Jack!" shouted Crossman.

Jack looked up from his work and saw a black Buick coupe slowing to a stop.

"It's going to take me a few minutes to get out this tube and stow my gear," Jack said. "Why don't you just go on, Happy? I'll be OK. Really, I will."

"I'm not just going to leave you on the side of the road!"

"There aren't many cars coming by—you'd better take this ride," Jack responded. "I'll thumb into town later and get the tube fixed."

Stuart ran to the car and spoke a few words to the driver, who nodded his head and set the parking brake. Crossman ran back to Jack, who was sitting Indian-style with the Harley's wheel in his lap.

"It's been a swell ride, Jack. Breakdowns and all."

"Yes, it has. And I'm going to miss having you with me."

Jack set down the wheel and stood up. Crossman reached out and shook Jack's grease-covered hand, then grabbed his belongings, turned around, and ran back to the waiting car, leaving Jack alone on the side of the Lee Highway.

Thirty minutes later, Jack had finessed the inner tube out of the wheel well and draped it around his neck with his thumb pointing toward Luray. He mopped his brow occasionally with grease-covered hands, which splotched his face with stains that made him look like a coal miner. The tube around his neck evoked images of *The Rime of the Ancient Mariner*, and it was this dismal sight that compelled the next car to stop and offer him a ride to a Luray gas station—which unfortunately didn't open until ten.

Jack waited out front until a 1932 Ford AA truck came bouncing up the dusty drive.

"Is that yo' cycle I seen on the road?" asked the owner in a thick Virginia accent.

"Yes sir," Jack replied, "I had a blowout."

The man looked the tube over and frowned.

"Rubba looks fine, but yo' valve stem's busted open."

The station owner unlocked the front door and rummaged through the shelves behind his desk. He pulled out a small box marked 19 x 4.00 and set it on the counter. Jack looked at the box and asked how much it cost.

"I usually charge two-fifty, but seeing as yo' broke down and all I can let ya have it for two dollas. That's what I paid."

"Do you have a welder here?" asked Jack. "I think this valve stem can be repaired. I can work all kinds of welders."

"Closest welda is over in Harrisonburg, but yo' right. Could probably fix that stem right up fo' a lot cheapa than a new one."

"How far is Harrisonburg?" asked Jack.

"Thirty-two miles."

Jack thanked the man, then walked back to the Lee Highway and stuck his thumb in the air. An hour and a half later he was sitting on the grass in front of Vickers Metal Shop eating half a pepperoni stick, a hunk of cheddar cheese, a Kaiser roll, and a bar of Hershey's chocolate from the local grocer.

Stan Vickers came out from his shop and handed him the tube.

"Good as new," said Stan. "I put the stem through an old tire rim and used a spot weld so it wouldn't damage the rubber. Then I cleaned it up with a bench grinder so it'll be sure and fit through your rim."

Jack paid the man fifty cents and walked across Route 11 to hitchhike his way back to the Raspberry. By late afternoon the tire was repaired and Jack was on the move again, riding southwest through the stunning valley that separates the Blue Ridge Mountains from the Alleghenies.

Jack hadn't counted on the heat and was seriously rethinking his route. While in Harrisonburg, he had traced alternate roads in his *State Farm Atlas* as he drank deeply from his canteen, and finally decided to turn north as soon as possible. He would take Highway 50 westbound and then head north toward the Great Lakes. This would make for a cooler ride, and he could also visit his cousins in Minnesota.

He turned onto Route 33 and rode over the Appalachians into West Virginia, then took Highway 220 thirty miles north to Petersburg where he stopped at an auto camp for the night.

With Stuart Crossman gone, Jack had the nine-by-nine-foot cloth all to himself and devised a clever method of folding his blankets inside the tarp to create a completely weatherproof cocoon. He also found that his mother's woolen seat cover made a fine pillow.

After dinner at the local diner, he sent another quick card to his parents:

Sun. June 25, '39
Petersburg, W. Va.

Dear Folks:

Got an early start but had tire trouble right away which took the greater part of the day to fix. OK now but didn't make much mileage. Had to go via thumb from Luray to Harrisontown [sic]—32 miles each way—to get the tube valve stem fixed. Having supper here and staying nearby at an auto camp where the man didn't charge me 50 cents (Fox and Ox Camp). Beautiful country—high mountains all covered with trees. Everyone around here talks so southern & the old folks crowd around the bike & look at it, touch it & discuss among themselves thereupon. Expect to meet Rt. 50 at Mt. Storm W. Va. and go west on it.

Love,
Jack

The sun dipped behind old Chimney Top west of town as Jack rode back to camp. He parked the Raspberry beside the shelter cloth, changed into underclothes, and crawled inside.

An hour after sunrise, he began reorganizing his belongings on top of a picnic table. As he packed the saddlebags and lashed his sleeping gear back onto the Raspberry, he realized he hadn't bathed or washed his clothes in five days.

Just outside of Petersburg, Jack found a dirt road that disappeared into the forest next to a small tributary. It was the south fork of the Potomac River. The Raspberry's springs squeaked and squealed as Jack followed the path, which came to an abrupt stop across the river from a hilly area called Stillhouse Gap. Jack looked to see if anyone was watching, then took out soap and towel, stripped naked, and jumped into the Potomac.

The morning sun offset the chill of the river as the greasy film accumulating on Jack's hands, face, and neck began to loosen with liberal use of soap and water. He dried himself off with his towel, wrapped it around him, and then washed his clothes with the same soap bar.

He pulled two sticks from a pile of driftwood and used his rope to lash them onto both sides of the Raspberry like miniature flagpoles. Then—wearing only his undershirt and shorts—he tied the wet clothes to the sticks and rode onto State Highway 42 northbound. In forty-five minutes he was in Mt. Storm and his shirt, shorts, pants, and socks had all blown dry.

At Highway 50, Jack turned due west toward Parkersburg, West Virginia. He'd just crossed Backbone Mountain Ridge when the rear wheel sent out a tooth-jarring clatter. Pulling off of the road, he discovered the Raspberry's rear chain guard bolt had rattled off. This allowed the chain guard assembly to rest on top of the rear sprocket.

Jack reached into his saddlebag and pulled out a length of bailing wire. He cut off a couple of inches with his pliers, threaded the wire through the mounting holes, and twisted both ends together. This would hold until he could get to a hardware store and replace the bolt.

His stomach began to growl as he continued west on Highway 50, and five miles later he happened upon a small grocery store in the small town of Aurora, West Virginia.

The Aurora General Store was an oblong, two-story wooden building with four plate-glass windows in front and a wide set of stairs leading up to its wooden double doors. Jack looked the shelves over and saw a variety of standard goods: Boraxo Powdered Hand Soap, Clabber Girl Baking Powder, Junket Quick Fudge and Icing Mix, Maxwell House Coffee, Post

Toasties Corn Flakes, 1-Minute Quick Mother's Oats, Ivory Soap, fresh bread, milk and cheese, apples, candy, flypaper, candles, washboards, mousetraps, and a hundred other items.

"Do you carry any nuts and bolts?" asked Jack, putting the Raspberry before his grumbling stomach.

"Sorry, son," said the proprietor, a man named McCrum. "You'd have to go to the hardware store. Is it something for your bike?"

"Yes, sir," Jack replied. "Her hardware has a bad habit of shaking off on the road. My chain guard is being held on with bailing wire now."

"Are you headed west? If it's motorcycle parts you need, there's a Harley-Davidson shop in Clarksburg—fifty miles down the road."

"Really?" said Jack. "That would work out just right."

As Jack considered what he'd buy for breakfast, he recalled how hungry he'd been while fixing the tire the day before.

"Say, would you have some kind of food I could keep in my saddlebags that wouldn't spoil? You know, something I could carry in case I get stuck in the middle of nowhere?"

The grocer thought for a moment.

"Well, if it were me, son, here's what I'd get. Take a few tins of these sardines packed in oil. They don't take up much space and have their own can opener. And a box of pilot biscuits."

"How about a stick of pepperoni?" asked Jack.

"Well, it won't go bad—but it'd make your bags smell pretty good to a 'coon or a bear."

"Chocolate?"

"Probably make a mess in this heat. Here, take a handful of horehound drops instead. Do you have a canteen?"

"Yes, sir."

"Then get a bottle of these halazone tablets and drop one in after you fill up from a stream. And here are some raisins and nuts that you can store in this can."

Jack bought four tins of sardines, a box of pilot crackers, the horehound drops, halazone, and a half-pound of shelled peanuts and raisins.

A hot wind blew in his face as he continued west on Highway 50, and the Raspberry rolled into Clarksburg at high noon. For several minutes

Jack stared at the shiny new motorcycles parked outside the Harley-Davidson shop. There was only one other VL in sight—a 1936 model with nine thousand miles on the odometer. The other bikes were brand-new 61EL Knuckleheads with four-speed transmissions, recirculating oil systems, tank-mounted dashes, and overhead-valve engines. Their only common parts with the VL were the generator, mudguards, and a few standard nuts and bolts. The Knucklehead was an entirely new bike—solid, fast, and reliable.

"That's a 1930 VL, ain't it?" asked one of the servicemen. "Looks like she's been around the block a few times."

"Yes," Jack replied, "and she's got a lot farther to go."

He bought three quarts of SAE 70 and a handful of nuts and bolts. He repaired the chain guard and then spent an hour snugging down every nut, bolt, or screw he could find.

Ten miles later, Jack suddenly felt a hundred sharp *thwacks* on his face and chest, as if someone had thrown a handful of pea-gravel at him. He rolled to a stop to assess the situation and noticed a half-dozen stunned honeybees crawling on his cotton undershirt. He had collided with a swarm at forty-three miles per hour.

Jack brushed off the remaining bees, climbed back on the Raspberry, and kicked the starter. To his surprise, the motor backfired. The resulting recoil from the kickstarter sent his right leg into the air.

*Spark advance must be in the wrong position*, he guessed.

The Raspberry started on the next kick and Jack thought no more about it as he puttered into Parkersburg, where he mailed another note to his parents:

June 26, 1939

Dear Folks:
    At Parkersburg, W. VA now. Will take Rt. 21 north and camp wherever seems convenient. Hot today, but traveling is comfortable. Hope all is OK at home. Didn't stop much today except for when I gave the bike a general going over at a Harley shop in Clarksburg.
                                Love, Jack

Just past Newcomerstown, Ohio, Jack came upon a series of signs spaced at fifty-yard intervals:

A WEEK-OLD BEARD

. . .

SO MASKED HIS FACE

. . .

HIS BULL DOG CHASED HIM

. . .

OFF THE PLACE

. . .

BURMA SHAVE

Jack laughed as he realized he hadn't even brought along a razor. Fifteen miles west of Coshocton, Ohio, he saw another sign:

Mohawk Dam
U.S. Army Corp of Engineers
September 1937

He followed the highway to the top of the new dam and shut down the Raspberry. Below the spillway, the Walhonding River rolled through a broad valley past a grove of buckeye, beech, and oak trees at a place called Possum Hollow. Jack turned around and followed a dirt path a quarter-mile upriver, then finessed the Raspberry fifty yards into the woods. Off came the blankets and ground cloth, and in ten minutes Jack had a cozy camp. He studied his atlas and noted the small settlement of Walhonding was just three miles up the road, so he fired up the bike and made his way through the woods back to Highway 36.

Jack was mildly disappointed to find no restaurant in Walhonding, but the town did have a general store and a modern service station, with three bright-red, glass-topped gas pumps out front. He walked over to the store and paid twenty cents for a T-bone steak in white butcher paper, a quarter-loaf of bread, a few stalks of celery, and an oatmeal cookie.

He rode back to camp through the lush Muskingum watershed as the

John Brown Motolamp cast a faint orange tinge on the road ahead. He started a campfire and impaled the steak on a green branch sharpened with his Barlow knife. The meat—cooked over an open fire—had a primal, minimalist taste, and Jack felt safe and secure sandwiched between the motorcycle and his campfire as the Raspberry stood watch like a steadfast sentinel.

As he drifted off to sleep, Jack heard a barred owl hooting at the moonrise over Coshocton County—and he realized he was living every boy's dream.

★ ★ ★

**FIVE HUNDRED MILES** to the east, the opening strains of "Moonlight Serenade" drifted over the waters of Long Island Sound as Glenn Miller led his orchestra on yet another sold-out night at the Glen Island Casino. At the New York World's Fair, Trylon and Perisphere reflected bright white as Aaron Copland's music played continuously inside the Hall of Pharmacy.

# 9

**S**CARSDALE JACK NEWKIRK strode across the tarmac at Naval Air Station Pensacola toward a waiting line of Boeing F4B-4 biplanes. His flight suit made the heat and humidity seem even more stifling, and all the pilots were anxious to get airborne that morning so they could have some wind in their faces.

Some five dozen cadets were in various stages of flight training at NAS Pensacola during the summer of 1939. Many were cocky and overconfident. Some were edgy and anxious, and a few seemed astonished they'd made it this far. They came from all over the country, with a few from Europe, Finland, and even a young man from South America.

One of the cadets from Class 121-C was a skinny kid from Texas.

"I'll have to be honest, friend," said Scarsdale. "I can hardly understand a word you're saying. Where'd you say you're from?"

"San Antone. Home of the Alamo, boy! Damn proud of it too. Evah been to Texas?"

His name was David Lee Hill. His friends called him Tex.

"No," Jack replied, "but my brother Bobby lives in Houston."

"Hell, that's just down the coast!" exclaimed Tex. "We oughta fly ovah and pay him a visit!"

Jack smiled and started to say something when their instructor interrupted them.

"All right, boys. Live ammo today. Your birds have their guns filled to the gills. We'll be working on ground targets to the east. The object will be strafing and conserving ammo."

The Boeing F4B-4, called the P-12 by the army, had been relegated to a trainer after its combat usefulness expired. It wasn't a hotrod—topping out at 190 miles per hour—but it served its role well as a weapons trainer.

After the briefing the men climbed into their cockpits and fired up the 550-horsepower Pratt & Whitney radial engines. They flew east over the Florida coast and bore down on a range of old automobiles and wooden buildings. Scarsdale Jack got a kick out of watching the targets explode as he hammered them with his .50-caliber machine gun.

★ ★ ★

**NINE HUNDRED MILES** to the north, young Jack awoke to the sound of a large fox squirrel scolding him from the branches above. As he broke camp and packed up the bike, he detected a stronger-than-usual gasoline odor wafting up from the Raspberry. A telltale drop clung to the bottom of the tank. He looked closer and discovered a small crack above the fuel petcock that had allowed the tank's contents to drip out overnight. Thankfully, the reserve tank was full and contained enough gas to take him back to Walhonding.

Jack rode three miles to the Walhonding service station—an impressive, modern facility, considering the remoteness of these Ohio woodlands. Three cherry-red gas pumps stood like soldiers at attention on a yellow and white concrete base. Two spacious shop buildings were attached to either side of the garage, and a small, cantilevered roof covered the main entryway.

"Would you fellows have any welding equipment?" Jack asked politely. "I've got a leak in my gas tank."

"Sure do," said the man at the desk, "but my welding man won't be here for an hour."

He wore a blue shirt stained with axle grease and a name patch that said "Red."

"I could probably do it myself, actually," Jack boasted. "I'm a metallurgy student."

Red chuckled.

"Ol' Pete is pretty particular about who touches his tools. Best wait 'til he gets here and see what he says. I'll take a look at what you got, anyway."

Jack and Red walked out the door and stood over the Raspberry.

"You'll have to take off the tank, of course," remarked Red. "It's empty, you say?"

"Yup," Jack nodded.

"Well, there's probably enough vapor in there to send it through the roof if it sees a spark," cautioned Red. "We'll want to blow it out real good with the compressor first."

"Good idea."

"Why don't you go to work removing that tank," Red suggested. "Ol' Pete will probably get here by the time you're done."

Jack pushed the Raspberry to a shady spot at the west end of the building beneath a medium-sized maple. He laid his tools on a shop rag, selected the proper crescent wrench, and started to remove the fuel petcock from the bottom of the main tank. The crack at the threaded joint crunched back and forth with the sickening sound of a tooth extraction.

As Red came out to check Jack's progress, a grizzled figure emerged from the woods.

"Here comes Pete now," said Red.

"What's the shotgun for?" asked Jack.

"Ol' Pete hunts squirrel and possum on his way to work. Stores 'em in the fridge if he gets any. Takes 'em home at night."

"Mornin' Red," said Pete. "What we got here?"

"The boy needs some welding on his gas tank. Name's Jack."

"Nice to meet you, boy," said Pete as he extended a rough right hand.

Jack passed the tank over to Pete.

"Hmmm, maybe weld it. Maybe solder," Pete murmured. "I'll take it into the shop and get to it. Either way, I'm afraid it's going to mess up that pretty paint job, boy."

For the next hour Jack sat beside the service station and ate a light lunch as Pete fiddled with the tank inside. Automobiles occasionally pulled up for gas—Model As, Model Ts, AA trucks, and the rare Buick. Some of these cars still had the old hand-starters, and Jack got up to help a woman wrestling with the crank until he saw Red was already on the way.

"There," said Pete as he strode out of the garage. "Tight enough for a moonshine still."

"How much do I owe you?" asked Jack.

"Fifty cents oughta do," Pete replied.

Back on Highway 36 again, Jack crossed the Walhonding River via an imposing steel bridge supported by concrete buttresses at the riverbank. The bridge's metal grating buzzed under his tires and caused the front wheel to weave unnaturally. Looking skyward he was surprised to see a dried deer carcass caught in the steel cross members twenty feet above.

*Now how did a deer jump all the way up there?* Jack wondered.

As he rode west through the broad valley, it occurred to him the deer hadn't jumped at all, but had been deposited by floodwaters of the Muskingum watershed. The Mohawk Dam had been built two years earlier to control these floods.

A mile north of Mt. Vernon on Route 13, he saw a man on the side of the road with a small canvas bag and his thumb in the air. Jack hadn't paid much attention to hitchhikers, but now that Stuart Crossman was gone he had room on the buddy seat for a passenger.

"Where ya headed, Mac?" asked Jack over the rumbling Raspberry.

"Mansfield," he replied. "But I'll ride as far north as you can take me, even if it's only a couple of miles. I'm tired of walking."

"Sure," said Jack. "We can tie your bag to my luggage carrier."

The man introduced himself as Jimmy. He was taller than Jack—about six-one—and his sturdy, muscular frame made Jack look like a ninety-eight-pound weakling beside Charles Atlas. He had a weary, worldly look, and Jack thought he resembled actor Edward G. Robinson.

"What brings you to Mansfield?" asked Jack as he tied Jimmy's bag to the Raspberry.

"I have a fight up there tonight," replied Jimmy. "I'm a boxer."

"Wow!" Jack exclaimed. "Who are you fighting?"

"Don't know yet. It's an exhibition put on by the prison warden. Either way, I'll get paid. It's good money, but it's kept me on the move over the years."

Throughout the Depression, boxing's popularity was second only to baseball.

"Say," asked Jack, "did you hear Joe Louis mop up the mat with Max Schmeling last year?"

"Did I hear it? Hell, I saw it! I was at Yankee Stadium with my trainer."

"You were there?" Jack exclaimed with wide eyes. He pulled out his *State Farm Atlas.*

"I think I can take you all the way to Mansfield," he said. "I was headed to Marion, but it's just as easy for me to go north first."

"I'd appreciate that, friend."

They shouted back and forth over the Raspberry's V-twin for forty-five minutes until Jack finally dropped Jimmy off in front of the Ohio State Reformatory.

"That looks more like a castle than a prison," observed Jack, as he stared at the building's rich stonework and architecture.

"Better to see it from outside than in," laughed Jimmy.

*Likewise,* thought Jack, *far better to shake this man's hand than get punched by it.*

The Raspberry rolled into Upper Sandusky in an early-evening drizzle as Jack looked for a place to eat and camp for the night. He parked at a small diner that was serving a twenty-cent special of chicken, mashed potatoes, gravy, and greens. Cold and clammy after his wet ride, he ordered a cup of hot chocolate and a piece of pie. His dinner cost him forty cents altogether, including a tip for the pretty young waitress.

After spending the night in the town gazebo, Jack was up with the rooster and packed his damp gear back onto the Raspberry. The morning sky was overcast but it had stopped raining, so he took advantage of the weather and settled into the saddle for the cruise into Indiana.

An hour and a half later he saw a road sign ahead:

KEEP RIGHT ON THIS ROUTE
FOR NEW YORK CITY AND THE WORLD'S FAIR!

*Whoever put that sign up is nuts,* Jack thought. *The fair is back that way.*

At Norwalk, Ohio, he finally looked at the map. He was about to ask for directions when he made a startling discovery. Without sun, mountains, or landmarks for a reference, Jack had turned the wrong way on Highway 20 and ridden sixty-two miles in the wrong direction. Disgusted, he filled the Raspberry with gas and oil and tore like a madman back across the Ohio farmland. He turned onto U.S. Highway 6 at Fremont and rode all the way to the Maumee River before he was forced to stop for gas at Bryan, Ohio.

The rain started again about ten miles southwest of Goshen, Indiana. Jack pulled into a farm and asked if he could camp for the night. An Old Order Amish man named Amos Zuck told him to park the Raspberry in the woods and lay his shelter cloth under a nearby oak.

It was a dreary camp, and after eating cold salami and bread for dinner, Jack got out pencil and paper, crawled under his tarp, and wrote his first extended letter home:

Wed June 26(?), 1939

Dear Folks:

I didn't have the opportunity to get a card off to you today since I traveled all morning and most of the afternoon. The rest of the time it's been drizzling just enough to keep me off the road. I waited for a while at a filling station & at the moment I'm lieing under the shelter cloth while the rain patters sharply upon it.

I've had lots of 1st hand experience at repairing under various conditions by now since several things of one sort or another have gone wrong with the bike. The worst so far was the tire trouble. Instead of being a simple puncture (which I could mend on the spot) it had to be a valve stem that was ripped off. The nearest place it could be fixed was 32 mi. away over the mts. Took all morning up to about 2:00 to be off. The drive & wheel sprockets have to be replaced soon & something is wrong with the ignition—I can't quite figure out what's the trouble. I've retarded it as far as it can be & still get good performance at running speed & yet it kicks back when I start the motor.

Well now for something a little more cheerful. Trip to N.Y.C. was very enjoyable. Made connections with the Fishers without any trouble & did the Fair up brown that afternoon. Started off next morning—but I don't need to tell you this cause you've probably had Stuart up already and or will have when he gets home & he'll tell you all about our travels.

Well when I left him I headed north toward Toledo & arrived there O.K. Then I did something I never thought I was capable of. I got on route 20 all right but I went in the wrong direction. I was twisted up for 60 odd miles before I realized my mistake. That ate up a good 3 hrs & some 3 gals gas. Don't tell anybody will you. That happened today & I'm still kicking myself for such a fo pah. It's getting too dark to write so I close with love.

Jack

P.S. Mosquitoes are fierce.
During July I'll send my cards to the lake.

# 10

AFTER A WRETCHED NIGHT in the Indiana drizzle, Jack folded his two woolen blankets inside the shelter cloth and prepared to set off as a hoard of mosquitoes swarmed around his face. To his dismay, he discovered that the starter pedal had slid off the Raspberry's kick-start lever, leaving just a five-inch-long shaft of metal. It was no doubt somewhere along U.S. Highway 6 between Bryan, Ohio, and Nappanee, Indiana. Undaunted, he would just have to make do without a starter pedal from now on. He started the Raspberry and rode back up the cow path, where Amos Zuck and his wife, Mima, were walking toward him. Mrs. Zuck was carrying a basket covered with an embroidered tea towel.

"We thought you might be hungry, friend," said Amos.

Jack cut the engine and set the Raspberry down on its jiffy stand. The springs squeaked as he lifted his weight off the saddle.

"That's mighty nice of you," he replied. "I didn't get much to eat last night."

The three of them sat down on a log as Mima Zuck unpacked the basket in the morning sun. She brought out apples, sausage, milk, and a breakfast mush she'd made from oven-roasted field corn. Zuck was a solid man—twenty-three years old—and wore a broad-brimmed straw hat, a blue shirt, and a pair of black pants held up by suspenders. Mima was a couple of years younger and wore a plain blue dress, a white bonnet, and black shoes that bore a slight discoloration from the milking parlor floor.

"What brings you to these parts?" Amos asked as he stared at the Raspberry's black and yellow, New York license plate.

"I'm on my way to California," Jack said between mouthfuls. "I'm going to see the world's fair in San Francisco."

Mima's eyes lit up. She had never traveled more than fifty miles from Nappanee.

"California!" she exclaimed as she recalled her geography. "How I would love to see the Pacific Ocean."

"I heard about a big fair in New York," said Amos. "Didn't know about anything out west."

After breakfast, they walked back to the Raspberry and Amos gave it a good look.

"Seems complicated," he smiled. "I'd think a horse would be simpler, yah?"

"Sometimes I think the same myself!" Jack chuckled.

Cumulus clouds began to form along U.S. Highway 30 that afternoon as Jack ducked under a bridge to wait out the showers and write another postcard:

Thursday
June 29, 1939
Aurora, IL

Dear Folks:

Did ya get my letter? Struck Rout 30 at Valparaiso, IN and expect to follow it all the way to DeWitt, Iowa then follow 61 (or 52) north to Minn. where I hope to spend a few days with the Leavenworths and Aunti Diesner. The ride across Indiana and Illinois was uneventful except for an occassional short heavy sun shower. Have to resprocket pretty soon.

Love, Jack

He crossed the Mississippi River at Fulton, Illinois. While he'd seen some big rivers back east, this incredibly long bridge made him understand why they called it the "mighty" Mississippi.

Around sundown Jack began looking for a place to spend the night and noticed a roadside sign a few miles south of Maquoketa, Iowa:

BE SURE AND VISIT<br>
SCENIC MAQUOKETA CAVES<br>
STATE PARK JUST OUTSIDE TOWN

Maquoketa Park—to Jack's delight—boasted a solid, newly constructed stone lodge, a walkway system, a stone picnic circle and several hexagonal picnic shelters where he could lay out his shelter cloth and blankets. A sign at the entrance said that members of the Civilian Conservation Corp—the CCC—had constructed the facility.

The CCC was part of FDR's New Deal, designed to combat poverty and unemployment by sending young men to work on conservation projects in rural areas during the Depression. CCC enrollees worked forty hours per week and were paid thirty dollars per month, with the requirement that twenty-five of that be sent home to their families. Members lived in camps, wore uniforms, and lived under quasi-military discipline. At time of entry, two out of three enrollees were malnourished and poorly clothed. Most had no more than a year of high school education, and few had much work experience. They lived in wooden barracks. They rose when the bugle sounded at 6:00 AM, reported to work by 7:45, and after a lunch break worked until 4:00 PM. Late afternoon and evening activities centered on sports and classes. On weekends there was bus service to town or home, or they could attend dances or religious services in the camp. The CCC provided two sets of clothes and plenty of food; discipline was maintained by the threat of dishonorable discharge.

The shelter at Maquoketa Caves State Park had all the amenities Jack could ask for, including a water pump, clean outhouses, and a roof over his head. After setting up camp under one of the picnic shelters, Jack hopped on the Raspberry and rode back into town for dinner at the Caveman Café. For twenty cents, Jack got a bowl of lamb stew, two slices of white bread with butter, collard greens, and a glass of milk. A radio played in the background, and Jack sat up at attention when he heard a familiar announcer from a thousand miles away:

> The National Broadcasting Company invites you to listen to Glenn Miller's music: *(Cue orchestra to Moonlight Serenade)*
> 
> Your favorite NBC station is inviting you to listen to Glenn Miller's music, with the waters of Long Island Sound breaking gently a few yards from the Glen Island Casino, just off the shore road at New Rochelle, New York.

The new King of the Swing Trombone and ace arranger, Glenn Miller and his Orchestra, presenting their interpretations of the melodies of the moment.

And now, Glenn Miller plays an old dance form, which in recent weeks has gained at least a modicum of popularity due in no small manner to you know who: The Barrel Polka!

For the first time since leaving New York, Jack felt a twinge of homesickness. He thought of his mother and father and how they would soon head north and spend the rest of the summer at the lake. He wondered if they missed him.

Lost in thought, Jack bit down hard on an object that tore into the roof of his mouth and made him bleed over his napkin. It was a bone from the lamb meat, cut sharp by the butcher's blade, which had found its way into the stew. He fished the bone out of his mouth and set it aside. The waitress apologized profusely and gave him a free piece of pie, which Jack ate gingerly as he listened to the full fifteen minutes of Glenn Miller's broadcast.

As he fell asleep that night, Jack realized he'd traveled an entire day with no mechanical breakdowns.

The Raspberry kicked his leg into the air at startup the next morning and Jack began to suspect this was a problem that wasn't going away. U.S. Highway 61 took him north across the mighty Mississippi at Dubuque, Iowa, and then crossed the river again at Lacrosse, Wisconsin, where Jack paralleled the western shore all the way to Lake City, Minnesota.

Lake Minnetonka, home to his Aunt Bertha and Leavenworth cousins, was only two hours away. As he approached the Twin Cities, he topped off the Raspberry's gas and oil tanks and scrawled out a hasty postcard:

June 30, 1939

Dear Folks:

    Arrived in St. Paul at 7:30 & haven't as yet gone to Leavenworths but shall now. Don't know whether I'll stay a while or go on tomorrow.

                              Love, Jack

He stayed several days in Minneapolis with his cousins, who pampered him like a prince. They celebrated his arrival with a huge dinner and then took him to the Excelsior movie theater, where they watched John Ford's *Stagecoach* starring John Wayne as the Ringo Kid.

Just before he rode away, Jack penned another postcard to his parents:

Dr. & Mrs. B. L. Newkirk
Glen Island P.O.
Lake George, New York

July 3, 1939
Lake Minnetonka, MN

Dear Folks:

Having a wonderful time at Woodside & expect to leave this afternoon or tomorrow morning. Stayed a few days with Leavenworths and went to a movie. Spent a day with the Diesners and enjoyed one of Aunty Burtha's famous spreads. They've been swell to me. Expect to take the southern route to Yellowstone.

Love, Jack

That afternoon, he rode southwest until he reached U.S. Highway 14 at New Ulm. The sun was an hour from setting as he followed a sign pointing to Lake Shetek State Park, where he took a gravel road several miles south and set up camp in a grove of trees above a broad, marshy area.

Angry clouds gathered overhead as Jack settled in for the night. He built no campfire, as the coming rain would likely put it out before he got a chance to enjoy it. With his faithful Raspberry parked upwind, Jack folded his blankets inside the shelter cloth, swatted mosquitoes, and hunkered down. Thunder boomed from the northwest as sheet lightning illuminated the clouds in a spectacular display of nature.

He heard the patter of raindrops on the shelter cloth swell to a roar as the drizzle turned to downpour and sent rivulets of water careening off the top of his cloth onto the grass below. Within fifteen minutes the storm cell passed and the rain diminished to infrequent, random *plops*. It had been like a symphony; a light, tentative intro followed by a thundering midsection and climax, then ending in a soft, redemptive pianissimo.

Jack stuck out his head. The mosquitoes were gone and the air was ripe with the fresh scent of ozone—as if Mother Nature had run a sanitized cotton mop over the entire county. Inside his cocoon, Jack had remained safe, warm, and dry.

But there was something about this place that made him uneasy—and a tangible feeling of eeriness began to settle around him. A screech owl called over the retreating rain, and residual lightning flashed from the east, illuminating the bottomland in short bursts. In these split seconds, Jack imagined he could see shadowy figures skulking through the slough below.

He fell into a fitful sleep. At three in the morning, he woke up with a start. He'd been dreaming. He had heard inconsolable weeping and children crying out, *"Mother—Mother!"*

The owl called again. *Tu-who; tu-whit, tu-who.* It moved closer and perched in a branch above him. Jack wriggled closer to the Raspberry.

*Something happened here.* He shuddered.

*Something terrible.*

# 11

AFTER READING JOHN STEINBECK'S novella *Of Mice and Men*, composer Aaron Copland knew he was fortunate to have been hired to write the music for the film, which was to feature some of the most recognized names in Hollywood: Burgess Meredith as migrant worker George Milton; Lon Chaney, Jr., as the hapless Lennie Small; and Betty Field as the vampish Mae. The project was, Copland said, "an American theme, by a great American writer, demanding appropriate music." In the summer of 1939, Copland made plans to leave New York and travel to California, where he would spend six weeks scoring the movie. *Of Mice and Men* would eventually earn Copland two Oscar nominations—and praise from many formerly unsympathetic critics who now said his work established "the most distinguished populist music style yet created in America."

Twelve miles from where Copland's music played at the New York World's Fair, it was standing room only at the Glen Island Casino, where Glenn Miller's popularity had skyrocketed. Miller realized this had been one of the best business decisions of his career, as the national radio exposure more than made up for the low pay. On any given evening during the summer of 1939, Glenn Miller could be heard on radio stations all across the country.

★ ★ ★

BACK IN PENSACOLA, Scarsdale Jack Newkirk and his friend Tex Hill were discussing the finer points of bailing out of an airplane. Neither had ever used a parachute in distress, and the object that morning was to jump out of a mock cockpit and land safely on the ground.

"No, Newkirk!" barked the instructor. "You need to roll with the fall or you'll break a leg. Now climb back up there and try again!"

Scarsdale shot Tex a sheepish grin, shrugged his shoulders, and climbed back up the ladder.

"What are you looking at, Hill?" the instructor screamed. "Get up there with him and jump—do it *now*, ladies! Just because you're hot shots in the air doesn't make you any better on the ground! Always remember: you're a soldier first. The aircraft is just one of your tools. Lose your plane and you'll have to be as tough as any Marine to get back to friendly territory—because in a matter of minutes any one of you prima donnas could be transported from your air-conditioned skybox to hand-to-hand jungle fighting. Do I make myself clear, Mr. Eagle Scout?"

"Sir, yes sir!" shouted Scarsdale.

"What about you, preacher's kid?"

"Suh, yes suh!" echoed Tex.

★ ★ ★

**THIRTEEN HUNDRED MILES** away, young Jack Newkirk rolled into Pierre, South Dakota, and ate lunch at a park overlooking the Missouri River. Overhead flew a banner celebrating the state's fiftieth anniversary of its admission into the union. Another sign read:

> ON SEPTEMBER 25, 1804 CAPTAINS MERIWETHER LEWIS AND WILLIAM CLARK PASSED THIS POINT BY KEELBOAT WHILE LEADING AN EXPLORATORY EXPEDITION TO THE PACIFIC OCEAN. THEY RETURNED IN SEPTEMBER OF 1806.

Yet another sign said:

> YOU ARE NOW ENTERING THE MOUNTAIN TIME ZONE. PLEASE SET YOUR CLOCKS BACK ONE HOUR.

Something about the word *mountain*—and to be standing where Lewis and Clark stood—excited Jack. Others had certainly come before, but for him this was terra incognita—the undiscovered country—and he could hardly wait to tell his parents about it.

Highway 14 took an abrupt left turn an hour west of Pierre, and after riding twenty miles due south, Jack came upon the small town of Midland, South Dakota. He went into the drugstore and bought a Butterfinger bar and a Pepsi-Cola for ten cents, then walked down Main Street. The place had an earthy smell: coal, wheat, and a slight odor of sulfur. There was fresh horse manure in middle of the road, along with confetti and candy wrappers, and Jack realized that a parade must have come down Main Street earlier in the day.

He continued fifty yards down the street and stopped beside a roadside hotel with a sign extending over the sidewalk:

FOR YOUR HEALTH'S SAKE
HOT MINERAL BATHS
STROPPEL HOTEL
MIDLAND, SO. DAK.

Jack stared at the sign and rubbed his sore legs with the palms of his hands.

"Howdy," came a voice from the covered porch.

"Uh, howdy," replied Jack. It was the first time on the ride anyone had used that salutation.

"Was that you on the bike?" the man asked as he set down an armload of lumber. "I heard you riding past."

"Yes, sir. I'm headed west. Don't know how far I'll get today."

"The name's John Stroppel," the man said, and extended his right hand.

"Jack Newkirk. Nice to meet you. Say, do you own this place?"

"That I do—my wife and I. We're fixing it up to take better advantage of the hot springs."

"What do you charge for the mineral baths?" ventured Jack.

"Well, we were planning on charging twenty cents," he said as he looked Jack over, "but we're still sort of under construction. If you want to come in and soak awhile, be my guest."

"Really?" Jack exclaimed. "That would be swell!"

He ran back to the Raspberry and got his towel and washcloth. Inside the bathhouse, Jack waded down a set of stairs in his undershorts and then submerged himself in the hot mineral water. The weightlessness was euphoric. He closed his eyes in an attempt to savor the moment, then took a deep breath and felt several vertebrae pop into place.

Jack looked around at Stroppel's handiwork—he'd built two adjoining bathhouses and plumbed water from an artesian hot spring into each building with three-inch pipes. This provided a constant stream of hot mineral water through two separate thousand-gallon cisterns fashioned out of solid concrete. Cinder blocks lined the perimeter to make a weatherproof enclosure. Stroppel had painted the interior light blue and installed a four-by-six array of opaque glass squares that allowed natural light to enter the room. A network of handrails had been made from plumbing fixtures and one-inch galvanized pipe.

Jack soaked in the mineral baths for a full hour, then dried off, got dressed, and climbed back on the Raspberry after heartily thanking Stroppel and his wife.

U.S. Highway 14 merged with Highway 16 thirty miles later at Phillip Junction. Jack rode directly into the sun, which was only two hours from dipping below the western horizon. This cast a golden glow over the prairie, and Jack wished he had his Kodak Bantam camera and a roll of Kodachrome film. Roadside animals also liked this time of day, and on more than one occasion Jack had to beep his horn at browsing deer.

He came upon several prominent road signs a few miles east of Cottonwood:

ONLY 20 MILES TO WALL DRUG!
FREE ICE WATER FOR ALL TRAVELERS

and

SPECIAL SEATS
. . .
RESERVED IN HADES
. . .
FOR WHISKERED GUYS

...

WHO SCRATCH

...

THE LADIES

...

BURMA-SHAVE

and finally,

Take next left to visit the new
Badlands National Monument

Eager to see the Badlands, Jack turned south at Cottonwood and topped off the Raspberry.

Sunset was forty minutes away as he rode through Interior, South Dakota. The Raspberry had behaved well that day, so Jack decided to ride into the heart of the Badlands and spend the night off the beaten path. He turned down an old road that wound through spectacular clay-stone formations with sharply eroded buttes towering on all sides. The road followed a dry creek bed that quickly narrowed to the width of wagon wheels. After a mile or two, it descended into a valley where buffalo grass covered a vast expanse of open prairie.

No motorcycle tire had ever touched this ground.

Jack turned off the wagon trail, rode across the prairie, and parked the Raspberry between two imposing bluffs, miles from anyone. The last of the sunset crept up the ruddy buttes as he put out his shelter cloth and gathered dry, curly sage wood for his campfire. The sage had a strong, feral odor, and Jack had no way of knowing that fifty years earlier a group of Lakota Indians had gathered just south of this camp for one final Ghost Dance—and fifty years in the future, director Kevin Costner would use this location to film *Dances with Wolves*.

With the shelter cloth spread between the Raspberry and the campfire, Jack sat beside the tiny blaze and stared skyward as a thousand lights emerged one by one. He saw an occasional shooting star, a precursor to the meteor showers that would soon rain fire in the summer skies. As he watched the light trails dissipate, he remembered that this was Independence Day—July 4, 1939. His thoughts traveled back to New York City, and he thought of all the fireworks he was missing. But nothing, he thought, could match the magnificence of these surroundings, and he wouldn't trade this scene for all the fireworks in the world.

Jack closed his eyes as the moonlight reflected off his face—and he could feel the afterglow of the Midland mineral baths as he drifted off into a deep, deep sleep.

★ ★ ★

**BACK IN NEW YORK,** Trylon and Perisphere reflected red, white, and blue as rockets exploded over the Lagoon of Nations. Earlier that day, Mayor LaGuardia had cut the ribbon for the new FDR Boardwalk at Staten Island and attended a parade complete with bathing beauties and gussied-up babies. The New York Yankees played the Washington Senators in a doubleheader at Yankee stadium—but if Jack had known about it, it would have broken his heart.

That day, July 4, 1939, saw Lou Gehrig—the Pride of the Yankees—deliver the most heart-wrenching speech in the history of the game. Lou Gehrig—the Iron Horse—the larger than life hero Jack had listened to since age six, reluctantly stepped up to a multitude of microphones, and in brave acquiescence to a terminal disease, tearfully choked out his farewell to baseball:

> Fans, for the past two weeks you have been reading about a bad break I got. Yet today, I consider myself the luckiest man on the face of the earth. Look at these grand men! Which of you wouldn't consider it the highlight of his career just to associate with them for even one day? I might have been given a bad break, but I've got an awful lot to live for. Thank you.

# 12

**THE NEXT MORNING** Jack couldn't resist scrambling up the rugged buttes beside his campsite in South Dakota's Badlands. He breathlessly made his way to the top, only to see more of the same for miles upon miles. Upon returning to camp he retrieved a postcard he'd bought the previous day.

*Why they're called "Badlands"*
*©Rise Studio #708*

On the opposite side, he penciled a note to his parents:

July 5, 1939

Dear Folks:
   Photo doesn't take in enough. There are miles and miles of rolling green country slowly turning brown and sprouting cacti. Air is hot but dry and therefore a cool wind. Climbed all over these things. Sure gives one a lost feeling. Dried my things that had been wet from

the night before. Beginning to see sage brush and sand. Still hot, but skys have been blue all over all day.

Love, Jack

P.S. Heading next to Yellowstone

He was reluctant to leave this place, but the sun was rising and the heat would soon become unbearable. With his fire dead and scattered, he loaded the Raspberry and struck out across the dusty prairie. He looked all the part of a Pony Express rider. His saddlebags—straight off a horse—were little different from those made in 1860.

As the Raspberry bounced along the dry creek bed, Jack suddenly heard a rasping sound followed by a surge in rpm and loss of momentum. He took a quick look back—just in time to catch a glimpse of his drive chain slithering along the ground behind him like a black rat snake.

Jack's heart sank. He was miles from anyone and could count on no help from passersby. After cutting the engine, Jack put the gearshift into neutral and muscled the bike to a shady spot under the west side of a gray-red pinnacle. To an archaeologist, this would be a gold mine of fossils and artifacts, but all Jack could think of was fixing his motorcycle.

He walked back to retrieve the chain, which was covered with a crust of dirt and looked like the flour-coated liver strips his mother used to fry. A quick inspection revealed one of the links had broken. The whole thing would have to be cleaned before it could be repaired and installed, or it would grind itself to uselessness in no time. Not a problem at a service station, but in the Badlands, he might as well have been on Mars.

On the ride down the creek the previous evening, Jack had passed an old campsite where some cowboys had left a large coffee can beside a fire ring. He walked back up the trail to get it. The words *Chase & Sanborn* were barely visible over the faded blue and red paint, but the can looked like it would still hold liquid.

Jack's Scout training began to kick in as he carried the can back to the Raspberry. He recalled that a large river lay to the south. With his canteen, halazone tablets, sardines, nuts, and pilot biscuits he could probably last a week out here with little discomfort.

Back at the bike, Jack got out his tools and removed the fuel line from the main tank. With the coffee can under the petcock, he opened the valve and drained a couple of pints of gas into the container. Next he got out a shop rag and cleaned off the chain as best he could. He swished the chain around in the gasoline and within a few minutes it was almost entirely free of filth. He swung it around his head like a Viking wielding a mace, and although this did a fine job of drying it out, it dribbled gas over his head and shoulders. He set the chain aside, fished a No. 50 master link from his saddlebag, and got out his chain-break tool.

To get the drive chain back on the bike, the Raspberry's chain cover had to be removed, which first required the removal of three nuts and the left footrest. Jack then had to loosen the rear wheel and slide it forward through the center stand so there would be enough slack to stretch the chain over both forward and rear sprockets. It was a dirty job, and by the time Jack snugged up the rear wheel and tightened the chain, his face and hands were covered with grease. He used the remaining gas in the coffee can to clean off his hands, then wiped them dry with his shop rag.

This job had taken nearly three hours and Jack was hungry, hot, and thirsty. He packed his tools, puttered back up the wagon trail, and then took the dirt road back into town. He went straight to the Interior Café's restroom to wash his hands and face. As he sat at the table with his fifteen-cent lunch, the waitress noticed he smelled a lot like gasoline.

The *State Farm Atlas* showed roads out of Interior in all directions. Jack was so taken by the scenery that he decided to take Road 40 west to the town of Scenic and double back through the Badlands. Along the way he passed a saloon with a sign on the porch roof:

INDIANS ALLOWED

The Raspberry coughed occasionally on the dusty roads leading to Wall. The carburetor had no air filter to speak of, only a small metal canister that swirled the air around before it hit the intake. Harley VL owners referred to this as the "rock catcher."

After several cups of ice water at the Wall drugstore, Jack discovered they also sold thick chocolate milkshakes. His mouth started to water and he licked his lips, but he couldn't quite bring himself to part with another fifteen cents. Instead, he filled the Raspberry with gas and oil, and then took Highway 16 west to Rapid City where he found a Harley shop.

"I've been having problems with my ignition," Jack explained. "The starter kicks my leg back and the engine runs rough at low speeds."

"Let's take a look," said the mechanic, whose name patch said "Sam."

"How old is this thing?" Sam asked.

"It's a 1930."

"Oh, a '30 VL," he moaned. "They were all lemons. You must have switched out the flywheels and headlights."

"I just got her a month ago," Jack replied.

Sam removed the timing cover and gave a few disapproving grunts.

"Everything looks OK. Hard to say what's wrong. Could be the condenser going bad. Just to be safe, kid, I'd replace the entire timing assembly—camshaft and all."

"How much would that cost?"

"Let's see," said Sam as he thumbed through his catalog. "Parts and labor would run about eleven dollars and fifty cents."

"Eleven-fifty?!"

"Yep, maybe more if I find anything else in there. I wouldn't skimp on this if I were you. There's some rough country out west. This bike will let you down sure as shootin' unless you fix it here and now."

"I can't afford eleven-fifty."

"Well, then, my advice would be to quit while you're ahead. This old gal just ain't up for a run to California. Now, we could take her in, fix her up, then try to sell her on consignment. You could catch a train back to New York and we'd wire you the money later."

Jack was getting hot under the collar.

*Quit? Quit!*

He might break down, run out of money, or get hurt—but he'd never just quit. He was going to California, by God—and he was going to see the San Francisco World's Fair.

"I think I'll just keep heading west and take my chances," Jack replied.

"I wish you the best of luck, then."

Out of Rapid City, he had a choice of riding Highway 14 through Deadwood or heading south on Highway 16 through Custer. Both roads met again at Newcastle, Wyoming. All things being equal, he preferred the northern route, as the air might be a little cooler. Besides, the name Deadwood had a tantalizing ring to it, and he remembered a movie he'd seen called *The Plainsman* starring Gary Cooper as Wild Bill Hickok.

Jack turned north onto Highway 14 and in forty-five minutes came upon a small town called Sturgis. He hadn't planned to stop, but he saw a motorcycle shop as he puttered down Junction Avenue. He pulled in front of the store and cut the engine, hoping to get a second opinion on the ignition problem.

"Howdy," said Jack as he walked through the door.

"Howdy," came the reply. "What can I do for ya?"

"I wondered if you might take a look at my bike. I think I'm having some ignition trouble."

"Let's go take a peek."

"Great—my name's Jack. I'm from New York."

He extended his right hand.

"You can call me Pappy, and I'm from right here."

"Just 'Pappy'? Hey, you're not *that* old!"

"None of us clubbers go by our Christian names," Pappy grinned. "You gotta earn your name around here."

"What do you mean by 'clubber'?"

"We started a little motorcycle club a couple of years back. Call ourselves the Jackpine Gypsies."

"That's swell," said Jack. "I haven't seen many cycles on my trip so far."

"Well, you come by in a few weeks and you'll see plenty. We put on a rally here last year and got nearly two hundred riders. It was so popular we're going to try it again. We're looking at maybe five hundred this year."

Jack's eyes widened.

"Five hundred motorcycles?" he gasped. "All in the same place?"

"That's the plan. Now, let's go out and see what you got."

As they walked out the door, Pappy looked down at the Raspberry and frowned.

"Oh—we don't really service this type. Just Indians, mostly—"

Jack clenched his lips with a look of disappointment. Pappy saw it and quickly responded.

"But a bike's a bike. And a biker's a biker. I wouldn't leave a man with a broken cycle. Not out here. Where you headed?"

"San Francisco. I'm going to see the fair."

"Well hot damn and fried eggs!" Pappy exclaimed. "Pearl! Come out here and look at this! This boy's takin' his bike from New York to San Francisco!"

Jack started the Raspberry, revved it a few times, then shut it off and explained the problem as he removed the timing assembly cover. He told Pappy about the serviceman in Rapid City.

"Oh, humbug," Pappy scoffed. "That fella doesn't know the butt end from the barrel. Nah, these condensers generally don't go bad. I'm suspecting your breakers. Next time you get to a Harley shop, you pick up a spare set of breaker points. They're cheap. Might make all the difference."

"OK, will do. What do I owe you for your time?"

"Don't worry about it, brother—you just ride safe and stop by on your way back. The rally starts the second week of August. Hope to see you here."

"That would be swell. I'll do my best to get back," Jack promised.

"Did you say you're headed to Deadwood and then west?"

"Yes, sir."

"Hell, boy—you can't come this far and not see Mt. Rushmore. They just unveiled Teddy Roosevelt a few days ago. Spend the night in the Black Hills and head south tomorrow."

Blue skies gave way to menacing clouds on the western horizon. Anticipating another soggy night, Jack didn't dawdle in Deadwood. The signs to Mt. Rushmore led down a narrow road marked Alt 85 that turned to dirt a few miles out of town, and Jack hoped to find a restaurant along the way so he wouldn't have to eat sardines for supper.

As he motored down the dusty road, he saw an old man gingerly walking along the right shoulder carrying a square-bottomed, brown paper sack. The man turned around slowly as Jack approached, hesitated, and then casually stuck out his thumb. His salt-and-pepper beard reminded Jack of Gabby Hayes, the jocular sidekick of Hopalong Cassidy.

"Can I give you a ride, old timer?" Jack asked respectfully as he lifted his goggles.

"Where are you headed, boy?"

"South—to see Mt. Rushmore. But I don't think I'll make it tonight; I was just going to camp along the road. Do you know if there's any place to eat farther on down?"

"No, son. Not much between here and Custer. Besides, it'll be dark by the time you get there. And you don't want to miss any of this country."

The old man's eyes looked the Raspberry over from stem to stern.

"Tell you what," he said. "I've got beef and potatoes here in my bag. You give me a ride home and I'd be glad to share my supper with you. I make a pretty good miner's stew."

"Sounds swell," Jack replied, and got off the motorcycle to help the old man climb aboard.

"You're welcome to sleep in my barn," the old man continued. "Got fresh hay bales up top. Looks like you'd be in for a wet night otherwise. Now, how do I get on this old horse? Never ridden on one of these things."

The old man set his grocery sack on the ground as Jack helped him get on the bike.

"Where do I put my feet?" he asked.

"Oh," said Jack, "you can just rest them on the footboards here. But let me kick the starter over first."

Jack handed the man his grocery sack, then got aboard and folded out the stub of the bike's missing starter pedal. After firing up the motor, he shifted into low gear and continued down the road with his passenger.

"The name's Eli," he shouted over the sputtering V-twin.

"I'm Jack!"

Eli directed him down several dirt roads, and Jack took detailed mental notes so he could find his way out in the morning. They creaked to a stop in front of an old ranch house surrounded by ponderosa trees, a grassy valley, and a creek. The house and outbuildings were beginning to show their age, but it was clear this was once a thriving operation. A gray, weathered barn with a gabled roof stood fifty yards away next to a corral with broken, rough-cut timber hanging from the posts. Jack saw a honey-brown Jersey cow munching on hay in the barn.

"Looks like you just spared me a walk in the rain, boy," said Eli as he climbed off. Raindrops sizzled as they began to splatter on the Raspberry's exhaust manifold.

"Best push your cycle into the barn," he continued. "You can make your sleeping palette up top on the hay. You'll find a ladder to the left. I'll go in and start supper."

Jack pushed the Raspberry into one of the vacant stalls, then unpacked his blankets and shelter cloth and carried them up a fixed wooden ladder to the barn's second story. The place had an amalgam of smells that reminded him of Caldwell's dairy farm back home: Fresh hay from the first cutting. Cow manure. Dried crib corn and silage. Ozone from the oncoming thunderstorm.

Jack arranged several hay bales into a fort, then folded his blankets inside the shelter cloth and put his woolen seat cover where his head would rest. He climbed back down the ladder and went into the house.

"So, do you run this place all by yourself?" asked Jack. "Any wife or family?"

"Wife's passed on. Got a boy in Cheyenne. I hire some men to help me around the ranch, but mostly I'm here by myself these days."

The old man put a fresh loaf of bread on the table, took some butter from a wooden crock, then checked the bubbling stewpot that sat on the cast iron cook stove.

"Let's give it a few more minutes," he said. "It's my own recipe. I use beef stock and some spices, then thicken it up with cornstarch. While that's boilin', I fry up the meat and potatoes and add it to the stew base. Doesn't take as long that way and tastes better, in my opinion."

"Sure smells good," Jack agreed.

When the stew was ready, Eli got two wooden bowls and placed them on the table. He filled both bowls and cut off two thick slices of bread. Jack was about to start eating when he saw the old man bow his head.

"Father, may we be grateful for the blessings thou bestows, and gracious in understanding when thou dost not. Amen."

"Amen," echoed Jack.

The meal would have been respectable in any restaurant, and the old man was full of stories.

"So did you grow up here—in the Black Hills?" Jack asked.

"Came to Deadwood with my pap and ma'am in the spring of '76. I was ten years old at the time and I tell you, it was no place for a boy. Crazy town. Wild and lawless. I saw a lot of 'em come and go—Wyatt Earp, Hat Creek Gang, Jesse James—I seen 'em all. Saw General Crook's men come through after Custer got whupped at Little Big Horn. But the biggest thing for me that summer happened one afternoon in August. We were loadin' up the wagon, ready to head home, when someone comes runnin' out of Mr. Mann's saloon yellin', 'Someone just shot Wild Bill!' We all ran over and I tried to jump up and see what was goin' on. Sure enough, a man named McCall had crept up behind Wild Bill Hickok and shot him in the back of the head. They ended up hangin' that coward and buryin' him with the knot around his neck."

"Wow!" Jack exclaimed with wide eyes. It was clear this old man was from a bygone era, and Jack wondered what he'd think of the 1939 New York World's Fair with its television, microwave oven, photocopier, and Electro the Motoman with his electronic dog, Sparko.

"When did you get this spread?" Jack inquired.

"Came here with my wife and boys in 1910. We had a good operation. Over six hundred acres and a few hundred head of cattle. Times were good, for the first few years, anyway."

"What happened after that?"

The old man looked down, sighed, and then looked up again.

"Son, have you ever heard of the Custer Wolf?"

"No, sir."

The man paused again.

"Let's go sit by the fire and I'll tell you about 'im."

Heavy raindrops pelted the roof of the ranch house. The old man brought out two plates, each with a square of gingerbread, and then sat down beside Jack in an armchair by the fireplace. He reached above the mantle for his pipe and lit it with a wooden, strike-anywhere match.

"It was sometime in the fall of 1915," he began. "That's when I first heard it. It didn't sound like any proper wolf. No, this one was different—it was the song of the devil—straight from the Book of Jeremiah:

> A voice was heard in Ramah, a sound of crying in bitter grief. Rachel weeping for her children, refusing to be comforted, because they are no more.

"That's when the killing started. First it was Meyer's spread over on Boxelder Creek. Then the ranches around Deerfield. That next spring he hit my place. Early one morning, about sunup, I was ridin' out to check on some calves when I saw a dozen cattle lying on the ground—all dead. I thought lightning must have struck, but there hadn't been any thunderstorms. My dog started to growl and my horse was acting real spooky."

Jack edged forward in his seat as firelight danced upon his face. The old man took a puff from his pipe and continued.

"Well, my dog took off like a shot over the hill—I called but he kept runnin'. Then I heard him yelp, and when I reached the top of the hill I looked down and saw him fighting with a white wolf beside another dead cow."

A flash of lightning momentarily overpowered the kerosene lamp. The thunder boomed three seconds later.

"I pulled out my six-gun and emptied it at the wolf—accidentally shootin' my dog in the process. He went limp and the wolf dropped him like a piece of garbage. Then he curled his lips and bared his teeth as if to taunt me. With a flip of his head, he disappeared into the woods. That's the only time I ever saw him."

"So you lost a dozen cows to that creature?" asked Jack.

"A dozen! No, boy, that was just the beginning. Over the next five years he'd make the rounds, killin' everywhere he went. Sheep down in Hot Springs, horses in Pennington County, cattle at Castle Creek. He visited me six or seven times, nearly ran me bankrupt. All in all, he cost the ranchers some twenty-five thousand dollars in dead livestock. And this killin'—it wasn't done for food—it was pure meanness. He hardly ever fed off the carcasses."

"Twenty-five thousand dollars? Couldn't anyone catch him?"

"Not this one, son, no sir. And we tried everything. Poison, traps, dogs, guns. He was just too smart. He even enlisted the help of coyotes in his murderous rampage. They weren't partners, though. Those coyotes were his minions. They'd follow at a distance and warn him whenever we'd approach. In return, he'd let them feed off his kills. The government had a five hundred dollar bounty on his hide and that brought all kinds of folks to these parts: professional hunters, gentlemen's sons."

"Finally," Eli sighed, "a man named Williams come out of Wyoming. He tracked the wolf for seven months solid, and finally got that son of the devil in October of 1920. But by that time a lot of us stockmen were close to broke. With the Custer Wolf and the rabies outbreaks, boy, those were tough years."

The next morning Jack awoke to the sound of Eli shouting beside the old corral.

"Come on down, boy! Get yourself some of these pancakes. You'll need to eat if you're fixin' to ride that motorbike all day."

Jack steered the Raspberry down the dusty lane to road A85, where he turned south again toward Mt. Rushmore. After another twenty minutes, he shut off the engine, kicked down the jiffy stand, and sat gazing at the imposing figures carved into the side of the mountain. Just as he'd been told, Teddy Roosevelt had been dedicated that previous Sunday—July 2, 1939.

★ ★ ★

**BACK IN NEW YORK CITY,** a sculptor named Korczak Ziolkowski had entered one of his works into a contest at the 1939 New York World's Fair. It was a marble bust of pianist Ignace Jan Paderewski—and it won first prize. A short time later, Ziolkowski received a handwritten letter from a member of the Lakota Sioux Indian tribe:

Dear Sir:
    According to the newspaper notice I note you have won honors at New York World's Fair in sculpture work. A number of my fellow chiefs and I are interested in finding some sculptor who can carve the head of an Indian chief who was killed many years ago. Proposition

is mine to be pushed by these certain chiefs and myself under my direction. Would you care to correspond with me on this project? There is a great [deal] to be explained of course. Perhaps you can help me in some way? This is to be entirely an Indian project under my direction. Please write at your earliest convenience.

This is a matter of long standing in my mind which must be brought before the public soon. The main thing now is to know if some one can do the work when money raised.

Please write me at your earliest convenience advising whether or not you can correspond in this manner.

Yours truly,

Henry Standing Bear
South Dakota

Ziolkowski agreed to work with the Indian chief, and several years later the first rock was blasted from what would become Crazy Horse Memorial—a reminder, in the words of Standing Bear, that "the Red man has great heroes, too."

# 13

**J**ACK CONTINUED INTO Custer County and back toward U.S. Highway 16. As he leaned the Raspberry to negotiate a curve, he saw a black Packard Sedan coming straight at him. He caught a glimpse of the driver, who was casually pointing out something to his wife. Jack swerved—and at the last instant the driver did the same. He felt the Raspberry's rear wheel slide from under him and time seemed to stop as he realized he was going to collide with the car.

He saw the spare tire in front of the driver's door.

He saw the running boards coming at him fast.

Then he felt a *whack*.

To his astonishment he found himself riding down the road again as if nothing had happened.

He had been extraordinarily lucky. The Raspberry's rear wheel had struck the rear wheel of the Packard, and the opposing forces righted the motorcycle from its skid. Any earlier and Jack would have been under the running board. Any later and he would have hit the rear fender.

The Packard drove on, but the incident left Jack shaken as he pulled over to the side of the road to let his nerves settle. His hands trembled as he realized what a close call it had been, and he wondered why some drivers seem to ignore motorcyclists.

He headed back to the Mt. Rushmore visitor's center to wait out the afternoon drizzle, then rode south to Custer State Park where he decided it wasn't worth riding any farther in the rain. He set up camp, got out pencil and paper, and wrote a note to his parents:

July 6, '39

Dear Folks:

Hope you'll excuse the "stationery"—it's the best I have. I'm now lieing under my shelter cloth after making camp in the rain getting me & mine nicely wet in the process. Mosquitoes are fierce & it's going to be a drizzle all night but I get a kick out of it all yet.

Had no rout trouble but kept dashing in & out of garages & farm yards between showers. At present I'm surrounded by the biggest grasshoppers I ever hope to see. Long as small green frogs. They were all over the road for 100 miles across S. Dakota & nearly knock my head off when they hit me. Rode through a flying swarm of bees a few days ago. Felt like someone had thrown a handful of stones at me hard.

Had a swell time at Lake Minnetonka & now I'm going to write both families & thank them.

Love,
Jack

P.S. Storms sure are funny here. Very black clouds—look like a sea upside down.
Following 16 (went through Badlands) to Yellowstone.

The bugs surrounding him were *Melanoplus sanguinipes*—the migratory grasshopper—and the scourge of many a South Dakota farmer during the Great Depression. In the spring of 1939, an infestation of *Melanoplus* nymphs had resulted in an extraordinary mass migration of adult grasshoppers. They swarmed in the millions, and nearly blocked out the Dakota sun as they traveled up to sixty miles per day. Upon landing, they laid waste to thousands of acres of wheat, barley, oats, alfalfa, clover, corn, and range grasses.

Jack had ridden the Raspberry right into the thick of it.

The next morning Jack continued on Highway 16 west into Wyoming. The *State Farm Road Atlas* told him all roads to Yellowstone would take him through Gillette. For this reason he'd given his Minnesota cousins a forwarding address of the Gillette post office. After a couple of hours' ride through the Wyoming prairie, Jack stopped in Gillette where, sure enough, there was a letter from his father waiting for him:

Mr. Jack Newkirk
~~1701 Girard Ave. N.~~ pls fwd to
~~Minneapolis, Minn.~~ General Delivery
~~c/o H. D. Diessner~~ Gillette, Wyo.

Anxious to beat the heat of the day, Jack stuffed the letter into his pocket and rode on through Spotted Horse and Buffalo, Wyoming.

He was out of the prairie now, and the ride from Buffalo into the Bighorn National Forest was dotted with pine forests and mountain meadows with creeks full of trout. The highway turned to gravel a few miles east of Muddy Pass, and Jack saw a dirt path heading southwest through a high valley. According to his atlas, this detour went through "Beautiful Scenery" and joined up with Highway 16 again at Powder River Pass. This would add a dozen miles to the trip, but it would take him through the heart of the magnificent Bighorn Mountains.

Jack set off down the narrow lane and puttered along at ten miles per hour. After five miles he splashed through the middle fork of Crazy Woman Creek. Farther ahead he came to the north fork of the Powder River. The water came up to his footboards this time, but the Raspberry seemed to enjoy the cool bath on her hot tires.

Five minutes later the engine began to buck and cough. The explosive backfires seemed utterly out of place in this mountain wilderness, and Jack instinctively looked around to see if anyone was watching. But there was no one to be seen, and the V-twin died before he even had a chance to shut off the ignition. He pushed the Raspberry off the trail and under a tree, sat down on a nearby rock, and replayed the sequence over and over in his mind.

★ ★ ★

**IT WAS HOT** and humid that evening at Santa Rosa Island on the Florida coast—and two hours later by time zone as Tex Hill, Scarsdale Jack Newkirk, and a South American pilot named Fernando Guzman prepared their Boeing F4B-4s for takeoff at Naval Air Station Pensacola.

During the preceding weeks they had practiced dogfighting, bombing, strafing, and destroying fixed targets, but the mission tonight involved no weapons. This was an exercise in navigation and landing designed to prepare them for nighttime carrier operations.

Two other pilots showed up and pre-flighted their aircraft, and they all took off in loose formation over the Gulf of Mexico. One by one, they headed toward preselected destinations, aided by compass, radio, timepiece, and a variety of panel instruments.

But a large, unseasonable—and unpredicted—cold air mass was settling over the Florida Panhandle, and within thirty minutes the temperature had dipped below the dew point. Fog began to blanket the area, and the Pensacola tower broadcast an urgent call.

"All aircraft, NAS Pensacola. Repeat. NAS Pensacola calling all aircraft. Return to base immediately. Repeat. Return to base immediately. Ground fog forming over the runway. Repeat. Heavy fog over the runway."

"You hear that, Tex?" Jack crackled over the radio.

"Roger. I'm five minutes out. See ya on the ground."

"Where's Nando?" Newkirk asked.

"I'm over Point Dixie," came the reply. "Turning west now. Where you, Jack?"

"West of Valparaiso—I'm right behind you," Jack answered. "Sweep me a path, amigo. I'll follow you in."

★ ★ ★

**YOUNG JACK KNEW** the difference between fuel starvation and ignition issues and was fairly certain the Raspberry's problem had nothing to do with the fuel system. The creek crossings could have gotten something wet, but he dismissed this theory because he'd ridden hundreds of miles in the rain with no problems. He then remembered what Pappy told him in Sturgis about the breaker points, and with a heavy sigh, got out his toolkit once again.

A blue Steller's jay landed on a nearby tree, eyed him curiously, and uttered a raucous cry. Breezes passing through the pine trees sporadically drowned out the babbling of the creek. Jack unpacked his shelter cloth and set it on a patch of grass in the sun, then arranged all his tools on the cloth like a surgeon preparing for an operation. In a desperate hope that the problem might be heat related, he turned on the ignition and kicked the starter one more time, but the engine just gave a halfhearted cough, backfired, and died.

Jack had broken down due east of Ten Sleep Canyon in Wyoming's Bighorn National Forest. The "road" was little more than a stock trail, and his atlas described it as "unimproved dirt—inquire locally." The atlas also described Wyoming as extremely remote—a hundred thousand square miles with just more than two hundred thousand people in the entire state.

It was then that he sensed that subtle, taunting voice again.

*You little fool! Did you really think you could make it to San Francisco? Now you're stuck out here and nobody's going to help you!*

★ ★ ★

**TEX HILL AND** two other pilots touched down in a dark mist that nearly obscured the runway lights. Within minutes the field was covered in heavy fog.

"Remaining aircraft," called the tower, "airfield below visibility minimums. Attempt no landing. Repeat. Attempt no landing. Proceed to your alternate."

"I'm on final approach," Guzman responded. "I think I can make it."

"Exercise extreme caution," said the controller. "Field well below minimums."

Fernando Guzman could see two faint, blurry lines below him. He lined up his F4B-4 between them and descended into the mist with one eye on his level flight indicator. The aircraft's landing light turned his surroundings into a bright sea of white so he shut it off. Guzman was lost in a blanket of fog and could no longer make out the runway. He prayed to the Virgin Mary as he slowed his descent to 150 feet per minute. Frantically attempting to keep his aircraft straight and level, he expected at any moment to feel the reassuring terra firma under his wheels. As his wings entered ground effect, a random gust tipped them to the right. With no outside reference, Guzman overcorrected and sent his left wing into the ground. The airplane cartwheeled and burst into flames, killing the pilot instantly.

Scarsdale Jack Newkirk looked down at the runway and saw a faint orange glow pulsating under the fog.

"Nando! Nando!" Scarsdale shouted. "No!"

★ ★ ★

**A LUMP WAS** forming in young Jack's throat as he stared intently at Harley-Davidson engine casing 30V8229C. The sun was about to set. His eyes began to well up with tears and he wished his father were with him. It was then he remembered the letter—a letter from home. He wiped the tears from his eyes and opened it with his Barlow knife:

Professor Burt L. Newkirk
17 Rosa Road
Schenectady, NY

Dear Jack,

This is Sunday evening. Ginny and Marion Emily are here and mother and Ginny have been putting up currant jelly. They picked something like a bushel of currants and will have together around 75 glasses of jelly. They put mint in them so they'll be pretty tasty. Ginny will take about half of them back with her.

We are getting your cards and have had one letter. You may be in Minneapolis by this time but if you leave before this arrives you will no doubt have a forwarding address.

Sorry you are having so much trouble with the cycle but suppose that is hardly avoidable with one so old. Did I speak to you of "shakeproof" washers? They are pretty good—better I think than ordinary spring lock washers, but the crown washer with cotter pin is the only thing I know of that is really positive.

Mother and I have been to the lake twice for several days each time. The boat leaks some but not a great deal. I fixed the place where the cooling water leaked out. The engine runs very well but it needs new piston rings and a general overhauling—bearings taken up etc. I made a couple of rubber gaskets for the pump and that is working nicely. The awning to cover the canoe racks is sewed but not set up yet so we are keeping your canoe on the porch and the others under the porch. We have not gone for ice yet but I set a box in the ground near the ice house and this keeps the butter fairly hard.

We appreciate your cards and letter. Keep them coming. We go back to the lake soon. Send mail there.

We all send love and best wishes, Dad

Jack sniffed and read the letter over several times. In some way, at least, he felt his father was out here in this wilderness with him. He shut out the voices of anxiety and doubt and wrote down a list on the back of the envelope.

CONS:
- Broken-down motorcycle miles away from the nearest road in Wyoming's Bighorn Mountains
- Nobody knows where I am

PROS:
- I am not injured
- I am not lost
- I have food, water, shelter, and the ability to make fire

He soon realized the pros far outweighed the cons. His surroundings were not his enemy—they were his allies. Hazelton Peak to the north protected him from harsh winds that swept over the prairie. The pine trees provided shade, windbreak, and fuel for his fire. The creek provided drinking water, and the rocks would make a fine fire ring and store heat overnight. At worst, he'd have to walk a few hours back to Highway 16. But it was getting late and he didn't want to get caught in the dark.

★ ★ ★

"NEWKIRK," CRACKLED the Pensacola tower, "advise amount of fuel on board."

"Uh," said a flustered Scarsdale Jack, "about an hour, I think—"

"The Pensacola airfield is closed to all traffic. Warrington, Milton, and Eglin also below minimums. We suggest Crestview to the northeast. Good luck, son."

Scarsdale was in borderline shock from the loss of his friend—and he was in serious trouble.

To bail out over the Gulf of Mexico and risk being lost at sea was an unpleasant proposition. He'd rather take his chances on the ground. He banked the airplane to the northeast and headed inland over the Choctawhatchee National Forest toward the small airstrip at Crestview. Forty-five minutes later he was circling over what, to the best of his dead reckoning, should have been the airfield, but it was nowhere in sight. He hoped to see some lights or cars on the road below, but the cloud cover had moved inland and was obscuring the ground.

Jack swallowed hard. He knew what he had to do, and reluctantly maneuvered the fighter several miles south where he hoped it would at least go down in an unpopulated area. He continued to circle and search for any sign of a road, until his engine finally coughed, sputtered, and died. He made one last radio call, said a quick prayer, and then jumped out of his airplane into the blackness of Florida's remote Choctawhatchee swamp.

★ ★ ★

YOUNG JACK GOT UP from his cramped position and stretched his legs. He kept fixating on a word he'd read in his father's letter: *shakeproof*. Nearly every problem he'd experienced had something to do with vibrations—a field in which his father was an expert. The ignition trouble had gotten progressively worse, so it very well could be related to vibration in some way.

Jack decided to make camp and work on the bike in the morning. He built a fire and set his shelter cloth and blankets beside it. He took a quick bath in the creek and washed his clothes, then hung them from a stick to dry by the fire. Next he walked around and gathered enough wood to last the night. As twilight gave way to firelight, he realized the psychological value of a campfire should never be underestimated.

Digging into his saddlebag, Jack grabbed a can of sardines and pilot biscuits from the Aurora General Store. After dinner he sat by the fire and sucked on a couple of horehound drops, then went to the creek and brushed his teeth. He dropped a halazone tablet inside his canteen and shook it a little, then thought over his plans. If he couldn't fix the Raspberry within two days, he resolved, he'd hike out and thumb a ride into Buffalo or Cody.

He walked over to the bike and flipped on the Raspberry's John Brown Motolamp. The headlight bathed the campsite in a soft amber hue that seemed foreign in this primal forest. Jack's mouth slowly formed into a wide grin. Looking up, he lifted both arms into the air and shouted triumphantly to the stars.

"Wilderness of Wyoming! I am a visitor from the World of Tomorrow—courtesy of the 1939 New York World's Fair!"

Jack awoke the next morning to a red-tailed hawk screeching overhead. He watched it circle a few minutes and felt a pang of envy about Scarsdale and the adventures he must be having in Florida.

Then he went straight to work on the Raspberry.

He removed both plugs. One looked blacker than the other, but they both produced a spark and their gaps were correct, so he set them aside and moved on to the next theory.

The V-twin's crankcase had a threaded plug that allowed the rider to check the ignition timing mark. Jack removed it and took a measurement: five-sixteenths of an inch—right on the money.

He scratched his head and thought of his father's letter again. Could something have shaken loose in the timing circuit? He stared at the timing circuit some more and wiggled the breaker points with his fingers. To his surprise, he felt one of the points yield.

His heart began to pound.

He pushed down on the starter shaft with his hand and watched the circuit breaker cam rotate. Astonished, he discovered the top breaker point no longer lifted off the lower one as it should have.

Jack removed the top breaker point and examined it closely. The cam follower was a small, rectangular piece of fiberglass riveted to the metal breaker. Through the years—clacking up and down a dozen times per second—the rivet had worked loose and was so sloppy that the cam follower just sloshed around on its axis.

Bingo! This would cause the ignition timing to go haywire!

He remembered what Pappy said at Sturgis. New breaker points would do the trick, but the closest set was probably a hundred miles away. He stared at the part again. It was a piece of stamped aluminum about the size of a peanut shell. The loose rivet was recessed underneath the breaker point. If he had a hammer and center punch, he could mash down the rivet and cinch the cam follower against the breaker point—but a hammer and punch were two tools he didn't carry.

Then he remembered the rocks he'd seen along the creek.

Jack walked to the water's edge and—like David preparing to battle Goliath—carefully selected three stones of proper size and shape. He walked back to the Raspberry and placed the breaker point on one stone like an anvil. A narrower stone would be his center punch. The third stone—a fist-sized boulder weighing about two pounds—was his hammer.

He practiced the motion a few times, then stood up and paced up and down the creek bed.

He knew he'd have only one shot at this. If he hit it wrong, he'd shatter the cam follower and disable the bike entirely.

# 14

**S**CARSDALE JACK NEWKIRK'S parachute carried him toward the ground slowly enough to spare his life, but still fast enough to cause injury if he landed incorrectly. In the darkness, he couldn't see his landing zone, but he heard the sickening crash as his airplane corkscrewed into the earth. He yelled down to see if he could gauge the ground proximity by echo and one minute later his legs crunched against a fallen tree, tearing the medial collateral ligament in his right knee.

Scarsdale cried out in pain as he tried to stand.

He had only a vague idea of where he was—somewhere in the Choctawhatchee swamp north of Eglin Field in the Florida Panhandle. His government survival kit contained a flashlight, pistol, knife, food, flares, matches, compass, and a few other items designed to keep him alive until he could be rescued. Scarsdale found a relatively dry patch of ground, wrapped himself inside his silk parachute, and spent a damp night among the mosquitoes.

At dawn he found himself surrounded by longleaf sand pines, swampy grassland, and a maze of waterways. According to his map, he was in the Yellow River Basin, but he wasn't sure if he was north or south of the river.

As an Eagle Scout, Jack was already an expert in survival, but his military training had honed these skills even further. He knew his best plan was to stay put and make himself as visible as possible to the rescue team. Limping over to a clearing, Jack spread his parachute on the ground and weighed it down with sticks. He broke off some dry branches from the sand pine trees and kindled a fire under the overcast sky.

The weather deteriorated and before long thick raindrops began to pelt his flight jacket. He had a thin seven-by-seven-foot poncho with grommets on each corner, and he used his parachute cord to stretch it tight against the surrounding trees. This protected him from the brunt of the rain shower and provided cover for the sizzling fire, but the approaching thunder gloomily announced there would be no rescue today.

Scarsdale knew the most important factor for his survival now was psychological. His injuries were not critical, and he could last a couple of weeks on body reserves and the rations in his survival kit. Water was everywhere, and he had fire and shelter. Thankfully, there were no enemy soldiers to evade. Even so, Scarsdale knew that defeatism and surrender were the enemy now—and they could be every bit as formidable.

He leaned against a log and warmed his hands as rivulets of water dripped off the tarp overhead. His thoughts traveled back to New York and he wondered what his family was doing. They all seemed more important to him now, and he resolved to spend more time with them once he got out of this mess. Scarsdale vaguely remembered someone saying that young Jack was taking a Harley from coast-to-coast to visit both world's fairs.

He caught himself smiling at the kid's audacity—and wished that at that very moment he were with him on the back of that motorcycle. Two Jack Newkirks. Twenty-five and nineteen. Riding along as kindred spirits of the open road.

★ ★ ★

**EIGHTEEN HUNDRED MILES AWAY,** young Jack walked back to the Raspberry and looked down at the three rocks beside his precious breaker points.

He wondered what Scarsdale—an Eagle Scout—would do in his situation.

Jack took another drink from his canteen. The sun was up and it felt good on his shoulders.

Finally, he knew he could put if off no longer and once again put the center-punch rock in his left hand and the breaker point underneath it. With the hammer stone firmly in his right, he practiced the motion a dozen times. Then, with all the seriousness of the first cut on the Cullinan diamond, Jack brought the stone down with a solid *whack!*

He gingerly removed the breaker from between the stones and tested the cam follower.

It was rigid. The rivet held it against the breaker body as though it were a new part.

Jack breathed a sigh of relief and sat down on his shelter cloth, weak from the prolonged stress. Then he installed the breaker points back inside the timing assembly.

*Vroom; vroom—vrooom . . . putt-putt-putt-putt-putt-putt-putt . . .*

Jack raised his fists toward the sky.

"Yes!" he shouted over the purring V-twin. "*Yes!*"

★ ★ ★

**TWO DAYS PASSED** before Scarsdale Jack saw the sky. He heard the drone of search planes in a grid pattern, but they were too far off to see his smoke and he wasn't going to waste a flare. By the fourth day, Scarsdale realized that they weren't looking in the right place and he decided to make his way north. He saw that Highway 90 ran east-west and it couldn't be more than a few miles away. But with an injured leg, he'd be lucky to make a mile a day.

He fashioned a walking stick out of a tree limb and strapped some basic tools to his belt. He left his parachute spread out on the ground with a note nearby:

> Aircraft destroyed. Pilot Jack Newkirk OK but I have sprained my knee. Will walk due north toward Hwy 90 but will follow south bank of Shoal River if I encounter it en route.

After slogging four hours through the muggy Choctawhatchee, Jack was thirsty and hungry. He found a pool of water nearby, but it was stagnant and probably contained parasites. Three feet from the pool, Jack dug a shallow pit with his hands. In ten minutes it was full of clear water filtered by the surrounding soil—it was the Indian spring Jack had learned about in the Boy Scouts.

Depending on his longitude, Jack realized he might run into the

Shoal River before he reached Highway 90. This didn't appeal to him, as the area was known for twelve-foot alligators. He plodded north and looked for any sign of civilization.

Just before sundown he came upon a creek twenty feet in width. Beside the bank he saw the snouts and eyes of a group of alligators. He killed one of them with a single shot from his pistol and limped over to retrieve it. The water boiled as the others scrambled to escape.

Half-dazed, he thrust the limp reptile over his head and screamed wildly.

"There, you slithering sons of bitches! Do you see what I can do? I am Scarsdale Jack Newkirk, by God! So stay out of my way—all of you!"

That night, Jack ate alligator meat roasted over an open fire.

The next afternoon Jack was plodding northward when he looked up and saw a group of turkey vultures circling above. He shook his stick at them, laughed hysterically, and screamed.

"A bit early aren't you, you bald-headed bastards! I'll show you how an American acts in a pinch!"

He was feverish, but his rant was not altogether a result of high body temperature. He knew he must not surrender to defeat. His vocalizations made him feel less alone, and his defiance in the face of hardship gave him a greater will to go on.

He'd been in the Choctawhatchee nearly a week when he heard the faint sound of a diesel motor to the east. He followed the noise and eventually stumbled into a field where a man was sitting on a green John Deere Model B tractor. The man jumped off and ran over to him as the motor popped at a hundred rpm.

"Say, are you that navy pilot they've been looking for?"

"I suppose I am, brother," Scarsdale sighed wearily.

★ ★ ★

**THE RASPBERRY ATE UP** the miles with a new vigor as young Jack rolled into Worland, Wyoming—the western terminus of U.S. Route 16. He felt strangely sad to bid goodbye to this highway. It had been an agreeable companion, and had guided him faithfully through some of the most scenic parts of the country. From Worland, an eastbound traveler could follow this road all the way to Milwaukee, then board a ferry steamer across Lake Michigan and follow Route 16 to its eastern terminus in Detroit—nearly fifteen hundred miles away.

Jack turned north and made his way to Route 20, then rode an hour into Greybull and headed west again. The ignition issue was solved, but to his dismay, about fifteen miles east of Cody, he noticed an unfamiliar rattle. Here he found a Harley shop, spent seventy-five cents on a new set of breaker points, and then asked the mechanic if he could take a look at his bike.

"Bad rattle!" shouted the service manager, as he frowned over the chugging V-twin. "Sounds like your main bearing is going bad. But I can fix it. Got the parts right here."

"How much would it cost?"

"I think I could do it for about fifteen dollars."

As Jack rode away, he didn't quite know what the man meant by "main bearing"—but the number fifteen had been clear enough.

Clouds masked the sun as Jack approached the east entrance of Yellowstone Park. The Raspberry chugged up Sylvan Pass as the sky began to spit snow, and Jack pulled over and put on every piece of clothing he had. The Yellowstone entry station charged a whole dollar, which Jack felt was unduly high considering he got into the New York World's Fair for seventy-five cents. Nevertheless, he reluctantly handed the ranger a precious, limp dollar bill.

By five o'clock he reached the eastern shore of Yellowstone Lake, the first large body of water he'd seen since Minnesota. According to his odometer, he'd traveled 250 miles since Ten Sleep Canyon. A "Free Auto Campground" sign jumped out at him at the village of Fishing Bridge.

By Sunday morning the clouds had moved off and given way to blue skies—but it was still unseasonably cold.

"You wouldn't have any old newspapers, would you?" he asked at the gift shop.

The clerk went to the back office and brought out a small stack of week-old papers. Jack thanked the woman, went outside to a picnic table, and wrote a letter to his parents:

Sunday July 9, 1939

Dr. & Mrs. B. L. Newkirk
Glen Island P.O.
Lake George, N.Y.

Dear Folks:

    I'm near Electric Peak, highest mountain in Yellowstone Park. It's over 11,000 ft and both the Raspberry and I notice the thin air. Had to adjust the mixture and have had a few other break downs I'll tell you about later.

    Getting colder all the time. Ran through snow yesterday. The motor has developed an awful bang & rattle. I think the main crankshaft bearing is going fast. Will try to make it to Butte but have my doubts. This will mean a considerable setback—both monetarily & temporary.

Love, Jack

    He dropped the letter in the mailbox and then layered newspapers inside his jacket and pants. This provided an excellent windbreak, and the only parts of him that got chilled were his gloved hands, which he would stop and warm against the V-twin's crankcase at five-minute intervals.

    As he rode past the Grand Canyon of the Yellowstone, the Raspberry started to pop and lurch. From the sound of it, Jack knew only one cylinder was firing. He pulled to the side of the road and took out both plugs. They said "Champion" on one side with the Harley-Davidson bar and shield on the other. The plug marked No. 3 looked black and worn, while the one marked No. 4 was relatively clean.

    As Jack sat down to weigh his options, he heard the familiar sound of an approaching V-twin. He looked up and saw a shiny Harley-Davidson VL with a South Dakota plate and two riders. It was a 1936 model—three years old—and Jack immediately noticed subtle differences between the two. This bike was painted Sherwood Green with silver trim around the mudguards. Its spokes and rims were polished chrome as opposed to the Raspberry's, which were an oily black.

"Everything all right, brother?" ask the rider, a man in his late twenties. An attractive blond sat behind him on the buddy seat.

"Oh, I think I'm having some spark plug trouble," Jack replied. "But I think I can get to the next service station. I'm headed west."

"Mind if I take a look? That's a 1930, isn't it?"

"Yes, it's a 1930. And I'd sure like to get your opinion on my engine problem."

The morning sun cast long shadows over the Yellowstone River's Grand Canyon. The men spoke beside the Raspberry while the blond took pictures of the scenery with her Kodak Brownie camera.

"Looks like you've got a mismatched set of plugs," said the rider. "Best not to mix 'em. One will run hot and the other one cold. Here, I've got a spare No. 4 in my saddlebags. Just take it. Then brush off that No. 3 and save it for an emergency."

The man went over and fished out the plug from his saddlebags and handed it to Jack, who screwed it into the rear cylinder head. After replacing the plugs, Jack kicked over the starter and both cylinders came to life. He revved it a few times and cut the ignition.

"Gee, thanks a lot, buddy. What do I owe you?"

"Oh, you don't need to pay me. Just help the next fellow on down the road. That's the code."

It was the same thing he'd been told by the man in Goshenville, Pennsylvania.

Jack spent the rest of the day riding a leisurely figure eight around Yellowstone Park.

That evening, as the sun dipped below the Madison Plateau, Jack set up camp at Old Faithful's free auto campground. He used the remaining light to scribble out another letter to his parents:

July 9, '39
Sunday Evening

Dear Folks:
   Upon entering Yellowstone Park after bumping over about 65 miles of dirt roads and construction the motor began to rattle terribly

as though a main bearing had come loose and was clanking around. Scared me rattling at any speed much over 30 so I kept below that all through the park. Then a cold running spark plug gave me trouble. It quit on the way to the Grand Canyon but a fellow cyclist and his wife stopped & gave me an extra one he had.

The hot springs were darned interesting. I had to retrace one road & the second time I went over it there was a 6" hole in the road with steam coming out of it that hadn't been there before. Someone had put a stick with a red flag in it.

Animals galore, of course. Gas is 30 cents per gallon and it's a long way to any good garage. But there are surely some wonderful sights here. As I rode by Yellowstone Lake there were often boiling, bubbling springs & miniature geysers on one side of the road & the cold cold lake on the other. Seems queer doesn't it? So hot & so cold within 30 ft of each other. Saw Old Faithful sprout and got off a lot of cards. Grand Canyon surely is deep.

Will try to get to a garage in Butte to address motor trouble.

Love, Jack

Jack left the park at West Yellowstone the next morning and rode north. Montana's state speed limit was simply posted as "Reasonable and Proper"—and in the Raspberry's condition, Jack figured thirty miles per hour was both.

An hour later he hit U.S. Route 10, a major east-west highway between Detroit and Seattle. As he approached Whitehall, Montana he saw a sign along the road:

> Lewis and Clark traveled through this area
> on their way to the Pacific Ocean.

Jack arrived in Butte, Montana in midafternoon. It had taken nearly seven hours to ride the 190 miles from Old Faithful, and he blamed his snail's pace on the "main bearing" that forced him to cruise at thirty. This increased his gas mileage, but made for a long ride across the Treasure State.

He pulled off the road at the next service station where the sign out front said "Consumers Oil Co." Gas was eighteen cents per gallon—about half what it cost in Yellowstone Park. After topping off the tanks, he pushed the Raspberry alongside the building and examined the motor. A serviceman came out and stood beside him.

"Trouble with your cycle?"

"Yes, sir. She has a terrible rattle above thirty miles per hour. The man at the shop told me the main bearing is going bad."

"Hmmm," the serviceman said as he held his chin and looked over the bike. "Well, I'm no motorcycle mechanic, but have you checked your motor mounts? We have a lot of cars come through with rattle problems after a few hundred miles over the road between here and Cody. It's usually because something shook loose."

The man walked back to service a customer while Jack knelt in the dirt and peered down between the V-twin's crankcase and the frame. To his surprise, he saw that both bolts holding the left side of the motor to the frame were gone. He checked the other side and discovered the rear bolt was also missing. Just one bolt, the drive chain, and a few cables, wires, and linkages were all that held the throbbing V-twin to the frame.

"Is there a hardware store in the neighborhood?" Jack asked.

"Yep, just a couple of blocks up Harrison Avenue. Did you find a problem?"

"I think so, but I'm a little embarrassed. You were absolutely right."

Jack headed up Harrison Avenue and walked by a soda shop. He peered inside and saw that a chocolate milkshake cost twenty cents, so he passed it by. At the hardware store, he bought a set of three nuts, bolts, and lock washers. Back at the service station, he sat beside the Raspberry and wrote another postcard:

July 10, 1939

Dear Folks:
  Found the motor to be loose on its mountings. Am letting it cool and then will replace bolts and tighten it all up. Hope that was the trouble. Grand weather & scenery. Moscow next via 10S, 10, 95.
                    Love, Jack

The bike ran as smooth as ever. Jack was relieved, but at the same time deeply chagrined, as he knew such a straightforward problem should have been addressed long ago. A few days earlier, he'd diagnosed and repaired a complex ignition issue with three stones from a creek bed, yet the simple matter of loose motor mounts had escaped him.

Each of the Raspberry's mechanical incidents taught him something valuable, and what he took away from this one was that some of the biggest problems often have the simplest solutions and the advice of "experts" should always be taken with a grain of salt.

# 15

THE RASPBERRY ROLLED into Moscow, Idaho, just before noon the next day.

Jack found his brother, Horace, working on a radio at Mac's Electrical Repair Shop surrounded by a pile of equipment. A turntable to his left spun a 78-rpm recording of Glenn Miller's "Running Wild."

"Jack!" shouted Horace, setting down his soldering iron and extending a right hand. "Why, you look all grown up."

"I've had some adventures, all right!"

"Well, let's get some lunch and you can tell me about 'em."

Horace Newkirk had just completed his first year of graduate work at the University of Idaho. He didn't have much time for gymnastics, yet his compact frame was still firm and muscular. He was twenty-eight years old, soft spoken, and easygoing; Jack couldn't remember a time when his brother had raised his voice in anger. The boys hadn't seen each other in more than a year and were anxious to catch up.

They rode the Raspberry to a nearby diner and ordered lunch.

"You've seen the baby?" asked Horace.

Their first niece, Marion Emily Cain, had recently been born to sister Ginny.

"You bet," said Jack, "and she's walking now. They're worried she's going to tumble into the lake, so Dad rigged up a rope and life jacket so he can read on the dock while Emily plays. Looks just like a puppy on a leash!"

"I hear Scarsdale's down at Pensacola flying navy planes," said Horace. "He must be having a great time, that lucky son of a gun."

"You know, I haven't seen him since he left Rensselaer."

"How are Mom and Pop?" Horace asked.

"Fine," Jack replied. "They're spending the rest of the summer at the lake, and . . . hey, wait! I've got a letter from Dad right here in my pocket."

Horace went back to work that afternoon while Jack repainted the Raspberry's gas tanks with a can of ruddy-red enamel his brother had lying around in the garage. This covered up the scars from the Ohio welding job, but it also covered his nice blue and red paint scheme with the Rensselaer surveyor's logo.

Jack sat in bed that night and went over his finances. He had just sixteen dollars to his name and was still a long way from San Francisco. The money would probably last to the Golden Gate Exposition, but the ride home was another matter. Horace mentioned a desire to drive to New York in his Ford at the end of the month, so after talking it over, Jack penned a note to his parents:

July 11, 1939

Dear Folks:
    Arrived in Moscow this morning & found Horace right away. Will stay here a day or so & maybe take a few trips around here with him. Then I'll go on to California and return here at end of month and come home with him and sell the bike if necessary.
                    Love, J. B. N.

The thought of parting with the Raspberry sent a shudder down his spine, but Jack told himself it would probably never come to that.

★ ★ ★

**TEX HILL POKED** his head into Room 114 of Naval Hospital Pensacola.

"You're looking pretty skinny there, boy!"

Scarsdale Jack slowly opened his eyes and stared up from the hospital bed.

"Well I could still whup you, Hill," he said weakly. "Bum leg and all. To say nothing of what I'd do to you in a dogfight."

Tex laughed and sat down beside the bed.

"They say you got malaria," said Tex.

"That's what they say," Jack replied. "Guess I'll be here awhile."

"Don't you worry about it, friend," said Tex and placed his hand on Scarsdale's shoulder. "We'll keep an airplane warm for you. You'll be back up before you know it."

"Not in time for graduation," Jack muttered.

"That don't matter none," said Tex. "No shame in being held over. Besides, you'll probably get to fly one of them new Grumman hotrods—the Wildcat. You lucky cuss."

A nurse came by and checked Scarsdale's vitals. She gave him a few pills, wrote some notes on his chart, and then made her way to the next patient.

"Too bad about Guzman, eh?" offered Hill.

Scarsdale Jack paused, looked out the window, and clenched his jaw slightly.

"Yeah, too bad," he sighed. "Guzman—good man."

Scarsdale wondered how many more of his friends would go down. It was clear now that this wasn't just a game—and that he'd come a long, long way since his first awkward flights over Lake George.

★ ★ ★

**YOUNG JACK SPENT** two days with Horace in Moscow, Idaho, before he climbed back onto the Raspberry and rode south. He crossed the Snake River at the bridge between Lewiston, Idaho, and Clarkston, Washington, and spent the next few hours cruising along Route 410 through the fertile fields of southern Washington State. He tried to identify the crops as he puttered along at forty-three miles per hour: wheat, asparagus, spinach, potatoes, onions, green peas, alfalfa, barley, corn, string beans, lima beans, and grapes.

Jack had crossed many of the country's major rivers—the Hudson, the Susquehanna, the Ohio, Mississippi, Missouri, Yellowstone, and the Snake—but there was a singular grandness about the Columbia, the largest river flowing into the Pacific Ocean.

A Shell Oil station outside of Umatilla, Oregon, had a 7-4-1 sign out front and Jack pulled in to fill the Raspberry's tanks. He also got two free maps, one of the state of Oregon and another of the city of Portland. Printed on top of both maps were the words:

## In 1939 plan to see all the West and the GOLDEN GATE INTERNATIONAL EXPOSITION on San Francisco Bay

He was on the home stretch—the Pacific Ocean was less than a day's ride away, and he could almost smell the salt air.

U.S. Route 30 along the Columbia River Basin crawled with migrant workers as Jack rode west. He passed large trucks with wooden cargo beds, precariously overloaded with tired men in dusty shirts and denim overalls. A few Apple Annies sat alongside of the road desperately peddling fruit from their weathered baskets. It was a scene straight out of *The Grapes of Wrath*—a stark reminder that the nation was still in the grips of the Great Depression.

West of Umatilla, Jack saw a man on the side of the road with his thumb in the air.

He wore a cotton shirt with the sleeves rolled halfway up a pair of muscular forearms. An old leather belt held up oversized brown trousers. His feet were shod in a pair of dusty work boots, and a brimmed denim newsboy cap covered his head. The man carried a canvas drawstring bag the size of a watermelon.

"Where are you headed, friend?" Jack shouted over the Raspberry.

"Down the road, son. Just down the road."

"Well, I'm going to Portland if you want a ride."

"Not goin' that far, boy," he laughed, "but I'd sure appreciate a ride down to Willow Creek. Got some work there, I hear."

"Climb on then. I'll tie your bag to the rack. You can hold the handles on the seat here and put your feet on the running boards."

The men headed down Route 30 with the Columbia River off their right shoulder. It was difficult to converse over the wind and motor noise, but Jack learned his passenger was from Arkansas and had come west for the past six years to gather crops up and down the Columbia Basin. It was a hard life, but the man lived tolerably well and was able to send some money home.

After fifteen miles, the man asked Jack to drop him off at the junction of Route 30 and State Highway 74.

"Thank you kindly, son," he said as he shook Jack's hand. "You know, ain't too many folks stop for a colored man."

The Mountain Time Zone gave way to Pacific Time at the Idaho border, giving Jack an extra hour on his watch. He now had twelve hours of daylight and could make five hundred miles per day if necessary. As he sped past the Dalles, Jack saw a sign to the right:

LEWIS AND CLARK CAMPED HERE

An hour later Jack was staring at the two-year-old Bonneville Dam, an engineering marvel that not only provided electrical power and flood control, but also made the Columbia River navigable for one hundred eighty miles upstream. Its single-lift lock was the largest in the world.

Jack stopped at a barbershop outside of Portland for a shave and haircut.

The barber shaved Jack's face clean and wiped it off with a hot towel. Then, without a word, he raised the barber chair, placed a damp cloth on the back of Jack's neck, and subtly attempted to scrub off three thousand miles of grease and road dust.

Back at the Raspberry, Jack looked over his Shell Oil map of Portland, where he'd made a large pencil mark on N.E. Faloma Road and written the words *Cousin Walter Smith*.

Jack weaved his way through Portland and found Faloma Road on the north side of town just south of the Columbia River. Cousin Walter was just about to leave work when Jack rumbled into the factory yard. They didn't quite recognize each other.

"Walter? Walter Smith?"

"Jack Newkirk?"

"That's me. All the way from the New York World's Fair!"

"Well, get off that bike and come on in!" exclaimed Walter as he shook Jack's hand vigorously.

"No," Smith continued, "on second thought, just stay right on your bike and follow me home. Let me run in and call the wife and tell her we're coming. Oh, dang it, I've got a meeting after dinner tonight I can't get out of. Anyway, I'll think of something. Darn good to see you, Jack!"

Overwhelmed by this enthusiastic welcome, Jack gladly followed him back to the corner of Thirty-seventh Avenue and Shaver where Walter lived with his wife and daughter. Supper was still an hour off, so Jack cleaned up, went into the guest room, and studied his atlas.

The dinner conversation centered around Jack's ride and any news of the family.

"So once you visit San Francisco," Walter asked between bites, "are you going to ride all the way back to New York?"

"That was my plan," replied Jack. "But I'm running out of money. I'll be lucky to make it back to Moscow. From there I can catch a ride home with Horace."

"Would you have to sell the bike, then?"

"I might be *forced* to sell her," Jack lamented. "Horace and I would need gas money."

"Walter," suggested his wife, "Jack should stop and see the Pomeroys."

"Great idea, honey," he replied. "Jack, we know some folks down by Medford who have a son about your age. His name's Pete, and he's working now—not going to college—so I'll bet he has some money to buy your bike if you end up having to sell her."

They heard a knock on the door. Walter got up to answer it and returned with a man about twenty years old who was dressed for an evening on the town.

"Jack, this is Charlie. He works for me at the foundry. He says he'd be glad to take you around and show you some of the city tonight, if you're up for it. I've got to get to my meeting."

Walter quietly slipped a dollar into Charlie's hand so Jack wouldn't see it.

"Well—thanks, Walt," said Jack. "That's swell of you guys. I'd like to see Portland, sure."

Charlie and Jack drove to Madrona Park next to the Willamette River and watched planes take off and land from the Swan Island airport and its adjoining seaplane basin. Charlie then drove Jack to a dance club near downtown Portland just as the sun began to set.

"This is a swell place," said Charlie. "They got some hot dames here who can't say no—I mean it's a dime a dance. They have to dance with you if you give them a ticket. You can swing, can't you, Jack?"

"Yeah, sure."

They paid fifteen cents to get through the door, then bought five dance tickets each and sat down at the bar. Charlie bought Jack a root beer as the jukebox belted out tunes from Benny Goodman, Kay Kyser, Glenn Miller, and other popular bands of the day.

A few girls looked over at Charlie and smiled. He smiled back, nodded, and held up his beer glass in a mock toast.

"OK, let's get to it!" said Charlie after finishing his drink. "I'll introduce you."

They walked over to the line of taxi dancers and Charlie began to make small talk. Several girls circled around him hoping they'd be the first to be picked, and Jack began to feel self-conscious beside his good-looking companion.

"Who's your little friend, Charlie?" one of them finally asked.

"Oh, this is Jack. He's from New York. He's my boss's cousin. Come on girls, let's stop yakking and get dancing."

The jukebox started to play Louis Armstrong's "Ding Dong Daddy from Dumas." Charlie took a girl by the hand and ran out to the dance floor. Jack meekly offered one of the girls a dance ticket. She took it, but he caught a glimpse of her rolling her eyes at the other girls with a sigh of acquiescence.

Things changed, however, once the dancing started. For the past few years, Jack had attended swing dance school with his friend Emmor Caldwell in New York—and had become a first-rate dancer. He knew the latest steps from New York's hottest clubs, and a lot of these moves hadn't yet made their way west.

The group of taxi dancers stopped what they were doing and stared.

Jack did the Foxtrot, the Collegiate Shag, the waltz, and the Big Apple. He threw in a few moves like the Boogie Back, Spank the Baby, the Rusty Dusty, and the Suzy Q. Only a few of the girls had the skill and stamina to do a good Lindy Hop, and Jack was able to pick them out right away as he watched them perform on the floor.

"Who is that kid?"

"He's from New York!"

"Hey, Jack," yelled Charlie, "you sure know how to shake a leg!"

"Feels great after sitting on that Harley for three thousand miles!"

Charlie dropped Jack off at Smith's house at midnight. Jack fell into bed and didn't get up until eight that morning. After breakfast Walt took him on a tour of his brass foundry and tried to persuade him to stay a day or two. Jack was anxious to head south, but promised he'd stop by on his way home. He climbed on the Raspberry and fired up the motor.

"Wait," said Walter, "let me get your picture."

Walter Smith snapped the photo, then put an envelope into Jack's hand with a letter inside:

E. H. Pomeroy and
Pete Pomeroy
Pineridge Orchard
Old Stage Road
2 ½ miles West of Central Point, Oregon

Dear Pete,

This is introducing my cousin Jack Newkirk from New York.

He is on his way to San Francisco. He is coming back this way from Frisco and needs to sell his cycle on the coast and will go home with his brother by automobile.

I told him to see you before selling his machine. $100 is all right for this cycle as this model is selling in Portland now at around $150 at the dealers. This is a 1930–74 in. and seems to be in fairly good condition.

    With best wishes
    —Walt

After Jack left, Walt went into his office and penned another letter:

Dr. Burt L. Newkirk  AIR MAIL
Glen Island
Lake George, New York

Dear Uncle Burt,

    Jack arrived here safe and sound on the evening of July 13th. He took a bath, had a night's sleep, and had breakfast with us.

    Took him to the foundry this morning and then he was on his way south. I wanted him to stay awhile but he would be on his way.

    His motorcycle is running O.K. so should not have much trouble with it. Seems to be a careful driver so the trip ought to do him lots of good.

                       With best regards,
                         Walter

    Jack headed southeast on State Highway 50 and within two hours had climbed from sea level to four thousand feet at Wapinitia Pass in the heart of the Cascades. Surrounded by eight-foot snow banks, Jack put on all his clothes and started to look for newspapers when a man driving in the opposite direction told him how hot it was in the valley below.

    An hour later, road construction detoured him around the small town of Maupin and onto a dirt road though a semi-arid stretch of wheatland and pasture. The temperature was nearly ninety and Jack began to get nervous about his fuel supply. He hadn't filled up since Portland and had switched over to his reserve tank a few miles before the road construction. The Raspberry was not likely to make the next service station. Jack slowed down to thirty to conserve gas, and after about fifteen miles came upon the small settlement of Bakeoven, Oregon.

    It wasn't a town, really. It was more like a small assortment of wooden ranch buildings. No store, no phone, and no gas station. He was in trouble.

    After parking the Raspberry in the shade, he sat down and studied his atlas. He might be able to squeak into Shaniko, but the Raspberry would most likely start coughing a few miles short of town. He was about to head out when a man on a horse appeared from one of the fields.

    "Howdy," said Jack.

    "Afternoon," replied the old cowboy. "Hot one, ain't it?"

    "It's actually not bad if you've got a forty-mile-an-hour wind in your face."

"I wouldn't know about that," the cowboy laughed. "I don't usually get this ol' boy off a trot."

He wore a weathered Resistol cattleman's hat made of finely woven straw. Its scalloped leather hatband was trimmed with braided horsehair and flashed with concho accents. He carried a rifle in his scabbard—a .30-30-caliber Winchester Model 94. The smell of dust and horse sweat made Jack think he had been transported into a Western movie.

"Would you know if there's a gas station anywhere about?" Jack asked. "I believe I'm about to run out."

The horse looked down its nose at the Raspberry and snorted, and Jack thought of how far he'd come since his encounter with the mounted Capitol policeman at the White House.

"Well, no, son. Closest service station is Maupin or Shaniko. Twelve miles, give or take."

"I might make that distance. Hate to have to walk in this heat, though."

"Can't blame ya. Listen, I've got a few hundred gallons in the overhead tank I keep for my machinery. Be glad to sell you some if you need it. I'd have to charge you twenty cents a gallon. That's what it costs me to haul it out here."

"Oh, that would be swell. I'd sure appreciate that, sir."

"The name's Jim. Jim Hinton. Nice to meet ya."

"Jack Newkirk. Do you run this spread?"

"Yup. Born and raised here. Cattle, sheep, wheat—it's kept me pretty busy."

"How old is this town?"

"Oh, a little older than me. I was born in '74 in a cave over yonder. Town was new then."

"Born in a cave? Boy, that's something!"

"At least I had a roof over my head. My daddy was born on the Oregon Trail."

Jack rode out of Bakeoven with two gallons of gas in the Raspberry's main tank. He joined U.S. Route 97 again and two hours later arrived in Bend, Oregon. By suppertime he was overlooking Crater Lake. Just as in Yellowstone, the park entry station charged him an entire dollar to get in. Jack grumbled to the park ranger that he had to pay the same as the carload of six people ahead of him and suggested there should be a lower entrance fee for motorcycles.

"I'll bring it up at the next meeting," said the ranger.

He went to the visitor's center and bought a hot dog and a soda, sat down and penned a note to his parents:

July 14, 1939

Dear Folks:

Started from Moscow yesterday. Rode down Columbia River and passed one town with no buildings. Stayed at Walter Smith's last night. Sweltered through Bakeoven, Or. at 2:00 & now am shivering through 8 to 10 ft. snow drifts across the rd. Got off and ran up one. Rare air made itself apparent at once. Am writing this from Rim Drive overlooking Crater Lake. Hope to reach Frisco. Horace is looking fine & has lots of work to do.
                Love, J. B. N.

About an hour before sunset, Jack rode out of Crater Lake National Park on State Highway 62. A couple of miles later, he pulled off the road, weaved through a few hundred yards of Douglas firs, and set up camp in the Rogue River National Forest west of the Cascade Mountains.

He'd been asleep for three hours when he felt pressure bearing down on his feet as though someone had set a sack of cement on them. He looked up groggily and saw an unmistakable silhouette in the moonlight.

*Bear!*

"Damn you, get off my bed!" Jack blurted out at full volume into the starry night. It was the harshest language he could muster.

The bear jumped up and ran off, then stopped twenty yards away to look over his shoulder. Jack hopped on the Raspberry, honked on the horn, and switched on his John Brown Motolamp. The light made an eerie reflection in the black bear's eyes, and by its size Jack could tell it was probably a second year cub that had recently left its mother.

He kicked the starter over a few times. After the V-twin fired up, he used a trick he'd learned along the road. Revving the engine, he shut off the ignition and held the throttle open, filling the combustion chamber and exhaust manifold with undetonated fuel. When the pistons had almost stopped turning over, he switched on the ignition again. This resulted in a loud bang and a plume of flames like Buck Rogers' rocket ship.

Jack repeated this performance a few times and then shut everything down. He could hear the bear crash through the woods in the opposite direction—far away from the fire-breathing dragon he'd stumbled upon. Jack looked around to make sure the pyrotechnics had not ignited anything on the ground, then crawled under his blankets again and nestled his back against the Raspberry's crash bar.

On Saturday morning he continued down the Rogue River Valley on Route 62. By nine o'clock he was in Medford treating himself to a rare restaurant breakfast, where the waitress pointed out how to get to Old Stage Road. Jack rode two and a half miles west of Central Point until he saw the sign:

### Pineridge Orchard

Jack was surprised to see a couple of young men in the driveway working on two shiny Harley-Davidson Model 61EL Knuckleheads. One of the bikes was painted solid blue with white trim on the mudguards. The other was green with silver trim. Both had Harley-Davidson "flying bullet" decals on their tanks, and a chrome-plated instrument console sat on top with a speedometer that went up to an optimistic 120 miles per hour.

"Hey, fellows," said Jack as he cut the Raspberry's ignition, "is this the Pomeroys?"

"Yes," said one of the boys as he set down a crescent wrench. "I'm Pete Pomeroy."

"I'm Walt Smith's cousin Jack. He said you were a man who likes to ride motorcycles."

"Every chance I get," said Pete. "Same with June here."

The other boy got up from under his Harley and extended a gritty right hand. Jack didn't mind—his hands were even dirtier.

"I'm DeWitt Carlson, Jr. Most folks just call me June. Where'd you ride from?"

"New York City."

"New York?" June exclaimed.

"Yup," Jack replied. "I wanted to see both fairs so I just pointed west and kept on going."

"The New York World's Fair?" Pete exclaimed. "You've come far, brother."

"Feels like far," Jack replied. "Walt sent this letter, but I guess he didn't know you both had new Knuckleheads. So never mind that part about buying my bike."

As Pete Pomeroy read the letter, a tall, stately woman walked out of the house.

"Did you say you're Walter's cousin?"

"Yes, ma'am."

"I'm Mrs. Pomeroy, Pete's mother. Welcome to Central Point."

"You live in a beautiful spot, ma'am. I've seen all kinds of country and I believe you have one of the best seats in the house."

As Jack spoke with Mrs. Pomeroy, Pete handed the letter to June and pointed to the middle of the page. June looked it over, raised his eyebrows, and nodded. They stood by politely until Mrs. Pomeroy finished speaking.

"Hey Jack, Walt says you're headed to San Francisco," said Pete. "Is that a fact?"

"You bet. I've come this far and I aim to get there, rain or shine."

"Are you going to the Golden Gate Fair?"

"That I am."

"How'd you like some company?"

"Oh, now Peter," interjected Mrs. Pomeroy, "I'm sure this young man's on a schedule. You mustn't impose. Besides, you both have jobs."

"Hey," Jack grinned, "it would be swell to have some company!"

"Mom?" Pete implored.

"Well I can't speak for June, but if it's all right with your father, then it's all right with me."

"Gee, thanks! Jack, how soon were you going to head south?"

"No set schedule, really."

"Could you wait a day or two? June and I have some work to do on our bikes—and we need to clear things with our boss."

"Sure."

"Jack can stay with us a couple of days, can't he, Mom?"

"He most certainly can."

# 16

TEX HILL BEGAN to wrap up his last few weeks of Pensacola's Class 121-C as Scarsdale Jack Newkirk lay in bed at the Naval Hospital recuperating from malaria and a torn knee ligament. During the course of their training, a camaraderie had developed that would last a lifetime. Some of Newkirk and Hill's fellow cadets included Robert "Buster" Keeton, George "Pappy" Paxton, John Hennessy, Joe Rosbert, Bert Christman, "Gil" Bright, Frank Lawlor, and Tommy Cole. All eyes were on the coveted Naval Aviator wings, that golden badge of courage awaiting those who didn't wash out during thirteen months of rigorous instruction.

Despite the intensity of the schedule and some tragic losses, Jack's year at Pensacola did have its lighter moments. Tex was fond of buzzing Lover's Lane along the Florida shoreline where teenagers gathered to park. Bert Christman was a skilled artist who had just come off an eighteen-month stint for the Associated Press, where he drew a comic strip called *Scorchy Smith*.

One day Christman sketched an extremely unflattering caricature of an unpopular instructor. He captioned it "Ol' Brassbottom" and passed it to Scarsdale. Newkirk erupted in a fit of uncontrollable laughter that caused the instructor to turn away from the chalkboard.

"Something funny, cadet?"

"No, sir," chuckled Jack as he tried to maintain a straight face.

"Then pay attention!"

"Yes, sir."

The instructor turned around and Jack took one more look at the drawing. This made him laugh even harder and tears came to his eyes. He crammed the paper into his pocket and tried to regain his composure, but it was too late.

"Newkirk, go sit in the hall until you can control yourself. And I'll be expecting a higher score from you when you're tested on this material, you got me?"

"Yes, sir," Jack laughed as he made a hasty exit.

History would record that NAS Pensacola's Class of 1939 produced a veritable dream team of naval aviators. Bert Christman, Jack Newkirk, and Tex Hill grew to be fast friends—and each would not hesitate to trust the other with their lives.

★ ★ ★

**TWO AND A HALF MILES** west of Central Point, Oregon, three teen-aged boys excitedly prepared their motorcycles for a five-hundred-mile ride down the Redwood Highway to the 1939 Golden Gate International Exposition. Pete and June tweaked and polished their twin Knuckleheads while Jack fiddled with the Raspberry's carburetor.

"Hey Jack," said Pete, "you know how to adjust chain tension on these bikes?"

"Oh sure," he replied. "It's no big deal. Here, I'll show you."

Early the next morning, they lined up their Harleys in front of the house for a photograph and then rode off to the west with a cloud of dust in their wake.

*Two Knuckleheads and a Flathead*

Both Oregon and California had maximum speed laws of forty-five miles per hour. This worked out well for Jack, who preferred to cruise at forty-three, but Pete and June felt hobbled by the limit. Their Knuckleheads could hit a hundred miles per hour—a claim proven by Harley-Davidson test riders on the back roads of Wisconsin. Nevertheless, neither Pete nor June was inclined to test the limits of their parents' goodwill, so they kept the speed just under forty-five as they puttered in loose formation down U.S. Route 199.

At noon they rode out of the Siskiyou National Forest east of Crescent City, California, where they were stopped at the Redwood Highway entry station. An inspector looked them over for signs of Citrus Canker Disease, Cotton Boll Weevil, and Oriental Fruit Moth. Satisfied the boys posed no threat to the state's agriculture, the inspector sent them to the next station where they were required to obtain a nonresident permit for the State of California.

Jack could smell something in the air. It was fresh, new, cool, and exotic. The boys rode their Harleys into Crescent City, got off the Redwood Highway, and followed Pacific Avenue to Pebble Beach Drive. For a hundred yards they rode on top of the hard sand as the waves left a line of foam that licked the Raspberry's tires.

At that moment, Jack realized he had done it. While the fair was still four hundred miles away, he could say in all truth that he had traveled from sea to shining sea—from New York Harbor to the Pacific Ocean. He had never been west of Minneapolis, but now he could say he'd crossed his country.

"What is it, Jack?" asked Pete as he saw Jack dabbing his eyes with his bandana.

"Nothing," Jack replied as the waves crashed against the sand. "Just glad to be here is all."

★ ★ ★

**FARTHER SOUTH—NEAR** San Luis Obispo and Agoura Hills, California—a film crew from the Hal Roach Studio was working on a scene for the movie *Of Mice and Men*. The job of the day was to film a group of barley wagons as they returned to the ranch at dinnertime—after which the lives of George, Lennie, Slim, Candy, Mae, and Curly would converge with tragic consequences. Director Lewis Milestone was anxious. After the scenes were shot, the movie still had to be edited and scored, and at this rate they'd be lucky to release the film by the end of the year. Milestone needed a screening copy by the first of October. This would allow six weeks for Aaron Copland to score it and then a month for duplication and distribution. Nineteen thirty-nine was shaping up to be a banner year for Hollywood, and Milestone wanted *Of Mice and Men* to be a part of it.

★ ★ ★

**PETE, JACK, AND JUNE** spent considerable time along Highway 101 gawking at the scenery and taking pictures of the coastline. When the highway curved inland, they found themselves surrounded by enormous redwood trees. Pete knew it would be fruitless to try to capture them with his tiny camera, so he didn't even try.

Ten miles north of Eureka, June spotted some tourist cabins and motioned Pete to pull over.

"Think this would be a good place for the night?" he asked.

"Looks good to me," said Pete. "Can't beat the view. What do you think, Jack?"

It was an awkward situation. The cabins only slept two, and Jack didn't want to pay for a room or presume upon his friends to pay for his lodging. He also didn't want to make them feel like tenderfeet.

"Listen, fellows," he said, "I've been camping on the ground for the last four weeks. I sleep better that way. Why don't you get the room and I'll spread out under the tree here. I could still use the sink and shower—then we don't have to get two rooms."

"Aw, Jack," said Pete, "I hate havin' you sleep outside if it starts raining."

"Don't worry about me—I've spent lots of nights in the rain. If it gets bad I'll come in and sleep on the floor."

They unpacked their bikes and settled in and then rode to a seafood stand by the beach. Jack spent thirty-five cents on the Captain's Basket: French fries, shrimp, clams, scallops, and two chunks of fish fried in a light brown batter. They watched the sun go down over the Pacific as waves whooshed rhythmically over the rocks and sand. As the sun dipped below the horizon, the rumble of three V-twins momentarily covered the sound of the sea as the boys rode off the beach and back up Highway 101.

The boys rumbled through another large stand of redwoods the next morning as they curved inland through Humboldt County. The road forked at the town of Leggett, where they could choose to ride inland on Highway 101 or hug the coastline all the way to San Francisco on Highway 1. Jack favored the coastal route, but this meant twenty miles of gravel. Pete and June weren't keen on taking their bikes over the dirt, but promised they would ride Highway 1 on the way home as long as they turned off before the pavement ended.

They stopped for lunch at Willits and Jack dropped another note in the mail:

July 19, 1939

Dear Folks:

Stayed 2½ days with the Pomeroys at Pine Ridge, Central Pt. Oregon. They treated me like a king, took me to a swimming pool, dinner & movie the 1st night & on a picnic the next day. Pete P. (a friend of Walter S.) & his chum are now with me on the way to Frisco. The trees along the Redwood Highway are immense. One feels somewhat like a flea traveling through a toothbrush.

Love, Jack

After four weeks on the road, Jack and the Raspberry moved as one. As with a woman—subtle variations in body language, vocal inflection, facial expressions, or general behavior—Jack had learned to discern changes in the Raspberry's demeanor that could foretell trouble brewing. Few things escaped his attention.

He'd learned how to set the throttle and ride with his hands off the handlebars. He could stop on a dime and U-turn as gracefully as a fighter pilot. He could send a shower of flames and smoke out the rear pipe by fiddling with the ignition, and the engine rarely had to be kicked over more than three times before the V-twin came to life. Jack's right boot bore a permanent dimple from the stub of the kick-starter pedal that rattled off somewhere in Ohio, and he had become an expert at diagnosing and repairing mechanical problems on the road.

As the three Harleys rumbled south down Highway 101, Jack began to notice a faint knocking sound from his V-twin. It sounded like it was coming from the pistons.

A paved road took them through Sonoma County west to Jenner, where they hit the coast again and motored south toward Bodega Bay. Pete stopped to take pictures while Jack poked around the Raspberry to locate the source of the knock.

It was late afternoon when they found another row of tourist cabins north of Bodega Bay. Pete and June would stay inside while Jack put his shelter cloth and blankets out on the brown, coastal prairie overlooking the beaches below.

For the first time in weeks, Jack had trouble falling asleep. It wasn't the salt spray on his shelter cloth or the pounding surf that kept him awake. It wasn't his financial situation or concern about the Raspberry. No—his restlessness was pure excitement—like a six-year-old on the night before Christmas.

Sixty miles to the south, he could see the faint aura of two-dozen multicolored searchlights cutting through the nighttime sky. Jack knew they were from Treasure Island. And he knew that by this time tomorrow, he would be standing next to the Tower of the Sun at San Francisco's glittering Golden Gate International Exposition.

# 17

WITH THE MORNING came the mist. More than one hundred fifty miles of California coastline were blanketed in fog—from the head of the Navarro River, past the lighthouse at Point Arena, down to Anchor Bay, Fort Ross, and from Goat Rock at the mouth of the Russian River to Baker Beach on the San Francisco Peninsula.

At Sonoma Coast State Park, where Jack had made his camp, there was giddiness in the air.

This was the day.

Thursday, July 20, 1939.

Exactly four weeks earlier, he had stood before the towering Trylon and Perisphere at the New York World's Fair. Today, he would ride his Harley into the Pageant of the Pacific.

After a leisurely breakfast—longer than Jack would have liked—the boys mounted up and motored down Highway 1. Pete took the lead as Jack and June rode side by side, creating a V-formation like geese. The traffic was light and the boys weaved down their carefree highway like otters frolicking in a stream. Pete held out his arms and made flying motions. Jack stood on his footboards and held both hands over his head. June made wide turns back and forth across the road like a skier carving powder. The antics continued until June's handgrip bumped against Jack's handlebar, nearly sending both of them head over heels.

They puttered past the Muir Woods, up the Manzinita Bolina road, and down Coyote Creek where they rejoined Highway 101. They came to a stop just north of Fort Baker.

The sight below them literally took their breath away—and would be seared in their minds for the rest of their lives.

The Golden Gate Bridge was the most magnificent structure they had ever beheld. Remnants of the morning fog clung to the bridge's surface and made its orange-vermillion paint look fresh. They had had seen flat, black and white versions of the Golden Gate in books, but this scene was in living color.

The bridge had six auto lanes sixty feet wide with ten-foot sidewalks on either side. It hung 220 feet over the water with towers that reached 760 feet into the sky. It was the largest suspension bridge the world had ever known. Jack's jaw hung open and his eyes were round.

It was Pete Pomeroy who broke their stunned silence.

"You go first, Jack!" he shouted.

And as the Raspberry crossed the center of the Golden Gate Bridge, curious onlookers looked over their shoulders to behold a boy with a huge smile on his face, pumping both fists in the air, unblushingly laughing out loud, and shouting *"Yaaaahoo!"*

★ ★ ★

**TREASURE ISLAND'S GOLDEN** Gate International Exposition—the Pageant of the Pacific—was situated on four hundred level acres in a rectangle 5,520 feet long by 3,400 feet wide. A 900-by-110-foot causeway linked the man-made island to the three-year-old San Francisco–Oakland Bay Bridge. After the fair the island would serve as a permanent airport with a semicircular administration building and two hangars—a grand central air depot for the entire Bay Area.

The layout of the fair exploited the relatively warm weather of the area. While the New York Fair had its various zones, the San Francisco Fair had its outdoor courts and gardens. The four-hundred-foot Tower of the Sun was surrounded by the Court of Honor, Court of Reflections, Court of the Moon, Court of the Seven Seas, and the Portals of the Pacific. Twelve hundred gardeners maintained the lush Avenue of Palms, Treasure Garden, Court of Flowers, and the Garden Walk on Treasure Island's south and west sides.

Business exhibits celebrated the speed and convenience of modern technology. Manufacturers promoted the wonders of mechanization, international pavilions enticed fairgoers to visit foreign lands, and the Gayway amusement area featured a number of rides and exhibits. One of the Gayway's most popular was Sally Rand's Dude Ranch, hosted by a bevy of nubile young women who deliberately crossed out the D and replaced it with an N.

There was more food than fairgoers could possibly sample: seafood, barbeque, baked beans, Chinese, Japanese, Mexican, Dutch, Italian, corn on the cob, ice cream, custard, and hamburgers and hotdogs around every corner.

A post office sat inside the Administration Building, and a Western Union telegram station was available at the Electricity and Communications Building. The Bank of America had an onsite branch office open from ten in the morning to ten at night. The Administration Building contained a fully equipped hospital, staffed with doctors and nurses at all times. The Exposition stayed open until 10:00 PM and the Gayway until 2:00 AM.

The boys agreed that their first stop in San Francisco would be the Harley-Davidson shop near the corner of Hayes and Polk Street. June's muffler had developed problems and Jack wanted to get a mechanic's take on his engine knock. They were riding through the Presidio when a police siren suddenly blared behind them.

"You boys have any idea why I pulled you over?" the officer asked.

"No, sir," they responded in unison.

"It's the noise, boys. Your cycles are louder than anything I've heard in a long time. We have a noise ordinance here, and you just busted it."

"It's my fault, sir," said June. "Part of my muffler came off on the way down the coast. We were just headed to the dealer to have it looked at-honest to gosh."

"Which dealer?"

"The one in Hayes Valley. Can you tell us how to get there?"

The officer told them to go down Lombard Street, turn right at Van Ness and follow it all the way to Hayes. He let them off with a verbal warning and told them to be safe.

The boys craned their necks as they rumbled past the San Francisco Art Museum, War Memorial, Opera House, Auditorium, and the huge City Hall, which reminded Jack of the Capitol building in Washington, D.C.

They described their problems to the mechanic at the Hayes Street Harley shop.

"Well," he said, "the Knucklehead's easy. It just needs a new muffler. We got 'em in stock so I could have it done this afternoon. Now the VL, that's a different story. I think your pistons are loose and could collapse at any time. They might hold if you go slow, but I'd recommend replacing the pistons, rings, and rods. 'Course, we'd need to throw in a couple of head gaskets."

Jack needed to sit down before he asked the usual question.

"So how much do you think that would cost?"

The serviceman got his parts list and started typing numbers into an adding machine. After entering each figure, he pulled a handle that cranked the numbers into a series of gears and then stamped them onto a roll of paper. To Jack, each *kerchunk* felt like a punch from Joe Louis.

"Oh, I'd say it'd be about thirty-five dollars parts and labor. Could have it done for you by tomorrow afternoon."

June authorized the repair to his Knucklehead. Jack told the man he'd "think about it."

They grabbed their luggage and took a bus up Market Street to Powell. June had never seen a cable car, so they jumped on the Powell-Hyde line and rode over Nob Hill, Russian Hill, and down to Ghirardelli Square where they got off near Fisherman's Wharf. As they walked toward the Embarcadero, Pete saw a rooming house where they could stay for two dollars a night.

They registered and left their belongings in the room, then walked to Pier 33 where a large ship was docked. Jack stared at the oblong building and its imposing, arched entryway.

"Does all this make you want to be a sailor, Jack?" asked June.

"Not me," Jack replied. "You'd never catch me on one of these ships."

They caught a streetcar to the Ferry Building where they each paid a dime to ride across the bay to Treasure Island's West Terminal. Pete snapped pictures while Jack and June leaned over the rail and peered across San Francisco Bay. Alcatraz Island—the Rock—loomed forebodingly off the port bow. They suddenly heard the rumble of engines overhead. June looked up, shouted, and pointed to the sky.

"Look, fellows! It's the Pan Am Clipper!"

Pan American World Airways had ordered a dozen of these Boeing

314 Clippers for transoceanic routes across the Atlantic and Pacific. One of the largest aircraft ever built, it was the Ritz-Carlton of air transport. Four supercharged 1600 hp Wright R-2600 Twin Cyclone engines allowed it to cruise at 190 miles per hour with a range of more than 3,500 miles. It carried 4,200 gallons of gasoline and 300 gallons of oil. The seats could be converted to bunks for overnight accommodation, and the plane had a lounge and dining area staffed by chefs from the best four-star hotels. The *Honolulu Clipper* service between San Francisco and Hong Kong began in January 1939—a trip that took only six days one way. The *Pacific Clipper* flew between San Francisco and New Zealand. The *Yankee Clipper* made its inaugural trip across the Atlantic between New York City and Southampton, England, on June 24, 1939.

It was the peak of luxury: a one-way fare across the Atlantic cost $675— enough to buy a new 1939 Harley-Davidson 61EL with every conceivable option and enough gas to cross the country twice. All Clipper operations in the Pacific were based out of Treasure Island.

The boys disembarked at the West Ferry Terminal and paid fifty cents each at the Portals of the Pacific entry gate, then turned right and walked down the Court of the Moon. A photographer with a tripod-mounted camera snapped their picture, gave them a numbered claim ticket, and said they could purchase the photo for fifty cents.

They sat down at Treasure Garden to plan their day. June wanted to go straight to the Gayway amusement area while Jack wanted to see the Metals, Mines and Machinery building and its fifty-foot-high Treasure Mountain. Pete wanted to see Agriculture Hall and the Life History of the Redwoods. They agreed to split up and meet at six o'clock at the Tower of the Sun for dinner and to discuss any reconnaissance information they had gathered.

Jack went straight to the Western Union exhibit. He had an important telegram to send—a message that would take only a few minutes to reach its destination three thousand miles away:

DR & MRS NEWKIRK
GLEN ISLAND
LAKE GEORGE, NEW YORK

yippee-horah-eureeka-and other such expostulations. I made it. Treasure Island location is beautiful.

Jack in san francisco, calif.

And then—with a touch of gloating—he sent a letter to Dick Hill back at Rensselaer:

July 20, 1939

Well my friend I believe you owe me a dinner or some such recompense. I have made it from New York City to San Francisco on "the Raspberry"—the motorcycle you said could not make it around the block. We have had our adventures but she is a good old gal and I have grown quite attached to her. Wish you could be with us here at the fair.

Sincerely, Jack

The postcard to his parents was not so upbeat:

After dinner the boys rode both Ferris wheels, the Giant Octopus, the Cyclone roller coaster, and the *Circuit du Mont Blanc*—a French merry-go-round sensation. As the sun went down, they walked through the Pavilions of the Pacific and visited Hawaii, French Indo-China, and Japan. An outdoor theater with a newly invented bamboo screen projected moving pictures of native life and tourist attractions in the Japanese archipelago and the South Pacific.

There were ten thousand colored floodlights hidden in troughs, tree baskets, and shrubs throughout Treasure Island. Black light was projected onto invisible panels in niches and murals to produce pictures that stood out in a phosphorescent glow. Twenty-four military-grade searchlights had been mounted on neighboring Yerba Buena Island, which had created the scintillating display of color Jack had seen along the Sonoma Coast.

The three boys ate frozen custard, walked around the Court of Pacifica, and chatted about their plans for the future. At ten o'clock they were herded back toward the West Ferry Terminal. They jumped on the boat for the mainland, where a bus finally dropped them off a block from their rooming house.

They returned to the Harley shop the next morning. Jack had come up with a few theories during the night and wanted to discuss them with the mechanic, but Pete and June had to be back home by Sunday afternoon and needed to head north. Sensitive to their position, Jack tried to make things easier.

"Listen, fellas," he said, "I know you've got to get going, but unless I can fix things here I'll do nothing but hold you back. The man said I needed to keep it under thirty-five, and that wouldn't get us in until Monday at the earliest."

"But Jack, we wouldn't feel right leaving you here with a broken cycle."

"You fellows need to be at work on Monday—I don't have to be anywhere 'til school starts. Just shoot up Highway 101 and I'll stay here awhile and talk with the mechanic."

"OK," said Pete, "how about this? June and I will head out and have lunch at the Golden Gate. If you're not there by two o'clock we'll head north."

Pete and June started up their bikes and rode off with a wave.

"Don't forget," said Pete. "We'll be waiting for you at the Golden Gate!"

By midafternoon the Harley mechanic was growing impatient with Jack and his wacky suggestions for low-cost repair alternatives.

"Listen," the man said, "I told you it was loose pistons. You've got no other choice than to replace everything lock, stock, and barrel. I don't set the prices here and thirty-five dollars is what it's going to cost. That's all I can say, son."

Jack climbed back on the Raspberry and headed north.

Pete and June were long gone, and it was about seven hundred miles to his cousin's house in Portland. At thirty miles per hour, this would be a long ride.

Scattered patches of cypress trees clung stubbornly to the bluffs along Highway 1. As dusk approached, Jack piloted the Raspberry along a footpath toward the edge of a scalloped cliff overlooking the Pacific. Parking the bike, he picked his way down to the beach, where he gathered an armload of driftwood for his campfire.

He spread his shelter cloth and blankets between the fire and the Raspberry, then sat down and cooked a steak over the flames as he watched the sun sink slowly into the ocean. Jack knew there was no land to the west for more than five thousand miles—nothing until the Empire of Japan.

The sea air and sunset affected Jack like a narcotic. He leaned against the Raspberry, gazed over the water, and unwrapped a bar of Ghirardelli chocolate from the fair.

He knew he had a good life. He'd grown up among the lakes and mountains. He'd learned to run, swim, camp, fish, and canoe. He wasn't rich, but he didn't need money to make him happy—because at this moment his spirit was more content than Howard Hughes, William Randolph Hearst, and the Rockefellers combined.

Against all odds Jack had completed his goal of visiting both 1939 world's fairs. The Great Depression was mercifully releasing its grip, and the World of Tomorrow promised peace and prosperity for all mankind.

His short-term ambition fulfilled, Jack thoughts drifted toward the future. He'd finish his last two years of college and get a job with one of the companies he'd seen at the fairs. Then he'd find a girl—someone like Judy Garland, maybe—and they'd settle down and teach their children to swim in Lake George as his father had before him.

Yes, life was good, and Jack drifted off to sleep with dreams of Ferris wheels, pretty girls, and the road home.

★ ★ ★

Crotalus horridus *felt a primal urge to make his way back down Tongue Mountain. The cold nights of September were several weeks off, but the snake was more than two miles from his den near the peninsula the locals call Montcalm Point. His progress was unhurried—only a hundred yards per day—but his intent was unmistakable: he would return to the vicinity of his hibernacula and spar with other members of his species over territory and mating rights. The snake had grown so large that these contests were no longer fair—Crotalus could quickly dispatch any rival with a three-pronged blitz by swaying, wrapping, and throwing them to the ground. The smaller ones didn't stand a chance.*

# 18

JACK SPENT THE next three days riding up U.S. Highways 1 and 101 at thirty miles per hour as the Raspberry's pistons clattered ever louder inside her cylinders. On July 24, Jack stopped for lunch on Wecoma Beach where the highway left the ocean. He bid farewell to the Pacific and arrived at his cousin's house in Portland that afternoon.

After dinner they went out to the Raspberry and fired up the V-twin.

"That's piston slap if I ever heard it," said Walter Smith.

"That's what the mechanic said," replied Jack. "He said the pistons are slapping against the rods, cylinders, and so forth. The thing I don't understand is I'm getting solid compression. Why would I have good compression if the pistons are loose in the cylinders?"

"What did he tell you?" Walter asked with annoyance.

"He said the pistons had worn loose and were liable to collapse at any time. He quoted thirty-five dollars to replace all the parts—two pistons, rings, rods, and a couple of other parts."

"If there's one thing I can't stand," Walter groused, "it's some mechanic trying to buffalo a rider to think a problem's more complicated than it is. You don't have worn pistons, Jack. By 'piston slap' I mean your pistons are slapping up against a layer of carbon that's formed on the pistons and cylinder heads. I'll tell you exactly what we'll see when we take off these heads. There will be a mess of black carbon deposits caked onto the combustion chamber. We just need to clean things up a bit."

While Walt drove into town to get some parts, Jack removed both tanks, the spark plugs, and the fourteen head bolts and washers holding the cylinder heads onto the motor. By the time Walt came back, Jack had the heads resting neatly on his ground cloth.

"Don't worry about saving those head gaskets, Jack," said Walt as he stepped out of his car. "I've got new ones here. My friend let me have them at cost—just a buck and a half."

Walt had been right—both the cylinder heads and pistons were coated with a thick layer of carbon. He went into his garage and came back with a couple of screwdrivers, two knives, and a metal brush.

"Here, Jack," he said, "you start on the rear cylinder and I'll work on the front."

After fifteen minutes of scraping and brushing, Walt took a cotton shop cloth and wiped the cylinder walls clean of carbon dust and inspected the valves.

"Looks like everything's seating all right. Pistons and rods look fine, too, so we'll put the heads back over two head gaskets."

"Two gaskets?" asked Jack.

"Yup. That way we'll have more clearance between the pistons and heads."

Walt cleaned the spark plugs, sanded the points, and made a few more adjustments to parts he thought needed attention. They spent the next thirty minutes replacing head bolts, gas tanks, and spark plugs; then Walt told Jack to fire up the bike.

The Raspberry responded with a sultry roar of satisfaction and then purred like a kitten. The slap and knocking were gone, and the engine had a healthy new sound like an opera singer who had finally cleared a frog from her throat.

"There you go, Jack!" proclaimed Walt. "You're good as new and thirty-five dollars richer."

"Walter Smith—you're a mechanical genius!" Jack gushed.

The next day Jack and the Raspberry celebrated the engine's newfound performance by riding nearly four hundred miles to Moscow, Idaho, at fifty miles per hour, without a sputter. He dearly wished he'd known as much about the bike at the start of the trip as he did now, but he knew there is no substitute for experience. Of all his miles on the road, Jack could count only three days where the bike had not had some form of mechanical breakdown. And though he was not aware of it, his five weeks on the road had taught him priceless troubleshooting, engineering, and problem-solving skills.

★ ★ ★

**HORACE LOOKED UP** from his workbench at the tanned-face boy in the doorway.

"Jack, you made it! Let's go get some supper—on me."

"That's a good thing, brother," he laughed, "because I've only got two bucks and some change to my name."

They rode the Raspberry to a diner and discussed plans to get back to New York. Jack's atlas told them they were three thousand road miles from home. The most practical thing to do, they decided, was to take Horace's old Ford over the most direct route possible—U.S. Highway 10.

Highway 10 was one of the original long-haul routes between Seattle and Detroit. It ran through Washington state, Idaho, Montana, North Dakota, and Minneapolis, Minnesota. At Manitowoc, Wisconsin, the highway changed to a ferry route that transported automobiles and their passengers sixty miles across Lake Michigan to Ludington. Highway 10 ended two hundred fifty miles later in Detroit, where eastbound motorists could cross into Ontario, Canada, and follow Provincial Highway 3 along the northern coast of Lake Erie to Buffalo, New York.

To his disappointment Jack saw that this route would take them nowhere near Sturgis.

As usual, their biggest problem was money. Horace's Ford only got twenty miles per gallon, so they'd need one hundred fifty gallons to get home. This would be twenty-five dollars in gas and likely another five dollars in oil. They would be ten days on the road and needed to budget for food and lodging. Horace was as eager as Jack to save money by camping beside the car. They budgeted a minimum of sixty dollars to get home. Horace had about twenty saved from his job at the repair shop, but the rest would have to come from Jack.

They looked out the window at the Raspberry parked along the curb.

A prolonged silence followed.

"This is a college town, Jack," offered Horace. "You could probably get a hundred dollars for her. We can put an ad in the paper. We'll be here another week, so you'd have time to spruce her up and make her look as good as she runs."

The Raspberry's Motolamp stared up at them as if she could read their lips through the plate glass window. After Walter Smith's tune-up, she had never run better—she'd proven it on the all-day run from Portland to Moscow. She was certainly up to one last trip across the country if they would just give her the chance. Of all her owners—Frank Lombardi, Elliot and Marjorie Mills, Eustace Hetzel—none had demonstrated more devotion than this poor, teenaged boy with his burning desire to see his country. Jack Newkirk had rescued her from the edge of the junk heap—and taken her to the most monumental exhibitions in the history of the modern world.

For both of them, it had been the ride of their lives.

Jack swallowed hard and stared at his supper, deliberately avoiding eye contact with the Raspberry.

"Yes," he finally sighed, "I suppose it's the only thing to do."

★ ★ ★

**AS HORACE WORKED** on his radios, Jack cleaned, polished, and painted the bike. He put an ad in both the *Moscow Daily Star-Mirror* and the weekly *Moscow News Review*:

FOR SALE: 1930 HARLEY-DAVIDSON MOTORCYCLE VL BIG TWIN 74 INCH. LUGGAGE CARRIER AND BUDDY SEAT. RUNS GREAT. $100. 111 E. D ST.

During the next few days, Jack sat on pins and needles. He secretly hoped no one would respond, but he knew they needed the money. On Sunday afternoon, a man walked up to Horace's door on D Street and knocked.

"I understand someone here has a motorcycle for sale."

He was a college student by the name of Ron DeMarzio.

"That would be my brother, Jack," Horace replied. "I'll go get him."

Jack came out, threw his leg over the Raspberry, and started her up for DeMarzio.

"She sounds fine," said Ron. "Can you take me for a ride?"

"Sure," Jack replied. "Hop on. Have you ridden a cycle before?"

"Oh yeah," said DeMarzio. "Used to have one just like this until I wrecked it last spring. I know all about the VL, I've just never ridden on a buddy seat. You drive and I'll listen to the engine and the tranny."

They rode west to Main Street, turned right, and went a couple of miles north on Highway 95. Horace was waiting when they returned twenty minutes later.

"She'll do," said Ron. "But I'm a little tight on cash now. How about I pay you forty now, then I'll pay ten bucks every two weeks as I get paid from my weekend job at the rail yard?"

A lump began to rise in Jack's throat.

"Can you come up with fifty?" Horace proposed. "And we'll be gone for month, so I wonder if you could make the rest of the payments to my boss, Mac, at the repair shop on Polk Street."

"Mac's place? Sure, I can do that. Fifty bucks now and ten bucks every couple a' weeks for the next few months, eh?"

"That would work," said Horace.

DeMarzio shook Jack's hand to consummate the deal.

Horace began to draw up a bill of sale while DeMarzio took out his wallet and placed five ten-dollar bills one-by-one into Jack's open palm. After the paper had been exchanged, DeMarzio jumped on the Raspberry, lifted up the jiffy stand, and folded out the shiny new starter pedal.

The motor started on the first kick.

Jack thought back to the corner of Burdett and Tibbits in Troy, New York—where he'd spent fifteen minutes coaxing the bike to move for the first time. There was something disturbing about how readily the Raspberry came to life for this stranger. It seemed almost treacherous—perfidious—as if one disloyalty was now being countered by another.

Jack looked at the wad of cash and felt a pang of regret. He knew this moment had to come, but he wanted to scream:

*Wait! I've changed my mind!*

The Raspberry—that complex, cantankerous, wondrous mass of metal, rubber, leather, chrome, cables, paint, spit, and bailing wire—was riding out of Jack's life forever.

The lump in Jack's throat grew larger as he watched the Harley disappear down the dusty street. He began to breathe in and out through his nose in short, involuntary staccato as he tried to hide his emotions from his brother. Tears welled up in Jack's eyes, and Horace's thoughts flew back ten years to when Jack had to return his magical red canoe.

Horace put a muscular arm around his little brother.

"C'mon, kid," he said, "let's go get a big chocolate milkshake."

And three thousand miles away, a song had just been released that would become one of the Glenn Miller Orchestra's biggest hits:

*To you, my heart cries out, Perfidia*
*For I found you—the love of my life—in somebody else's arms.*
Perfida © 1939 by Alberto Dominguez and Milton Leeds
Peer International Corporation

# 19

**H**ORACE AND JACK left Moscow on the morning of August 1, 1939. By the next night they had motored to the middle of Idaho's Snake River Plain, north of U.S. Highway 30 between Twin Falls and Pocatello. After driving a mile or so across the prairie, they found an inconspicuous spot to camp. It was as remote and sparse as South Dakota's Badlands. To the north lay the Craters of the Moon National Monument with its bizarre caves, craters, and lava fields that looked like the bowels of hell.

Horace's Model A sat on a grassy plain beside their campsite. With the car as a windbreak, the brothers cooked soup over a camp stove and watched the sun go down. Coyotes began to howl and Jack could see their eyes glowing on the hillside in the moonlight. Horace looked at his watch, walked around to the back of the car, and returned holding a wooden box the size of a small suitcase.

"Whatcha got there, Newk?" asked Jack.

"I've got a treat, that's what," said Horace. "How'd you like to be in New York right now?"

"What do you mean?" Jack asked. "New York's thousands of miles away."

"Well—give me a minute and I'll bring New York to you."

Horace began fiddling with the knobs of a month-old RCA Model 94BP1 portable tube radio. The sound of static over squeals, music, and voices seemed out of place on the open prairie.

"You mean that thing runs on batteries?" asked Jack.

"Absolutely!"

"How'd you get it?"

"A fellow brought it into the shop last week. It didn't work and he wanted a floor model. Well, I asked Mac if I could work on it in my spare time. I just replaced the GE and Hytron tubes, soldered some cold joints, and she came to life. Only cost me two dollars in parts."

"That's really swell, Horace! How long do the batteries last?"

"Should last us the whole trip home, if we—oh, wait, here it is—listen, Jack."

The National Broadcasting Company invites you to listen to Glenn Miller's music. *(Cue orchestra)*

Besame music. Yes, Glenn Miller's music. Introduced now by his own original signature, "Moonlight Serenade," and presenting another program by the NBC network by Glenn Miller, foremost exponent of the swing trombone and one of America's ace arrangers. From the Glen Island Casino just off the shore road at New Rochelle, New York, right on the shore of Long Island Sound.

Jack clapped his hands together and broke into a wide grin. He could hear the dinner crowd in the background through the radio's three-inch speaker and the sound of ships' horns over the waters of Long Island Sound. Horace had brought New York right into the middle of Idaho's vast Snake River Plain.

As Glenn Miller's music drifted across the waters of Long Island Sound that night, the coastal town of Peconic, New York—on the northern end of the island—was just beginning to quiet down. A sixty-year-old man with unkempt hair, a rumpled undershirt, and rolled-up pants stoically put his signature on a letter that he would deliver the next day.

```
To Mr. Franklin D. Roosevelt
President of the United States
August 2, 1939

Sir:
    Some recent work by Enrico Fermi and Leo
Szilard, which has been communicated to me in
manuscript, leads me to expect that the element
uranium may be turned into a new and important
source of energy in the immediate future. Certain
aspects of the situation which has arisen seem
```

to call for watchfulness and, if necessary, quick action on the part of the Administration.

I believe therefore that it is my duty to bring to your attention the following facts and recommendations: In the course of the last four months it has been made probable that it may become possible to set up a nuclear chain reaction by which vast amounts of power would be generated. Now it appears almost certain that this could be achieved in the immediate future.

This new phenomenon would also lead to the construction of bombs, and it is conceivable that extremely powerful bombs of a new type may thus be constructed. A single bomb of this type, carried by boat and exploded in a port, might very well destroy the whole port together with some of the surrounding territory.

I understand that Germany has actually stopped the sale of uranium from the Czechoslovakian mines which she has taken over. That she should have taken such early action might perhaps be understood on the ground that the son of the German Under-Secretary of State, von Weizsäcker, is attached to the Kaiser-Wilhelm-Institut in Berlin, where some of the American work on uranium is now being repeated.

Yours very truly,

Albert Einstein

★ ★ ★

ON AUGUST 9, Horace and Jack paid fifty-five cents to cross the Ambassador Bridge over the Detroit River into Canada. At the Canadian customs station, Horace was told he could not bring his .22-caliber revolver into the country. They had to drive back over the toll bridge, find a post office to ship the pistol home, and cross into Canada again via the Detroit-Windsor tunnel, where Horace complained to the customs officer that he had to pay three separate tolls.

After driving two hundred fifty miles along the north shore of Lake Erie, they crossed over the Niagara River on the Peace Bridge connecting Fort Erie, Ontario, to Buffalo, New York.

At Niagra Falls, Jack bought a postcard and scribbled a few lines to his parents:

Dear Folks:

Spent a beautiful night under the stars among the eroded lands & howling coyotes. We're making nice progress but gas is high and mileage is low. Sure kills me to see this car eat gas after riding the bike. Gas is expensive out west but went down to 8 gal for 95 cents in Wisc. We're pressing on slowly because of a broken left rear spring and Horace's newly installed piston rings. I plan to take bus to Bolton Landing on Monday August 14 so would you please leave my canoe at Bell Pt.

Love, Jack

They arrived home at noon on August 12. A note pinned to the door invited them to come up to Lake George as soon as possible, but first Horace had a week's worth of work to do on his car.

Jack felt crippled without the Raspberry. He was no longer free to travel anytime he pleased, but was now at the mercy of train, trolley, and bus schedules. Nevertheless, school didn't start until September 14, so he had an entire month to fish, swim, and canoe up and down his thirty-two-mile paradise.

Two days later, a bus dropped Jack off at Bell Point Road and he walked a quarter mile to the lakeshore. There, on the dock, were his mother and father standing beside his blue Morris canoe.

His mother couldn't manage any words, so she just ran over and hugged him. His father put a hand on Jack's shoulder and gave it a firm shake.

"We thought we might never see you again, son."

They paddled two miles across Northwest Bay, past Montcalm Point, and east of Turtle Island to their camp along the lakeshore.

"So how did you know when I'd get here?" asked Jack.

"We checked the bus schedule," said his mother.

Before Jack was allowed to take off for the rest of the summer, his mother made him compile a journal of his trip. She plopped down every card, letter, ticket stub, and photo he'd mailed, and then gave him a letter Stuart Crossman had sent the previous week:

Monday Aug 7, 1939

Dear Jack:

Am I glad to hear that you are homeward bound. I believe I have received all your cards, the last one today, and have followed your itinerary with much interest—and quite a little bit of pride. Of course, there isn't much space on a postcard to even begin to write of the trip. If you are back in the city at any time, by all means be sure to call me. When I returned, I paid a visit to your folks. Naturally they were eager to hear about the trip and your mother showed me some of your postal cards; it was then that I learned of the disastrous Sunday on which I left you. I can picture your absolute misery and dejection. Many times I have looked back upon that Sunday and wished that I had been with you, if for nothing else but company. I am convinced I should have stayed. Will you forgive me?

I know you will be interested to hear of my return to N.Y.C. from Va. After leaving you, I walked thru the village, stopping on the way to have breakfast. I had two rides from Luray to cover the nine miles to the Skyline Drive, at which point I was very politely dumped and forced to thumb again. My face was very burned from the wind & sun, and in trying to find a roadside tree to shade myself I walked the entire road to the spring at the foot of the mountain. Fortunately, another ride, but only to Sperryville, ten miles. Another walk, looking for a shade tree. With all the billions of trees in the world, I can't understand why nature didn't grow one, just one, on that road for me.

At last, a young fellow from Baltimore, MD picked me up and took me into Washington where I arrived in time for 12:00 Mass. Had my clothes pressed in a "While You Wait" and then found a room. I remained overnight in D.C. until 4:30 the next afternoon. My only regret is that you were not there with me. I returned to N.Y.C. on Tues. via Greyhound Bus.

This vacation will always stand out as a memorable and most profitable one for me, and I know it must for you. Every moment was enjoyable—even those spent for motorcycle breakdowns. I will want to hear all the thousand of odd facts that you have become acquainted with, but most of all I want to see you again.

—Stuart Crossman

"You really want me to save all this stuff, Mom?" Jack protested.

# 20

A 1939 GAR WOOD Twin Cockpit Runabout slowly drifted down the channel south of Mohican Island in the Lake George Narrows. Her polished red-mahogany hull was rigid and watertight, and she looked more like a piece of fine furniture than a boat.

Two attractive teenaged girls sat on the bow and casually dipped their toes into the water. A third girl sat on the red upholstery of the rear cockpit and watched two boys argue near the open doors of the boat's engine compartment.

"I told ya we shouldn't have oughta!"

"Shut up, Lou. You want I should give ya a fat lip?"

"You and who else, Tony?"

The wooden boat drifted through the shoals toward the rocky shore of Fourteenmile Island. As they passed Ranger Island, they were surprised to see a blue canoe paddling around the lee shore. It was headed in their direction, and the skinny kid inside looked to be about their age.

"Do you fellows need any help?" he shouted.

"Yeah," Lou yelled back, "our engine died and we can't get it goin' again. You know anything about motors?"

"Oh, a bit, I suppose," said the paddler as he sidled up to the boat.

One of the girls smiled and offered to hold the canoe line. The two boys extended their hands and hoisted the barefoot stranger onto the polished deck of the Gar Wood.

"I'm Lou Imbergamo," said one boy. "This is my big brother Tony and these are Rose, Gina, and Martha."

"I'm Jack Newkirk," said the boy. "What seems to be the trouble?"

"Well," said Tony, "we took out the boat—"

"—without askin'," Lou interrupted.

"Yeah, yeah," said Tony. "Without askin' the old man. Anyway, we got half a mile out and our motor died. We can't get it goin' and I'm afraid we're gonna run the battery down."

Tony's brother, Lou, looked anxiously south toward Lake George Village.

"Our old man will kill us if he finds out we took the boat without askin'," he muttered.

Jack had been heading back to camp after a hike up Shelving Rock Mountain. He might have paddled on by, but he remembered the man outside of Goshenville, Pennsylvania, who'd fixed the Raspberry and taught him the biker's code: *Always help the next fellow on down the road.*

And a summer on a rickety motorcycle had turned him into an expert on engines.

"Mind if I turn it over a few times?" asked Jack.

"Sure, go ahead."

"We should cast the anchor first," Jack said. "It's about twenty feet deep here but there's a shoal a hundred yards south."

"That's a swell idea, Jack," Tony replied. "Where do you think they keep the anchor?"

"It's usually stowed underneath the seat cushions," said Jack.

He tossed the anchor overboard and cinched the line to a bow cleat after playing out eighty feet of scope. He ran the line through the chalk and casually tossed the bitter end into the forward cockpit. The others watched with fascination. It reminded them of the cowboy who'd roped, flanked, and tied a calf in ten seconds flat at the New York World's Fair.

Within a minute, the Gar Wood sat motionless with her bow in the wind.

"OK, let's have a listen to this motor," said Jack.

Tony Imbergamo looked at his watch and tried to calculate when his father would be back from New York City. Jack turned over the Gar Wood's six-cylinder engine and frowned as he heard the sound of coughing and wheezing. He knew almost immediately what was wrong.

"Your motor's not getting any gas, boys," Jack said. "Sure you haven't just run out?"

"The tank's almost full," replied Lou. "I checked it before we left."

Jack unscrewed the fuel cap and confirmed the tank was three-quarters full. It was plumbed with a soft, black, rubber fuel-priming bulb that could be squeezed and pumped with one hand. This rubber fuel bulb had a valve inside, and Jack tried to manipulate it by squeezing and crushing, but it was collapsed like a hot water bottle with the air sucked out. He knew this meant there was an obstruction somewhere in the line.

He shut off the petcock and removed the hose clamp from the upstream side of the bulb. After draining out a tablespoon of gas, Jack put the hose in his mouth and blew as if he were belting out a high C on his cornet. After a few seconds the resistance gave way and air flowed through the tube as easily as bubbles through a straw. He connected everything back together and gave the priming bulb a couple of squeezes.

With one twist of the key, the engine came to life.

A hoorah went up from the crew, and the brunette smiled at Jack in admiration.

"You had some crud in there," said Jack. "It was obstructing the flow. It'll be OK for a while, but you should check the filter screen and valve every hour until you see no more sediment."

"Man, you just saved our bacon!" Lou gushed.

"We owe ya a million bucks!" echoed Tony. "Can we tow ya home, at least?"

"Sure—I'm just across the lake."

From that day forward the Imbergamo brothers treated Jack Newkirk like a king. Every few days they'd roar into the bay and shout for him to come out for a ride. One August evening he was finishing up the dinner dishes when he heard the familiar sound of the Gar Wood Runabout approaching the dock.

"Jack—Jack!" shouted one of the girls. "Come on down. We're going to see the new movie in town. It's called *The Wizard of Oz*."

"What's it about?" Jack yelled from the porch railing.

"Who cares what it's about!" cried Tony. "It's got Judy Garland!"

"I'll be right down!" shouted Jack as he ran to get his sweater.

★ ★ ★

**ON AUGUST 31, 1939,** Jack's sister Ginny and her husband Bernard Cain drove to Lake George to spend a weekend at camp. That afternoon, Jack and Bernard took a hike up Tongue Mountain to get a bird's-eye view of the lake. They planned to return by sunset.

At that very moment—four thousand miles away in Gleiwitz, Poland—the Nazi Gestapo contrived an attack on a German radio station to create the appearance of Polish aggression. The Gestapo poisoned a well-known Polish sympathizer, shot his body multiple times, and left it at the scene. *Operation Himmler*—the Nazi's premeditated plan to invade Poland—had begun. The German Wehrmacht stood ready at the Polish border like a panther waiting to pounce.

★ ★ ★

*On Tongue Mountain,* Crotalus horridus *slithered down the twilight slopes and onto the trail. He sensed motion—and flicked his tongue in and out to identify the source of the vibrations. The summer air was warm and the snake could strike as fast as lightning. Suddenly, instinct told him to curl his neck back and lift his tail off the ground.* Crotalus *began to shake his rattle in a loud, deliberate, ominous buzz.*

The German battleship *Schleswig-Holstein* opened fire on Westerplatte in the Gulf of Danzig. The Luftwaffe hit the Polish town of Wielun with waves of Stuka dive-bombers as the German Tenth Army, Thirty-first Infantry, and First and Fourth Panzer Divisions rolled across the Polish border in a well-planned juggernaut.

*Jack Newkirk heard the unmistakable sound of* Crotalus horridus *in the fading light and skidded to a stop along the path of fallen oak leaves. Like freight trains hurtling inexorably toward a roundhouse, this moment had been years in the making. Jack locked eyes with* Crotalus *in a moment of primal, unadulterated hate—an enmity as old as the Garden of Eden, the dawn of man, and the Ancient Foe.*

Jack knew only that he had to kill it.

*Bernard Cain handed him a stout stick with a twisted, gnarled knot on* one end. Together they circled the rattling rope of death as it writhed on top of the dry leaf bed. Bernard struck the first blow, breaking the snake's back two feet from its buzzing rattle. Jack followed with several strikes to the head until—at last—Crotalus horridus *moved no more.*

★ ★ ★

**ON SEPTEMBER 4, 1939,** a gray-haired Burt Newkirk walked slowly up the rock path leading to his cabin on Lake George. He had a newspaper in his hands—and Jack saw they were trembling.

"Great Britain has just declared war on Germany," he said gravely.

He had seen some of mankind's worst calamities—the Battle of Little Bighorn, the Spanish-American War, the San Francisco Earthquake, the sinking of *Titanic* and *Lusitania,* and "the war to end all wars"—World War I. But this new conflict distressed him more than all others. The Nazis had created a foundation for war of immense proportions—and Burt knew his sons and nephews were of prime age to fight it.

★ ★ ★

**ON A CRISP SEPTEMBER** evening, young Jack Newkirk walked across the Rensselaer campus toward the hill overlooking Troy. *The Wizard of Oz* was still playing downtown at Proctor's Theater—and revisiting this world of beautiful witches, laughing munchkins, and good triumphing over evil might help Jack forget the events of the past few weeks.

Suddenly he smelled the acrid odor of smoke coming from the hillside. He saw orange flames and rushed toward them. A ten-foot pole with a swastika on top burned proudly for the entire world to see. With a fury that rivaled the killing of *Crotalus,* Jack savagely kicked the pole as if it embodied everything that had destroyed his World of Tomorrow.

The swastika crashed to the ground like the *Hindenburg.*

Jack could still smell smoke on his clothes as the pre-feature newsreel rolled. Most of these newsreels were informative, confident, and upbeat. This one, however, caught Jack completely off guard. It showed the 1939

New York World's Fair at twilight, accompanied by solemn music and commentary.

Jack began to cry.

It seemed to have been written just for him:

> *But the days grow short when you reach September—*
> *Trylon and Perisphere bravely symbolized the theme of the*
>    *New York World's Fair:*
> *The World of Tomorrow.*
> *But now, in the world of today, war has come and Europe is*
>    *already dark.*
> *The thirties are ending—another era is passing.*
> *Through the fun and fantasy of the Fair, something whispers:*
>    *"It is later than you think."*
> *The president has said, "Many voices are heard as we face a*
>    *great decision."*
> *Comfort says, "Tarry a while."*
> *Opportunism says, "This is a good spot."*
> *Timidity asks, "How difficult is the road ahead?"*
> *Shall we pause now and turn our back upon the road that*
>    *lies ahead?*
> *Shall we call this the Promised Land? Or shall we continue on*
>    *our way?*
> *For each age is a dream that is dying—or one that is coming*
>    *to birth.*

And on a lonely street in Moscow, Idaho, Harley-Davidson VL No. 30V8229C sat outside a small apartment in the rain. She was beginning to rust again. A streetlight reflected dimly off the chrome ring of the John Brown Motolamp, as raindrops rolled down its face and dripped softly onto the ruddy-striped fender like tears.

*Burt L. Newkirk*

*Horace L. Newkirk*

*"Scarsdale Jack" Newkirk*

*Young Jack Newkirk*

# PART II

## The Rising Son

*"Let them at least have heard of brave knights and heroic courage."*
—C. S. Lewis

# 21

A STORM WAS BREWING over the Bay of Campeche in the southern Gulf of Mexico—a major breeding ground for Atlantic hurricanes. The squall strengthened, moved northeastward, and made landfall in south-central Louisiana on September 26, 1939.

High winds and waves buffeted the shoreline from New Orleans to the Florida Panhandle, uprooting trees all along the coast. Scarsdale Jack Newkirk sat inside Naval Hospital Pensacola and watched the heavy rain pelt against his window.

*There'll be no one flying today,* he thought.

But in Europe, eleven hundred Nazi planes pounded Warsaw. The Soviets had invaded Poland in cooperation with the Germans, and after an intense sixteen-day battle, the Modlin Fortress north of Poland's capital surrendered.

In China, Japanese forces now occupied Manchuria, Shanghai, Nanjing, and Southern Shanxi. The city of Kunming, at the northern terminus of the Burma Road, was China's only lifeline to the outside world. The Chinese Air Force's Eighteenth Squadron relocated to Kunming to protect the virtually defenseless city against air attacks, but the Japanese quickly defeated the poorly equipped airmen. Japan ruled the skies, and within a few months the Chinese Aviation Committee reluctantly ordered a cessation to all aerial combat. Chinese leader Chiang Kai-Shek was overwhelmed, but he placed great hope in a hardy, leather-faced American—a former flight trainer by the name of Claire Lee Chennault.

Claire Chennault learned to fly during World War I and became Chief of Pursuit Training for the U.S. Army Air Corps in the 1930s. His methods and tactics were ahead of his time, and this earned him the ire of superior officers and, ultimately, an early retirement. But Chennault was an expert pilot and tactician. He led the Army Air Corps' official team of aerobatic stunt pilots "The Three Men on the Flying Trapeze." General Mow Pang

Tsu of the Chinese Air Force saw Chennault's final performance and made a point to meet him after the show.

In the spring of 1937, the Chinese government asked Chennault if he could evaluate and provide training to the Chinese Air Force. He was offered one thousand dollars per month plus expenses, a car, a driver, and an interpreter. Chennault's original contract was for three months. He would end up staying eight years.

★ ★ ★

**SCARSDALE JACK NEWKIRK** realized Eagle Scout training had saved his life—and his surly survival instructor had been absolutely right when he said everything could change in an instant. The war in Europe weighed heavily on his mind, and he knew America would be drawn into it sooner or later. He'd also seen horrific reports of Japanese aggression in China, where Imperial soldiers reportedly engaged in rape, looting, arson, and mass executions on an appalling scale.

He spoke to his sister, Janet, a few times from the hospital phone. Not one to beat around the bush, Janet confronted him directly.

"So tell me again why you joined the navy? Why not just fly for the airlines?"

"Pen," Jack replied, "in the first place, the U.S. Navy gives the best and most complete training available. Second, I couldn't ask for better friends than the boys down here. I wish you could meet them, sis—Bert Christman, Tex Hill, Bus Keeton, Fernando Guz—"

He paused and swallowed hard.

"Anyway," Jack continued, "I figure a war is in the offing and most of us Newkirk boys will be in it one way or another. We're all of prime age. Lou, Bobby, Horace—even little Jackie, I suppose. I, for one, would rather be in a plane than have to run a bayonet through some fellow."

"Now, Jack," said Janet, "let's hope it never comes to that. Even Lindbergh is speaking out against U.S. involvement in the war. Maybe this whole thing will blow over in a few months."

Tex Hill received his wings on November 1, 1939. Jack Newkirk got his several weeks later. They bid goodbye to their friends at Pensacola and headed off to their assignments, unsure if they'd ever see each other again. Tex was assigned to Torpedo Squadron Three (VT-3) on the USS *Saratoga* (CV-3) fresh from her recent overhaul. Scarsdale was snapped up by Fighting Squadron Five (VF-5), which flew Grumman F3Fs off the deck of the USS *Yorktown* (CV-5). Bert Christman was transferred to Bombing Squadron Four (VB-4) on the USS *Ranger* (CV-4) to conduct Neutrality Patrol operations in the Atlantic.

By this time Scarsdale Jack had flown in almost every aircraft in the navy's inventory. While the F3F was a fine airplane, all the buzz was about Grumman's new F4F Wildcat. Due on the *Yorktown* as soon as his leave was up, Scarsdale went home for one last family visit before departing for San Diego. From there he would be sent to a base he'd neither seen nor heard of—some place on the idyllic Hawaiian island of Oahu called Pearl Harbor.

The November 7, 1939, issue of *Look Magazine* contained a Special War Feature Section with a stern admonition that America should stay out of the war in Europe. North Dakota Senator Gerald Nye asserted, "America can stay neutral if we *keep our money out of war*" and "England and France made Hitler . . . let them face the problem."

The article continued with "Sons of the Poor Rule the World (Exceptions are Chamberlain, Roosevelt, Gandhi)," where the journalist gave a glowing sketch of Soviet dictator Joseph Stalin:

> Stalin is a shoemaker's son. Poverty and reaction to his religious education formed the basis of his revolutionary career . . . he would like to see all shoemakers' sons become Stalins. When I visited him, I was struck by the bare simplicity of his office. Well read, Stalin despises money, lives modestly.

*Look's* war feature ended with an ominous scenario on what might happen if America were to join in the fight against Hitler. The four-page spread profiled the fictitious, middle-class Hoagland family, whose father runs a small textile plant while his wife raises their five children: John, 28; Doris, 23; Jim, 20; Winifred, 17; and Chris, 13.

As soon as America enters the war, Mr. Hoagland's plant is seized by the U.S. Army to make military uniforms. To escape arrest by the American Secret Police, the Hoaglands are forced to burn many of their books, including Hemingway's *Farewell to Arms*. Newspapers, movies, radio—even their mail—is censored. John has a weak heart and escapes the draft, but is forced to work in a munitions plant. Jim is drafted and dies in a field hospital. A labor shortage requires Doris and Winifred to take low-wage work where they are forbidden to strike or change jobs. Young Chris joins a propagandist group similar to Hitler Youth and helps stone a classmate whose name sounds German. The Hoaglands rejoice when armistice comes, as they expect a postwar economic boom. Instead, a second Great Depression settles in.

But all of this could be avoided if America were to follow a firm policy of isolationism.

★ ★ ★

**IN LATE NOVEMBER,** young Jack received a letter from Pete Pomeroy:

Dear Jack:

I'm sorry I haven't answered your two swell letters before this but I just had time to get our motorcycle trip pictures developed last week.

June is thru working in the packing plant and made a couple of hundred bucks and bought a 1930 Plymouth. It has only been driven 32,000 miles by a minister so it is in good shape. We traded our '37 Buick Special for a '39 Buick Century. It is a swell car but it doesn't get very good gas mileage.

Well, how do folks feel about the war back there? Everyone out here seems to think that we will be in it before long but none of them want war. I certainly hope we don't get into it, I don't think it's any of our business 'less someone starts our way then of course we would have to, but to go to some other country and spend a lot of money and lives fighting their wars, I don't see it.

Yours,
Pete

★ ★ ★

**AMERICA ENDED THE** thirties with a blend of hesitant optimism and benumbed acquiescence. Both world's fairs announced they would proceed as planned for 1940, but New York changed its theme from "The World of Tomorrow" to "For Peace and Freedom."

Hollywood premiered several blockbusters just before the New Year, including *Of Mice and Men*, *Mr. Smith Goes to Washington*, and *Gone with the Wind*. To ring in the New Year, Glenn Miller performed with the Andrews Sisters over CBS radio live from New York City:

> Now all you Chesterfield fans get in the mood for 1940, because Glenn's going to play his most popular number of 1939: "In the Mood"!

Six weeks later, Miller shared the microphone with Martin Block, host of the nationally syndicated *Make-Believe Ballroom:*

> Glenn, the purpose of this pleasant visit is to notify you and all of your friends that your band has been voted America's number one band on my last *Make-Believe Ballroom* poll. Congratulations, Glenn, and on behalf of the *Make-Believe Ballroom* and its listeners, here is a bronze plaque. It's presented with our best wishes to Glenn Miller: America's #1 Dance Band!

That spring, composer Aaron Copland was commissioned to score a second film for United Artists, a screen adaptation of the Thornton Wilder play *Our Town*. The movie would be nominated for six 1940 Academy Awards, including Best Original Score.

★ ★ ★

**SCARSDALE JACK NEWKIRK** rapidly distinguished himself within his *Yorktown* squadron by winning awards in both pistol marksmanship and aerial dogfighting. In April 1940 the *Yorktown* participated in Fleet Problem XXI, a large-scale, two-part military exercise that would define future warfare in the Pacific. The first phase was dedicated to plans and estimates, screening and scouting, and coordination of combatant units. The second phase included convoy protection, seizure of advanced bases, and engagement between opposing fleets. It also included two exercises where air operations played a crucial role: Fleet Exercise 114 proved that airplanes could be used for high altitude tracking of surface forces, and Joint Air Exercise 114A prophetically pointed out the need to coordinate the army and navy to defend the Hawaiian Islands.

Midway through the mission, Scarsdale Jack sat down in his quarters on the *Yorktown* and penned a letter to his father:

AIR MAIL HAWAIIAN ISLANDS TO USA
TO: Louis H. Newkirk, Esq.
Mutual Life Building
43 Cedar Street
New York, New York

24 April 1940

Dear Daddy—

The 'war' seems to be over as we are now anchored back in La Haina Roads between Maui and Molokai and Lanai. Tomorrow we are going into Pearl Harbor near Honolulu on the Isle of Oahu. Then the fun begins. There will have to be a lot of it to make up for this last week, as it has been a humdinger.

A week ago last Monday we weighed anchor at La Haina and put out for Point X, which turned out to be damn near the equator. It was terribly hot and as we had to darken ship every nite to keep from being torpedoed, that means closing all the portholes. You can imagine what the sleep we got was like—not so hot. To top that off we had to take off before dawn, without lights, to be able to intercept enemy bombers which usually attack as soon as it's light enough to see the target.

One morning when we had climbed to about 22,000 feet we could see the sun. It was a regular ball of fire; behind us at 180° from the sun was the moon which was full and of a greenish hue. Quite a picture on a Sunday morning as you rendezvous up there smoking oxygen and navigating. Stan, my section leader, and I found an uncharted Isle in our sector when we were on patrol that day. More later.

Love, Johnny

Jack fell in love with the Hawaiian Islands—and while many locals viewed these swaggering navy pilots with misgiving, Jack's disarming smile and good nature brought him friends both on and off base.

One of these was a Honolulu surfer named Ke'akaokalani.

"Wow," said Jack, "that's a mouthful! What's your name mean in Hawaiian?"

"That's just the first part," the surfer laughed. "The whole thing is Ke'akaokalani Ka'aumoana Christianson. It means 'heavenly shadow of the seafarer'—but you can just call me 'Lani.'"

During his time off, Jack learned to surf at Waikiki Beach and Kapi'olani Park ten miles southeast of Pearl Harbor. When Lani thought Jack knew enough to keep from getting killed, he took him to Waimea Bay on the northern shore of Oahu. After a day of surfing, Jack, Lani, and a few others cooked a feast on the steep volcanic hills overlooking the ocean, then slid down on huge leaves to the beach below and watched the sun set over the Pacific.

It was also in Hawaii that Jack formed a friendship with another *Yorktown* pilot—a Marine from Fighting Squadron Two by the name of Greg Boyington.

They were an unlikely pair on shore leave. Boyington was stocky, muscular, and pugilistic. Newkirk was tall, lean, and more likely to talk his way out of a fight than to start throwing fists—an ability Boyington secretly admired.

Walking down the streets of Honolulu one day, Jack stopped in front of a jewelry store where a brilliant string of cultured Mikimoto pearls hung around a navy-blue-velvet bust. He stared at them intently, mesmerized by the soft light reflecting off each satin orb.

"What's up, Scarsdale?" teased Boyington. "Got a sweetie down in Chinatown?"

"Come in with me," said Jack, ignoring Boyington's reference to Honolulu's red-light district. "Even a leatherneck like you could get cultured in a place like this."

They walked inside and the proprietor stared at Boyington like he was the proverbial bull in a china shop.

"I'll take that string of pearls in the window," Jack said as he peeled off bills from his wad of cash.

"You gotta be kiddin' me!" Boyington laughed. "Who'da thought you'd be a softie for some Betty back home? Unless you're plannin' on wearin' those pearls yourself."

"Only for you, Greg," Jack quipped. "Come on now. We'll be late for the boys at the Wiki Waki Woo."

But Scarsdale didn't have a girl back home. The string of pearls had been an impulse buy. He only wanted a souvenir to memorialize his time at Pearl Harbor. If that special girl came along, he'd give them to her. If not, he'd give them to his sister, Janet.

A few weeks later Fighting Squadron Five took off on maneuvers over the Pacific. They were thirty-five miles out to sea when an updraft slammed Scarsdale's plane into a large canvas sleeve-target that took a chunk out of his tail section. Jack managed to nurse the airplane back to base, where he pulled off a miracle landing that astonished his commanding officer.

"Why didn't you just bail out, Newkirk?" he asked.

"I'd have been a fool to go overside so far out in the water, sir," Scarsdale explained. "Although I suppose that might have made the sharks happy."

# 22

IN MOSCOW, IDAHO, Horace Newkirk was reaching the limits of his patience. A year earlier, a University of Idaho student had ridden off on his brother's 1930 Harley-Davidson, promising to make monthly payments until the fifty-dollar balance was settled. The money never appeared, so one Saturday morning Horace decided to pay this deadbeat a visit.

He walked a mile down Main Street, turned south, and then went another mile to the railroad tracks. A block away, he saw the Raspberry parked under a streetlamp.

She was in terrible shape. Her fenders were bent and rusted, the chain was drooping on its sprockets and the John Brown Motolamp had been smashed—its flat glass lens shattered into a thousand pieces along some dirt road. She looked to Horace like a battered woman.

"Hey, DeMarzio—Ron DeMarzio!" Horace shouted. "I'd have a word with you."

A disheveled young man appeared from behind the screen door.

"What do *you* want?" DeMarzio shouted back, clearly hung over from a Friday night spree.

"You owe my brother fifty dollars. Now pay up or I'm taking the bike!"

DeMarzio stepped outside and stood defiantly between Horace and the Raspberry.

"That was the deal," Horace continued. "One hundred dollars. You'd pay half up front and ten dollars a month until she was paid for. We haven't seen a red cent since you rode off."

"This thing isn't worth a hundred dollars," DeMarzio scoffed.

"Not after what you've done to her!" Horace shot back. "It'd take twenty or thirty bucks just to bring her up to par. My brother sold you a solid bike for a hundred dollars. You looked him in the eye, shook his hand, and promised to pay him. So now you've got two choices: pay me fifty right now or I'll give you twenty for her as is."

"I don't have fifty dollars," DeMarzio hemmed and hawed. "And even if I did, I wouldn't give it to you."

"Then I'm taking the bike," Horace said flatly.

"You and who else, Milquetoast!"

Horace Newkirk was gentle by nature, but the recollection of his little brother sobbing as he watched the Raspberry ride out of his life made him burn with anger. Years of gymnastics training had made Horace strong, balanced, and as fast as a cat.

"Get out of my way," Horace warned.

"Aw, go dry up, you sissy. You and that skinny brother of yours."

Horace answered DeMarzio with a swift punch to the gut. DeMarzio fell to the ground with the wind knocked out of him, and Horace grabbed his shirt, pulled him close, and gruffly stuffed a twenty-dollar bill into his front shirt pocket.

Horace swung his leg over the Raspberry, primed her cylinders, flipped the ignition switch, and bore down on the kick-starter lever. DeMarzio watched blankly as the Raspberry sputtered down the street, across the railroad tracks, and out of sight.

That night Horace sent a letter to his brother:

May 5, 1940

Dear Jack:

As you know, payments for the Raspberry were never forthcoming so today I took it upon myself to repossess her. The manner in which this was accomplished is not of great importance; just know that she is safe with me now in the garage.

I received only $60 for my car which of course was on its last legs. I don't know how I will get home this summer after I graduate but I wanted to suggest this: supposing I send you $40 and you sign the title of the Raspberry over to me. This way I can license and ride her back to you this summer. I believe I can do that and still afford to get home. Of course, it will cost me, too, some 20 or 30 dollars to put it in the shape in which I would want to use it. The tires, chain, and sprockets amount to over $15, and I don't know what I'll run into later. Today I bought a new Motolamp (which D. smashed) for $5.

If you like this idea, drop me a line as soon as possible and I'll send the necessary red tape for you to sign along with a check. The weather is dandy here for a ride across the country.

Your brother, Horace

Over the next few weeks, a deal was struck:

May 12, 1940

Dear Horace:
Yes, yes—by all means bring the Raspberry back to New York if at all possible! No payment to me is necessary. I have listed the "sale" price of one dollar on the enclosed title. This should be enough for you to get the paperwork in order and you can transfer ownership back to me once you come home. Be assured I shall never make the mistake of selling her again. How I envy you on your ride east. Let me know if you would like me to mail you my *State Farm Atlas*. I recommend the route through Yellowstone, Ten Sleep, and the Black Hills. If you pass through Sturgis, SD please stop at the motorcycle shop on Junction Avenue and give my regards to a man they call Pappy. His advice served me well on the road (and off). Please Tell him I'm sorry I didn't make his cycle rally but I will get back there someday (if it's still going on).

Your brother, Jack

Horace's response went out a week later:

May 19, 1940

Dear Jack:
Your letter was very generous, but I think I shall send you $20 which a fellow will pay me at the end of this month as the final

installment on my car. If you paid the original owner (Hetzel?) $40, I sure don't know where you got it! But with this $20 you can settle up with yourself or somebody, a little bit anyhow.

Before I start on such a trip home, I shall have to replace the chain and both sprockets. One tire has a big bulge in the side and will have to be replaced. The other can be retreaded. I find now that the battery is almost gone, too. The chain is badly stretched and cracked (side links) in a couple places. Sprockets have sharp points with some broken off. There are other smaller (I hope) items, many of which I probably have not found yet. I'll probably tear it all apart and put it together before starting. It really isn't in too good shape and, of course, DeMarzio did it no good.

Your brother, Horace

★ ★ ★

**THE NAVY GAVE** Scarsdale Jack two weeks leave from the *Yorktown*, which he used to visit his brother Bobby in Houston, Texas. One Saturday they took a trip to Galveston with a carload of friends for a day at the beach, and Scarsdale promptly started to show off his surfing skills from Hawaii. As he rode the waves, he began to notice one of the girls in particular.

Her hair wasn't exactly brown; it seemed more blondish to Jack. She looked to be about twenty and had full, red lips and a lilting laugh, and it didn't escape his attention that she looked fine in a swimsuit. It took a few hours for Jack to overcome his shyness, and even then it was the girl who finally broke the ice.

Jack ran up from the beach with the surfboard under his arm.

"Looks like a lot of fun out there," said the willowy blond.

"Well, there's one way for you to find out, and that's to let me teach you," Jack ventured. His heart pumped rapidly as he awaited her response.

"Oh, would you? I've always wanted to try," she fibbed.

"My pleasure," said Jack, trying to sound confident as his nervousness shifted to anticipation.

"I'm John Newkirk," he said, and thrust out his right hand. "My friends call me Jack. My dad calls me Johnny."

"I'm Jane," she said. "My mother and father named me Virginia Jane Dunham, but nobody calls me Virginia—just Jane."

"Well then, Jane Dunham, let's get started."

They stood waist-deep in the water as Jack explained the basics of the board: the nose, the rail, and the tail. He showed her how to lie facedown and paddle out past the breaking waves. As they made small talk, Jane explained that she was from Lansing, Michigan and had lived in Houston for less than a year.

After an hour Jane was actually able to stand on the board for brief periods before laughing and falling backward into the water. Jack made a pretense of catching her and encouraged her to keep on trying—and he secretly hoped she enjoyed his arms around her as much as he did.

The other boys watched from the beach.

"I'd say your brother's been smitten, Bobby," said one.

"High time," said Bob Newkirk. "All this flying has crimped his social life. Too bad she lives here and he's on some aircraft carrier in God knows where."

★ ★ ★

**EIGHTEEN HUNDRED MILES** to the northeast, the younger Jack Newkirk paced the porch deck of his family's Lake George cabin. He anxiously checked his watch again, then walked down to the dock, lifted his blue Morris canoe into the water, and placed two paddles inside.

Horace was scheduled to arrive at four o'clock.

At two forty-five, Jack jumped in his canoe and paddled through the Narrows to Bolton Landing. An hour later he was walking down Sagamore Road, where he turned left at the T and went south along Route 9N to Rogers Memorial Park so he could get a better view of the road.

Jack remembered something his mother once told him—something about if you love something, set it free. And this day, the Raspberry was returning to him.

He vowed nothing would ever cause him to betray her again.

After a few anxious minutes, Jack's heart started to beat faster as he heard a far off, rhapsodic rumble roaring up the road.

It sounded a lot like the Bronx cheer.

★ ★ ★

**A NERVOUS NATION** watched as events unfolded in Europe and the Far East. Germany invaded Luxembourg, Belgium, Holland, and France. Adolf Hitler pompously paraded down the Champs-Élysées, literally dancing with glee as he shook hands with Nazi officers and signed autographs in the shadow of the Eiffel Tower.

British Expeditionary Forces and the French Army valiantly attempted to hold the Maginot Line as the Nazis planned Operation Sea Lion—an outright invasion of Great Britain. Prime Minister Neville Chamberlain resigned in ignominious impotence and was replaced by First Lord of the Admiralty, Winston Churchill.

Churchill's leadership, the Royal Navy's control of the English Channel, and the Royal Air Force's brilliant performance in the Battle of Britain held the Nazis at bay for the time being.

In the Far East, Japan continued its relentless bombing of Chinese cities like Kunming while Japanese troops occupied much of central China and the surrounding nations. All airfields in French Indo-China were now available to the Japanese military, and Hanoi was now one of the most strategic staging areas for Japanese operations in Southeast Asia. Ki-21 Sally bombers regularly pounded Chinese targets and were often accompanied by Ki-27 Nate fighters as well as the occasional combat prototype of a new aircraft, the Mitsubishi A6M Zero.

Thousands of Chinese were massacred in and around Nanking, where Japanese officers allegedly held a "contest" to see who among them could be the first to behead a hundred people with a sword. Facing a stalemate with Chinese troops, the Japanese adopted *Jinmetsu Sakusen*—the "Burn to Ash Strategy" known as the Three Alls: Kill All, Burn All, Loot All. The Chinese skies were so undefended that Japanese student pilots out of Canton were allowed to conduct bombing practice with live ordnance. After decimating the Chinese Air Force, arrogant Japanese pilots began to complain that they had no worthy opponents.

In the fall of 1940, distraught Chinese leader Chiang-Kai Shek sent for Claire Chennault.

The Chinese Air Force was virtually nonexistent, and unless the bombings could be stopped, Chiang Kai-Shek worried China would have to surrender. He sat down with Chennault and put forth a plan: Could China buy some of the latest American fighters and hire American pilots to fly them?

Chennault was pessimistic, but Chiang Kai-Shek was persistent. He put Chennault and General Mow on the Pan American Clipper out of Hong Kong and after considerable island hopping, they reached Treasure Island in San Francisco and took a series of flights to Washington, D.C. They discovered President Roosevelt had already been looking for a way to help China in her struggle against Japan.

While Chennault, General Mow, and a few high-level advisors faced extraordinary levels of red tape, they ultimately convinced the president to sanction a clandestine group of American pilots to fly American fighters with Chinese markings and engage the enemy over Chinese skies. Roosevelt subsequently diverted a shipment of a hundred Curtiss P-40 Tomahawks bound for Great Britain and sent them to China instead.

Chiang Kai-Shek had his airplanes.

Now he needed the pilots to fly them.

# 23

YOUNG JACK NEWKIRK graduated from Rensselaer Polytechnic Institute in the spring of 1941. A few weeks later, he accepted a job at Bethlehem Steel in Pennsylvania as a junior metallurgist. He loaded up the Raspberry with his meager belongings and rode toward Philadelphia, retracing the route he and Stuart Crossman had taken two years earlier. This time, however, Jack went nowhere near Queens. The 1939 New York World's Fair was gone forever. Trylon and Perisphere had been dismantled and the resulting scrap metal delivered to military factories for war use.

★ ★ ★

SCARSDALE JACK NEWKIRK bid goodbye to his Hawaiian friends, and the USS *Yorktown* departed Pearl Harbor on April 20, 1941, in company with destroyers USS *Warrington*, USS *Somers*, and USS *Jouett*. They went through the Panama Canal on May 6 and arrived in Bermuda on May 12. The *Yorktown* conducted patrols in the Atlantic—from Bermuda to Newfoundland—and over the next few months logged 17,642 miles enforcing American neutrality.

Scarsdale was now flying the Grumman F4F Wildcat, a low-wing monoplane fighter capable of cruising at 320 miles per hour and climbing to almost forty thousand feet. It came from Grumman's plant in Bethpage, New York, on Long Island—only a few miles from Jack's hometown.

When he wasn't flying, Scarsdale was preoccupied with thoughts of the girl he'd met in Texas, Jane Dunham. They'd become inseparable during Jack's time in Houston and had corresponded regularly over the last six months. The navy had a policy that no pilot could marry until two years after earning his wings, so Jack reluctantly put such thoughts out of his mind.

Scarsdale, of course, had not been the only one with a burning desire to fly at an early age. Living legends like Charles Lindbergh, Richard Byrd, Amelia Earhart, and Clarence Chamberlin had inspired a generation of boys to make flying their lifelong ambition.

One of these boys was Charles Alfred Anderson, who at the age of six had been awestruck by a barnstorming Curtiss biplane near his home in Virginia's Shenandoah Valley. Anderson applied to Drexel Institute Aviation School but was not accepted. He approached several private flight instructors for lessons but couldn't find anyone who'd take him. A few years later, Anderson tried to join the army with hopes they would teach him to fly. This, too, failed, and he soon began to realize his biggest difficulty was not money, time, or ability—it was the fact that he was born black.

Anderson devoured every book he could find on airplanes. He was bound and determined to fly, but discovered most pilots wouldn't even take a colored boy for a ride, much less teach him the fundamentals of flight. By age twenty-two, Anderson knew the only way he was going to fly was to buy his own airplane and teach himself. He pooled his savings with money borrowed from family and friends and spent twenty-five hundred dollars on a two-place, high-wing Velie Monocoupe that cruised at eighty-five miles per hour. After gleaning as much information as possible from books, magazines, airshows, and local airports, Anderson taxied his airplane to the end of the runway and launched himself into the sky. His first few landings were hair-raising but he survived them—and other pilots finally began to take him seriously.

Al Anderson earned his private pilot's license in 1929 and Orville Wright himself signed it. In 1933 Anderson became the first Negro to earn a commercial pilot's license and in 1940 was named Chief Flight Instructor at the Tuskegee Institute in Alabama.

One spring day in 1941, Anderson was prepping a line of students for civilian pilot training when a boy came running out of the hangar building.

"Big news, Chief Anderson! The president's wife is payin' us a visit!"

"What's that you say, boy?" asked Anderson, whom his students simply called Chief.

"The president's wife—Mrs. Roosevelt! She's comin' to visit us here at Tuskegee!"

An official line of cars pulled up beside the airfield. A handful of stoic men stepped out, scanned the area, and then opened the door of the limousine. Out came Eleanor Roosevelt in a white blouse, spring jacket, and hat topped with a small bouquet of faux flowers.

"Welcome to our airfield, Mrs. Roosevelt," said Anderson as he proffered his right hand.

She took it, and the two began talking about the subject of flying.

"Chief Anderson," she finally said, "I've heard it said that colored men cannot fly airplanes. What is your response to that?"

"Well, Mrs. Roosevelt," Anderson smiled, "I'd say you just climb into my airplane and see for yourself."

"I believe I'd like to do that!"

The Secret Service protested vigorously, but the First Lady would have none of it. She had a point and she intended to make it. One of the agents rushed to a phone and put in a Code Red to the president, who interrupted a cabinet meeting to take the call.

"Just what's so urgent, Edward?" asked an annoyed Franklin Roosevelt.

"Mr. President," he panted, "what should we do? Your wife is about to go up flying in an airplane with some Negro!"

*First Lady Eleanor Roosevelt takes flight with Chief Anderson*

FDR's face changed from irritation to a bemused grin.

"Now, now, Edward," Roosevelt chuckled, "don't worry. Eleanor will no doubt do what she wants down there regardless of what I might say. Just let her be—I'm sure I'll hear all about it when she gets back."

★ ★ ★

**THE USS *YORKTOWN*** docked at Norfolk, Virginia, and Scarsdale Jack Newkirk gladly took a few days shore leave. He went straight to the base athletic club and hit a few tennis balls around with some men he'd met in the locker room. As they showered up, Jack glanced at a newspaper someone had left on the bench:

Japanese Bomb Chunking Again—Thousands Killed!

"Lousy Japs," muttered Scarsdale. "They never hit a guy who can fight back."

"Aw, can it, Mac," said one of the sailors. "The Chinks can fight their own battles without us buttin' in. What happens outside the U.S. is none of our business."

"Well I'll make it my business if this keeps up," Scarsdale snapped. "Someone's gotta stand up for the little guy. I'm sick of watching these people get pushed around. The Japs are tossing Chinese babies into the air and catching them on their bayonets, for God's sake!"

"So you gonna lick the Japs single-handed?" asked another man.

"I don't know what I'm going to do," Jack fumed. "But I tell you what—I'm getting tired of living the easy life while thousands of innocent people get hammered."

"Well good luck to you, Sir Galahad," mocked the sailor.

Jack shot him a daggered look and the seaman decided not to push his luck.

At the far end of the room sat a man who'd been listening to every word Scarsdale uttered, and shortly before the *Yorktown* resumed patrols in the Atlantic, Jack was quietly approached by a man who introduced himself as Commander Rutledge Irvine—retired.

Several weeks later, Janet Newkirk got an unexpected visit from brother Jack, who asked if she could join him for dinner at the Rainbow Room, high above Manhattan on the sixty-fifth floor of 30 Rockefeller Center.

"This is certainly a pleasant surprise," said Janet. "How do you rate, Jack, that you get so much time off from the navy?"

"Sis, as of this week I'll no longer be in the navy."

"What happened?" she gasped. "That's all you've ever wanted! They didn't kick you out, did they?"

"No, no!" Scarsdale laughed. "Nothing like that. I've been given an offer I can't refuse."

"What's that?"

"Well, I'm not at liberty to explain everything, but I can tell you that in July I'll be sailing for China. I've accepted a position with the Central Aircraft Manufacturing Company—CAMCO. When I get back in a year, I'll be reinstated to the navy with no loss in rank or pay. In the meantime I get paid at least six hundred dollars per month plus bonuses."

"Wonderful! But China? Surely you're not making the trip alone. What's this all about?"

"No, I won't be alone. Not by a long shot. I'll be with a lot of my fellow flyboys. They're calling us the American Volunteer Group—the AVG."

"All right, I won't press you on your 'secret mission' but I hope you'll write Dad or me and keep us up-to-date. When do you leave?"

"My last official duty is tomorrow. I have to ferry a new plane from the Grumman plant on Long Island over to Naval Air Station Norfolk—in Virginia. Then I'll visit Bobby in Houston on my way to San Francisco. After that, it's off to China."

"So after tonight, I won't see you for more than a year?"

"Well, why don't you look out your window tomorrow about two o'clock. I'll say goodbye to you from the cockpit of a brand spankin' new Grumman F4F Wildcat."

"Don't fly too low, Jack. The police have planes now, you know."

"What?" Jack laughed out loud. "You expect me to be afraid of them in the bird I'm flying?"

They walked to the window and stared down at the specks walking the streets of New York.

"This is about the height you pull out of a power dive," Jack remarked. "You can see how tight it has to be gauged. At the speeds we're traveling, you'd hit the ground in half a second. That's why it's too bad if you get hit or black out."

"Makes my skin crawl," said Janet, and she turned her eyes away from the window.

After dinner Scarsdale Jack spent the rest of the evening writing a letter to Jane:

June 15, 1941

Miss Jane Dunham
Houston, Texas    AIR MAIL

My Darling:
    As I told you in my last letter, I will be arriving in Houston at the end of this week, at which time I hope to explain the queer circumstances that have led to my visiting you again on such short notice. Leave it to say that I now have new responsibilities, not only diplomatic ones, but setting an example in our small force that our adversary will realize the caliber of any future action our country may take, and think twice before encroaching on the policies which it is our mission to set up and protect.
    With regard to us, I have spent much of the past year thinking of our times together and dreaming of times to come. My deepest regret in my new capacity is that I will be compelled to be apart from you.
    I will phone you before I leave as I hope you can arrange the time off from your job to spend some days together with me, as I have something I would put up to you before I leave for the east.
                    With all my love,
                      Jack

Unbeknownst to Jack, Jane was also writing a letter at the same moment:

June 15, 1941

Lt. John V. Newkirk
c/o USS Yorktown CV-5
NAS Norfolk, Virginia

My Darling Jack:

I am lying next to the stuffed bear you won for me at the carnival. I miss you terribly but when it gets unbearable I hug my bear tight and make believe you are in my arms once again.

I understand you cannot tell me the nature of your new assignment but I hope it will not separate us for too long.

I have arranged to take the time off from work at the end of this month when you are here. Of course you will want to spend some time with Bobby so I'll not presume to have you all to myself. I shall be glad to meet you at the airport as you asked.

'Til then, I remain faithfully yours,
Janie

The next morning Jack walked to Grand Central Station and caught a bus across the Queensboro Bridge, past Madison Square Garden Bowl, and onto the Grand Central Parkway. He stared out the window as he rolled past the remnants of the New York World's Fair in Flushing Meadows, and after a few transfers arrived at the Grumman Aircraft factory in Bethpage, Long Island. A navy captain gave him a quick glance.

"Are you the hotshot from the *Yorktown*—Newkirk, they said?"

"Yes, sir," Scarsdale saluted. "Lt. Jack Newkirk reporting for duty."

"All right, here's the drill. This Wildcat needs to be delivered to Norfolk today. You know how to get there, I take it?"

"With my eyes closed, sir," said Jack.

"She's been flight tested and fueled. There's obviously no ordnance on board, so just sign these forms and you're good to go."

"Yes, sir."

"Now Newkirk," he said, "no funny business. Just take the plane straight to the ground boss at Norfolk. Understand?"

"Yes, sir," said Scarsdale as he attempted to subdue the grin spreading over his face.

"Clear!" yelled Jack, and the Wildcat's fourteen-cylinder, twelve-hundred-horsepower Pratt & Whitney radial engine roared to life. He took off and headed south-southwest until he was out of sight. Then, just west of Massapequa, Jack snapped the airplane into an aileron roll and made a beeline for Manhasset Bay on Long Island's northern shore. He crossed Long Island Sound at two hundred miles per hour, saluted his ancestors from the Dutch ship *Moesman,* and performed a double barrel roll. The groundskeepers at the Glen Island Casino looked up, squinted, then raised their hands and waved. Jack inverted the Wildcat and waved back.

He zoomed past New Rochelle and followed North Avenue toward Scarsdale, climbing two thousand feet in just over a minute as he circled the city for one last look at his school, church, and boyhood home. After breaking out of the holding pattern, Jack turned south and did a power dive down to five hundred feet, which increased his airspeed to two hundred fifty miles per hour.

He followed the Bronx River Parkway and buzzed Yankee Stadium, where the Yankees would go on to beat the Cleveland Indians 6–4 by the end of the game that day. Jack then crossed the Harlem River into Manhattan and headed straight down Lenox Avenue toward Central Park. Four blocks to the west, he could see his old school at the Cathedral Church of St. John the Divine, and he began to sing "Amazing Grace" at full volume inside the cockpit.

He pushed the throttle to the firewall. Startled patrons lifted their heads and waved wildly as Scarsdale Jack zoomed over Central Park and did an Immelmann turn over Carnegie Hall to gain altitude for his final assault on the city. At precisely two o'clock, Jack roared past an office high atop Rockefeller Center, where a woman inside jumped up and down and waved uselessly out the window as she strained to get one last glimpse.

"Hey—that's my brother!" shouted Janet to a stunned typewriter salesman.

Scarsdale climbed over the Chrysler Building in an upward corkscrew and drew a bead on the Empire State Building as if he were preparing to attack King Kong.

"Bang, bang—you're dead!" yelled Jack as he squeezed the trigger on his empty guns.

After buzzing Ellis Island and the Statue of Liberty, he broke off and followed the coast to Norfolk, where he signed his navy discharge papers before anyone had time to complain.

★ ★ ★

**REAR ADMIRAL ARTHUR COOK,** commander of aircraft in the Atlantic Fleet, was on the phone with Washington.

"Damn it, Frank, they're taking some of my best men!" he moaned. "I don't want to come up short if the Jerrys torpedo a few of our ships anytime soon. Just what's going on here?"

"Can't say, Art," said Secretary of the Navy Frank Knox, "but it's straight from the top. Anyone from the American Volunteer Group has to be released. No questions asked."

"Well," grumbled Cook, "whatever this is, it's bigger than me—and it had better be for a damned good cause!"

# 24

SCARSDALE JACK ARRIVED in Houston the last week of June. Jane met him at the airport and they went straight to Bobby's house. After settling in, Jack and Jane drove to their favorite restaurant and got a private booth.

"So, my dear," asked Jane, "what's all the hush-hush about? Is the navy going to take you away from me all summer, now?"

"It's going to be a little longer than that, I'm afraid."

"But why? Are they teaching you to drive submarines next?"

Jack laughed at her innocence, but then began to speak solemnly.

"Janie," he said, "I've been selected to serve in the Far East. I volunteered, in fact. We're called the American Volunteer Group—the AVG. It's my chance to make a difference. To do something I believe in. But . . . it means I'd be gone over a year, darling."

Janie began to cry softly and dabbed her eyes with the red-checkered napkin from her lap. Jack stopped talking, reached across the table, and gently laid his hand on top of hers. This caused her to burst into tears, and her chin lowered to her chest as she trembled in muted sobs.

Jack sat in awkward silence as he watched this beautiful young girl absorb the gut punch he'd just given her. Janie's reaction only strengthened his love for her. She didn't scream. She didn't get up and walk out. She took the news with dignity and grace. Jack knew more than ever that he wanted to spend the rest of his life with her.

"Does this mean it's goodbye for us, then?" Janie sniffled.

"Not if you'll marry me," said Scarsdale.

"Oh, Jack," said Janie, "we've been over that. The navy won't allow anyone to marry within two years of their wings."

"But Janie, as of last week, I'm no longer in the navy. Their silly rules don't apply to us anymore—we could get married tomorrow!"

Jane looked up from the table and her tear-streaked face pleaded desperately for Jack to continue. A potent silence hung in the air.

"Janie," Jack choked, "I love you. Will you marry me?"

She began to cry out loud and tears flowed freely, only this time she was laughing and smiling—eyes closed running the gamut from despair to joy in just a few minutes.

"Yes," she sobbed. "Yes, Jack, I'll marry you."

The waiter stuck his head into the booth.

"Everything OK here?" he asked awkwardly.

"Sure, Mac," Jack laughed through tears of his own, "everything's swell! Couldn't be better!"

And he left him a five-dollar tip.

*Virginia Jane Dunham, wife of Scarsdale Jack*

Over the next two weeks Jack and Janie rushed to make arrangements for a church, dress, cake, and a few wedding guests. Jane's family was in Michigan and most of Jack's were in New York, so the wedding party would be sparse. Jane had to quit her job in Houston, but she had a sympathetic boss who wrote a glowing reference letter for any future employer.

On Saturday July 5, 1941, John Van Kuren Newkirk and Virginia Jane Dunham were united in marriage at the First Presbyterian Church of Houston, Texas. They stayed two nights at the Lancaster Hotel and then caught an early flight to San Francisco where they checked into the Mark Hopkins Hotel at the crest of Nob Hill.

They took the elevator to the AVG reception at the hotel lounge. Jack began to introduce himself as Janie met some of the other AVG wives. Jack occasionally stole a glance at Janie as she spoke, and he was impressed by her ability to make friends just as fast as he could.

"Jack, who's that rough-cut man over there?" Janie asked. "He certainly looks capable, but I wouldn't want him mad at me."

"That's Claire Chennault," said Jack. "He'll be our commander—and I hope he never gets mad at me, either."

Chennault, sensing he was being talked about, gave a friendly glance to Janie, then smiled and nodded his head. He gave Jack a quick once-over and continued mingling with the guests. Fifteen minutes later, Janie saw Jack engaged in a lively discussion with Chennault, as both men made fluid airplane motions with their hands like Tai Chi.

Jane took the trolley to a Union Square beauty shop the next day to get her hair done as Jack and other AVG members attended a meeting with Chennault in the hotel. After this brief session with the new recruits, Chennault was driven to Treasure Island where he took the Pan Am Clipper back to Hong Kong.

Some of the AVG wanted to go out on the town. Jack politely declined and explained he'd be spending an entire year with this motley lot so he'd rather have one last dinner with his wife. That evening Jack and Janie jumped on a streetcar and took it to the Golden Pheasant Restaurant at the corner of Powell and Geary Street.

"Oh, it seems so expensive, Jack!" Janie gasped.

"Honey, this could be our last night out for a year," he said. "Don't worry about the prices. You order whatever you want—because I certainly intend to. Tonight we're going to eat, drink, and dance like there's no tomorrow!"

Jack ordered the grilled sea bass steak dinner and a pint of Piel's beer for a dollar. Janie had the broiled eastern rock lobster and a glass of California Tipo wine for a dollar twenty-five. For dessert, both ordered a raspberry crème brûlée topped with a mint leaf and thick shavings of Ghirardelli chocolate.

They'd just finished dinner when a shout rang out from the band assembled on stage.

"Yes, indeed!"

THE GOLDEN PHEASANT — POWELL AT GEARY — SAN FRANCISCO, CALIF.

The Golden Pheasant came to life as the bandleader cued the drums, bass guitar, piano, and muted brass in a spirited cover of a popular Tommy Dorsey tune. It was one thing to hear these songs over a scratchy monophonic speaker, but it made Scarsdale's hair stand on end in excitement to hear them live, in full surround-sound, reverberating off the walls.

"Come on, Janie!" he yelled. "Let's dance!"

Jack grabbed her hand and they rushed out to the dance floor. On stage, a man and woman started singing into their shared microphone:

*It comes out if it's in you, yes indeed!*
*Makes you shout, Jack, it sends you, yes indeed!*
Yes Indeed © 1941 by Sy Oliver • Embassy Music Corporation

On Thursday July 10, 1942 Jack and Janie Newkirk had breakfast with their new AVG friends at the Hotel Bellevue on the corner of Geary and Taylor Street. The conversation was light, as most of the women were on the verge of tears. After breakfast, the men stood outside the hotel and talked among each other.

If the AVG's mission was supposed to be a secret, it certainly wasn't a well-kept one. Robert Sandell, an army pilot, told Scarsdale that on his way to breakfast he'd overheard a cigarette girl speaking with the elevator operator.

"Yes," she'd said, "they're all going to China to keep the Burma Road open. They're sailing today on the *Jagersfontein*."

Scarsdale chatted with a fellow navy flyer named Jim Howard while another man took movies of them with his 16mm camera. Finally, a bus pulled up and the men loaded their baggage. The bus drove them to the Embarcadero as Janie and a few others followed in a car. They took pictures at the pier as the Dutch ship *M.V. Jagersfontein* waited patiently for the passengers to board. Jack took Janie aside, and they stood at the rail and looked out toward Treasure Island and San Francisco Bay.

For a long time, neither of them spoke.

"Janie," Jack finally said, "I've been saving something for you."

He reached into his suit pocket and pulled out an oblong case. Janie took it, opened it, and drew in a quick breath.

"Oh, Jack—they're beautiful!" said Janie as she began to cry.

Scarsdale held her closely and rocked back and forth, kissing her forehead and wiping her tears with a handkerchief from the front pocket of his suit jacket.

"They're from Hawaii," he said. "And there's one pearl for each week we'll be apart. When I get back, each one will stand for a year together for the rest of our lives."

"Will you put them on me?" Janie sniffed.

"Right now?" asked Jack.

"Of course."

At ten o'clock, the *M.V. Jagersfontein* backed away from the pier as Janie waved goodbye to her husband of less than a week.

"Don't forget to look up," she shouted through her tears. "I'll be waiting for you at the Golden Gate!"

The ship turned unhurriedly and headed into San Francisco Bay. Janie jumped into a car with two other AVG wives and drove frantically along the Embarcadero, then raced down Van Ness, Lombard, and through the Presidio to the Golden Gate Bridge. They parked their car and ran in high heels to the bridge's crest. Each carried a large roll of solid, ten-inch-wide crepe paper that Janie had bought the day before.

As the ship approached, the wives looked down and saw their men standing on deck. Janie leaned out over the rail with the pearls dangling from her neck. Clutching the open end of the paper, she hurled the roll toward the bay and let go after the paper played out. The two others did likewise, and three dancing streams of colored ribbons—red, white, and blue—floated gently down toward the *Jagersfontein* like three kite tails billowing in the wind.

Scarsdale felt his eyes getting moist. He slowly raised his right hand high into the air, fingers outstretched in a salute he'd learned as a boy from his family—a salute to its newest member—Virginia Jane Dunham Newkirk.

The *Jagersfontein* passed under the Golden Gate Bridge and out to sea, and the wives watched until it became a speck on the horizon. Three hours later, Janie boarded a Greyhound bus for Los Angeles to begin her new job. As the bus lumbered down Highway 1 past Big Sur, Janie ran her fingers slowly up and down the necklace counting each pearl like a set of rosary beads. There were fifty-two of them.

# 25

ONE WEEK AFTER leaving San Francisco, the *Jagersfontein* pulled up to a dock in Honolulu and disgorged her restless passengers. Scarsdale Jack went directly to Pearl Harbor to visit some old friends while some of his shipmates lined up in front of the local cathouses like customers at a Monday meat market.

Shortly after the *Jagersfontein* left Honolulu, the passengers were surprised to see two U.S. Navy cruisers pull alongside. The USS *Salt Lake City* and *Northampton* had been sent as escorts after a Japanese radio broadcast informed listeners that the *Jagersfontein* would be sunk before it reached Rangoon. The navy ships stayed with the vessel until the Dutch gunboat *Java* took over near Australia.

On July 24, another ship departed San Francisco Bay with an additional AVG contingent. She was the *Bloemfontein,* sister of the *Jagersfontein,* both built in Amsterdam in 1934. Among the *Bloem* passengers were Bert Christman and Tex Hill, two of Jack's fellow 1939 Pensacola cadets. They shared the ship with a group of missionaries who soon began to irritate the AVG. Army pilot R. T. Smith wrote: "The . . . missionaries—'Holy Joes' to us—are driving us nuts with their constant gathering around the piano and singing hymns by the hour. So we drive them nuts by playing hot swing records on the phonograph."

The *Bloemfontein* was followed by yet another Dutch ship—the *Boschfontein*—which carried twenty-five of the AVG from San Francisco to Singapore, including army pilot Charlie Bond and Scarsdale's old friend from the Marine Corps, Greg Boyington. Coincidentally—before her recent rebuilding and rechristening—the *Boschfontein* had been called the *Nieuwkerk*.

Upon disembarking, Jack sent a letter to his wife:

## AIR MAIL TO UNITED STATES OF AMERICA

August 11, 1941
Mrs. Jane Newkirk
523 S. Westmoreland Avenue
Los Angeles, California

My Darling:

    We have docked at Singapore and are now to be transported to Rangoon in Burma. I trust by now you received my little packages from Hawaii, Australia, and Batavia. The journey has not been so horrific as some made out it would be. I miss you and cannot wait until we are together again.

                    All my love–
                    Jack

    It was like a high school reunion when the AVG members assembled in Burma.

    "Boyington—you old Devil Dog!" shouted Newkirk as he patted him solidly on the back. "Geez, take a shower, will ya? You smell like a dozen rotten eggs soaked in whiskey."

    "I don't smell half as bad as you look, Scarsdale. When's the last time you combed your hair?"

    "Say, Jack," said Bert Christman. "Seen any good comics lately?"

    "Minute Man!" Scarsdale exclaimed. "I'll get you yet for having me kicked out of class."

    "You're lookin' skinny as ever, boy," said Tex Hill.

    "Well, it's not exactly your mama's home cooking around here," Jack replied. "You'll see what I mean soon enough. Makes me long for that swill we used to choke down at Pensacola."

    "So who let Newkirk into this outfit anyway?" Boyington taunted.

    But something about Scarsdale Jack Newkirk had impressed Claire Chennault, who divided the AVG into three squadrons and immediately named Scarsdale as leader of one of them—the Second Pursuit Squadron or, informally, the Panda Bears. Scarsdale's position came as a surprise to some. Jim Howard, for example, had two years seniority on Jack and mildly grumbled that he had been passed over. Scarsdale softened the blow by naming Howard his deputy. For squadron personnel, Scarsdale picked off most of the navy men right away, including Tex Hill, Bert Christman, Robert "Buster" Keeton, Tommy Cole, Frank Lawlor, John "Gil" Bright, Ed Rector, and George "Pappy" Paxton.

The First Pursuit Squadron—Adam and Eve—would be led by Robert "Sandy" Sandell.

Arvid "Oley" Olson's Third Squadron called itself the Hell's Angels.

Chennault's chief of staff, Harvey Greenlaw, had brought along his wife, Olga, supposedly as official keeper of the daily AVG war diary. At thirty-three years old, Olga Greenlaw was exotic and attractive—and according to Boyington, never far from her Elizabeth Arden makeup kit. The presence of an attractive woman among rowdy, mostly single men made for complex dynamics within the AVG. Harvey and Olga's tempestuous marriage only compounded this.

The AVG spent most of the fall of 1941 assembling their P-40s and training in aerial combat techniques Chennault had gleaned throughout many years of observing the enemy.

The P-40 Tomahawk was an all-metal, low-wing, single-seat fighter aircraft built by Curtiss-Wright of Buffalo, New York. It featured self-sealing fuel tanks and armor plating behind the pilot's seat, and was powered by a 12-cylinder Allison engine that generated 1100 horsepower and a maximum speed of 360 miles per hour. The engine lacked a supercharger, so the P-40 performed best at low altitudes. It didn't have the agility of the light Japanese fighters, but the P-40 could capitalize on Japanese weaknesses in combat. This was precisely what Chennault intended to teach his men.

"Never get into a dogfight with a Nate," Chennault warned, "and especially a Zero if you ever see one. You can't match them, turn for turn. Instead, you've got to hit them with a fast dive, which they cannot match."

The P-40 was a rugged aircraft compared with its light, wooden, and unarmored Japanese counterparts. It carried two .50-caliber machine guns in the nose and four .30-caliber guns on the wings and was designed to "slug it out, absorb gunfire, and fly home." They were painted standard olive green and brown on top with a gray underbelly. After assembly, all American insignia was replaced with the Chinese Air Force symbol—a twelve-pointed blue and white star.

Charlie Bond of the First Squadron had seen a magazine photo of a P-40 in North Africa painted with shark's teeth. Pilot Erik Shilling, after speaking with a Chinese missionary, heard that as an island people the Japanese had an almost religious phobia about sharks. This idea was passed by Chennault, and before long the nose of each P-40 displayed an intimidating mouthful of teeth with a red eye above it, giving the plane a startling resemblance to a tiger shark.

Each squadron further decorated their aircraft with markings befitting their monikers.

The First Pursuit Squadron—Adam and Eve—used a green apple with a snake and a naked "Eve" pursuing a uniformed "Adam." The Second Squadron exploited Bert Christman's artistic talents and painted caricatures of panda bears on the P-40s' sides. The Hell's Angels adopted red silhouettes of naked women with halos and wings.

During a lull in training, Scarsdale Jack wrote a letter to his father:

September 27, 1941

TO: Louis H. Newkirk, Esq.
Mutual Life Building
43 Cedar Street
New York, New York

Dear Daddy:
    I am well and as busy as ever. My sense of humor has declined, I'm afraid, but I am still healthy and have been promoted to squadron commander. There are many things about the life of our group which would be very interesting to you, but this is war and I cannot talk about that. However, there are many interesting things about the country which I can write about. Last Sunday, in Rangoon, a pilot

from China National Airways (marvelous organization), his stewardess, our flight surgeon, our Chinese fever doctor, and I all went to the zoo. We got full of beer, teased the leopards, fed the elephants, and then saw the snakes. You have no conception of what snakes are until you have been out here—makes our slithering friends on Tongue Mountain seem mighty tame. There are the banded krait, who is no less nasty than his compatriots the cobra, pit-viper, Russell's viper, and bamboo snake—and none of them have rattles. There is also the matter of pythons, but they are practically harmless. At the zoo we saw them eat whole chickens, and we also saw a crocodile eat a baboon—really a bestial performance.

We killed a seven-foot cobra in the officer's barracks the other night, and two nights later when one of my boys went down in the jungle, I had to take a party out and find the usual mess. Our guides deserted us and we wandered around in the jungle until nearly dawn. We ran across a bunch of vipers and I shot two with my pistol; the sergeant got another. It was a horrible night, and I really missed my old hunting boots. The ones I had on (riding boots) are no good anyway, and were too short to boot (ha! ha!).

Love to all—Johnny

The accident Jack alluded to, but could not disclose, was a midair collision between two of his Panda Bear pilots. Gil Bright had been flying over Toungoo, Burma, when he saw a P-40 in the distance. Consistent with training protocol, Bright rocked his wings to challenge his rival to a mock dogfight. The pilot of the other Tomahawk was Johnnie Armstrong, a plucky youngster from Hutchison, Kansas. Armstrong made a head-on pass toward Bright. At the last second, Bright made a quarter-roll to starboard and expected Armstrong to do likewise. Instead, Armstrong forged ahead and the resulting collision caused each airplane to lose a wing. Bright slung open his canopy, unbuckled, and was ejected by centrifugal force. His parachute opened and Bright watched helplessly as both aircraft crashed into the jungle.

Scarsdale organized a rescue party, and on the way to the crash site came upon Gil Bright riding back to base on a bicycle borrowed from one of the locals. They spent the rest of the night searching the jungle—an experience that painfully reminded Scarsdale of the Florida swamps. In the morning, they found John Armstrong's body still strapped in his cockpit.

It was the second week of September. The AVG had yet to engage the enemy, but they were already losing men and aircraft. Armstrong was Scarsdale's first fatality as squadron leader. Tragically, it would not be his last.

A few days later, Jack wrote a note to his wife and another to brother Bobby:

October 5, 1941
(Our 3-month Anniversary!)

Dear Janie:
   Some wonderful news has just come out, so hold your breath (but not too long). There is a possibility you may be able to come out here in a few months. If this looks like it has a chance of coming to pass, I will send details at that time.
   Either way, we have all made many tentative plans for the future. A big reunion house party in Honolulu next summer, in case we can't get you all out here before that.
   Life in Burma is not what you and I have grown accustomed to. Cooking is done over charcoal fires. Bathrooms, pure water, sanitary kitchens are very few and far between, so you can perhaps visualize some of the personal discomforts of this place. We are all supposed to be diplomats, while at the same time doing a great deal of supervising, teaching, entertaining and bargaining.
                                   All my love, Jack

P.S. We will have our 2nd Anniversary together, won't we darling?

October 5, 1941

Dear Bobby:
   This is a land of strange contrasts. There seems to be poverty and luxury to an unbelievable degree with no intermediate stages.

The many idols of gold and silver—all studded with great jewels—are surrounded by desperately poor, half-starved coolies bowing and scraping before all this magnificence. It is difficult to find rags to clean our planes, as the coolies all take them home to clothe their families with. It is easy to see how the enemy could presume upon these poor fellows and subjugate them with the brutal tactics we have heard all too much about.

Love to all, Johnny

# 26

**AS MONEY BEGAN** to trickle in from young Jack's job at Bethlehem Steel, he could finally afford to replace some of the Raspberry's key components during the non-riding winter months, including the battery, drive chains, sprockets, tires, pistons, and front mudguard.

On December 5, 1941, Jack took a weekend auto trip with some work buddies. They spent Saturday night at a cabin in the Kittatinny Mountains of New Jersey, then hiked Sunday morning and had lunch overlooking the Great Appalachian Valley. The Sunday afternoon drive home was full of friendly banter.

Rod Malloy turned on the radio. Swing music filled the car as it rolled down Highway 8 toward the Delaware River. All of a sudden a distressed voice preempted the music:

> We interrupt this program to bring you a special news bulletin. The Japanese have attacked Pearl Harbor Hawaii by air, President Roosevelt has just announced. The attack apparently was made on all naval and military activities on the principal island of Oahu . . . and just now comes the word that a second air attack has been reported on army and navy bases in Manila. Thus we have official announcements from the White House that Japanese airplanes have attacked Pearl Harbor in Hawaii and have now attacked army and navy bases in Manila.

"Damn it! Those back-stabbing S.O.B.s!" shouted Scarsdale Jack Newkirk eight thousand miles away in Toungoo, Burma. He slammed his fist onto the table, let loose a string of epithets that shocked even the navy men, then stood up and paced back and forth with his jaws clenched in rage. Pearl Harbor was more than just a spot on a map. It had been his home. As far as he was concerned, the Japanese might just as well have raped his sister.

The American Volunteer Group immediately took on a new dimension. Their country was now at war—and Chennault knew he had to move fast.

He sent pilot Erik Shilling to take photos over Bangkok as Panda Bears Ed Rector and Bert Christman flew escort. Chennault was stunned by what he saw. At least twenty-five Japanese ships were already unloading troops, tanks, artillery, and armored cars. Fifty planes sat wing-to-wing on the Thai airfield. The Japanese clearly planned to move on Rangoon and Singapore—but with no bombers at their disposal, all the AVG could do was protect what few aircraft they had. And with Washington preoccupied with Pearl Harbor and the Nazi threat, there would be no more men, airplanes, or supplies for the foreseeable future. The AVG was on its own—the only American force on the Asiatic mainland to oppose Imperial Japan.

The 650-mile Burma Road—China's vital supply line—started out in Burma and ended in Kunming, China. To defend it, Chennault would need the AVG at both ends. On December 12, he dispatched the Hell's Angels to Rangoon and six days later sent the Panda Bears and Adam and Eves over the hump to Kunming to set up new headquarters.

Upon arrival the American Volunteer Group was appalled at the condition of Kunming. Scarsdale Jack watched in revulsion as a horrific scene played out before his eyes.

A recent Japanese bombing had strewn the streets with bodies, burning cars, and debris from collapsed buildings. Dazed survivors stumbled around like zombies as the stench of death and burning tires permeated the air. Shell-shocked victims unable to walk took refuge in doorways and storefronts and raised their hands pleadingly to passersby.

An oversized pickup truck with wooden rails lumbered through the streets gathering dead bodies, and its stack of corpses swayed back and forth as the truck's tires rolled over fallen bricks and broken timber. At one point, the truck nearly upset as the mound of bodies shifted too far to one side. This brought a strong berating from a Chinese soldier—a veteran of many Kunming bombings—who admonished the workers to pile the bodies in staggered fashion like cordwood, not randomly on top of each other.

Two feral dogs fought over a human leg, and another had part of an arm in its mouth as it scampered down an alley with its gruesome prize. The dogs looked as if they were the best-fed residents of the city.

An old Chinese woman—sensing Scarsdale was some kind of leader among this strange group of men—groveled at his feet and shouted unintelligibly, "*Kongxi! Bu jing bao! Bu jing bao!*" This made Jack feel extremely uncomfortable; she was like the biblical woman in Galilee who sought to touch the robe of Jesus Christ.

"What's she screaming about?" yelled Scarsdale as he snapped out of his stupor.

"Uh, she want help from air raid," explained his translator. "No more air raid she want."

He walked past a broken building surrounded by a dozen dead children with twice as many wailing parents. This had evidently been a school. Rescue workers used shovels to pry up the wreckage in vain hope some of the children might still be alive. They hefted a thick wooden beam off a corrugated metal sheet while a frantic Chinese couple looked on. Then the men peeled back the metal as if turning the page of a book.

The young couple collapsed to the ground—inconsolable—as they beheld their five-year-old daughter lifeless in the rubble. Scarsdale stared intently at the girl's face. It was coated with white dust from the bomb's fallout that made her look like a porcelain China doll.

He wanted to go and cradle her, but he was in shock.

Scarsdale realized he had to get out of there. He walked a few blocks north with some of his Panda Bears to an undamaged part of the city, where he made a feeble excuse to use the toilet. He walked into a hotel restaurant, shut himself inside one of the bathroom stalls, then vomited and began to weep. He held his face in his hands and his body was racked with sobs. He recalled a decade earlier when he'd received his Eagle Scout badge and made a promise to Rear Admiral Richard Byrd—a promise to live by the Knight's Code:

*DEFEND the poor, and help them that cannot defend themselves.*
*NEVER break your promise.*

As Jack thought about the meaning of the oath, his grief and anger turned into resolve.

"*I am a knight!*" he shouted in his mind. "*My armor is the cockpit of a P-40 Tomahawk. My horse is a 12-cylinder Allison engine. My lance is a bank of six machine guns. And now I'm coming after you, you monsters. That's my promise. And all hellfire is coming with me!*"

The Chinese were not the only casualties in Kunming that day. Gone forever was the innocence of a young man from Scarsdale, New York, who had just turned from Boy Scout to warrior.

Bert Christman, generally more intuitive than the others, saw Jack's red eyes and weary face as he walked back out to the street. Bert approached him and put an arm on his shoulder.

"Don't worry, Scarsdale," said Christman. "We'll get 'em next time."

"You're damn right we will," Scarsdale choked as his lower lip quivered.

The next day Jack received a letter from Janie dated December 5, 1941, in which she innocently asked when he might be able to come back on leave. He missed her fiercely and sat down to compose the most serious letter of their short life together:

December 19, 1941

My Darling:

By now you know the President has declared war against the Japanese. My dear, you have no idea of what war really means back in the security of the States, and I hope you never will. To this end, I also hope you will understand what follows in this letter.

There are certain things in every man's life which he cannot bear to leave undone if he is manly. Murder and bullying of peaceful, innocent peasants is one of those things I cannot stand for. Until I have done all in my power to relieve the situation I cannot leave it for the other fellow. Until I have done all in my power I shall not return.

Besides, this task is ours only, for now we are the only ones who are qualified to do it, and we need every ounce of manpower, every financial and material support, and every mental uplift or the whole thing will be impossible. Without that, we cannot beat a team united, supported, and coordinated as those others are in their hatred of us and the freedom we stand for.

Please don't think I am going to stay here forever without you, for that is quite impossible. Next fall we will meet as planned in Manila or Honolulu. It is awfully hard to make plans just now, but we can count on that as a starter. If I were to go back to you now, and you were familiar with the circumstances out here, you would lose respect and that would not make you happy. I dream that you and I shall someday raise our children to respect all men, but to fear no one.

All my love,<br>Jack

To date, the American Volunteer Group had lost three pilots and many aircraft to accidents. Between Pearl Harbor and the Kunming slaughter, the AVG smelled blood—and they were itching to get the Japanese in their sights.

They wouldn't have to wait long.

On the morning of December 20, 1941, ten twin-engine Japanese Ki-21 Sally bombers fired up their motors at an airstrip northwest of Hanoi as the crews laughed, joked, and taxied toward the runway. Once airborne, the rear gunners came forward and served hot tea to the pilots and bombardier as they crossed into China's Yunnan province. They had no fighter escorts. For the past few years, the Japanese had enjoyed supremacy over the Asian skies, and this day's mission to Kunming would be routine—just as it had been three days earlier when they'd pounded the city with no opposition.

When the formation was about sixty miles from Kunming, the crew made a final check of the bomb bays and manned their stations in preparation for the drop. Bored gunners watched with amusement as rookies fiddled with the complicated bombsights. They were fifteen minutes from the drop when all hell broke loose.

"*Ahhh! Koukuuki! Katakidoushi!*"

Japanese gunners frantically manned their stations and watched in horror as four screaming shark-toothed Tomahawks descended from above.

"Shark Fin Blue," crackled Scarsdale Jack Newkirk over the radio. "Bombers sighted fifty miles east of base."

"Huh? These can't be Japs," broadcast Gil Bright. "There's no escort."

"Look, you damn fool!" yelled Bert Christman. "Look at the red balls on their wings. It's the Japs, I'm tellin' you!"

Christman was answered by several seconds of agonizing silence.

"He's right, by God," shouted Scarsdale. "Engage, engage!"

"I'm on 'em," said Ed Rector.

The four P-40s charged haphazardly toward the Japanese formation as chaos ruled the skies. The AVG pilots practically tripped over each other as they attempted to maneuver, shoot, and keep out of the others' way. The Japanese shifted from complacency to combat in a matter of seconds and the entire formation turned abruptly to the south. Claire Chennault listened to the unfolding drama from his command bunker in Kunming.

"Son of a bitch!" shouted Scarsdale. "They saw us! They're dumping their bombs like crap from a cow!"

"Don't let 'em get away!"

*Pum-pum-pum-pum-pum-pum-pum-pum—*

"Hey! Watch where you're shootin' for God's sake! I'm on your side, remember?"

"Sorry, Chief—"

"Hell's bells! My guns are jammed!"

"Did you turn on the damned switch?"

"Whoops—"

*Pum-pum-pum-pum-pum-pum-pum-pum—*

The Japanese jettisoned their loads and ran for home. Instead of falling on Kunming, the bombs exploded harmlessly on the ground below as astonished Chinese peasants chattered and pointed to the sky. But the Sally was a fast airplane and the Curtiss P-40 would have a tough time overtaking it in level flight. This didn't stop Ed Rector, who throttled forward and gave chase—determined to "get one of the bastards."

Scarsdale called off the attack and sheepishly headed back to base with Christman and Bright. His indecision had probably cost them some victories, but he knew he had an ace in the hole: his Panda Bears had chased the bombers straight into the open jaws of Sandy Sandell's Adam and Eves, who circled in ambush over the Japanese path of retreat.

The First Squadron pounced wildly on the bombers and sent three of them spiraling to the ground as horrified Japanese crews stared at the strange enemy planes with Chinese markings and gaping jaws. Six other bombers were heavily damaged, and they limped away from the fight toward their base. It was later reported only one of them made it home.

Thus, with a large degree of awkwardness, misapplied tactics, and dim-witted errors, the American Volunteer Group prevailed in its first battle of the war. Later that day, Chennault called Scarsdale into his office. Jack steeled himself for a scolding. His respect for Chennault bordered on adoration, and he hated to let the Old Man down.

"All right, Newkirk. First, you hesitated to engage the enemy. Second, you failed to turn on your gun switches. Either mistake could cost lives—your own included—understand?"

"Yes, sir."

For a moment Jack thought about offering to step down as squadron leader.

"But," Chennault continued, "this was your first time in combat. I've seen it a hundred times. Buck fever. I'd rather you get it over with now than choke up in a dogfight later on. I know you won't make those mistakes again."

"No, sir, I shall not."

"That'll be all, then. And Jack—" said Chennault with a grin.

"Yes, sir?"

"Good job today. Next time—you get 'em all."

"Yes, sir!"

The citizens of Kunming staged a celebration with fireworks, a parade, and huge quantities of food. Wreckage from the downed bombers was carried triumphantly through the streets by hoards of grateful Chinese, who now treated the American newcomers like heroes. For as long as the AVG was in China, Kunming would never be bombed again.

As Scarsdale watched the festivities, he was surprised to see the old woman who just days earlier had pulled on his pant leg and pleaded for help. She stood tall this time and ran over to him with both thumbs up.

"*Ding hao! Fei hu! Fei hu!*" she exclaimed.

"What's she shouting now?" asked Scarsdale as he shook his head in confusion.

"Uh," said his interpreter, "she say that everyone now calling you 'The Flying Tigers.'"

# 27

AS 1941 CAME to a close, Franklin Roosevelt and Winston Churchill met at the South Portico of the White House to light the National Christmas Tree and address the nation.

> **CHURCHILL:** Fellow workers, fellow soldiers in the cause, this is a strange Christmas Eve. . . . Almost the whole world is locked in deadly struggle. Armed with the most terrible weapons which science can devise, the nations advance upon each other. May we cast aside, for this night at least, the cares and dangers which beset us and make for the children an evening of happiness in a world of storm.

> **ROOSEVELT:** Fellow workers for freedom: The year 1941 has brought upon our Nation a war of aggression by powers dominated by arrogant rulers whose selfish purpose is to destroy free institutions. They would thereby take from the freedom-loving peoples of the earth the hard-won liberties gained over many centuries. But our strength, as the strength of all men everywhere, is of greater avail as God upholds us. Therefore, I do hereby appoint the first day of the year 1942 as a day of prayer, of asking forgiveness for our shortcomings of the past, of consecration to the tasks of the present, of asking God's help in days to come. Against enemies who preach the principles of hate and practice them, we set our faith in human love and in God's care for us and all men everywhere.

Throughout the previous decade, America had embraced a collection of heroes during the gloom of the Great Depression: Jesse Owens, James "Cinderella Man" Braddock, Will Rogers, Seabiscuit, Joe Louis, Babe Ruth, Joe DiMaggio, Lou Gehrig, and many more.

Now—in the throes of war—America desperately needed heroes again.

And eight thousand miles away, a legend was being born over the Asian skies.

The Flying Tigers admirably defended Rangoon against the Japanese aerial armada. On Christmas Day 1941, twelve P-40s from the Hell's Angels intercepted seventy-one Ki-21 Sally bombers and three dozen Ki-43 Oscar fighters and shot down twenty-eight Japanese aircraft without the loss of a single American pilot.

On January 3, 1942—weary of waiting for the Japanese to strike—Newkirk set out to take the war to the enemy. He handpicked three Panda Bears—Tex Hill, Bert Christman, and Jim Howard—and then took off from Mingaladon Airfield in Rangoon for the Raheng Aerodrome in Thailand, fifty miles inside enemy lines and across two rugged mountain ranges. Christman's plane soon developed engine trouble and forced him to return to base. This left Newkirk without a wingman, but he pressed on with Howard and Hill across the Dawna Mountains into the rising sun. Fifteen minutes later, they spotted the target. A string of Japanese bombers and fighters was parked by the runway, some with their props spinning—sitting ducks. Newkirk zoomed over the airfield and put the sun at his back, ready to hammer the parked planes with his .50-caliber machine guns.

Suddenly he realized he was not alone over the airstrip. He'd been so fixated on the planes on the ground that he hadn't noticed several Japanese fighters maneuvering above the field. All thoughts of strafing went out of his mind as Newkirk pulled out of his dive and set his sights on the nearest plane, which he identified as a "Type 0"—the Mitsubishi A6M Zero Chennault had warned him about. It was his first combat dogfight—and he knew any Zero could easily outmaneuver his Tomahawk. There was no margin for error, but his dive speed gave him the advantage. Newkirk flipped on his gun switches, lined up the sights, and squeezed the trigger in several short bursts. The rounds tore through the enemy's thin airframe and engine block and smoke billowed from the cowling. The Japanese plane began to yaw wildly, then made an attempt to turn left before it inverted and crashed into the jungle below.

In the meantime, Jim Howard sent incendiary rounds toward the field. One of the bombers exploded as a few others caught fire. Howard was so preoccupied with his ground targets that he was completely unaware of the Japanese Ki-27 Nate on his tail that peppered his Tomahawk with bullets. Luckily, wingman Tex Hill had seen the Nate latch on to Howard. Hill positioned himself behind the Nate, and in the heat of first combat completely forgot Chennault's instructions about "short bursts" and sprayed the Nate like water from a fire hose. It exploded before his eyes—and after flying through the resulting fireball Hill saw a second Nate coming straight at him. He felt a few thuds and knew his plane had been hit. With a squeeze of his finger, Hill opened up all six machine guns into the oncoming fighter. The enemy aircraft coughed smoke, rolled over, and plunged to the ground.

Newkirk glanced below as Howard made a second pass. Curiously, grandstands flanked the airfields—grandstands filled with what appeared to be panicked spectators. The Flying Tigers had evidently interrupted an air show—a Japanese demonstration of aerial power to impress the local Thai officials. The crowd certainly got more than they bargained for.

Then Newkirk abruptly spotted another Japanese fighter—an older Mitsubishi A5M—on his left flank with machine guns blazing. Newkirk took evasive action and the enemy flew right over his nose. The A5M immediately reversed course with an Immelmann turn in a deadly game of chicken. Newkirk held his course and poured lead into the oncoming plane. Just as they were about to collide, debris began to fly off the Japanese airplane. The A5M arched skyward, stalled, and corkscrewed into the jungle.

The airfield was on fire, four enemy fighters had been shot down—and Scarsdale Jack Newkirk, David Lee "Tex" Hill, and James "Jimmy" Howard returned to base in what historians would later recognize as the first American offensive mission of World War II.

The Panda Bears and Hell's Angels celebrated at Rangoon's Silver Grill that evening. During the previous months Newkirk had assembled some of the Flying Tigers with singing skills into a barbershop group he called "The Four Hoarse Men of the Apocalypse." After dinner and a few drinks, they commandeered the Silver Grill's microphone and took the stage. They got razzed at first—until the others realized they actually had some talent.

"Hey, Tex," whispered Erik Shilling, "those boys ain't half bad."

"Scarsdale spent a few years in that New York choir school," said Tex Hill, "St. John the Divine. Yup, Jack's got a good set of pipes."

"I'll be damned," said Shilling. "Scarsdale—a choir boy."

They ended the impromptu performance with "Down Among the Sheltering Palms" with Jack's rich baritone voice on the solo. By this time the club owner had started to record the event on the Silver Grill's 78-rpm record machine:

> *Down among the sheltering palms*
> *O honey wait for me, O honey wait for me*
> *Meet me down by the old Golden Gate*
> *Out where the sun goes down about eight*
> *How my love is burning, burning, burning*
> *Can't you see I'm yearning, yearning, yearning*
> *To be down among the sheltering palms*
> *Oh honey, wait for me*

Recalling his final glimpse of Janie on the bridge, Scarsdale nearly always choked up on "meet me down by the old Golden Gate" so the group changed the line to "don't you forget that we've got a date," and this solved the problem.

Scarsdale's bunk was beside Bert Christman's that night.

"I'm sure sorry I had to drop out on you, Jack," Christman whispered. "I've been kicking myself all day about it."

"You can't be blamed for a bum engine, Bert. Don't worry. We'll have plenty of chances."

"I just hate being on the ground when I know you're all up there fighting."

"I know how you feel. I can't stand inaction."

The heat of the day was beginning to let up as a welcome breeze blew through the barracks.

"Jack, do you believe in God?"

"Of course I do."

"What do you think God would make of what happened today?"

"What do you mean?"

"The Bible says 'Thou shalt not kill' doesn't it?"

"Yep," Jack muttered as he thought of the two Japanese pilots he'd sent spiraling into the jungle.

A few more AVG members crept into the barracks and carefully shut the door so as not to wake the men.

"Bert," whispered Jack, "you remember that story about the Good Samaritan?"

"Yeah," said Christman. "A bunch of thugs beat up some poor guy on the road. They left him for dead and nobody would help him—except that Samaritan."

"I wonder what God would say if the Samaritan had come along an hour earlier—when the fellow was actually getting beat up. Do you stand by and watch him get pummeled or jump in and stop the bad guys?"

Christman propped himself on his elbows as he listened to Jack.

"We live in a crazy world," Jack continued. "I guess I think of it this way: By taking out those Japs, we probably saved a few hundred innocent people who never hurt anybody. We didn't start this fight—but hopefully we'll finish it. And hopefully nothing like this will ever happen again. Don't forget what we saw in Kunming last month."

"You know, Bert," Jack continued after a long pause, "I've been having this dream—"

"About what?" asked Christman.

"Can you quiet down over there?" someone protested. "We're trying to get some sleep."

★ ★ ★

**IT TOOK NO TIME** for the press to pick up on the Tigers' successful raid. Clamoring for positive stories of America's involvement in the war, a bevy of correspondents rushed to cover Rangoon and Kunming—*Time-Life, United Press, Associated Press,* the *New York Times,* and the *Chicago Daily News.* The legend of the Flying Tigers grew larger with each new article and broadcast. A San Francisco radio station transmitting from the Fairmont Hotel described the Tigers as "the hardest fighting outfit in the world." *Time Magazine* wrote "man for man, plane for plane, anything labeled U.S.A. could whip anything labeled Made-in-Japan." *Time* made a claim of ownership to "Scarsdale Jack," reminding readers that he had once been their office boy in New York. Walt Disney Studios created an official AVG moniker—a winged Bengal tiger, claws extended, flying through a large blue V for Victory.

For the first few weeks of the war—before Butch O'Hare's valiant fight off the *Lexington* and Jimmy Doolittle's daring raid over Tokyo—Scarsdale Jack Newkirk became one of the most written about pilots in the nation. Headlines described him as *The Scourge of Burma*, *The Scorpion from Scarsdale*, and his self-given nickname, *Danger*. Admiral Byrd reminded friends that he had personally given Scarsdale Jack the Eagle Scout medal. Even Eddie Rickenbacker, the famed World War I ace from Bronxville, followed the exploits of the Flying Tigers.

America had its heroes again. And they had wings of steel.

The Newkirk family, of course, couldn't have been prouder. Janie scoured the papers and magazines for any mention of her husband. Louis saved all his son's letters in a fireproof cabinet. Professor Burt Newkirk cut out articles, pasted them into a scrapbook, and sent duplicates to young Jack at Bethlehem Steel, who in turn took them to work to show his friends. And at the Naval Shipyard in San Francisco, Horace proudly answered yes whenever asked if he was related to Scarsdale Jack, that famous naval aviator off the *Yorktown*.

The Japanese were far less enthralled with Newkirk, Chennault, and the Flying Tigers. The day after the Tak raid, an embarrassed Japanese Air Force launched a retaliatory strike that they hoped would snuff out the Flying Tiger nuisance once and for all.

On January 4, 1942, a fleet of thirty Japanese fighter aircraft jumped several P-40s patrolling the Mingaladon airfield. Three of Newkirk's Panda Bears were shot down, though fortunately none of them lost their lives. Bert Christman's plane was riddled with bullets and the earphones were shot off of his head, which was grazed in two places. Christman had plenty of time to think about it as his parachute carried him to the rice paddy below.

For the next four days the Japanese sent waves of fighters and bombers to punish the Tigers. The fighting was fierce and AVG ground crews listened intently over the radios as the battles unfolded in the sky.

"There!" yelled Scarsdale. "Ten o'clock low. Don't take the bait, Christman, don't take the bait! Good—good! Now dive on him or he'll slip away."

While the AVG pilots got most of the glory, Scarsdale was keenly aware they'd be nowhere without their ground crews, and he'd include them in the action during brief lulls in battle.

"Hey Bailey, Blackwell!" he crackled over the radio. "That new prop governor's running real smooth—thanks, boys! And Pistole, you oughta see your .50s ripping into those Sallys like a swarm of mad hornets!"

The Japanese continued the onslaught until January 8 when they realized they were losing approximately ten of their own aircraft for each enemy P-40. That afternoon, Scarsdale led a half-dozen Tigers back to the aerodrome at Tak to strafe the enemy airfield again. He summarized the raid in his combat report:

> Left the base at 1635 and flew in loose line astern with weavers at an altitude of 10,000'. While crossing the border we were able to take advantage of a cloud . . . dove straight into Tak aerodrome out of the sun . . . I saw four enemy aircraft, a few trucks, and several ground personnel. On the next dive, I attacked an I-97 fighter which was parked by the operations building. It was silver coloured and had branches on it, and when I looked back, it was in flames. On the same dive, I fired on a truck which was driving across the field. The truck swerved and ran into the burning plane. On the next dive, I fired on a plane across the field from the building, several pieces fell out of it and it collapsed on the ground. During this process I heard two "plunks" in my fuselage. The rest of the planes were heading back so I left also.

Jack later discovered the plunks were bullets from riflemen stationed at the field. Panda Bear John Petach circled around and "dispersed" them with his machine guns.

The fighting let up in mid-January as the Japanese attempted to rebuild their stunned air force. For added safety, the Flying Tigers moved off base to live in the relative luxury of homes offered by appreciative residents of Rangoon. Jack stayed with a British major and his wife. Bert Christman and Ed Rector took up with executives from the Burmah Oil Company. Greg Boyington lived in the palatial estates of two Scottish oil barons, Jim Adams and Bill Tweedy, who knew they had much to lose should the Japanese capture the Burmese oil fields.

Claire Chennault was in a Kunming hospital with a serious bout of bronchitis when he received an encouraging radiogram from the leader of the Panda Bears:

> **GENERAL CHENNAULT:** THE MORE HARDSHIPS, WORK, AND FIGHTING THE MEN HAVE TO DO THE HIGHER THE MORALE GOES STOP THEY SEEM TO THRIVE ON ADVERSITY STOP THE SQUADRON IS BECOMING MORE UNIFIED EVERY DAY END NEWKIRK

On January 20, six Panda Bears escorted half a dozen British Blenheim bombers to the Japanese forward airfield at Mae Sot in Thailand. En route they ran into six enemy fighters and Newkirk promptly shot down two of them. Thus, with five victories in less than three weeks, Scarsdale Jack became the first Panda Bear ace and one of the first American aces of the war. Christman attempted to engage the enemy but ran afoul of two Japanese Nates who riddled his Tomahawk with bullets, destroyed his windshield, and forced him to limp back to base.

At Rangoon's Silver Grill that evening, Christman took Jack aside and bought him a drink. An attractive Burmese woman, accompanied by a balding pianist, stood at the stage mic and belted out "Blue Moon" with an accent that made the popular tune sound almost comical.

"That girl needs some help," prodded Christman. "Why don't you get your boys up there and show her how it's done?"

"It hasn't been the same since we lost Merritt," lamented Jack. "Now that we're a trio the owner's calling us 'The Unholy Three.'"

After a little more chitchat, Christman got down to business.

"Jack," he said, "what is it about my flying? I haven't bagged any Japs yet. All I seem to do is get myself shot down."

"Oh, Bert, some of it's just dumb luck," Jack consoled. "You're a good pilot. You'd have washed out back at Pensacola otherwise."

"I suppose," said a dejected Christman as he nursed his drink, "but the proof's in the pudding, as they say."

"There's just one thing, maybe," Jack hesitated.

"What is it?"

"Well, your flying is top notch, but I think you could be a little more forceful in your attacks. This is no place to be a gentleman. When you engage the enemy, pounce on him like a terrier on a rat. This is a dirty, brutal business. There's no way to sugarcoat it. It's you or him—remember that."

"So you think I need more of a 'killer instinct?'" Christman pressed.

"I never thought of us as killers. On the contrary, when we allow the bad guys to escape, we've just condemned all the innocent people he'll kill in the future. We don't want any more Kunmings or Pearl Harbors. And neither of us want to leave our bones here."

"That's a fact," Christman sighed with a faraway look. "I sure miss Colorado. Have you ever seen the Rockies?"

"Not yet," Jack replied.

"Well, when this is all over, you come out and go fishing with me. I know some great places along the Cache La Poudre River."

"That would be swell. I love to fish. Any hunting out there?"

"Elk the size of Paul Bunyan's ox."

"OK, it's a deal," said Jack. "You show me the Rockies and I'll show you the Adirondacks. You'd love Lake George. The water's so clear you can find your fish just by looking down."

"That's settled then," said Christman. "In the meantime I need to start pulling my weight around here. I've been shot down twice with nothing to show except busted-up Tomahawks."

"Tell you what," Jack replied, "on our next mission I'll stick close and talk you through some of what I've learned about the Jap pilots."

"Thanks, Jack."

"But don't think for a minute that you're not pulling your own weight, Bert. I'm damn proud to have you as one of my flight leaders, and I'd go into battle with you any day."

A photographer named George Rodger was hanging around the Mingaladon airfield shooting photos for *Life Magazine*. He captioned many of the pictures himself and described the Tigers as "a new type of fighting man." The craggy faced Chennault would typically strike a dour pose whenever photographed, as if to say, "Don't tread on me." Newkirk followed suit and scowled at the camera from the shotgun seat of Jim Howard's Jeep. Rodger's photos eventually came to the attention of Prime Minister Winston Churchill, who reportedly said, "God Almighty, I'm glad they're on our side."

On January 23, 1942, the air raid siren interrupted Rodger's photo session. Panda Bears Jack Newkirk, Gil Bright, "Pete" Petach, Bert Christman, Ed Rector, Jim Howard, and a few others rushed into the sky to intercept the aerial assault. They were dumbstruck by what they saw. The Japanese had assembled over three dozen fighters and an equal number of bombers to exact revenge upon the Flying Tigers.

At ten thousand feet, Jack targeted a bomber formation and shot one of them down as they approached the field. True to his promise, he kept in close contact with Bert Christman.

"Good—now get in among them, there! Dive! Dive! You can get on his tail now! Blow him out of the sky, or by God he'll come back at us later! Stay with Rector, understand?"

A group of Nate fighters broke off and attacked the P-40s. One of the Nates lagged behind and Jack shot off its wing with a single burst from his .50-caliber machine guns. But Scarsdale had flown into a trap, and three Nates began to perforate his plane with machine gun fire as he lost sight of Christman in the melee. Jack's engine sputtered, lost power, and began to overheat. He dived toward the field and faked a death spiral as smoke poured out of his cowling. The Nates, confident they had shot down Jack's airplane, broke off to engage the remaining P-40s.

Jack pulled out of the spin fifteen hundred feet above the Mingaladon airstrip and discovered his flaps wouldn't extend. This caused him to overshoot the runway and his Tomahawk nosed into the ground, bending the propeller and damaging the airframe. Jack extricated himself from the bullet-riddled aircraft and ran frantically toward the flight line as he wiped blood off his face from a cut on his forehead.

"George!" he panted, "I need another bird—right now!"

"We don't have one, Jack," said crew chief George Bailey. "They're all up in the air."

"You gotta have something, for God's sake!" Jack pleaded as he panted and paced from the sprint across the airstrip.

"Well, there's 8140—but she's got a bad tail wheel and a rough idle, among other things. No way she'd pass inspection."

"Is she fueled and armed?"

"Yes, but Jack, she's got a couple of bullet holes in the tail we haven't patched up and—"

Jack jumped into the P-40 and took off toward the fighting. His face clenched in anxiety as he tried in vain to reach Christman over the radio.

"Bert, you there? Rector? Can you copy?"

As Jack climbed through twelve thousand feet, he saw Ed Rector and Bert Christman encircled by a swarm of Japanese fighters. Three Nates pummeled Christman's P-40. They shot away his control surfaces and ruptured the coolant lines. Prestone covered his windscreen and the engine rapidly overheated, and the elevator and rudder no longer responded. Out of options, Christman unbuckled his harness, opened the canopy, and jumped over the side.

Jack watched in horror as a Japanese Nate lined up his sites on the target floating helplessly to the earth. A line of tracer bullets arced toward Christman and riddled his body as faint puffs of red exploded from his chest, neck, and head.

"Bert! No! No!" Jack shouted uncontrollably, his face wracked in anguish and guilt.

Jack latched on to the Nate, squeezed his trigger, and the enemy arched toward the ground. The Japanese bombers were under such heavy attack that they abandoned the airfield objective, jettisoned their bombs, and turned for home. Jack dived on a retreating bomber, blew off its tail section, and set the starboard engine on fire. As he streaked past the bomber, Newkirk stared the doomed Japanese pilot in the face—and extended his middle finger with unmitigated rage.

Allen Bert Christman—aged twenty-six, cartoonist, Flying Tiger, friend—hung limp in his harness and crumpled unceremoniously to the ground, as the billowy parachute gently covered his lifeless body like a shroud of white linen.

# 28

**O**N FEBRUARY 10, 1942, Glenn Miller stood in front of a microphone at the CBS Playhouse on West Forty-fifth Street in New York City. RCA executive Wallace Early was on hand to present Miller with an unusual award as radio host Paul Douglas spoke to the millions of fans tuned in:

**DOUGLAS:** I want to present Mr. W. Wallace Early, the manager of record sales for Victor and Bluebird Records—Mr. Early.

**EARLY:** Thanks, Paul. It's a pleasure to be here tonight, and speaking for RCA Victor, we're mighty proud of "That Chattanooga Choo Choo" and the man who made the record, Glenn Miller. You see, it's been a long time—15 years in fact—since any record has sold a million copies, and "Chattanooga Choo Choo" certainly put on steam and breezed right through that million mark by over 200,000 pressings, and we decided that Glenn should get a trophy. The best one we could think of was a gold record of Chattanooga. And now, Glenn, it's yours with the best wishes of RCA Victor Bluebird Records.

**MILLER:** Well, thank you, Wally. That's really a wonderful present.

**DOUGLAS:** I think everyone listening in on the radio should know, Glenn, it actually is a recording of "Chattanooga Choo Choo," but it's in gold—solid gold—and it's really fine.

**MILLER:** That's right, Paul, and now for the boys in the band and for the whole gang—thanks a million two hundred thousand.

Glenn Miller's dogged persistence, bolstered by the miracle of radio, had turned his orchestra into the most popular musical group in the nation—and the recipient of the industry's first-ever gold record. On his occasional trips to Colorado to visit his parents, Glenn Miller always made a point to see his old teacher and mentor, who had long since retired from teaching and now cut hair for a living.

"Hey, what's knittin', kitten?" asked Miller from the doorway of the barbershop.

"Zero, Nero," came the reply. "Come on in, boy. What can I do for you this trip?"

"Just a trim and shave, Boss. We're all going out on the town!"

Ft. Morgan, Colorado, was a cow town compared with Miller's New York City, but Boss was used to Glenn's dry humor and tried to match it note for note as he worked the clippers.

"Ever dream you'd be getting a shave and a haircut from your old band teacher?" he asked.

"No more than I dreamed I'd flunk my first college music course," Miller replied.

"Surely you're not blaming me for that?" Boss chuckled.

"I wouldn't dream of it," said Miller with a wry smile.

"Do you remember when we talked about dreams?" asked Boss.

"I do," said Miller in a more serious tone, "I'll never forget it."

Boss dabbed a thick froth of Burma Shave onto Miller's face and carefully cut his whiskers with a straight razor.

"Been listening to much radio lately?" Glenn asked.

"No, my set went out and I haven't gotten around to fixing it. Besides, seems all they play is some guy named Glenn Miller."

"Well," Miller laughed, "you might listen for a new arrangement we recorded a while back. I kept thinking about you the whole time."

"Which tune?" asked Boss. "How am I supposed to recognize it? Not 'Chattanooga' again!"

"No, no. You'll pick up on this one from the title alone," said Miller. "It's got your name all over it."

"Whatever you say, boy."

★ ★ ★

**BACK IN NEW YORK CITY,** famed conductor Andre Kostelanetz had commissioned composer Aaron Copland to compose a musical portrait of an "eminent American" as part of a patriotic war effort. Copland chose Abraham Lincoln. He not only wrote the music, but much of the narrative, which included excerpts from Lincoln himself:

> Fellow-citizens, we cannot escape history. . . . The fiery trial through which we pass, will light us down, in honor or dishonor, to the latest generation. . . . We—even we here—hold the power, and bear the responsibility.
> 
> He was born in Kentucky, raised in Indiana, and lived in Illinois. And this is what he said. This is what Abe Lincoln said:
> 
> "The dogmas of the quiet past are inadequate to the stormy present. The occasion is piled high with difficulty, and we must rise—with the occasion. As our case is new, so we must think anew, and act anew. We must disenthrall ourselves, and then we shall save our country."

*Lincoln Portrait* premiered in the spring of 1942. A radio broadcast narrated by Carl Sandburg came shortly thereafter. For the CBS Masterworks recording, Copland chose actor Henry Fonda to be the narrator, revisiting Fonda's role from the 1939 film *Young Mr. Lincoln*.

★ ★ ★

**A THOUSAND MILES** southwest in Tuskegee, Alabama, an "experiment" was underway that would change the course of military aviation. Popular opinion—and a handful of "scientific" studies—purported that Negroes lacked the intelligence and dexterity to handle the complex machinery and demanding psychological environment of aerial combat.

Eleanor Roosevelt thought this was rubbish.

In a series of legislative moves—no doubt influenced by FDR's conversations with his wife—the Army Air Corps set out to create an all-black unit of combat aviators. The 99th Fighter Squadron was formed at the Tuskegee Institute, where Charles Alfred "Chief" Anderson was the chief flight instructor. Their airplane was the Curtiss P-40—the same planes the Flying Tigers were making famous in headlines all around the world.

In the first months of 1942, Chief Anderson's class produced five black aviators who proudly wore the silver Army Air Corps wings Anderson had been denied fifteen years earlier. With the country now at war, several other squadrons out of Tuskegee joined the 99th Fighter Squadron to form the 332nd Fighter Group—the legendary "Tuskegee Airmen."

★ ★ ★

**IN THE INDUSTRIAL TOWN** of Bethlehem, Pennsylvania, young Jack Newkirk was nine months into his job as a junior metallurgist at the Bethlehem Steel Corporation—the second-largest steel firm in the United States, which had produced many of the steel rails connecting the nation. During the 1920s and '30s, Bethlehem Steel helped build some of America's most prominent landmarks: Madison Square Garden, the Chrysler Building, Rockefeller Center, Trylon and Perisphere, and San Francisco's Golden Gate Bridge. With the country now at war, Bethlehem began to produce war materials, including armor plating, cannons, airplane cylinders, and more than eleven hundred ships for the U.S. Navy.

Burt Newkirk began to grow anxious about his sons and their roles in the war.

Horace was in San Francisco at the Hunters Point Naval Shipyard. With his physics training and knowledge of electrical theory, he had become an expert in demagnetizing ships—an art form known as "degaussing" that prevented vessels from triggering enemy mines. This expertise caused the draft board to recommend that Horace be classified as II-B: a draftee deferred as necessary to national defense.

Young Jack was a different story. Twenty-one years old, healthy, and willing to serve, he was a prime candidate for the draft. He started making noises about becoming a pilot like Scarsdale, and Burt suddenly realized it might have been a mistake to pass along so many newspaper clippings idealizing his son's famous namesake.

Throughout the winter and spring of 1942, Burt Newkirk wrote a series of quietly desperate letters to his son, often with inconsistent attempts to steer Jack toward technical service in the military or—as with Horace—a strategic position as a civilian:

> Yesterday I sat at lunch with Dr. Baker and he said the draft is going to take all the men under 30 yrs of age regardless of their technical qualifications. I asked him what he thought you ought to do, i.e. wait for the draft or apply for a commission in some branch of the service. He thought you should do the latter. . . .
>
> It appears to me that it would be a courteous thing for you to write to Lieutenant Commander Cole that you have been advised that you ought to stick to metallurgy and consequently you will not push your application for the appointment as ensign in engineering. . . .
>
> This morning I spoke with Captain Richardson, the R.O.T.C. officer here at Rensselaer and he was emphatic in recommending that you apply for a commission. . . .
>
> Of course, I can't give you any advise at this distance, but I do feel pretty sure that you should not allow yourself to be taken by the draft if you can help it because the army organization is expanding so rapidly now that they must be swamped with men having special qualifications that they have no means of using to good advantage. . . .
>
> Jack, if you must go into uniform it would be best surely to go where you think you can do the most good. I think it is a part of the contribution that each of us should get into the job that he can do the best, whatever our abilities.

Jack was so wrapped up in his new job that the war seemed a world away. Surely the draft board, if they ever called, would assign him to a position commensurate with his qualifications. Jack shrugged off most of his father's anxieties and enjoyed the bachelor's life. With warriors like Scarsdale pounding the enemy, the war could be over in a couple of months.

★ ★ ★

AS SQUADRON LEADER, Scarsdale Jack had the onerous task of filling out Bert Christman's personnel report. After delaying as long as possible, he sat down dutifully at the typewriter:

**TO:** Chief Personnel Division U.S. Navy Dept. Washington, D.C.
**NAME:** Christman, Allen B.
**RATING:** Flight Leader
**DATE OF BEGINNING ONE YEAR CAMCO SERVICE:** September 15, 1941
**RATING ON PERSONAL CHARACTERISTICS:**
  Initiative - Above Average
  Force - Average
  Aggressiveness - Superior
  Intelligence - Superior
  Endurance - Superior
  Alertness - Above Average
  Cooperation - Superior
**MILITARY BEARING:**
  Neatness - Superior
  Courtesy - Superior
  Obedience to orders - Superior
**BEHAVIOR OF INDIVIDUAL UNDER FIRE:** This officer was twice shot down yet displayed no lack of courage and was always eager to engage the enemy. The third time, he was shot down and killed. He always made cool, well-calculated decisions under fire.

**WOULD YOU DESIRE TO HAVE THE INDIVIDUAL CONTINUE TO SERVE UNDER YOUR COMMAND?** Yes.
**DO YOU RECOMMEND PROMOTION OF INDIVIDUAL UPON RETURN TO ACTIVE SERVICE?** I would have.
**REMARKS:** This officer was one of the highest assets that the squadron had and his death is a loss far more serious than the loss of his companionship.

J. V. NEWKIRK (UNIT COMMANDER)
2ND PUR. SQ., AVG
KUNMING, YUNNAN, CHINA
FEBRUARY 20, 1942

**CONCURRED:**
C. L. CHENNAULT
(GROUP COMMANDER)

By the end of February 1942, Japanese soldiers had overrun eastern Burma and were approaching Rangoon. Without bombers and fresh supplies, the beleaguered Flying Tigers and the British Royal Air Force could no longer hold off the Japanese onslaught. Chennault ordered the remaining Flying Tigers to grab whatever they could from the Rangoon docks and move two hundred fifty miles north to Magwe.

Greg Boyington's Scottish hosts took off on foot with small bundles on their backs as Greg shook his head in dismay. The wealthy oil executives had been reduced to a pair of refugees.

"Anything I can do for you here after you go?" Boyington shouted.

"Aye," yelled Jim Tweedy, "set a match to the place! I dinna fancy no Jap sleepin' in me bed."

The evacuation of Rangoon was pure bedlam. Waterlines, telephones, power—nothing worked. Vicious gangs roamed the city and looted everything in their path. The British opened the doors of the asylums and released criminals, lepers, and mental patients into the streets. Chennault ordered chaplain Paul Frillman to lead the first convoy out of the city. Frillman recorded some of what he saw:

We came upon a leper at a downtown gas station. It was an American station, exactly like those selling this brand in the United States. The leper with his filthy rags, his great lion head and thickened features, looked as if he had escaped from a medieval dungeon. He was laughing insanely as he pumped the gas into the street, shaking the hose above his head to make the fluid scatter and sparkle in the sunlight.

The Adam and Eves headed for the relative safety of Magwe. The Panda Bears and Hell's Angels rested and regrouped in the sanctuary of Kunming—and anticipated the certain battles that would accompany the Japanese offensive.

On the evening of February 28, the AVG Flying Tigers were guests of honor at a banquet hosted by Generalissimo and Madame Chiang Kai-Shek. This was a profound gesture of respect by the Chinese—the equivalent of King George and Queen Elizabeth asking the Tigers to dine with them at Balmoral Castle. As dinner was about to be served, two Chinese waiters opened the double doors to reveal Scarsdale Jack Newkirk dressed smartly in a brand new uniform. Flanked by Jim Howard and Arvid Olson, Scarsdale marched into the banquet hall and called the room to order. Everyone stood up as Chiang Kai-Shek and his wife entered the room.

Kai-Shek's wife, Soong May-ling, was educated at Wellesley College in Massachusetts and spoke excellent English. Petite, attractive, and articulate, her refined mannerisms immediately endeared her to the Flying Tigers.

"Colonel Chennault, members of the AVG, and other friends: as your honorary commander, may I call you 'my boys'?

"The whole Chinese nation has taken you into their hearts. I want you to leave a true impression on my people of what Americans really are. Everything you do will have repercussions on the country I love best next to my own—America!"

Her words evoked thunderous applause from the floor.

"I would like all of you to get up and drink a toast to the two great sister nations on both sides of the Pacific. These two sisters have now a bond of friendship and sympathy which serves us well in the crucible of war, and which will serve us equally well when the victory is ours."

Chiang Kai-Shek began to speak through his interpreter: "My gratitude to the American Volunteer Group is infinite. For the past few years, China has been locked in a desperate struggle of life and death and you alone have come here to defend us. We have always resolved to fight, but we lacked the air arm you are now providing. I am very pleased to present you boys with five hundred dollars bonus for every airplane shot down from the air. But I shall be pleased also to give you a bonus for each plane destroyed on the ground as well."

The Flying Tigers roared in a standing ovation as Chiang Kai-Shek returned to his seat.

★ ★ ★

**BY MID-MARCH, SCARSDALE** Jack had destroyed ten enemy airplanes and was given half-credit for another he had strafed on the ground. His record was officially 10.5, making him one of the first double aces of the war. This also brought him $5250 in bonus pay, all of which was sent back to Janie to deposit in their nest egg account. The bulk of his monthly $750 salary as squadron leader was also sent home, and Jack and Janie wrote back and forth to each other about how they would use this money for their dream house after the AVG returned from their mission.

★ ★ ★

**BACK IN NEW YORK,** Scarsdale's father, Louis Newkirk, received a message from a woman named Clare Boothe Luce, the wife of *Time* and *Life Magazine* publisher Henry Luce. She thought the family might be interested to know that Scarsdale Jack would be featured in *Life Magazine*'s March 30, 1942, issue as part of an article on the Flying Tigers. Mrs. Luce also mentioned she had visited the Tigers and was in possession of a 78-rpm record Jack had made with his barbershop group in Rangoon.

Louis contacted Burt, who reluctantly told his son about it.

Young Jack could hardly believe it—*Life Magazine!* He would have some serious bragging rights to his friends at Bethlehem Steel.

# 29

ONE WEEK BEFORE the *Life Magazine* article hit the newsstands, young Jack Newkirk went to the garage below his apartment and removed the nine-by-nine shelter cloth that covered the Raspberry. He pushed the motorcycle into the sun, took off the rear wheel, and removed its balding tire with the help of two tire irons from his toolkit. The old inner tube, festooned with patches, was set aside for a spare. He repeated the procedure with the front wheel and the Raspberry stood naked on the pavement, held up only by the rear stand and a block of wood. Then Jack went back into the garage and carefully retrieved the 4.00 x 19 Goodyear Sport Special All Season motorcycle tires he'd purchased the previous fall.

They were literally worth their weight in gold.

The Imperial Japanese Army had cut off America's primary source of rubber, and tires were now precious commodities. Gasoline was rationed as well, but contrary to popular belief it wasn't because of an oil shortage, as America produced 98 percent of its crude oil domestically. The primary motivation for gas rationing was to conserve rubber.

As deliberately as a surgeon, Jack placed the new inner tubes inside the Goodyear tires and finessed them onto the rims. He inflated each tire to the recommended 20 psi and put them back on the Raspberry. Jack put five squirts of fresh oil into the crankcase with the manual oil pump, then filled the transmission with SAE 70 to three-fourths of an inch below the filler opening. After hitting each Alemite point with grease, he reinstalled the battery and primed the cylinders.

The Raspberry roared like a tiger, and Jack immediately took off for an afternoon ride across the Delaware River and back. His forty-five mile trip used up one gallon of gasoline. In an automobile, it would have required three—and three gallons per week was all that was allowed for nonessential travel in the spring of 1942.

The next afternoon Jack was outside his apartment polishing the Raspberry when he looked up to see his friend Rod Malloy walking down the street.

"Hey, Jack. You got the scooter out of mothballs, I see."

"You bet," Jack replied, "and she runs like a top. I went up around Phillipsburg yesterday and put almost fifty miles on her. Only used a gallon."

"That's what I wanted to talk to you about. You know, with my new job I've got a lot of miles to cover this summer and my car drinks like a fish. Not sure how I'm going to make out with the gas rationing and all."

Jack continued polishing as Malloy shuffled his feet.

"How much did you pay for her, anyway?"

"Forty dollars," he said tersely.

"Well, I'd offer you three times that much—especially with those new tires. A hundred and twenty bucks, Jack. Cash on the barrel. What would you say?"

"I'd have to say the same thing I said last time, Rod," Jack sighed. "The Raspberry's not for sale. She never will be. I made that mistake once before."

★ ★ ★

**SCARSDALE JACK WOKE** up in a cold sweat at the AVG hostel in China's Yunnan Province. It was the middle of the night and he'd just had the dream again. The vision had played out with such realism that he was trembling in his bunk.

In his dream Jack floated down the streets of Kunming surrounded by wreckage from an aerial bombardment. He stopped at a fork in the road and to his right saw the remains of a school building. The lifeless body of a five-year-old Chinese girl lay within the rubble, and her alabaster face was covered with white powder. The other path led to a lush garden with thick green grass and a fountain surrounded by lotus flowers. Janie was there—holding out her arms as if to embrace him. A small table was set with tea and pastries, and an even larger one was lavished with bottles of chilled wine and huge quantities of steaming food.

As Jack started toward Janie, he glanced one more time at the face of the child, and at that instant the little girl's eyes flew open. For a long time she lay motionless, staring directly into Jack's eyes. Then her face began to crumple as tears flowed down her cheeks. She extended her slender arms upward, and from a distance, Jack heard her mournful plea.

*Help me . . . Help me!*

Jack heard the whine of incoming bombs, and with a final, anguished glance toward Janie, rushed toward the little girl and shielded her with his body. He felt the explosion rip through the air and everything went black.

It was the same dream. Every time.

★ ★ ★

LIFE MAGAZINE FINALIZED its Vol. 12, No. 13 and sent it to the printer. Twelve-year-old Shirley Temple graced the cover, and the magazine contained a special feature article:

FLYING TIGERS IN BURMA

The article's introductory paragraph proudly embellished the exploits of the AVG:

One shining hope has emerged from three catastrophic months of war. That is the American Volunteer Group of fighter pilots, the so-called "Flying Tigers" of Burma and southeast China who paint the jaws of a shark on their Curtiss P-40s. Outnumbered often ten to one, they have so far shot down about 300 Jap planes, killed perhaps 800 Jap airmen.

As promised, the article featured a prominent photograph of "Scarsdale Jack" Newkirk along with a short biography:

Squadron Leader John V. Newkirk, 28, of Scarsdale, N.Y., went to New York Cathedral Choir School, was Eagle Scout, Time, Inc. office boy, graduate of Rensselear Polytechnic. He trained as Navy flier at Pensacola, Fla., married Lansing, Mich., girl.

Another caption exaggerated Scarsdale's official combat record by more than doubling it:

> Flying Tigers pose in jeep car on the flying field. Newkirk, the man making a face, has shot down 25 Japs so far, had seven or eight when the picture was taken at the end of January.

★ ★ ★

**MARCH 24, 1942,** was a special day for young Jack Newkirk in Bethlehem, Pennsylvania, as it was the first time in months that the weather permitted him to commute on the Raspberry.

It was also his twenty-second birthday.

Jack rode the Harley from his apartment on East Market Street to the Bethlehem Steel factory, where his colleagues fawned all over the bike.

"No gas rationing worries for you," said one.

"You say she carried you from New York City to San Francisco? That must have been one swell trip!" gushed another.

The boss let Jack off work early that day. In his mailbox was a birthday note from his father who, as usual, had included another admonition about what Jack should do in the war effort:

> Yesterday I saw Dr. Hotchkiss again for a short talk. He implied that you ought, without fail, to get the proper blanks to fill out for Navy Ordnance or Army Ordnance and go as far as you can toward an appointment. He thinks technical men of your age will be drafted and be given short training as private soldiers and their technical educations will just not count. This looks foolish . . .

★ ★ ★

**MARCH 24 BEGAN** early for the small cadre of Flying Tigers eight thousand miles away in Namsang, Burma. Three days before, the Japanese had bombed and strafed the airfield in Magwe, fatally injuring AVG crew chief Johnny Fauth and pilot Frank Swartz. Chennault ordered ten Tigers to retaliate. Jack Newkirk volunteered with Panda Bears Whitey Lawlor,

Hank Geselbracht, and Robert "Buster" Keeton. Bob Neale, Charlie Bond, Mac McGarry, Ed Rector, Bill Bartling, and Greg Boyington made up the Adam and Eve contingent.

It would be one of the most daring raids in the history of the AVG.

Chennault's plan was to strike the Japanese-occupied airfield in Chiang Mai, Thailand—one hundred twenty miles behind enemy lines. Intelligence reports indicated numerous enemy aircraft parked at Chiang Mai, with the possibility of another large group farther south at either Lamphun or Lampang.

The Tigers took off in the pre-dawn hours hoping to surprise the enemy on the ground. As they approached Chiang Mai, the Panda Bears turned south toward Lampang. Scarsdale spotted enemy activity at the Chiang Mai railroad depot and lit it up with incendiary rounds from his .50-caliber machine guns, alerting the Japanese that the dreaded Flying Tigers had come to pay a visit. Enemy airmen rushed out to their planes—just in time to see the Adam and Eves hurtling down with their guns blazing.

The P-40's twin .50-caliber M2 Browning machine guns were formidable weapons. Each cartridge launched an explosive thumb-sized bullet toward its target at more than three thousand feet per second with twelve thousand foot-pounds of energy—five times that of a .30-06 rifle. Through a combination of physics, fluid dynamics, and kinetic energy, the human body literally explodes when struck with such force. The P-40 could fire fifteen of these .50-caliber rounds per second, resulting in devastation on a massive scale. Even so, the lack of bombs made attacking a well-defended airfield an exceptionally dangerous proposition. Instead of an anonymous strike from a safe altitude, a strafing run was more like a knife fight.

Finding no aircraft at the auxiliary airports, Scarsdale turned back toward Chiang Mai to join the Adam & Eves, who continued to pound the main airfield with continuous waves of machine gun fire. Bob Neale and Charlie Bond made multiple runs over a long row of Japanese fighters and killed several pilots frantically attempting to get their planes airborne. Boyington made two passes, and the resulting pillar of fire shot a thousand feet into the air. Enemy tracers and anti-aircraft fire flew all around them. Mac McGarry's P-40 was hit and began to cough smoke, forcing him to bail out over the jungle.

South of the field, Scarsdale was blowing the holy hell out of any target of opportunity he could find. He strafed barracks, railcars, trucks, fuel barrels, oil dumps—anything that looked Japanese. As he approached Chiang Mai, he saw a column of military vehicles lined up near the bridge spanning the Kuang River. A machine gun nest had been set up on both ends of the bridge and lines of tracer bullets began arching toward Scarsdale's P-40.

A Japanese armored vehicle quickly halted alongside the road. The driver jumped out and barked orders to the young machine gunner as Scarsdale looped overhead to set up an attack.

The sight of the gaping shark's mouth diving straight at him with guns blazing caused the young private to lose control of his bladder. Nevertheless, he pointed his anti-aircraft gun skyward, pulled the trigger, and sent a stream of 20mm projectiles toward Scarsdale Jack.

"Open wide you yellow-bellied S.O.B.—" Scarsdale shouted as he hurled six streams of lead at the incoming firestorm.

He was thinking of Pearl Harbor, Kunming, and Bert Christman.

Suddenly Jack felt a strange shock, as if he'd been struck by lightning. His mind whirled in confusion. The control stick didn't respond and everything seemed to be in slow motion. He instinctively reached up to unbuckle his harness and bail out as the earth rushed up at an astonishing speed.

He saw Janie crying and waving from the Golden Gate.

He saw the alabaster face of the Chinese girl buried in the rubble at Kunming.

And then there was nothing but black as Scarsdale Jack Newkirk plunged into oblivion.

The P-40 crashed into the ground at three hundred miles per hour, burst into flames, and bounced across the field like an incendiary bomb. The Allison engine tore off of its mounts and rolled a hundred yards ahead of the flaming wreck as Jack's lifeless body tore through the Tomahawk's shattered canopy like a rag doll. A wave of Japanese soldiers rushed over to the wreckage as another group ran to retrieve the American's remains.

That evening, the young Japanese machine gunner from the armored car was given a ceremonial cup of sake served in a wooden *masu*—honored in front of his company for demonstrating extraordinary bravery in the face of death.

# 30

*The blood-dimmed tide is loosed, and everywhere
The ceremony of innocence is drowned... Surely the
Second Coming is at hand. The Second Coming!*
—William Butler Yeats

**B**URT NEWKIRK WALKED slowly up the sidewalk toward his house on the corner of Athol and Rosa Roads in Schenectady, New York. His soft, gray hair blended with sullen clouds overhead, which were on the verge of sprinkling rain over the leafless landscape below. In his right hand was the March 25, 1942, issue of the *New York Times*. He stopped to steady himself against an oak tree as he absorbed the headlines:

FLIERS IN BURMA SMASH 40 PLANES

A.V.G. PILOTS SCORE

"SCARSDALE JACK" KILLED

KUNMING, China, March 24–Pilots of the American Volunteer Group smashed forty planes at the Thai airport of Chiengmai today in a dawn attack that caught the Japanese by surprise.... The enthusiasm of the returning American pilots over the success of the raid was dampened, however, by the death of their squadron leader, Jack Newkirk. His plane was seen crashing near the Japanese airfield at the end of a low dive and his mates believe that a burst of machine-gun fire from a Japanese gun mounted on a parked truck near the airfield got him.

Burt walked inside, set the newspaper down, and sighed wearily as he reached for a pair of scissors, then carefully cut out the article and set it aside for the family scrapbook as he'd done so many times before.

The telephone rang. He knew all-too-well who would be on the other end.

"Son," he said reassuringly.

Burt heard sniffling over the background static.

"Dad—"

"Yes, son."

Burt waited patiently as Jack gathered his composure.

"They killed him, Dad. On my birthday. Why'd they have to kill him—on my birthday—"

"I don't know, son. This is war. Bad things happen. I don't understand it either. Do you want to come home for a few days?"

"No!" he shouted. "I'm going to join the navy. I'm going to be a pilot."

"Jack, now listen to me. Scarsdale had been flying since he was a teenager. He was the best we had and they still got him. The country can use you in other ways. Metals, engines, ships, engineering, problem solving."

"No!" Jack repeated. "I've made up my mind. I'm going to quit Bethlehem Steel, go to California, and join the navy."

"I'm asking you not to do that."

"I'll do whatever I want!" Jack shot back defiantly as he wiped the tears from his cheeks. "I'm twenty-two now, you know."

Burt heaved a sigh of defeat. Jack was of age and there was nothing he could do about it.

"There's something I need to ask you," Jack continued.

"Yes?"

"I need some money. The plane ticket to San Francisco is $125. I can pay you back when I get my enlistment bonus and—"

"I can't do that, son," Burt interrupted.

"Dad—Horace is already out there! I can't just sit here while the other boys are in the thick of it!"

"Jack, I can't finance a flight to California until you've exhausted your possibilities of serving right here—as a civilian, maybe. Look at me: I'm sixty-six and Pratt & Whitney says my work with superchargers is of vital importance to the war effort. So there are many ways to serve. You don't have to be a pilot, understand? Jack?"

Burt waited for a reply, but Jack slammed down the phone and ran outside crying into the Pennsylvania rain. He paced in front of his apartment as amber rays poured from the streetlamps along East Market Street. The reflection in a shiny circle of chrome caught his eye.

*The Raspberry!*

★ ★ ★

**A PESKY REPORTER** from the *San Francisco Call-Bulletin* cornered Janie in the United Airlines office on Geary Street near the Golden Pheasant Restaurant. A photographer snapped her picture as she stared listlessly at the floor, eyes red from crying. In her pocket was a string of fifty-two pearls, which she idly rubbed between her thumb and forefinger like a set of rosary beads.

The article appeared that evening:

ACE OF 'TIGERS' KILLED
IN RAID ON JAP AIRPORT

Hero's Widow Dazed

Bride Hears of Death Here

KUNMING, China, March 24 (AP)—Mrs. Newkirk, pretty young bride of the slain Burma hero, was in San Francisco visiting friends when she heard this morning of his death in action.

She hurriedly checked out of her hotel and booked reservations on a United Airliner for Los Angeles, where she has made her home and worked in a defense training school since the fortunes of war took her bridegroom to the Orient.

As she waited at United's downtown office for the limousine to take her to the airport, she found it difficult to restrain her grief. "I can't talk about it," she cried. "I just want to get back home."

★ ★ ★

**AVG SECRETARY OLGA** Greenlaw heard a knock at her door in Kunming. Claire Chennault—as close to tears as she'd ever seen him—walked in with an armful of flowers. Her husband Harvey followed with a potted cherry tree adorned with blossoms the Japanese call *sakura*.

"Jack Newkirk is dead."

Olga was speechless, but somehow managed to swallow her tears. During the next few days, stunned AVG members revisited the Chiang Mai mission with stiff upper lips as they recalled their squadron leader.

"We burned the hell out of those Jap planes," said Bob Neale. "Caught 'em just as they were about to take off. But God, did we pay through the nose! Did you see what got him, Bus?"

"Machine gun in a Jap armored car, I think," said Keeton. "I saw him diving on it when he went in."

"Could have been target fixation," said Charlie Bond. "Maybe he just didn't pull out in time."

"Not Scarsdale," said Frank Lawlor. "He was a navy man. I could see it if he'd been diving toward water where it's tough on depth perception—but not on a ground target."

A few moments of silence followed as it all sank in.

"Anybody notice him acting funny over the past few days?" asked George "Pappy" Paxton.

"Hell, yes!" blurted Boyington. "For the past week or so he just wasn't the same guy. Not the friendly, smiling Jack I'd come to know in Honolulu on the *Yorktown*. The night before the Chiang Mai raid he just didn't want to talk at all—about anything."

"He gave me his pipe just before he left," said Sam Prevo, the flight surgeon. "Told me to keep it as a souvenir."

"He gave me his whipcord cloth," added Paxton.

Tex Hill cleared his throat.

"Well, Jack left a letter with the Old Man just before he took off. Said he wanted me to lead the Pandas if anything happened to him. Hope Howard's not too upset—"

"Then there was that toothbrush thing," Boyington muttered. "I was standing beside Scarsdale in the washroom. A little RAF sergeant came up and said the water was all right to wash in, but don't drink it or use it to brush your teeth with. No sooner did that Brit leave than Jack dips his toothbrush into the water and starts brushing away."

"No kidding?" asked Lawlor.

"So I said, 'Jack, you knucklehead, didn't you hear what that guy told us?' Scarsdale just shrugged and said, 'It probably won't matter after tomorrow.'"

"That Jack was a wild one," Paxton shook his head. "A daredevil, really, almost to the point of recklessness. But I sure as hell wouldn't want to be a Jap in his sights."

"Too damn bad none of us are technically military anymore," said Keeton. "Scarsdale would have been a hell of a contender for the Distinguished Flying Cross. Now he'll never get it."

"I heard him talking with Christman one night," said Red Probst. "He was goin' on about some dream he'd been having."

"Well, there's no way he had a death wish," said Greenlaw. "Jack had too much to live for. Wife back home and all."

AVG chaplain Paul Frillman spoke up.

"Jack seemed mighty angry after Pearl Harbor and Kunming—especially after Christman went down. I was a little worried. The day before he left, he asked me to update his will to provide for his wife."

"Scarsdale just got the call, I guess," Boyington offered flatly as he stared into space.

"I dunno," he muttered. "I suppose any bugs in that water just burned up with him."

Greenlaw shot Boyington a dirty look. She didn't think it was funny, but knew him well enough to understand how he processed grief.

But Scarsdale had not burned up inside the wreckage of his P-40. His body was thrown clear of the cockpit and landed in a rice paddy in the Mae Ping basin south of Chiang Mai. The Japanese buried it nearby after celebrating the end of "the immortal Jack Newkirk."

Chiang Kai-Shek and Soong May-ling sent a letter of condolence to his family in New York. Chennault did likewise. In New York, Jack's sister received a note from the plaza where she worked:

Dear Janet:

I told about your Flying Tiger brother on several occasions. Of course, you have read the fine things said about him in several books that came out recently. I believe one of these was by a South African correspondent named Gallagher and was entitled "Action out East."

If we can find the excerpts from my broadcasts we will be glad to send them to you.

Sincerely yours,

Lowell Thomas
Rockefeller Center

Babe Ruth signed a baseball and gave it to Jack's father, Louis, who auctioned it off for twelve hundred dollars in war bonds. Bond revenue from Scarsdale residents purchased twelve Republic P-47 Thunderbolts, which subsequently flew in formation over the city's Memorial Day parade. Each Thunderbolt bore a name such as "The Scarsdale Avenger," "The Scarsdale Scorpion," and "The Scarsdale Battler." Rensselaer Polytechnic Institute posthumously awarded Jack Newkirk its first Albert Fox Demers Medal for distinguished service, where President William Hotchkiss pronounced him the college's "greatest hero of all its thousands of alumni in its 118 years."

New York's Westchester Board of Supervisors moved to name the new Westchester County airport at Rye Lake after Scarsdale Jack. The U.S. Navy created the "Scarsdale Jack Unit" at its pre-training camp in Chapel Hill, North Carolina, and fifty men from Westchester County joined up.

The August 1942 issue of *Wings Comics* ran a two-page, full-color spread that raved about Jack's "dauntless blows against the Japs." Not to be outdone, rival *Zip Comics* inducted him into its Hall of Fame with an effusive, six-page feature:

OUT OF THE HORRORS OF SIX MONTHS OF ACTUAL WAR COMES THE SHINING HOPE OF AMERICA'S ULTIMATE VICTORY—A HOPE EMBODIED IN MEN LIKE "SCARSDALE JACK" NEWKIRK! SO LONG AS MEN OF NEWKIRK'S BRILLIANT

CALIBRE, ON LAND, ON THE SEA, OR IN THE AIR—CONTINUE TO SOCK THE ENEMY WITH HARD-HITTING YANKEE PUNCHES—OUR CAUSE OF FREEDOM FOR ALL WILL BE WON!

★ ★ ★

**ON A DUSKY STREET** in Bethlehem, Pennsylvania, a young man stood stoically on the curb as another counted out six crisp twenty-dollar bills and placed them one by one into his hand.

A weathered, worn, well-traveled Harley-Davidson VL Big Twin—Serial No. 30V8229C—stood anxiously behind them. Rod Malloy climbed onto the Raspberry and fired up her seventy-four-cubic-inch V-twin engine. Young Jack Newkirk shoved the wad of bills into his pocket, grabbed his duffle bag, and walked resolutely down the street in the opposite direction while the rumble of the Harley faded into the distance. Three days later he was staring at the hustle and bustle of the new military base on San Francisco's Treasure Island.

In an ironic twist of fate, Jack realized the Raspberry had now brought him to this place twice—but for two profoundly different reasons.

# 31

IN AUGUST 1942, Army General Charles Young received a surprising and unsolicited letter from the RKO Building in New York City:

> Dear General Young:
>
> For the past three or four years my orchestra has enjoyed phenomenal popularity until we have reached a point where our weekly gross income ranges from $15,000 to $20,000. . . . I would be entirely willing to forego it for the duration. I should like to go into the army if I could be placed in charge of a modernized army band. I feel that I could really do a job for the army in the field of modern music. I hope you will [also] feel that there is a job I can do for the army. If so, I shall be grateful if you will have the proper person contact me. With kind personal regards, I am,
>
> Respectfully yours,
> Glenn Miller

General Young's quick reply praised Miller's "willingness to make personal and patriotic sacrifice for the duration of the War." After formally submitting his application, Miller received a telegram on September 10:

> Capt. Glenn Miller. Your appointment announced. Reporting date October seven. Full details to reach you with orders. Congratulations and good wishes.

Two weeks later Miller broadcast his farewell show from the Central Theater in Passaic, New Jersey. The orchestra's last number was forever burned into the hearts and minds of millions—an unblushing anthem to the frolicking freedom of youth and Depression-era ingenuity:

*Moppin' up Soda Pop Ricky's to our heart's delight*
*Dancin' to swing-a-roo quickies, Jukebox Saturday Night!*
Jukebox Saturday Night © 1942 by P. McGrane
& A. Stillman • Chappell & Co.

*Jukebox Saturday Night* parodied several musical numbers of the day, including a spirited imitation of trumpeter Harry James' *Ciribiribin*. At the end of the number, Miller stepped up to the microphone and the audience went wild:

> **MILLER:** Well that lad that imitated Harry James really did a job. The reason—'cause it was Harry James himself. Harry, come on over here and say something.
>
> **JAMES:** Well hello, Everybody.
>
> **MILLER:** Harry, naturally we're very reluctant to give up our Moonlight Serenade. But since I got a date with Uncle Sam coming up I can sincerely say I'd rather have you take over our regular Tuesday, Wednesday and Thursday spot than anyone I know. So next Tuesday—get to work, mister.
>
> **JAMES:** Well, Captain Miller, coming from you that's an order. But seriously Glenn, I'm sure everyone agrees with me that you're doing a mighty fine thing in joining the army.
>
> **MILLER:** Thank you very much, Harry. That's swell. You know folks it makes me feel a little sad to leave Marion, Tex, Skip, The Modernaires, this wonderful gang of boys in the band, and all our friends listening. But there's a lot of swell guys in the outfit I'm going in, and maybe all of us can get together again after this thing is over. In the meantime, I'll see you all in the army and we'll say goodbye in the best way we know how.
>
> *(Cue Moonlight Serenade)*

*Down Beat* magazine recorded the emotional event:

> VOCALIST [MARION] HUTTON BROKE DOWN, STARTED CRYING, AND RAN OFF THE STAGE. MOST OF THE BRASS SECTION WASN'T DOING

MUCH BETTER. MILLER, FAMED FOR HIS TACITURNITY, TURNED AWAY FROM THE BAND TO KEEP FROM CRACKING UP HIMSELF—ONLY TO FACE ROWS AND ROWS OF KIDS BAWLING THEIR EYES OUT.

As Glenn Miller prepared for duty, composer Aaron Copland began to compose one of eighteen fanfares commissioned by Cincinnati Orchestra conductor Eugene Goossens.

"It is my idea," wrote Goossens, "to make these fanfares stirring and significant contributions to the war effort."

While Goossens' other seventeen composers for the most part submitted works based on bugle calls, triple-tongued staccato bursts, folk songs, and other traditional fanfare material, Copland delivered a distinctive, three-minute piece for brass and percussion that would become one of history's most enduring compositions.

Copland began his fanfare with sudden strikes from the kettledrums—evocative of the bombs that had fallen on Pearl Harbor one year earlier. The drums were punctuated by a Chinese gong that sustained its cry between each drum hit. Then, as if from across the ocean, three unaccompanied trumpets sang out the main theme in unison—a striking metaphor for the three intrepid squadrons of isolated airmen in Asia known as the Flying Tigers. The trumpets were then coupled with horns in two-part harmony, though the fundamental theme remained the same throughout. Trombones joined the mix, and finally, a tuba grounded and supported all the other instruments in a sweeping anthem of brass and percussion.

Copland wrote the fanfare for the ordinary American—for those "doing all the dirty work in the war." He wrote it for the defenders of Wake Island, Dutch Harbor, and Bataan—for Rosie the Riveter, the families planting victory gardens, and for a group of colored men in Tuskegee, Alabama, who wanted to show the world they could fly. He wrote it for an underpaid professor in New York who solved the vibration problems in the B-17's superchargers, for a group of Navaho Indians who'd become codetalkers, for the Virginia Jane Dunhams of the world who gave their men even more reason to come home alive—and for that handful of men who gave their lives protecting thousands of unknown Chinese.

Aaron Copland wrote his fanfare for the millions of Americans who, rather than fixating on their differences, focused instead on what they had in common.

"Fanfare for the Common Man" premiered on March 14, 1943.

"Its title," wrote an ecstatic Eugene Goossens, "is as original as its music."

Physically, Copland was built much like Scarsdale Jack Newkirk: lanky, wiry, and "rather delicate" compared to the Charles Atlas physiques idealized in magazines.

In his element, however, each man was a veritable giant.

By surrounding himself with a shark-toothed P-40 Tomahawk, Scarsdale Jack inspired millions during a time of national crisis. Aaron Copland did much the same—but with only staff paper and a pencil.

*Aaron Copland composes by candlelight*

★ ★ ★

**YOUNG JACK SPENT** one year training in San Francisco as a U.S. Navy specialist. After his resentment subsided, he realized his father had been right and he should put his natural abilities to work instead of rushing to become a pilot.

His technical background, water skills, weapons expertise, and physical fitness qualified him for a position in an elite Naval Diving Unit at Tiburon in San Francisco Bay. They received rigorous training in artillery, anti-aircraft weapons, small arms, psychological operations, jiu-jitsu, diving, ship degaussing, and explosive ordnance demolition. His training qualified him for a wide variety of assignments, and upon completion he was told he could expect to be deployed anywhere at anytime.

Jack was assigned to the navy's Lion 4 Advance Base Unit, and the name's implication wasn't lost on him: his cousin had been a Tiger—Jack was now a Lion. In late 1943, Lion 4 received orders to sail for the Japanese-held Admiralty Islands in the heart of the South Pacific.

A large Dutch transport sat at Pier 33 ready to carry a thousand young Americans to fight the Japanese. She was the *M.V. Bloemfontein*—the same ship that brought Tex Hill, Bert Christman, Ed Rector, R. T. Smith, and dozens of Flying Tigers to the Orient. The *Bloemfontein* backed away from Pier 33 and aimed her bow toward the harbor entrance. Jack stood on deck and took one last glance to starboard.

Treasure Island was a shell of her former self. The Tower of the Sun was gone. The Court of Honor, Court of the Nations, and Treasure Garden had been buried in asphalt. The Golden Gate International Exposition had been replaced with Treasure Island Naval Base and the "glittering spec-ta-cle" of 1939 was forever gone—as was that wide-eyed nineteen-year-old boy who once walked her paths.

As the ship passed under the Golden Gate Bridge, Jack saw three girls waving from the rail two hundred feet above. He raised his right hand with fingers outstretched, and his face slowly widened into a firm, resolute smile.

# 32

*Had he and I but met by some old ancient inn,*
*We should have sat us down to wet*
*Right many a nipperkin!*

*But ranged as infantry,*
*And staring face to face,*
*I shot at him as he at me,*
*And killed him in his place . . .*

*Yes; quaint and curious war is!*
*You shoot a fellow down*
*You'd treat if met where any bar is,*
*Or help to half-a-crown.*
                        —Thomas Hardy, "The Man He Killed"

**T**HE ADMIRALTY ISLANDS are a group of eighteen landmasses and atolls in the South Pacific's Bismarck Archipelago, north of Papua New Guinea and the Solomons. Manus Island, the largest in the Admiralty chain, is sixty miles long and twenty miles wide with an interior mountain range that reaches twenty-three hundred feet above sea level. Its entire area is covered with rugged jungles of dense, lowland tropical rain forest.

In early 1942, the Japanese attacked the nearby port of Rabaul and established a major base from which they launched sorties to such objectives as Guadalcanal and the Coral Sea. They subsequently advanced on New Guinea and pushed toward Australia, capturing Manus Island on April 10, 1942. By the summer of 1943, and under direct command of General Douglas MacArthur, the Allies mounted a campaign to reclaim the region and leave "over 100,000 [Japanese] troops in isolated impotence"—cut off from supplies and reinforcement. MacArthur referred to the recapture of the Admiralties as "putting the cork into the bottle," as this would be one of the last steps in the campaign.

Only a shallow channel separated Manus and neighboring Los Negros Island. Together, they formed the strategic Seeadler Harbor—a major prize for the Allies. On February 29, 1944, the U.S. Army's First Cavalry Division assaulted the beachhead at Los Negros as navy guns pounded Japanese positions on shore. The First Cavalry met considerable enemy resistance, but by six o'clock that night more than a thousand Allied soldiers had landed. General MacArthur came ashore and decorated the first man to hit the beach that morning, Lt. Marvin Henshaw from Troop G. While the Los Negros beachhead landing was a success, reconnaissance teams reported that Lorengau—Manus's capital town—was still "lousy with Japs."

Bombers from the Fifth Allied Air Force pounded Lorengau and other strongholds and sent the enemy fleeing into the jungle. Without reinforcements and supplies, however, the Japanese realized it was simply a matter of time before Allied forces reclaimed the Admiralties.

After frantically grabbing whatever they could, a small group of Japanese soldiers rushed inland through the dense undergrowth toward the village of Rossum. They defended their positions with skill and tenacity from camouflaged bunkers and treetops until they ran low on ammunition. A team of Americans from the Eighth Cavalry caught up with them at the end of March, and during the brief firefight that followed, the panicked Japanese expended their ammunition and frantically looked toward their commanding officer.

He barked his final orders, then staunchly drew his *katana*—the sword of the Samurai—and raised it high above his head as he yelled *banzai!* A U.S. Army sergeant watched in shock as the screaming apparition rushed at him headlong, sword uplifted, and ready to cut him in half.

The sergeant squeezed off a quick burst from his Thompson submachine gun and the Japanese officer crumpled facedown into the dirt. Two Japanese enlisted men, upon seeing their commander fall, quickly disappeared into the jungle of Manus Island without food, ammunition, or any means of communication.

Aboard one of the ships in Seeadler Harbor was Jack Newkirk of Lion 4 Advance Base Unit. The task at hand was to reclaim the harbor for Allied use, eliminate any enemy threat to Allied vessels and their crews, and set up a major, all-purpose naval base for the Pacific Fleet.

The smell of battle was still fresh as Jack stepped ashore. Palm trees had been splintered and tossed by artillery, and large water-filled craters pocked the landscape.

*If not for the war*, Jack thought, *this place might be a tropical paradise.*

Shell-shocked men walked around the docks of Lorengau, many wrapped in bandages and makeshift splints. Jack approached one man, an army sergeant, who was perched on a pile of crates trying in vain to light a cigarette with a rusty Zippo lighter.

"Give you a light, bud?" asked Jack as he produced a pack of matches from his shirt pocket.

"Thanks," the army man growled as he looked up slowly.

"Looks like you've seen some action here," said Jack as he held up a lighted match.

The sergeant laughed out loud and took a puff.

"Action? Sure. Welcome to hell, kid."

The older man stared out into Seeadler Harbor.

"Sure wish I had some proper cigarettes," he sighed. "These damned Cotabs are the pits."

"Here," said Jack, "I've got some Lucky Strikes in my sea chest. Glad to give you some."

Jack didn't smoke, but he'd been told cigarettes, magazines, and anything from the mainland would be highly prized in the field.

"Luckies?!" gasped the sergeant. "I'd swim to Brooklyn and back for a pack of those."

"Take 'em," Jack said as he fished through his belongings. "You look like you've earned it."

"Well, thanks, kid. You're all right."

"You from Brooklyn?" asked Jack.

"Yep, Flatbush Avenue. You?"

"Upstate. Schenectady."

The grizzled sergeant crushed his old cigarette into the hard coral soil, took out a Lucky Strike, and put it up to his nose in a long, drawn-out sniff.

"Look at us," he mused. "Two New Yorkers sittin' halfway around the world in this hellhole. Who'd of thought that five years ago?"

"That's a fact," Jack agreed. "All I could think of in '39 was fun and adventure. Say, did you go to the world's fair?"

" 'Course I did—it was just up the river in Queens. My favorite was Frank Buck's wild animals. I'm a hunter. I'm goin' out west to hunt after all this is over. Say, what else you got in that sea chest of yours?"

"I've got *Time*, *Life*, some Glenn Miller records, and a few comic books. Here, this one has Scarsdale Jack Newkirk in it."

"No kidding? Scarsdale Jack in the comics? That I gotta see."

They chatted a few minutes longer until a Jeep appeared to take Jack up the island.

"Nice to meet you, Mac," said Jack as he shut the sea chest. "Maybe I'll run into you again."

"Hey, thanks a lot kid," the sergeant replied. "Listen, I want you to have this. Don't know what I'd ever do with it."

The man handed Jack a long Japanese katana. To the untrained arm, it seemed surprisingly heavy. Jack pulled the sword from its sheath and examined the sharp metal blade.

"Careful," said the sergeant. "That could take your head off."

"Where'd you get it?" asked Jack.

"Jap officer. He came running at me swinging it over his head. Damndest thing I ever saw."

"Well, thank you."

"And another thing."

"Yes?"

"Forget whatever you've heard about the Japs being backstabbing cowards, monkey-faced Nips, or bucktoothed idiots. They are bold, fierce, and skilled jungle fighters—some of the best I've seen, except for the Ghurkas, maybe. Anyway, don't underestimate them. They don't surrender and they're pretty much suicidal. We figure there's still about a hundred 'n fifty hiding up there in the mountains, so stay frosty when you hit the interior."

"Yes, sir," said Jack, momentarily forgetting that he technically outranked the man.

A couple of miles inland, two young Japanese soldiers huddled in a makeshift shelter of branches and palm leaves. Both were tired, hungry, and still in shock after seeing their commander cut down in front of them as he bravely charged the enemy with his sword.

Between the two of them, they had an empty Arisaka Type 38 rifle, a bayonet, their wallets, some moldy pilot biscuits, a pair of binoculars, and a rubberized poncho stuffed inside a musty canvas knapsack. At the bottom of the knapsack, they were overjoyed to find a five-round clip of 6.5 x 50mm ammunition and another round floating around loose. They used the bayonet to hack branches and cut leaves for the lean-to and the poncho served as a roof layer. After a few wretched nights in the driving rain, a gnawing hunger began to set in. Their scanty ration of pilot biscuits was supplemented with large, green-shelled snails they found crawling high in the trees. The men soon realized these trees also provided excellent vantage points, and they picked out two spots a hundred yards apart for their respective guard stations.

Each man took turns holding the rifle and the six precious cartridges as the other scanned the area with the field glasses. Three miles below, they could see the Americans going about their business in Seeadler Harbor.

They agreed to split up during the day to search for food and each took turns carrying the gun. Most often they'd return with only a handful of berries, a lizard, a snake, or more snails, all of which they'd eat raw as they had no way of making fire. Late one afternoon, one of them came running back with a small bundle under his arm.

"*Toshio! Shokumotsu!*" the soldier shouted excitedly.

Earlier that day he had come across the body of a dead American from the Eighth Calvalry. After finding nothing of apparent value, he left the body where it fell and crept silently through the jungle to a clearing where enemy forces were milling about. As he'd done many times before, he lined up his sights on a random serviceman, clicked off the rifle's safety catch, and positioned his finger over the trigger.

As he contemplated pulling it, the aroma of hot stew wafted over him like the scent of water in the desert. Hunger—not the Emperor—was his driving force now, and primal instinct compelled him to think of little else but food. It was lunchtime and several hundred American soldiers were gathering loosely in the chow line.

It was then that he got the idea.

After stowing the rifle in the undergrowth, he crept back to the dead soldier's body, stripped off the uniform, and put it on himself. The Japanese imposter slipped in among the Americans and—head bowed furtively under a wide-brimmed jungle hat—he picked up an empty plate. To his astonishment, the mess crew plopped down a perfunctory pile of steaming rice and topped it off with beef stew and gravy. He inconspicuously snuck around the corner, wolfed down the food, and managed to grab a few K-ration boxes and shove them into his clothes. Back in the forest, he changed into his old uniform and rolled up the other with the food wrapped inside, and then snuck back to the hideout.

The two men stretched the pilfered K-rations into a week's worth of tiny meals. When they could bear the hunger no more, they decided to try the chow line trick again. The next time, however, the Japanese soldier made brief eye contact with one of the mess crew.

"Hey!" the man shouted. "That guy's a Jap!"

After a halfhearted struggle, the man was a prisoner—but contrary to what he'd been told, the Americans did not shoot him on sight, bayonet him, or gouge out his eyes. Instead, they sent him to the brig on the USS *Bush* where he was interrogated, fed, and given a clean set of clothes.

As Allied forces continued to mop up pockets of resistance on the lesser Admiralty Islands, Lion 4 moved heavy equipment onto the smaller islands of Ndrilo, Hauwei, and Pityilu on the opposite side of Seeadler Harbor. Boredom often set in at night, and the men would tune in to whatever radio broadcast they could find. More often than not, the clearest signal came from Japan:

This is your number one enemy, your favorite playmate Orphan Ann of Radio Tokyo, the little sunbeam whose throat you'd like to cut. This program tonight is especially dedicated to the boys of the 509th Group, which just landed on Tinian. Oh sorry, that's supposed to be a secret. By the way, fellas, what kept you so long?

"Tokyo Rose again?" groused one of the lieutenants. "Hey, Newkirk, change the damn station, would ya?"

Jack fiddled with the tuning knob, which sent a howl of whistles and static into the tropical air as he searched for another English-speaking station:

AND NEXT UP, WE HAVE THE LOVELY MURPHY SISTERS WITH A MESSAGE FOR THOSE POOR SAPS—UH, I MEAN JAPS TRYING TO HOLD OUT IN THE PACIFIC. GIVE IT UP, BOYS!

*You're a sap, Mr. Jap, to make a Yankee cranky*
*You're a sap, Mr. Jap, Uncle Sam is gonna spanky—*

As Jack lay awake in his Quonset hut, feelings of bitterness began to well up inside him.

*None of us should even have to be here,* he fumed, *and it's all the Japs' fault.*

They'd bombed Pearl Harbor, killed Scarsdale Jack, attacked Dutch Harbor, and then boasted how they'd use the new Alaska Highway for their eventual invasion of America. The idea of his countrymen subject to the brutality demonstrated at Nanking was more than he could endure.

He shut his eyes and tried to sleep—jaws clenched in a reflexive expression of rage.

West of Rossum, a lone Japanese soldier sat high in a tree overlooking Lorengau and Seeadler Harbor. His compatriot had never returned from the second infiltration attempt, so he had to make do with what little food he could forage from the forest or steal from the villagers. Loneliness was also a factor. He took out his wallet and stared at his only items from home: a small photo of his parents and two faint pink cherry blossoms—the *sakura*—he'd pressed in wax paper just before leaving his home in Nagoya to join the Imperial Army.

He leaned back against the tree and absentmindedly rubbed his solid brass, army issue, hand engraved dog tag, and then placed a hand on his shirt pocket and felt reassuringly for the clip of five 6.5 x 50mm cartridges. The sixth round was locked and loaded inside his rifle, ready to be sent through the heart of the next American to come through the jungle. He carried only one cartridge in the gun, avoiding any temptation to waste his precious ammunition.

He felt a twinge of guilt about running away after his commanding officer had been shot, but told himself he was much better off alive than dead. He was no coward, he kept telling himself. Hadn't he—after all—already proven his mettle in New Britain?

Two years earlier, during the Battle of Rabaul, he'd been ordered to round up one hundred fifty Australians—many wearing Red Cross armbands—and march them into the jungle beside the Tol Plantation south of the city. There, as his superior officer watched, he shot three of them in the back and bayoneted four others. By the time the massacre was over one hundred fifty prisoners lay dead.

A rustling in the leaves snapped the soldier out of his trance. He raised his rifle and sighted in on the movement, but instead of a man he saw one of the elusive feral pigs that roamed Manus Island. With thoughts of fresh meat, he impulsively pulled the trigger. The pig fell to the ground as the shot echoed throughout the hills south of Lorengau. Within an hour a leg of pork was roasting over a fire started by matches from the K-rations.

While the meat brought much-needed sustenance, it also brought a group of Americans, who heard the shot and homed in on smoke from the fire. He heard them coming, scampered up his tree, and hastily loaded a round into the rifle as he searched frantically for a target. His sights came to rest just below the top of a drab-green metal helmet among the leaves. Just as he squeezed the trigger he saw a flash from his enemy's M1 carbine. His own rifle kicked and belched fire, and suddenly he felt himself falling inexorably toward the earth.

For a moment he was back in Nagoya during cherry blossom season, and the fragrant air drifted into his nostrils like a woman's perfume. But then he heard the screaming of the men he'd killed at the Tol Plantation, and in his last moments of consciousness he was struck by the horrific awareness that the world may have been slightly better off had he never been born.

He was dead before he hit the ground.

Bounding through the jungle, swinging his sword like a machete through the undergrowth, Newkirk was the first to reach the body. From a distance, it was difficult to hear what he was screaming—but it sounded as if years of rage were being vented in this single, terrible moment.

★ ★ ★

**IN LATE 1944,** Lt. Jack Newkirk sits in his Quonset hut in the Admiralty Islands with an aerial photo of Lake George above his desk. A drab-green metal helmet hangs on the side of his plywood locker, which contains an M1 carbine, a .45-caliber M1911 pistol, a Samurai sword, and an enemy ammo clip with four 6.5 x 50mm rifle cartridges. On the wall—like a trophy of *crotalus horridus*—hangs the solid brass, hand-stamped dog tag of a Japanese soldier.

Jack's C.O. calls him outside for a photograph, and as he attempts a smile for the camera, there is—quite literally—a monkey on his back.

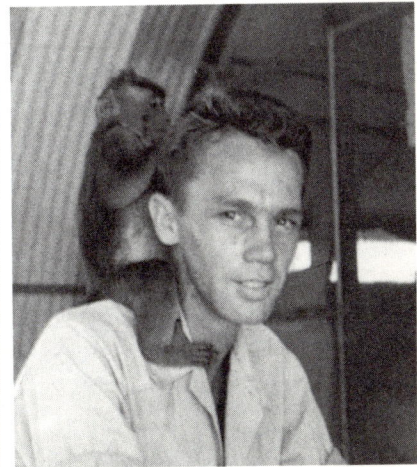

*Lion 4 Advance Base Unit in the South Pacific*

# 33

**WITH THE ENEMY** eradicated from the Admiralty Islands, Lion 4 set out to build a naval base for MacArthur's push to recapture the Philippines—and possibly invade the Empire of Japan. Seeadler Harbor was an outstanding facility. Its hook-shaped geography prevented enemy access except through a heavily guarded entrance between the two small islands of Ndrilo and Hauwei. Ndrilo—two miles long by one mile wide—was just five miles across the bay from Lorengau. In the absence of any immediate threat, Lion 4 searched for unexploded ordnance, placed sensitive magnetometers below the harbor entrance, and demagnetized countless ships.

On December 24, 1944, the men gathered around their radios to listen to President Roosevelt:

> It is not easy to say "Merry Christmas" to you, my fellow Americans, in this time of destructive war. Here, at home, we will celebrate this Christmas Day in our traditional American way because of its deep spiritual meaning to us; because the teachings of Christ are fundamental in our lives; and because we want our youngest generation to grow up knowing the significance of this tradition and the story of the coming of the immortal Prince of Peace and Good Will.
>
> The Christmas spirit lives tonight in the bitter cold of the front lines in Europe and in the heat of the jungles and swamps of Burma and the Pacific islands.
>
> We pray that with victory will come a new day of peace on earth in which all the Nations of the earth will join together for all time. That is the spirit of Christmas, the holy day. May that spirit live and grow throughout the world in all the years to come.

The men dolefully ate their rations and dwelt on the ghosts of Christmas past as the radio played Glenn Miller and the Andrews Sisters' "Don't Sit

Under the Apple Tree." After the song was over, they were stunned by a heartrending announcement:

> Major Glenn Miller, the well-known American bandleader, is reported missing. He left England by air for Paris nine days ago. Major Glenn Miller came over from the States early this year to direct the American band of the AEF, which has often been heard playing in the Allied Expeditionary Forces program of the BBC.

"Glenn Miller—dead?" asked one of the men incredulously.

The men stopped eating in a spontaneous and reverent moment of silence. A few of them fought back tears. Jack Newkirk was the first to speak.

"I saw him once."

"Really?"

"Yeah."

"When?"

"Senior year. It was an intercollegiate dance in New York—hundreds of girls. Glenn Miller was at one end of the ballroom and Tommy Dorsey was at the other."

"Man, that must have been one hell of a swingin' shindig."

"It was," Jack reminisced. "And no one could swing it like Miller."

★ ★ ★

**DURING THE NEXT** six months, Lion 4 demagnetized hundreds of ships in Seeadler Harbor, many of which went on to fight crucial battles in the South Pacific. In February 1945, U.S. troops recaptured Bataan and stormed Iwo Jima. In March, General MacArthur stood upon the liberated island of Corregidor, thus fulfilling his three-year-old vow of "I shall return."

On April 12, President Roosevelt died at his vacation retreat in Warm Springs, Georgia. While Jack disagreed with many of Roosevelt's policies—especially his merciless attacks on Herbert Hoover—he was more or less the only president whom Jack had ever known. Roosevelt had served during Jack's most formative years—from age twelve to age twenty-five—

and was the reassuring voice of the nation during its darkest times. The death of Franklin D. Roosevelt marked the irrevocable end of an era.

But unbeknownst to all but a handful of scientists and government officials, Roosevelt had secretly acted upon Albert Einstein's ominous letter of August 2, 1939—the placid night Jack and Horace had camped along the Idaho's Snake River Plain after an epic trip between two world's fairs. Shortly thereafter, President Roosevelt authorized an operation called the Manhattan Project—and the world would never be the same.

On the evening of August 6, 1945, a group of dumbfounded young men in the Admiralty Islands listened to a startling announcement blaring over the radio:

> The men who have applied the greatest weapon ever developed, the Atomic Bomb, are closed-mouth, serious, and highly impressed with the world-shaking magnitude of what they've done. We talked with Col. Paul W. Tibbets, Jr. of Miami, Florida, pilot of the B-29 that dropped the first atomic bomb in history. We asked him how he'd felt about it, and he said he didn't feel anything much, but you knew from talking to him that he sensed the meaning of that bombs away. The explosion was a big ball of fire. Anyone not having dark glasses would have received a visual shock several miles away. One of the crew members said "My God" when he saw what had happened:
> 
> "What had been Hiroshima was a white mountain of smoke and when we saw it first it was already up to 25,000 feet. About 1,000 feet off the ground it looked like boiling dust."
> 
> This one bomb is the equivalent of a two-thousand B-29 raid.

At the end of 1945, Jack packed up his sea chest and boarded the troop carrier USS *Comet* (AP-166) for transport back to the United States. As the ship steamed out of Seeadler Harbor, Jack took one last look west toward the lush, green hills of Manus Island. The sunset was a blood-red ball of fire, and somewhere beneath it lay the bones of a Japanese soldier beside two sakura blossoms pressed in wax paper.

A soft tropical breeze blew across the deck of the *Comet*. Jack sat down, removed the katana from its scabbard, and stared at it for several minutes as he idly rubbed the Japanese dog tag between his thumb and forefinger like a string of fifty-two pearls. The sword was soon dotted with drops of salt water, and Jack suddenly realized this was the first time he had shed tears since his twenty-second birthday.

★ ★ ★

**BACK IN NEW YORK CITY,** Janet Newkirk opened a letter from her brother in Houston:

Dear Pen:

I just received a copy of a letter from the American Volunteer Group addressed to you which tells us that Johnny's body was found and reinterred in Baarackpore, India. This may not mean much to you but while I was in the Army I lived there for two years and next to hell I don't know of any place that is filthier, smellier, dirtier, or less desirable for a resting place, even if he is in a United States Military Cemetery.

Whether you asked Dad in accordance with that letter to have his remains removed to New York or Scarsdale (I think St. James the Less), of course involves your and Dad's opinion, but them's my sentiments.

Affectionately, Bobby

★ ★ ★

**IN LATE 1961,** a son was born to former Navy Lt. Jack Newkirk and his wife Carolyn.

Silver-haired Burt cradled the new grandson in his arms and stared deeply into the baby's dark, unblinking eyes.

"I wonder what he will grow up to be," said Burt.

"We're going to name him Johnny," Jack announced.

Burt paused, looked up at his son, and then nodded in tacit understanding.

# PART III

## The Golden Gate

All we have of freedom
All we use or know
This our fathers bought for us,
Long and long ago.

—Rudyard Kipling

# 34

If there's a universal biker's road salute, I have yet to see it. Wrecker and Atch say they wave to passing riders by lifting their fingers off the handgrip. Black Dog raises his hand like he's being sworn in. Bear tells me pretty much anything goes except a fist with the middle finger extended—that's liable to get you stomped. And some riders simply extend their left arm as if to say *gimme some skin, bro!*

But it doesn't matter much on U.S. Highway 50—the "Loneliest Road in America"—because there's hardly anyone here to wave to at all.

I don't mind the distances. The run between Delta, Utah, and Fallon, Nevada, gives a man plenty of time to think. I've got no CDs, no satellite radio, no iPod, and no GPS. So as long as I'm thinking about it, I might as well make up my own salute—an American Biker's Salute:

Take the left hand off the grip and make a fist. Hit your sternum with the thumb side. Then straighten the arm, extend your first two fingers, and point to the asphalt.

I suppose it looks Romanesque, but the message is sincere:

*From my heart to yours, you and I are brothers of the open road.*

I think my biker bros would understand.

Wrecker, Bear, Atch. Julie, Nico, Black Dog. Jazda, Tony, ThorsBlood.

These are my people. And there are six million of us.

From Bellingham, Washington, to Key West, Florida, we ride our bikes with pride. Anyone who sits on a motor and two wheels is part of the brotherhood. Harleys, Beemers, rice-burners—it doesn't matter much in the end. All of us face the same wind and weather. We all share the same risks and rewards. And while we may disagree on the small stuff, at the end of the day we always stand by each other.

The biker is a dimly understood icon of popular American culture. And the spectrum is wide—from rich urban bikers (RUBs) and wannabes (posers) to the outlaw "1-percenters." Some simply see us as a tribe of troglodytes, but we generally reflect a broad cross-section of America. Consider the enigmatic Chris Langan (a burly Harley rider with one of the highest IQs on the planet), Senator Ben Nighthorse Campbell, the Reverend Chuck Swindoll, capitalist Malcom Forbes, singer Billy Joel, and host Jay Leno—all the way down to *Raising Arizona*'s proverbial "warthog from hell." Proud, independent, opinionated, and free, we don't go looking for trouble—but we don't back down if trouble comes to us.

Like anything else, there's always a marginal element that makes the rest of us look bad, but by and large the riding community stands for freedom, honor, and above all—respect. We can argue all day about politics or religion and still remain friends—but sit on a man's bike without asking and you've committed a cardinal sin.

To "ride bitch" means to travel as a passenger on a motorcycle, regardless of gender. A "greybeard" is an older biker—bearded or otherwise—who's earned his respect from many years on the road. And "bro" is probably one of the more misused terms of endearment, often tossed around by RUBs or posers looking for a fast track into the biker community. Some bikers have become hypersensitive about this.

"Hey bro. This seat taken?"

"What? Did you just call me 'bro'? Listen—I am not and will probably never be your bro. You've never bailed me out of jail, helped fix my bike in the rain, or stood up for me in a fight. So don't you call me 'bro'—ever!"

The term "ride safe" reflects a sincere wish from one biker to another for safe travel to his final destination. It's seldom used among strangers and is considered disingenuous if said too soon. "Ride safe" means more than just watching out for "cagers" (car drivers). It's more like a reluctant goodbye—as in *vaya con Dios*.

★ ★ ★

**I PULLED OFF** Highway 50 just inside the Nevada border and topped off my gas tank. As I sat in the shade nursing a Gatorade, a couple pulled up in a new Ford Powerstroke dually. They towed an oversized Savanna trailer—the kind with a slide-out living room and satellite antenna. They walked into the station and left their little brown dachshund inside the cab.

They returned a few minutes later and to their horror discovered all four doors had locked with the keys in the ignition. The woman grew frantic as the minutes ticked by, and the dog grew more and more lethargic in the sweltering heat.

*Help the next fellow on down the road.*

That's what the Old Man always said.

I put down my drink and walked toward the distressed couple.

Just then a police car drove up. *Problem solved,* I thought, and turned back to the Harley.

"Officer?" the woman asked. "We're locked out and our dog's inside—can you get us in?"

"Sorry, ma'am. We're not allowed to break into vehicles anymore. It's a liability issue. I can call AAA or get a tow truck—best I can do."

*Oh, for cryin' out loud. We're a hundred miles east of Buzzard Breath, Nevada. It'd take hours to get someone out here. By that time, these poor folks will have a roasted wiener-dog.*

The cruiser drove off in a cloud of dust. I stood up again and walked over to the truck as the couple eyed me nervously.

"You wouldn't have a cat in the trailer, would you?" I joked. "Maybe if we held it to the window, the dog would get excited enough to jump on the power-lock button."

The man managed a slight smile.

"No cats, I'm afraid."

"Well, let's see what we can do about unlocking your rig. I've got some tools in my bike."

"I'd appreciate that," he said. "Name's Bob Turner, by the way."

"My friends call me Johnny," I replied.

"You headed west?"

"Yes—to San Francisco."

"No kidding? That's where I'm going."

A man named Russ came over and offered the use of his cordless drill.

"Maybe," he suggested, "you could drill into the rear window latch and slide it open."

"Worth a try," I replied. "But I'd hate to chew up this man's cherry truck with a drill bit. Could you go inside and see if they have a clothes hanger? We can fish it through the door trim and try to hit the unlock button. I've done this a few times with my own Ford."

I grabbed the toolkit from the Harley as Russ went inside. Back at the truck, the dachshund panted and stared listlessly out the window as its tongue lolled and dripped saliva. The little bugger was starting to grow on me—he just might fit in the leather pouch behind my windscreen.

Russ emerged with a hanger. I fashioned it into a makeshift poker and wrapped my flathead screwdriver in a shop rag so it wouldn't chip Bob's paint. I worked the poker as Russ pried the door. After a couple of minutes we heard a dull *thunk*.

The truck's alarm howled in protest.

"We got it!" Russ exclaimed.

"Thank God," sighed Bob and his wife in unison.

A blast of hot air greeted us as we opened the door and scooped out the dog.

"Thanks a million," Bob said. "Can I buy you a beer or anything?"

"Oh no," I replied, "I already have a drink, thank you."

"Wish I could repay you somehow," he persisted.

"You can," I said. "Just help the next fellow on down the road. That's the code."

"What code?" Bob asked.

"The Biker's Code—my people," I explained. "We always look out for each other."

I walked back to the Harley to study my new *State Farm Road Atlas*. It was going to be a long, hot ride across Nevada. Fine by me.

I don't mind the distances.

Plenty of thinking time—and plenty of time to remember.

★ ★ ★

**THE OLD MAN** first put me on the back of a bike when I was six. I clung to him like a baby chimp, but after a few miles realized it was a stable platform with an exhilarating vantage point.

At age eight I joined the Cub Scouts. Our den mother was also the mother of a classmate of mine, Russell Hester. One night Russell and I went to his garage and looked at the family's lineup of motorcycles. I was awestruck—it never occurred to me they made bikes small enough for kids to ride. Russell had a candy-red Honda Z-50 Mini Trail and his brother had a CT-70. The shiny chrome, brilliant reflectors, and polished aluminum were hypnotic, and during the next few months I could think of little else. I began to pester my father for a mini-bike of my own, and several weeks later I overheard him discussing it with my mother. He said something about my being "born to the breed."

"But he's only eight," she protested.

★ ★ ★

**THWACK!**

Something hit my shin hard enough to give me a welt through the leather chaps.

*Thwack! Thwack!*

I pulled off the road near the crumbling Pony Express station at Cold Springs, Nevada, where the highway crawled with stubby, six-legged bugs as big as my thumb.

An invasion of Mormon crickets, I was told—*Anabrus simplex.*

Something like the Old Man's South Dakota grasshopper plague in 1939.

I set up camp outside Fallon, Nevada, and rode into town for dinner. The place was full of young pilots from the Naval Weapons Fighter School—TOPGUN—and I wondered if any of these kids had heard of a naval aviator off the USS *Yorktown* by the name of Scarsdale Jack.

The next morning I headed southwest toward Carson City. The temperatures were already in the nineties, but a mile-a-minute breeze made for an agreeable ride.

I was only a day away.

In twenty-four hours I'd be at the Golden Gate.

★ ★ ★

**I SUPPOSE AGE EIGHT** was a tipping point in my life. Besides becoming aware of two-wheeled motorized vehicles, it was also the year the Old Man announced we'd be moving to a ranch west of Denver. The distances around the spread were large, and I used this as yet another reason why I had to have a mini-bike.

It was also the first time I remember hearing what the Old Man called the "voices of my conscience." It was nothing audible—nothing schizophrenic, creepy, or outside the head. No, these voices were much more subtle. One was benevolent and kind. The other was insidious, shadowy, and alarmingly appealing. The first time I remember it was on the playground.

Janet Weismiller was a crippled girl in my third grade class—born with some disease our teacher called "the palsy." When she wasn't wearing her protective helmet, Janet looked remarkably like Shirley Temple, complete with cherubic face, curly brown hair, and dimples. And despite her affliction, Janet was always full of laughter and smiles.

But before she could go anywhere, Janet had to put on a complicated array of crutches, braces, and other contraptions designed to protect her from a fall and help her function more like the rest of us. A wave of compassion swept over me the first time I saw her shambling down the hall toward the lunchroom, hobbled by her *impedimenta* like a ballerina from Vonnegut's *Harrison Bergeron*. From that day forward I made a point of sticking close to her. I carried her books, opened her doors, and fetched her lunch tray. It seemed the proper thing to do.

One winter's day a group of boys encircled me on the playground.

*Johnny loves Janet! Johnny loves Janet! Johnny loves Janet!*

I suppose, as much as an eight-year-old can understand these things, I did love Janet. What I didn't understand was how love could sound like such a bad thing.

That's when I heard them.

*Ignore those boys*, said one voice, *it doesn't matter what they think.*

*You're a sissy*, said the other, *and nobody likes you. Especially when you hang with cripples.*

The boys continued their taunts and tears welled up in my eyes.

*Johnny loves Janet! Johnny loves Janet! Johnny loves Janet!*

I stared at the ground and felt like the rope in a tug of war.

*Johnny loves Janet! Johnny loves Janet! Johnny loves Janet!*

"I do not love her!" I finally shouted in frustration.

"Do too!" jeered Stewey Madison. "We saw you carrying her books and tray!"

I ran off the playground and into the lunchroom. Janet was inside, ready to make her way back to class.

"Hi," she beamed, "want to walk back with me?"

"No!" I snapped, "and I'm not going to carry your books anymore, open your doors, or anything else!"

"What's wrong, Johnny?" she asked as her face crumbled.

"Nothing!" I shouted. "Just don't bother me anymore."

She burst into tears as I walked away.

Later that night I thought about what I'd done. Life had dealt poor Janet Weismiller a pretty tough hand—and now I'd just broken her little heart.

After the Christmas break, I tried to find her to apologize, but discovered her parents had transferred her to a school more suitable to her needs.

While I'd go on to make more mistakes, from that day forward I was far less inclined to let others dictate my actions—especially when I knew what was right. The lesson was a victory of sorts, but it had come at a high price. And like the rattlesnake—the dreaded *crotalus horridus*—the temptation to violate my conscience would rear its head for years to come.

★ ★ ★

**U.S. ROUTE 395** is a north-south highway that runs through some of the most spectacular and rugged scenery in the American West. In the 1930s this road stretched from the Canadian border at Laurier, Washington, all the way to San Diego, where it merged with Highway 101 several miles north of Mexico. Significant portions of the highway were still unpaved when the Old Man followed this road down the Columbia River in 1939.

I got on Route 395 south of Carson City. It wasn't the most direct way to San Francisco, but it ran to Yosemite National Park, where the

Old Man had taken his enlisted men on a wilderness excursion just before they left for the jungles of the South Pacific.

★ ★ ★

**I WAS NINE** the summer we moved to the ranch. Obsessed with mini-bikes, I called every dealer in the Metro Yellow Pages and asked the price of their least expensive unit. More than one dealer addressed me as "ma'am" until they learned I was simply a wishful, fourth-grade boy.

One sunny afternoon the Old Man dropped my dog and me off at the local golf course. He gave me a dollar to buy some treats at the snack shack while he ran errands. As I stood in the shade eating chocolate-covered raisins, a soft puttering sound drifted up from the creek. A short time later, two boys rode up the bank on brand new Honda CT-70 trail bikes. Their engines idled as I gawked at their mud-spattered bikes.

They had everything I ever wanted—freedom, friendship, and endless country where they could ride their new mini-bikes. I could hardly contain myself—and the voices of conscience once again came to the surface.

*Talk with them,* said one, *offer them some of your raisins.*

*You'll never have what they have,* taunted the other. *They're privileged, you're not, and you never will be—those rich, spoiled brats! They don't care about anything but themselves!*

Resist though I might, I was soon awash in envy.

"Sick 'em, Trixie, sick 'em!" I shouted.

My terrier ran over and nipped their ankles. They kicked the dog, shifted into gear, then rode over and stopped in front of me. With a justifiable look of anger, they spat in my face and rode off in a cloud of dust.

When Dad returned, I cried to him about the "mean boys on the mini-bikes." He listened patiently to my side of the story and then gave me a lecture I wouldn't soon forget.

"Johnny, did you ever think about being nice to them?"

"No," I sniffed. "It's just that they had mini-bikes and I didn't."

"Son," he continued, "more often than not, people will be your friends if you give them the chance. You blew it this time. They probably would have offered you a ride."

He was right, of course. As with Janet Weismiller, I had followed the wrong voice.

Another screwup, but another lesson learned.

Three weeks later the Old Man pulled up in a trailer with a beat-up 1969 Vespa 50cc motor scooter. It wasn't exactly what I'd had in mind, but it had two wheels, a functional engine, and a headlight. Over the next two years, I rode that scooter in places its designers never intended.

The Vespa taught me how to repair a flat, troubleshoot an ignition, and tear down and rebuild engine components. When it finally succumbed to wear and tear, the Old Man promised me a modern trail bike if I kept up with chores and got good grades in school. I spent much of that winter drooling over the tattered brochure of a Suzuki Model TC-90—a single cylinder, two-stroke with dual gear ranges. It cost $399. I spent hours memorizing its specs and dreaming of mountain trails and fields of grass—and I didn't dare let my grades slip or slack off on chores. After school let out, I could hardly sleep the night before we picked it up.

For rural, pre-teen boys with mini-bikes, summer in the Rocky Mountains was heaven on earth. Like Roy Rogers and Trigger or the Lone Ranger and Silver, we began to associate each other with what we rode. Freddy Linneman had a Honda SL-70. Bobby Bukovic rode a CT-90 and Steve Oubre had an Elsinore 125. Alan Kinard's QA-50 didn't even come with a headlight, but he sat on it like he was king of the world. Jesse Roux raced motocross, and Ric Morr's SL-70 was almost like Freddy's. Tom Bellwood had a Suzuki TC-90 identical to mine, and Steve McCasland rode a Chaparral 80.

We learned how to avoid the county sheriff by sticking to dirt roads and trails; if it wasn't paved, it was fair game. Our fathers, of course, forbid us to ride on pavement. When we did have to cross asphalt, we'd always get off and push.

Our domain expanded immeasurably when we finally figured out how to reach the South Platte River by following old stagecoach roads and railroad beds. From the Platte, we could ride hundreds of miles through the Pike National Forest. When we ran low on fuel, we'd refill our tanks at an unmanned, coin-operated gas pump near Sprucewood—and we never left home without a few quarters in our pockets.

One summer's day Steve Oubre, Alan Kinard, and I set out to explore the area around West Bear Creek where we spent the day riding, swimming, eating, and bickering along the riverbank. The sun was low when we started for home twenty miles away. Steve and Alan typically rode faster than I did, and within a few minutes they were half a mile ahead in the forest. The trail went down an embankment and through a small creek. I hit a fallen aspen tree on the opposite side of the creek and dumped my motorcycle with its wheels facing uphill. Gas began to dribble from the gas cap and the engine stalled as I crawled—unhurt—out from under the bike.

All I could hear were the creek, the breeze through the aspen trees, and the fading sound of two mini-bikes a half-mile away. I tried to heft the motorcycle right side up, but it outweighed me by two to one, and my eleven-year-old legs weren't up to the job.

A raven uttered a raucous gurgle above me from its perch in a Ponderosa pine.

*Idiot,* some voice taunted, *now you're gonna spend the night here.*

I began to cry. I could walk out, but it was getting dark, and I was reluctant to leave my bike. Even on its side, it provided at least some semblance of civilization.

The faint putter of engines still floated through the forest, but there was something different this time. The sound wasn't moving away anymore—it was getting closer. Within a few minutes, my friends arrived on the scene and together we lifted my motorcycle upright.

I didn't know it at the time, but Alan and Steve had just become my first biker brothers—my "bros"—and had demonstrated one of the fundamental tenets of the Biker's Code:

*Never leave a brother behind.*

# 35

THE TEMPERATURE WAS 107 as my Harley descended the winding hills of Route 120 onto the brown, parched fields of California's San Joaquin Valley. One careless cigarette butt could turn this tinderbox into a wildfire. After two days on Highway 50, Silicon Valley rush hour between Fremont and Milpitas came as a shock. Interstate 680 was jam-packed with commuters and I hadn't seen another biker since Yosemite.

A bright light suddenly appeared in my rearview mirror—another Harley! The bike sped confidently between the cars as I remembered it was legal to split lanes here. The rider pulled up beside me. I looked over and saw long blond hair billowing from beneath a reflective helmet. I gave her an American Biker's Salute. She waved for me to follow. The presence of another biker in this heavy traffic was a balm to my frayed nerves, and we rode together until she exited at the Montague Expressway.

I made my way to San Jose where my former college roommate Robert lived with his wife, Judy. They put me up for the night, and I took a much needed shower. Judy gave me maps of the Bay Area, and I memorized as much as possible so I wouldn't have to stop every few blocks.

"So when do you officially start retracing?" asked Robert.

"Tomorrow," I replied. "First I'll ride around the Embarcadero and Treasure Island, then head north to the Golden Gate."

"Traffic shouldn't be bad on a Saturday," said Judy. "Have you spent much time in the city?"

"No," I said, "but it's got a lot of family history."

"And where do you pick up the Old Man?" Robert inquired.

"Montana."

"Why aren't you meeting him in San Francisco?"

"He's in his eighties, Bob. We'll be lucky to make the fifteen hundred miles we've got planned."

"I see. So you'll retrace—in reverse—his route between the 1939 New

York and San Francisco Fairs and pick him up on the road. How'd you decide which part he would ride?"

"I wanted him to see the heartland one last time. And we have to hit Sturgis. He said he had an old promise to keep."

The next morning I rode up the Junipero Serra Freeway to San Francisco's South of Market area and headed toward Union Square. A shiver ran down my spine as I stopped at the corner of Powell and Geary.

I recognized the façade from old photos.

The Elkan Gunst Building still stood, but the elegant restaurant it once held was long gone. A lump rose in my throat as I imagined Scarsdale Jack and his new bride laughing and dancing inside the Golden Pheasant Restaurant on July 9, 1941—blissfully unaware it would be their last night together.

The resentment brewing inside of me caught me by surprise.

*You could have known him,* something whispered, *if those Japanese hadn't killed him.*

I fired up the Harley and continued down Geary to Van Ness, then turned south and stopped in front of the War Memorial Opera House and Davies Symphony Hall.

★ ★ ★

**BY THE TIME** I was twelve, most of my mini-bike friends knew the local trails and back roads by heart. We gave names to landmarks and paths: Crack Rock, Butterfly Rock, the Whopper, the Dunn's Trail, the Grange Trail, the Woods Road, and Lover's Lane. The Front Range was our frontier, we were its cowboys, and our mini-bikes were the ponies. We carefully polished the chrome, lubricated the chains, and changed the oil religiously—as if the bikes themselves lived and breathed.

It seemed we'd just settled in when my father announced he had a one-year research job at the Cavendish Laboratory in Cambridge, England. It was bittersweet to leave Steve, Tommy, Alan, Bobby, Jesse, and Freddy, but mostly I'd miss that two-hundred-pound, two-wheeled pony.

At the British schools we wore uniforms, prayed before meals, and took careful notice of the long, thin cane behind our teacher's desk. As luck would have it, I arrived just as the class was to be taught the facts of life. Our teacher was a stodgy old coot named Mr. Eaton who, when describing the male member, actually used the term "tallywhacker."

"Any questions?" he finally asked our mortified class.

I happened to be scratching my head.

"Yes, Mr. Newkirk?"

"No questions, sir!" I gasped.

A couple of my British friends were choristers in the highly regarded King's College Choir. On weekends we'd take a double-decker bus to the theater near Market Square and then head off to King's College Chapel, where they'd sing in Choral Evensong as I listened from the stalls. The year in England had a major effect on my cultural education, and I came away with an affinity for classical music and British writers—as well as a slight East Anglican accent.

Back in America I returned to a routine of mini-bikes, chores, and schoolwork. When it came time to select a band instrument, it seemed a matter of practicality more than anything else. I couldn't see hefting a forty-pound tuba three miles to and from the bus stop each day. Even a clarinet or trumpet would get heavy—and neither would fit in a backpack with my books.

I asked for the smallest instrument available and the band director told me it was the flute. Its sound reminded me of the young voices I'd heard in King's College Chapel.

My choice brought immediate scorn from some of the boys.

"Newkirk, you fairy! Flute's a girly instrument. Only girls play flute, you sissy."

But my biker mentality was well into its development—and I wasn't about to take any guff from the football players.

"That's right, Nimrod," I shot back, "only girls play flute. So for the next few years you'll be sitting with the likes of Spinzig and Molsberry here. I'll be surrounded by cute girls. So blow that out your saxophone."

They looked over at Joey Molsberry, who had his index finger in his nose.

"Besides," I continued, "Kwai Chang Caine plays flute. You gonna call *him* a sissy?"

After a few years' practice I began to win some contests, and at seventeen I soloed with the National Repertory Orchestra under Carl Topilow, who had recently won the prestigious Exxon Arts Endowment competition on PBS.

He scared the bejeebers out of me.

Maestro Topilow was a professional—a world-class conductor and performer. I was an amateur and didn't want to embarrass him or his orchestra.

My piece was the Mozart Flute Concerto No. 2 in D major. As the strings and horn section played the opening strains, a nagging voice reared its head and shook its rattle.

*Just who do you think you are? You don't belong on this stage. You're just an imposter.*

The biker in me rose to the surface again, and I ignored the insidious voice of doubt. The performance turned out to be one of my better ones. It was also one of my last.

The classical experience exposed me to some gifted musicians—Jean-Pierre Rampal, Eugene Fodor, Michaela Paetsch—and it soon became clear that if I practiced very hard I might become good, but I would never be truly great. Content to keep music as a hobby, I entered engineering school that fall.

★ ★ ★

**I RUMBLED AWAY** from Davies Symphony Hall and parked the Harley at an outdoor Internet café near the former Hotel Bellevue. It was Saturday, July 16 and I had no set schedule. Places were much more important than dates on this trip.

The street was beginning to fill up with cars and pedestrians.

I felt another chill.

*Scarsdale stood here just before he got on the* Jagersfontein. *The Old Man was here before he got on the* Bloem. *Horace was at the naval shipyard, and in 1906 Burt walked down this street helping the earthquake victims.*

★ ★ ★

**I FIRST HEARD** about Scarsdale Jack when my schoolmate, Mike Vandeweghe, showed me a paperback entitled *The Flying Tigers* by Russell Whelan. He said the leader of the Second Pursuit Squadron—the Panda Bears—had the same name as I did and wanted to know if I was related.

"I don't know," I said, "I'll ask my dad."

Later that night I did just that.

My father got a far-off look in his eyes and remained silent for a while.

"Yes," he finally said. "Everyone knew about Scarsdale Jack."

He took me to the basement, moved aside several cardboard boxes, and pulled out a dust-covered, oblong sea chest. The surface bore faint, black stencil marks:

Ens. J. B. Newkirk, USN

A musty smell wafted up as he opened the chest. He took out an old uniform, a Samurai sword, a piece of brass engraved with strange characters, and a partial clip of 6.5 x 50mm rifle cartridges.

"Why is one of the bullets missing?" I asked.

He looked down at the floor as if he wished he'd never opened this Pandora's box.

"It's a long story," he said. "I'll tell you sometime, just not today."

"So tell me about Scarsdale Jack," I persisted. "Tell me some stories of the war."

"Maybe later," he sighed as he closed the box. "You read your friend's book first. Then someday I'll tell you the rest of the story."

I picked up the sword, pulled it out of its sheath, and slowly waved it through the air like Luke Skywalker in the house of Obi-Wan Kenobi.

"Careful," my father said. "That could take your head off."

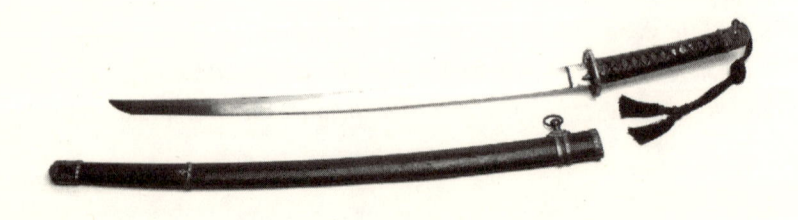

*Lower Manhattan (New Amsterdam) at the time of the
Moesman's arrival in 1659.*

Courtesy of the New York Historical Society

TRYLON AND PERISPHERE—*the two indelible icons of the 1939 New York World's Fair. Twin bridges across the Grand Central Parkway connect the main fairgrounds to the Transportation Zone. In the distance, the Empire State Building towers over Lower Manhattan.*

Courtesy of the New York Public Library

"Speed"

New York World's Fair 1939

*The World's Fair* Speed *statue symbolized the "rapidity with which human thought may be transmitted" through the modern marvels of radio, telephone—and a new technology called television.*

Created by the Grinnell Litho Company

*Harley-Davidson VL Big Twin No. 30V8229C—the "Raspberry."*

1939 Kodachrome slide from author's collection.

*Jack Newkirk and the "Raspberry" in Portland, Oregon on July 14, 1939.*

Photo by Walter Smith

*Pete Pomeroy with Harley-Davidson Model 61EL Knuckleheads along the Redwood Highway.*

*A Boeing 314 Clipper flies over the 1939 Golden Gate Exposition on Treasure Island. To the left, Pier 33 reaches toward Alcatraz as the two-year-old Golden Gate Bridge spans the entrance to San Francisco Bay.*

Photo by Pacific Aerial Serial Surveys, Oakland, CA

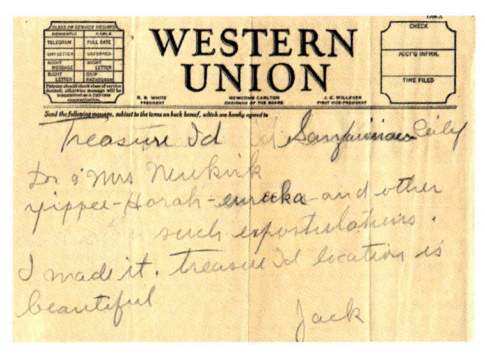

*A triumphant Jack Newkirk, June Carlson, and Pete Pomeroy explore San Francisco's Golden Gate International Exposition.*

Crotalus horridus *taken on the eve of World War II.*

*Claire L. Chennault,*
*Group Commander (L),*
*"Scarsdale Jack" Newkirk,*
*Squadron Leader (R)*

@ Flying Tigers Association
Used by permission.

*Greg "Pappy" Boyington* 　　*David Lee "Tex" Hill* 　　*Allen "Bert" Christman*

*AVG Flying Tigers patrol the China-Burma border in 1942.*

Photo by R. T. Smith @ Brad Smith. Used by permission.

"Scarsdale Jack" as idealized by comic books of the day.

From Zip Comics, August 1942

*A chance encounter with C. Alfred "Chief" Anderson of the Tuskegee Airmen.*

Aerial photo by Lucian Bartosik

*And after nearly seven decades, an Old Man keeps an old promise.*

\* \* \*

**I LINGERED AT** the Internet café longer than necessary as I subconsciously postponed the inevitable. Finally I took a deep breath, climbed onto the Harley, and rumbled toward the waterfront as if riding into battle. I rode to the crest of the Golden Gate Bridge, where the ghost of a young blonde had been patiently waiting for me. She wore a string of pearls—and I could swear I heard the foghorn of the *Jagersfontein*.

San Francisco.

New York City.

No two places have influenced my forefathers more than these. I wondered how they would influence me—and a somber group of Japanese monks gathering at Pier 33 would soon help me answer that question.

# 36

TREASURE ISLAND WAS originally built to host the 1939 San Francisco Golden Gate International Exposition. After Pearl Harbor the U.S. Navy seized the island in a "declaration of taking and deposit" to establish a base for "protection of navigation and commerce" and for "preparing and receiving and forwarding men to naval duty." During World War II the island served as the major departure point for sailors in the Pacific theater.

On September 30, 1997, the naval station was closed and the island returned to civilian use—but just a decade after the base closure, Treasure Island had the appearance of a ghost town.

I rode the Harley through its abandoned streets, derelict buildings, and dilapidated housing complexes. A boarded-up movie theater sat across from a ruined bowling alley. It felt like I'd stumbled onto an apocalyptic set of *Half Life 2: The Movie.*

I tried to imagine the Old Man as a fresh-faced nineteen-year-old standing underneath the Tower of the Sun with Pete Pomeroy and his friend June, none of them knowing that a few short years later young Jack would return to this place as a soldier. As I rumbled through what had been the Court of Reflections, I realized I had much reflecting to do myself. The peace rally at Pier 33 had shaken me to the core. The old Japanese man had seen right through my bitterness and resentment and I was emotionally exhausted.

I parked the Harley under a forlorn row of palm trees and stared into San Francisco Bay. Treasure Island was no more the glittering Pageant of the Pacific.

It was a wilderness.

★ ★ ★

**ONE SUNNY SUNDAY MORNING** when I was about twelve, I had been dragged out of bed with much grumbling on my part. I didn't want to go to church. I wanted to ride my mini-bike with the other boys. I fidgeted, stared out the church window, and looked at my watch, eager to get out and ride while the weather was good.

The preacher talked about Jesus Christ spending forty days in the wilderness, during which he heard a number of profane "voices" tempting him to do things contrary to what he knew was right. The preacher said these voices mixed truth with lies in a profound understanding of human weakness that—to this day—is used to confuse and attack us.

My ears perked up.

He then spoke about the apostle Peter: it seems when everything hit the fan and Christ was about to be crucified, Peter got cold feet and—on three separate occasions—shouted "I don't know him!"

*I'd never do that*, I thought self-righteously from the church pew, *Jesus was cool, hanging with the outcasts and all. If he came today, I think he'd come as a biker. I'd have treated him like a biker bro—and we always stand by each other.*

Three decades later I finally understood what the preacher had been talking about.

I've always counted myself among the majority of bikers who believe in the "Man Upstairs." But all I could think of now was my bitterness at Pier 33 and how readily I chose the low road.

I had gloated over the Allied victory in World War II.

I had mocked a group of Japanese monks who came in peace.

And I had dissed a couple of guys who simply asked for directions.

Three times—I might as well have shouted, "I don't know him!"

And I realized then that I was no better than Peter.

Burt, Horace, Scarsdale, the Old Man—all men of faith. They wouldn't be proud of me.

They'd be ashamed.

My face was fraught with fatigue as I rode back toward the exit of Treasure Island where a man at a small kiosk was selling postcards, film, and newspapers. As an afterthought, I pulled over to buy some postcards to send home.

The proprietor was an old Chinese man speaking Mandarin to another man who casually leaned against the booth. After selecting a couple of cards, I approached the register to pay. The old man nodded politely at first—but then did a double take the likes of which I'd never seen.

"*Fei hu!*" he gasped, staring at the AVG patches on my leathers.

Both Chinese men looked at each other as if they'd seen a ghost.

"*Fei hu!*" he repeated, "Flying Tiger?!"

"Yes," I replied pointing to my patches. "The Flying Tigers. I wear these in honor of Scarsdale Jack Newkirk, leader of the Panda Bear squadron. He was killed defending the Chinese in 1942. He was a cousin."

The old men became animated and chattered wildly in their native tongue. One of them turned to me and babbled in broken English as he grabbed my hands and shook them firmly.

"I from Yunnan Province—Kunming! You come to China—they treat you like hero for what you did!"

"But I did nothing," I replied. "I only share the name."

"But your family, your people—you only ones who save us from Japanese!"

The old man began to weep.

"Japanese bombs hit my family. Kill my mother. Then Flying Tigers come and no more bombs."

His frail body was overcome with emotion. He embraced me, and his tears soaked into my leathers.

"China still teach children about Flying Tigers in school," he sobbed. "You tell your people China never forget what you did."

★ ★ ★

**FROM THE GHOSTS** of the Golden Gate to the Atomic Flame to the Chinese survivors—this had been one of the most surreal days of my life. I made camp north of the Golden Gate and listened to the waves gently lap against the shore. Although I wouldn't pick up the Old Man for another fifteen hundred miles, I knew for sure now that I wasn't riding alone—Burt, Horace, Scarsdale, the Old Man. In a very real way, I felt as if they were all riding with me.

It was as if they wanted to show me something.

★ ★ ★

**FOG BLANKETED THE BAY** as I broke camp early the next morning. I rode across the Golden Gate Bridge one last time, then pointed the Harley northward and headed up Highway 1.

At Bodega Bay I turned inland to Santa Rosa where I planned to visit Horace's daughter—my cousin Nadenia Newkirk. Arriving early, I stopped at a Starbucks on D Street and parked the Harley face out. I went inside, bought a bagel, then sat down and watched through the window as a half-dozen bikers pulled up to another coffee shop across the street.

I'd just started to read the newspaper when a man and his two young children climbed into an SUV parked in front of my bike. His kids were fighting and I could see the man yell at them as he threw his car into reverse. I watched in horror as he backed up and crashed into my Harley, causing the bike to skid and teeter like a balanced rock.

All hell broke loose.

The bike's alarm howled and the lights flashed. The bikers across the street stood up and walked briskly toward the SUV's path of retreat. This would be no hit and run.

I jumped up—bagel in hand—and walked out the door.

At just under six feet and one hundred seventy-five pounds, I'm not exactly built like a linebacker. But a biker dressed in leathers and covered with patches usually evokes apprehension from just about anyone. From his shocked expression, I could tell I scared the heck out of this guy.

I walked straight toward him, took one last bite of my bagel, and tossed the remains into the trashcan for effect.

Voices began to tussle in my mind like two dogs tugging on a rag.

*Stupid yuppie doofus! He walked past your bike twice and now he's gonna expect you to believe he never saw it. Rip into him! Make an example of him and impress those bikers. Grab him by the collar and shove him against the SUV!*

But I remembered my failure at Pier 33 twenty-four hours earlier.

The street grew quiet. All eyes were upon me. I was on center stage and I knew it. The six bikers across the street stood at the ready—out of range, but watching my body language.

"You OK, bud?" I asked the shaken-up driver. "You look a little pale."

"I am so sorry, man," he said. "My kids were screaming and I was totally out of it."

"Yeah, I know what you mean," I agreed. "I've got a couple of those things myself."

The man put his hand to his forehead, then turned and leaned against his car.

"I can't believe I hit your bike!" he moaned. "I am so sorry!"

"Well," I said, "it doesn't look like there's any damage. Your spare tire just hit my handlebars and skidded the bike a little."

"Oh man," he sighed, "I thought you were going to kick my ass."

"Hey, it's just a machine," I said as I patted the man on the shoulder. "Machines are replaceable. People aren't. I'm sure from now on you'll be keeping an eye out for my biker brothers—both parked and on the road."

The bikers across the street stood down and walked back to their coffee; the other onlookers went back about their business.

"Thanks for your understanding," he said. "I really screwed up."

"So is that a 'Semper Fi' sticker I saw on your bumper?" I asked.

"Yeah," he said. "My stepson. He's in the Marine Corps."

"Do me a favor, will you? Tell him he's got the respect of a grateful American."

"Hey, I'll do that. Thanks, man."

"And don't forget to keep an eye out for motorcycles."

"I will," he promised, then got into his car and drove off.

"Hey bro," shouted one of the greybeard bikers from across the street, "come park by us!"

And for a moment, in the back of my mind, I thought I could hear three or four voices cheering.

★ ★ ★

**I CONTINUED NORTH** on Highway 1 past Point Arena. It was hard to imagine the Old Man had ridden all the way from the Golden Gate Bridge to Portland, Oregon, on this road at thirty miles per hour after a mechanic had told him the Raspberry's "loose pistons" were about to fail. I slowed down to thirty—and envied the Old Man's slower pace along this stunning stretch of highway.

I stopped for gas at the coastal village Elk, California, and struck up a conversation with two sisters named Cee J and Candice who ran the café, country store, and inn called the Greenwood Pier. Cee J was an attractive, long-haired brunette who radiated health and vitality. She walked me around the grounds to a spectacular overlook of the ocean, which, she informed me, had been voted one of the "Best Places to Kiss in Northern California."

"So you're headed north?" she asked.

"Yes," I replied. "For as long as I can keep my eyes open. About this time in the afternoon I usually have to eat some junk food or slam down a few caffeinated drinks to stay alert. You sell that stuff in your store?"

"Argh!" Cee J exclaimed. "Don't put that garbage into your body. Here, wait just a minute."

She ran inside, came out with pen and paper, and began to draw a complex map with mailboxes, trees, and ocean as reference points.

"Now let me show you something," she said gaily. "This is my favorite swimming hole on the Navarro River. I usually don't tell anyone about it, but you go up there and jump in the water. That'll do the trick."

I gave her an American Biker's Salute and headed off. After a few miles I turned inland and followed the river through a stand of redwoods and parked the Harley in the fern-carpeted forest. Cee J's map led me down a faded path to the riverbank where I peeled off my leathers and jumped—headfirst and buck-naked—into the cool, clear water of the Navarro.

Later that afternoon I happened upon some kind of carnival near Ft. Bragg. A handful of vendors hawked sports drinks, shoes, and fitness gear to passersby. At one of the booths was a blond kid in dreadlocks selling strawberry-banana smoothies at four bucks a pop.

He was clearly an extrovert—broad smile, animated conversation, and a valley-voice that reminded me of Crush, the "totally awesome" sea turtle from the movie *Finding Nemo*. The kid wore a T-shirt emblazoned with an iconic, messianic figure in a beret, who gazed at some far-off vista as if struggling valiantly toward a revolutionary nirvana. Parked behind his booth was a new compact crossover SUV—a Honda Element. As he turned around, I saw the U.S. flag sewn onto the seat of his pants.

I sat down in the shade and listened as he spoke to his customers. He ended each sale with some pearl of wisdom that could have come straight from the leftist manifesto.

"Thanks, dude! Shoot a logger, save a tree!"

"Take care, man. The road to hell is paved with capitalists!"

*All right*, I thought, *that does it. If this trustafarian is going to pollute the environment with his screed, then he can jolly well listen to a biker's take on things.*

I waited for a lull in the crowd and then approached his booth.

"Hey, man," I said. "Could I get one of those?"

"Sure, dude!" he beamed. "Four bucks."

I gave him the money and watched as he plopped a banana, some strawberries, pineapple juice, and ice into his blender. He poured the frozen concoction into a large red cup and gave me a straw. After an all-day ride in the sun, it tasted as sweet as ambrosia.

"You make a great smoothie," I said.

"Thanks. It's all natural, man."

"So this is all organic?"

"For sure! No carcinogens or toxins. I'd never put that kind of crap into my body."

I glanced wryly at the marijuana leaf decal plastered to his bumper.

The kid said he was a junior at UC Berkeley majoring in history and political science. After a couple of minutes, I steered the conversation toward what I was really interested in.

"So why do you wear that T-shirt?"

"That's Che Guevara, man! He's my hero—he's a revolutionary. Hey, you're a biker. Have you ever read *The Motorcycle Diaries*?"

"No, but I read something along those lines a while back. It said 'a revolutionary must become a cold killing machine motivated by pure hate.' He also said 'a people without hate cannot triumph against the adversary.'"

"That sucks, man," he said. "What bunghole said that?"

"Che Guevara," I replied.

"No way," he gasped.

"Way," I said. "Check it out. It's from his 1967 message to the Tricontinental."

"But Che wasn't hateful, man. He stood up for the little guy."

"Guevara? The 'Butcher of La Cabaña?' No, it's more like he stood up the little guys and shot them if they disagreed with his dogma. He oversaw hundreds of executions without due process."

The kid looked uncomfortable. He couldn't be more than nineteen.

"Besides," I continued, "it's not hate that allows us to triumph over the adversary. Hate *is* the adversary. Trust me on this one."

"So, like, what are you saying?"

"I'm saying you'd do well to pick a different hero."

"So who would you choose, man?"

"Well, if you really want a revolutionary, look no further than Thomas Jefferson. For an emancipator, there's Abraham Lincoln."

"Yeah, Lincoln was cool. He freed the slaves."

"For a humanitarian, there's Herbert Hoover."

"Hoover? You got to be kidding! He caused the Depression!"

"Oh, good lord," I laughed. "Is that what they're teaching you? I suppose you could argue, in twenty-twenty hindsight, that Hoover could have done more to mitigate it, but to blame him for the Depression is a gross oversimplification. Even before he was president, Hoover organized hunger relief that would make Bob Geldof look like a weekend hacker. Just Google 'Great Humanitarian' and Herbert Hoover's first on the list."

My intent wasn't to belittle this kid; I just wanted him to think for himself instead of blindly following his academic Svengalis. He made me realize that, as in 1939, youth in America are still hungry for heroes. If none come forward, they'll create their own—as did the Israelites in the barren desert. Guevara has become their golden calf. He is the hot chick across the dance club floor who beckons them with a wink and a nod, and they're in love before they've even met.

Che Guevara lost this biker's respect long, long ago.

"You know," I went on, "you said something to the last guy about free market capitalism. What was it, something about the road to hell?"

"Yeah," he said. "Capitalism only serves the rich by exploiting the little guy."

"I'd respectfully disagree," I countered. "The free market system is what allows the 'little guy' to rise to the top. And frankly, you're one of the best examples I can think of."

"How so, dude?"

"The banana costs you fifty cents. Juice and berries, about the same. The ice is negligible, and when you amortize your blender and other equipment, and figure time and overhead, I'd say you've got less than two bucks into each smoothie. You charge double that, and I'm happy to pay it. Everyone benefits, from the thirsty biker to the guy who picked the strawberries. But if you start charging too much, I'll buy from the next guy over, or better yet, open a stand of my own that competes with yours."

"I'm no capitalist, dude."

"But you are—and it's nothing to be ashamed of. You don't exploit anybody. You provide a service, sustain jobs, and make an honest profit doing so. Now that's my kind of American."

"Uh, thanks."

"There's just one thing."

"Yeah?"

"That flag. Most of us bikers see it as the symbol of liberty that a lot of good people died to bring us. Of course you're free to express yourself, but when you wear the flag upside down on your pants like that, it could be seen as a sign of disrespect among my people—especially the veterans. I'm sure you don't intend that."

"No, man, no disrespect intended."

"I didn't think so, but the next bikers who see it won't necessarily be of my good nature."

"OK," he said. "Thanks."

"Thank you," I replied. "And here's four more bucks. Could you make me another one of those smoothies?"

"Comin' right up, man!"

★ ★ ★

**THE SUN WAS LOW** over California's Highway 1 as the road bent reluctantly inland toward its terminus at the small town of Leggett. I set up my tent along the coastline and lay down to the sound of swishing waves breaking over scalloped bays. I knew the Old Man had also camped alone in this immediate vicinity, and I imagined both of us at nineteen—young, ambitious, optimistic—not so different from America in the summer of 1939.

# 37

**H**IGHWAY 101 THREADED me through the redwood forests and back toward the coast, where I caught myself humming an old Woody Guthrie tune:

*This land is your land, this land is my land*
*From California to the New York Island*

I turned inland at Crescent City and bid goodbye to the Golden State. From Death Valley to Mt. Whitney, from hippies to highbrows, California had reminded me that America is one of the most pluralistic nations on the planet.

The terrain changed noticeably on the east side of the Klamath Mountains as I motored toward Grant's Pass, Oregon, on Highway 199 where Pete Pomeroy, June Carlson, and the Old Man had ridden the morning of July 17, 1939. Interstate 5 took me to Central Point, where I stopped for directions to Old Stage Road—hoping there might still be some sign of the Pomeroy's Pineridge Orchard. I found no trace of it.

The Old Man never saw Pete or June again after they split up in San Francisco, and now I wondered what ever became of them. Did they go on to live happy, productive lives—or were they killed at Omaha Beach, Bataan, Wake Island, or Bastogne?

My front tire went flat just outside of Medford and I discovered a two-penny nail buried deep within the rubber. It was late afternoon and I'd hoped to spend the night at Crater Lake National Park, where a black bear had jostled the Old Man out of his sleep on July 14, 1939. Plugging the tire leak delayed me for an hour, but I still managed to get to Crater Lake in time for a sunset ride around Rim Drive. I set up my tent near Dutton Creek and spent a bearless night in the park.

The next morning I headed north to Bend, Oregon. A few miles out of town my tire started to leak again. I stopped at a gas station and asked if they could fix it.

"Nope, can't work on it," said the serviceman. "Our equipment isn't designed for those tires. You'll have to find a Harley shop."

I limped into a Wal-Mart parking lot, sat down on the curb, and stared at the tire as the sky began to spit raindrops. I wondered what the Old Man would have done in my situation—the tools I carried wouldn't even allow me to remove the wheel. I'd been there a few minutes when a man walked up in a Wal-Mart Sales Associate vest and a T-shirt that said "Harley-Davidson. Ride Free." He had a bushy handlebar mustache and a nametag that said "Bruce."

"Nice scooter," he said, "100th Anniversary Road King Classic."

"Thanks," I replied. "I'd like it even better with a firm front tire. Do you know if there's a bike shop around here that can fix a flat?"

"Yeah," he said, "there's a couple. But if you come into the store I'll show you what I do with my old Shovelhead."

I followed Bruce to the auto department and he began to grab items off the shelf.

"First, you should carry a couple of these bike-sized cans of inflator and sealant. But for now I'd just get a bottle of this gorilla snot and put it in your inner tube. You can use our air hose out back."

"Inner tube? I thought the Road King's tires were tubeless."

"Not on the Classic. It's a nostalgia thing, I guess."

"That explains why my plug didn't hold."

Bruce stood by in the drizzle as I went to work on the tire.

"Dang," I said. "One thing I don't have is a valve stem remover."

"Oh, I've got one in my bag. Hang on and I'll go get it."

In ten minutes I had a hard tire again.

"Probably be OK now," said Bruce. "But you might swap out that tube next time you get to a wrencher."

"I appreciate this," I said. "Not too many people would help out a biker in the rain."

"Hey man, that's the code," said Bruce. "Like my old man used to say, 'You only find out who your friends are when the chips are down.'"

I rode away reflecting on the wisdom of Bruce's old man—and on a ten-year-old incident that seemed to prove him absolutely right.

★ ★ ★

**KELLY WERBACH WAS** a senior at the nearby United States Air Force Academy and the daughter of one of my dad's fishing buddies. The more I got to know her, the more she fascinated me. Her legs were toned and muscular from years of playing on the academy soccer team, and she seemed to be that rare combination of Demi Moore, Mia Hamm, and Cyd Charisse—eye-catching, athletic, confident, and adventurous.

*Now that,* I thought, *is my kind of woman.*

Kelly had just been through the Academy's rugged and controversial SERE training: Survival, Evasion, Resistance, Escape. In SERE, cadets were subjected to what they might expect if captured by the enemy or forced to bail out over the Choctawhatchee swamp. As she explained the experience to me, I marveled at this mysterious combination of woman, child, and warrior—and I secretly wondered which one of us, if the chips were down, would be tougher.

Kelly was a few years younger than I was, and a very attractive catch at a college where the men outnumbered the women ten to one. I pretty much dismissed the idea of dating her. She was above my class. And she probably had some boyfriend on the Falcon football team with no neck.

But my confidence increased when I received a coveted invitation to her graduation, where the commencement speaker was to be the president of the United States. I arrived at Falcon Stadium early and sat beside Kelly's father and older brother, Kurt—both airmen themselves. Our conversation was pleasant enough, though I sensed Kurt was sizing me up. Kelly's dad beamed as the graduates marched out in their regal uniforms.

"Here, in this stadium," he said, "stand the finest men and women in our country. Nowhere will you find people of higher integrity."

I believed him.

At the graduation party that afternoon, Kelly told me she wanted to be a fighter pilot, but she had yet to fly anything but a glider. I'd been a pilot for years as part of my job, so on a whim I invited her flying. To my surprise and delight she accepted, and we made plans for a weekend run to Utah in a Cessna I flew for work.

The Cessna had just been overhauled, so I wanted to take it over the flatlands before crossing the mountains with such precious cargo. I invited Kevin Williams, a friend from high school, to fly with me to the town of La Veta, Colorado, for a shakedown cruise.

We landed at the remote airstrip and taxied toward the parking ramp. Tumbleweeds blew across the runway as pronghorn antelope grazed along its edges. It looked like a Western movie set. As we approached the ramp, I was surprised to see a lone figure in a cowboy hat and boots standing beside the runway—a Texan with a capital "T."

"Howdy," I said. "You know how far a walk it is to town?"

"Howdy," the man said back. "It's a couple miles. You boys need a lift?"

"Sure, if you're headed that way."

"Glad to give you a ride."

"I'm Johnny and this is Kevin."

"My name's Red. Red McCombs. And this here is Mr. Toby."

He patted the head of a small, salt-and-pepper dog sitting in the front of his Ford.

"So what's your line of work, Red?" I asked. "You live around here?"

"No, I'm from San Antonio. I sell cars, do a little radio, and I also work with sports teams."

"How'd you get here from San Antone?" I asked. "We didn't see any planes on the ramp."

"My Learjet just dropped me off. Only takes ninety minutes."

"So what kind of sports teams do you work with?" asked Kevin.

"Oh, I own the San Antonio Spurs. Used to own the Denver Nuggets. Thinkin' about football now."

Red McCombs spent the better part of an hour showing us around La Veta. As Kevin and I flew home that evening I felt good about the aircraft—and I was looking forward to my date with G. I. Jane.

To avoid any appearance of impropriety, I invited my friend Ric to join Kelly and me as an unofficial chaperone. The flight to Utah was uneventful, and that night Ric and I slept under the stars beside Lake Powell while Kelly stayed in a tent I set up for her.

When it came time to leave, Ric and Kelly loaded their gear into the plane as I performed the preflight inspection. I inserted a calibrated dipstick into each gas tank and logged a total of two and a half hours fuel on board—almost twice that needed to reach the mountain town of Gunnison where we planned to refuel and have lunch. Part of the preflight procedure was to flush any fuel line sediment out through the tank drain on the belly. The drain lever seemed sticky, and a small amount of fuel dribbled out onto the ground even after the valve was closed. It stopped after a couple of quick snaps, so I thought no more about it.

We'd been flying just over an hour when the engine quit.

The most frightening sounds I've ever known have not been the cry of a mountain lion or the bawl of an angry bear, nor the crash of glass and metal or the crackling of a forest fire. The most terrifying sounds in my life have been the quiet ones: the click of a firing pin on a dud round, the silence when I call for my little girls to come in from play, or the whir of a spinning propeller a thousand feet above the mountains.

"What's going on?" Kelly screamed as her face turned ashen white.

"I don't know," I said as I counted off the emergency checklist. Airspeed, eighty knots. Fuel valve, both tanks. Mixture, rich. Mags, both. Primer, in and locked.

The engine came to life briefly like a dying swan and then fired no more.

"Make sure you're buckled!" I yelled. "Looks like we really get to do this."

"You're kidding!" Kelly gasped.

"Mayday, Mayday, Mayday," I broadcast. "November 8817 Victor. Engine failure two miles west of Blue Mesa. Three souls on board."

My heart went into overdrive as I scanned the terrain below. Not good. Mountains to the right. Ridge in front. I could clear the ridge, but there'd probably be a downdraft on the other side. Not worth the risk. A rocky, sage-covered meadow to the left—but there were power lines running through it. Too dangerous. Highway 50 underneath—it's curvy, but it's the best bet.

"There's power lines down there!" Kelly shrieked.

"Saw 'em!" I shouted. "They don't cross the road."

Virulent voices of fear and panic rattled inside my head. They wanted me dead.

*Idiot! You're going down. Just like Scarsdale! But you're taking two others with you! You're all going to die!*

"We're all gonna die!" Kelly cried.

A sickening wave of terror washed over me—but something in the morass stood out.

*Just like Scarsdale—*

A Zen-like trance followed as I concentrated on a single spot on the mountainous road below. I sensed another voice—positive, cool, serene. To me, it sounded just like Scarsdale.

*You're fine, son. Good airspeed, solid airframe, and nobody's shooting at you. Put down full flaps and flare over the motor home. Just protect your fuselage. Piece of cake.*

The prop stopped spinning and I calmly shut off the master switch.

"We're all gonna die!" Kelly repeated.

Ric gave me thumbs up and nodded in silent confidence.

I skirted the rocky ridge, lowered the flaps, and picked out a narrow, seven-hundred-foot stretch of blacktop. This was my runway. I bled away excess altitude with a slip maneuver, then straightened out and flared over a white Winnebago that was crawling up the hill. The airplane touched down a hundred feet in front of it, bounced once, and brushed along the dirt bank as we rotated like a ballerina in a slow-motion pirouette. We came to rest on the side of the road in a cloud of dust.

"Everybody out!" I shouted.

"I can't believe it," Kelly gasped. "We just survived a plane crash."

Ric got out and stood at a safe distance as Kelly ran around picking up souvenir pieces of fiberglass that had scraped off the wingtip.

"Anybody hurt?" I asked.

"I'm OK," said Kelly.

"Me too," Ric added.

I stared at the airplane's underbelly. Fanning out from the fuel drain were dirty blue streaks of residue from an hour's worth of fuel leaked over Utah and Colorado.

The adrenaline had worn off by the time the paramedics arrived. They looked me over and then went on to Ric and Kelly. My hands started to shake as I sat down on the side of the road. I picked up a plum-sized stone and stared at it.

*It's so smooth*, I thought, *as though it's made a ten-thousand-mile journey down a river.*

A state trooper asked me to get in his car and said I could meet the others later at a local café. I wrapped my fingers around the stone and climbed into the cruiser. Ric ran over, put a hand on my shoulder, and spoke loudly enough for the trooper to hear.

"There aren't too many pilots who could've pulled off that landing, bro," he said. "You saved our lives."

"It wasn't just me," I said as I rubbed the stone. "I had some help from above."

An hour later I walked into the café where Ric was waiting.

"So did they give you a ticket?" he asked.

"No ticket. He just filled out a report, shook my hand, and said goodbye. Where's Kelly?"

"At the clinic."

"Why? She said she was fine."

"Now she says she has whiplash."

I walked toward the restroom to wash my hands and overheard two guys in ambulance uniforms chatting in their booth.

"So what'd you think of that chick from the plane?"

"Pretty hot. She's from the Air Force Academy."

"What happened, anyway?"

"She said the stupid bonehead ran the airplane out of gas."

"What an idiot."

"Yeah—and good thing she was in the plane."

"Why?"

"He was about to crash it into some power lines."

Back at the table, to our mutual astonishment, a neighbor named Phil happened to walk in. He was headed home—three hours by car. I asked if Ric could go with him while I waited for Kelly.

"No problem," said Phil. "Happy to help. I'm just glad you guys are OK."

Kelly showed up fifteen minutes later.

"I called my brother," she said coldly. "He'll be here in a few hours."

"That's good," I said. "Ric's going home with Phil, so you and I can ride back with your brother. You want something to eat?"

"He says you can't ride with us."

"What are you talking about?" I asked.

"Kurt's really mad and he doesn't want to see you. He's worried he might lose his temper and there will be a fight."

I could feel my face getting flush.

"I'm not worried about a fight," I said with restraint. "What worries me is leaving you alone in this town. You're my responsibility. That's something I'm sure your brother would respect."

"Listen, you're not welcome to ride with us. You need to leave—now."

It wasn't a request. It was a direct order from Second Lieutenant Kelly Werbach.

Technically, I suppose I had screwed up. I should have cancelled the flight the moment I suspected anything with the fuel system. Still, the incident left me less inclined to venerate any person or group who claims higher integrity than the rest of us.

A Wal-Mart employee in Oregon, who lends out his tools in the rain.

A Texas billionaire who drops everything to give a stranger a ride.

Compared to someone who'd abandon you a hundred miles from home, there's no question who the biker would call "bro."

★ ★ ★

**BAKEOVEN, OREGON, WHERE** the Old Man nearly ran out of gas, no longer appears on modern maps. Modern Highway 197, however, crosses the 1929-vintage Deschutes River Bridge and removes all doubt as to where the Raspberry's wheels rolled in 1939. To the east I could see abandoned segments of former State Highway 50 speckled with sagebrush and prairie grass.

I closed my eyes and imagined the Old Man puttering down this lonely stretch of highway—young, free, and blissfully unaware of the world-shaking war to come. He was also unaware that his cousin Scarsdale was at that very moment fighting for survival in a remote Florida swamp.

I rode on to Portland, Oregon, and located Faloma Road and the former site of Walter Smith's Interstate Brass Foundry. His metal shop is long gone, but Walt lived to a ripe old age and finally succumbed to a heart attack at work in the middle of some project.

There was nothing further for me in Portland, so I took Interstate 84 up the Columbia River to the Bonneville Dam—which had been open only a year when the Old Man puttered past it in 1939 and spent his nights nestled between two army blankets and a homemade shelter cloth.

I began to feel downright coddled in my modern tent and sleeping bag. Hotels—which were out of the question for the Old Man—were an occasional luxury for me, as I had to recharge my electronics every four to five days. As I looked for a place to sleep, I wondered if I would have had the tenacity to tough it out every night as he did at age nineteen.

★ ★ ★

**AT NINETEEN, I GOT** a bee in my bonnet to return to England where I'd gone to school, and to circumnavigate Great Britain by bicycle. I also wanted to visit Germany and Austria. My father and mother watched nervously as I loaded my bike, panniers, and helmet onto a Boeing 747 bound for London. Within a few days I was back in Cambridge preparing for the long summer's ride. Just before heading north, I stopped at the University of Cambridge for lunch. A man in a wheelchair approached the door and I held it open for him.

"Thank you," came a soft voice from the chair.

It was Stephen Hawking, the brilliant theoretical physicist afflicted with the same disease that forced Lou Gehrig to retire in the summer of 1939.

A couple of weeks later I had pedaled some six hundred miles north to Inverness, Scotland, where I turned south again and followed the shore of Loch Ness. I happened upon a group of men on antique motorcycles at a nearby fairground and saw several 1930s-era Harley-Davidson VL Big Twins.

"My father rode one of those across the United States in 1939," I said proudly. "He was just nineteen years old."

They asked what I was doing on a bicycle instead of a motorcycle, and I mumbled something about wanting to get the exercise. I explained that I was nineteen as well and was spending the summer peddling around Europe.

"Trying to one-up the old man, are ya?" asked a Scottish greybeard.

"No," I scoffed, "nothing like that. It's totally different."

But later that night at the Glen Nevis Youth Hostel, I realized the greybeard had been absolutely right. My father had proven himself at nineteen by crossing the country under all kinds of hardship. And while I couldn't duplicate his ride, I could try to do one better by traveling under my own power in a foreign land—with much of it in a foreign language. I had subconsciously set out to affirm that I was at least my father's equal.

★ ★ ★

I PULLED THE HARLEY into a resort lodge east of Portland near Stevenson, Washington. I'd been to this place before on business and remembered they served some of the best salmon I'd ever eaten. I went straight to the dining room—still clad in leathers from the day's ride.

"Table for one?" I asked. "Anywhere's fine."

The hostess took one look at me and swallowed hard.

"Uh," she hesitated. "Wouldn't you rather sit at the bar?"

"No, thanks," I replied, "I'm not a big drinker. I just wanted some of that salmon of yours."

"I really think you'd be more comfortable at the bar. The main dining room's filling up."

"But I'm a guest here," I protested. "And your dining room looks pretty open to me."

"We can certainly have someone bring you a sandwich at the bar."

I left the lodge and rode into Stevenson to find a dining experience with a little less *hauteur*. The town was hosting the annual Columbia Gorge

Bluegrass Festival. I struck up a conversation with some folks having dinner at a local burger house. They were members of a group called Looking Glass Bluegrass Band.

"Come on outside when you're done," said the banjo player, an affable army officer named Jackie Dunevant. "We'll play you a song, and you can be the first to buy our new CD."

Looking Glass stood in the courtyard and performed a lively rendition of Tony Hazzard's "Fox on the Run." A crowd gathered and threw money into Dunevant's banjo case as his daughter handled CD sales. After the set I sat down with the band and we talked music.

"So Jackie," I asked, "who's your favorite banjo player? Earl Scruggs? Béla Fleck? Pete Wernick?"

"Ron Block," he said without hesitation. "He can pick, he can sing, he can write. Plays a mean guitar, too."

"I'll have to check him out," I said.

"You do that," said Dunevant. "You won't be disappointed. He plays with Alison Krauss and Union Station."

I returned to the lodge that evening, put on a swimsuit, and soaked my bones for an hour in their outdoor hot tub. I closed my eyes and imagined how the Midland, South Dakota, mineral baths must have felt to the Old Man in 1939.

A rotund guy in a toupee climbed into the tub with me as a group of bikers roared down Highway 14 along the Columbia River a half mile below.

"You know the difference between a Harley and a Hoover?" he asked in an apparent effort to make conversation.

"What's that?" I replied.

"A Hoover only carries one dirtbag."

I burst into a fit of laughter.

In my leathers I looked so much like a biker that the hostess wouldn't serve me. In my swimsuit I looked so much like a yuppie that a stranger felt safe telling biker jokes.

# 38

I CAN'T THINK OF any biker brother who doesn't want his father to be proud of him—to measure up, so to speak. But this "measuring up" sometimes feels a lot like competition. If you don't think so, watch what happens when a teenaged boy and his dad grapple on the living room floor in a friendly wrestling match. At some point, it's not so friendly. The dad thinks he's being challenged. The boy just wants to hear his dad say, "Nice going." Deep inside every man's heart is that unquenchable thirst for affirmation from the old man.

Author Donald Barthelme dedicated his book, *The Dead Father,* to this often-volatile bond. And while modern psychology has stated that fatherhood is the fullest expression of masculinity, the poet tells us that "the Child is father of the Man."

It was a lot of food for thought as I rumbled up the Columbia Basin.

★ ★ ★

SOMETIME IN THE 1980S the Old Man and I were on our way to a weekend camping trip when a rope I'd tied to the luggage rack came loose and started flapping in the wind. I pulled over, fixed it, and climbed back into the car.

He was in a bad mood—something about work, he said.

"So did you fix it?" he asked.

"Yup, the knot came loose."

He started in on me about quitting the Boy Scouts after we'd moved to the mountains. The rope wouldn't have come loose, he groused, if I had learned how to tie proper knots.

Next, he began grilling me about my job. His career was in the era of the "Organization Man" and he couldn't understand why I was working for a small company instead of a GE or IBM. He also reminded me I wasn't getting any younger, and that I should probably find myself a nice girl pretty soon.

My blood was starting to boil.

"Yep," he sighed, "too bad you never made it to Eagle Scout—"

"Like Scarsdale?" I shouted.

"Now, I didn't say that."

I'd had enough—I let him have it with both barrels.

"Listen," I fumed, "you can't just have a son, name him Johnny, and think he'll magically inherit the courage of Scarsdale, the strength of Horace, and the intellect of Burt!"

I didn't give him time to answer.

"I hate to disappoint you," I said as a lump rose in my throat, "but I'll never be any of those men, much less measure up to all three! So you'll damn well have to settle for what you've got."

I was practically in tears. The nuclear weapon of paternal relationships is for a father to make his boy think he's ashamed of him.

The Old Man looked chagrined, as if he knew he'd hurt me deeply.

★ ★ ★

**SEVERAL YEARS LATER,** we were on a bicycle trip in Montana's Bitterroot Valley. I was a few miles ahead of him and stopped at the top of Chief Joseph Pass to wait. An older man, a CEO from some Fortune 500 company, stood beside his own bicycle as he fiddled with a camera.

"Piece of junk," he cursed, "I come all the way from New York for this view and now my camera freezes up."

"Mind if I take a look?" I asked.

The camera's CPU had locked up, so I removed the battery and used my multi-tool to hit the reset button under the access door. After reinstalling the battery, the camera beeped to life.

The man thanked me profusely, snapped a few photos, and started off down the pass.

The Old Man rode up a few minutes later.

"Johnny, did you fix that man's camera?" he beamed.

"I hope so," I replied.

"He stopped me just to say what a great son you must be—and that he'd hire you any day of the week."

My reaction took me off guard. Here I was, thirty-something and married, yet it still meant the world that my dad was proud of me.

★ ★ ★

**A FLOTILLA OF** windsurfers flew across the water near the Columbia River Gorge, often traveling faster than my Harley. Highway 14 took me past the Bonneville, Dalles, John Day, and McNary dams, which generate a combined power output of nearly six gigawatts. One of the dam workers pointed out that they also provide flood control, commerce up and down the river, and irrigation for land that would otherwise lie fallow. With all the talk of global warming, these clean sources of renewable energy made them seem even more impressive.

The sun was just above the horizon as I turned east onto Highway 12 where the Walla Walla River meets the Columbia. I stopped near the small town of Dixie, Washington, to snap a few pictures of a sprawling wheat field to the east.

"Everything OK, bud?"

I looked over to see a sheriff's deputy pull up beside me.

"Yes sir," I replied, "just taking pictures of the wheat. We don't see anything like this where I come from."

"Well, they're working it up the road a mile or so. Should make great pictures in this light."

"You a photographer?" I asked.

"Oh, I dabble. Best light around here is in the evening—but you'd better head up the road now or you'll lose it."

High on the hillside were two red combines cutting, threshing, and shooting streams of wheat into awaiting trucks. In 1939 this field would have been full of pitchfork-carrying laborers gathering wheat sheaves behind a horse-drawn cutter. The sheaves would then be loaded into primitive, belt-driven threshing machines. It could easily have been a backdrop for Steinbeck's *Of Mice and Men*.

*Wheat harvest near Dixie, Washington*

These days only four men are needed to handle the entire operation: two in the combines and two in the grain trucks. Each truck holds nearly six hundred bushels of Washington white wheat, 90 percent of which will be exported to nations hungry for the fruit of America's plains.

"Howdy," I said as I climbed off the Harley, "mind if I take some pictures of your operation?"

The man had just emptied a truckload of grain into a tall elevator by the flat river bottom.

"Don't mind at all," he said. "Climb into my truck and I'll take you up to the combines."

He introduced himself as Matt Lyons, farm boss and former ski champion. In his college days, Lyons carved the slopes with the likes of Jean-Claude Killy. Now he ran a thousand-acre wheat farm in the state of Washington, one of the nation's largest producers of wheat—ahead of Idaho, Nebraska, Oklahoma, and South Dakota.

Lyons's diesel-powered combines are marvels of modern efficiency. The wheat kernels are slung into a 150-bushel tank as the chaff is chopped up and spread over the ground in a cloud of golden dust. When the combine is full, the operator offloads the grain into a truck via a swinging boom as both vehicles move side by side so the harvest will not be interrupted. After four combine loads the trucks are full and its operators load the wheat into elevators. Eventually it will be turned into pancakes, pastries, cookies, crackers, flat breads, and cereals.

"Hey Charlie!" Lyons barked over his radio. "Time to head down. See you at the bottom."

Matt and I lumbered down the hill as the second truck followed over an ocean of stubby wheat stalks and down to the grain elevators. The door of the other truck swung open and a lithe young woman stepped out of the cab. Her long, flaxen hair was as amber as the waves of grain she was harvesting.

"Charlie?" I asked in surprise.

"Yes," she replied, "I'm Charlie."

"With all due respect, ma'am," I said, "you look more like a cover girl than a farm hand."

"Maybe," Matt laughed, "but Charlie drives the big rigs with the best of the men."

"Well, thank you both," she blushed.

She was eighteen years old.

I rode away reciting William Butler Yeats's poignant poem, "The Song of Wandering Aengus." Charlie was the archetype of Yeats's "glimmering girl"—the metaphor in his elusive quest:

> *Though I am old with wandering*
> *Through hollow lands and hilly lands,*
> *I will find out where she has gone,*
> *And kiss her lips and take her hands;*
> *And walk among long dappled grass,*
> *And pluck till time and times are done*
> *The silver apples of the moon,*
> *The golden apples of the sun.*

And I seemed to recall that Yeats died in 1939.

That evening I parked the Harley at the Farmer's Café in Waitsburg and walked in for dinner. As I sat at my table, the unmistakable voice of Sam Elliot came over the radio with a variety of ways to cook beef—something like Bubba's shrimp recipes from *Forrest Gump*: Beef Stroganoff. Beef Bourguignon. Irish Beef Stew. Beef Brisket. Chateau Brion. Saubraten. Roast Beef. Catalonian Beef Ragù. Mongolian Beef. Chicken Fried Steak. Steak Diane. Grilled Steaks Balsamico. Hamburgers. Sizzling Beef. Spicy Braised Beef. Barbequed Beef Ribs. Beef Wellington. Pepper Beef. Beef Jerky. Beef with Broccoli. Beef Burritos. Beef Fajitas. Beef Tacos—Do you see where I'm going with this?

"Beef," he declared. "It's what's for dinner."

The radio ad ended with a triumphant, instantly recognizable theme.

My face widened into a broad smile. I ordered a steak from the waitress—and the salty farmers at the next table gave me a quizzical look.

*Bravo, Mr. Copland!* I thought. *Bravo!*

★ ★ ★

**I FIRST HEARD** Aaron Copland's music as a teenager, when "Fanfare for the Common Man" was broadcast over huge loudspeakers during a parade. My hair stood on end as the brass and percussion echoed through the streets. I could have sworn I'd heard it before—and it sounded like everything I'd ever imagined about the Second Coming of the Messiah.

Like Glenn Miller, Copland liked to revisit old folk songs with creative arrangements. Miller's versions of "Danny Boy" and "Little Brown Jug," for example, were huge hits in 1939. About the same time, Aaron Copland discovered a collection of field recordings commissioned by the Library of Congress. They included old American ballads, fiddle and banjo tunes, hymns, and work songs from across the country.

Copland had a field day.

He took "Chimchack," an old children's song, and turned it into the popular "I Bought Me a Cat." A Shaker melody called "Simple Gifts" became a central theme for *Appalachian Spring*, and a solo fiddle tune called "Bonaparte's Retreat" blossomed into one of Copland's most popular works: the "Hoedown" from *Rodeo*. Today, "Hoedown" can be heard all over the country—from Emerson, Lake, and Palmer to the Bellagio Fountains in Las Vegas. The National Cattlemen's Beef Association adopted it for the "It's what's for dinner" campaign.

While my friends idolized the Rolling Stones, the Police, and other popular rock groups, for some reason I held up Copland as my hero.

None of my biker bros had even heard of him.

★ ★ ★

**I ROLLED INTO** Lewiston, Idaho, at dusk. Too lazy to look for a campsite, I stopped at a hotel on the outskirts of town and checked in. As I walked back to the Harley to get my gear, I saw a group of three or four guys standing outside of the hotel. One of them was holding a guitar case.

"So, are you guys with the band?" I asked off the cuff.

"Hey man," one of them laughed, "we *are* the band."

It was Tommy Tutone, the group that brought us one of the most famous phone numbers in rock 'n roll: *867-five-three-o-ny-ee-ine.*

★ ★ ★

**MOSCOW, IDAHO, WAS** one of the more important towns on the Old Man's 1939 route. It was his safety net should he ever get stranded out west. It was also where finances forced him to sell the Raspberry, and where—a year later—Horace angrily repossessed her after a deadbeat stiffed his little brother out of fifty bucks.

A Saturday farmers' market was underway at downtown Moscow's Friendship Square, where the stands overflowed with fresh produce, meat, flowers, nursery plants, handmade crafts and homemade baked goods. I stared at the abundant mound of bread and pastries and wondered if any of them had been made from Matt Lyons's wheat.

From out of nowhere, the incongruous sound of an *a capella* soprano began to drift through the air from a nearby alleyway. I went to investigate and found a slender brunette belting out Italian arias beside a trash dumpster. On the pavement next to her were a black cat, a black dog, and a beat-up red box with a smattering of bills and coins.

She introduced herself as Poeina from Seattle. We spoke for several minutes about music and I offhandedly joked that she should try out for *American Idol*.

"I did," she said, "I didn't even get to the second round."

After a year in Cambridge, I figured I knew a good voice when I heard it. And even over the hustle and bustle of Moscow's Farmers' Market, I believed Poeina had more raw talent than anyone I'd ever heard on *American Idol*. Somehow, the sardonic symbolism of classical music relegated to this back alley reminded me of the village names I'd run across in England.

Stratford-upon-Avon, Saltburn-by-the-Sea, Staunton-on-Wye, and Poeina-by-the-Dumpster.

She began to sing *Nel cor più non mi sento* from the Italian opera *La Molinara*. For a moment, I was Henry Higgins. Poeina was my Eliza. And we were proudly standing before the queen at the Ambassador's Ball:

> *Nel cor più non mi sento*
> *Brillar la gioventù!*
> *Caggion del mio tormento,*
> *amor se culpa tu.*

I rode out of Moscow, Idaho, with *Nel cor più non mi sento* echoing in my head. It occurred to me that I'd never bothered to find out what the words meant, and I resolved to ask the first Italian I met.

★ ★ ★

**IDAHO'S LOCHSA RIVER** along Highway 12 became more and more tempting as temperatures approached a hundred degrees. Recalling my swim in the Navarro, I pulled off the road and jumped into the water. As I swam across the river, I thought of the Japanese monks from Pier 33 and their walk to Alamogordo. I wondered how they were handling this heat. I climbed back on the Harley and chugged up Lolo Pass—where Lewis and Clark struggled two hundred years earlier—and silently gave the monks an American Biker's Salute.

★ ★ ★

**I CAMPED IN** a forest north of Butte, Montana—the town where the Old Man discovered his "awful bang & rattle" wasn't the main bearing at all, but a loose motor held on by just one bolt, a few wires, and some control cables.

By sunrise I was headed east on Montana's placid State Highway 2, formerly known as U.S. Highway 10S, where the Raspberry had "banged and rattled" westbound. This road follows the Jefferson River, which converges with the Madison and Gallatin at Three Forks, Montana, to form the mighty Missouri.

It is quintessential Lewis and Clark country. It's also Montana wheat country.

"*Nel cor più non mi sento!*" I yelled as I pumped both fists in the air. "*Brillar la gioventù!*"

I had no idea what I was shouting, but surely this song was an expression of unbridled joy and the passionate fullness of life—the *abbondanza* for which the Italians are so well known.

And for some reason, the bucolic scene along Montana's Highway 2 made me think of Niccolò Paganini.

Paganini was an Italian violinist born in the late eighteenth century. At age eight he began to compose his own music. He gave his first professional concert at twelve. While Paganini had some growing pains—a gambling problem, for example—he quickly became an international superstar, playing to packed audiences all over Europe. His compositions, style, and ability were so radical and revolutionary that lesser violinists swore he had sold his soul to the devil.

Around the same time, an Italian luthier named Giuseppe Antonio Guarneri del Gesù crafted an extraordinary violin out of spruce wood and Bosnian maple. The one-of-a-kind instrument became known as *Il Cannone*—the cannon—for its booming, resonant, and exceptional tone. In a rare and astonishing convergence of greatness, the priceless violin known as *Il Cannone* eventually found its way into the hands of Niccolò Paganini.

"I heard an angel sing," said composer Franz Schubert, "when Paganini played his Adagio. An artistic comet of this magnitude will never again cross the heavens."

"What a man! What a violin! What an artist!" exclaimed pianist Franz Liszt, who then cloistered himself in his apartment for two years to practice and write music.

To this day, many consider Niccolò Paganini to be the greatest violinist of all time. Some still believe he sold out to the devil. *Il Cannone* is kept in the city of Genoa and travels only under armed escort—and with an insurance policy of forty million dollars.

"That the greatest instrument made by the most celebrated maker would fall into the hands of the greatest performer in history," wrote virtuoso Eugene Fodor, "is true justice of destiny."

As I rumbled along Highway 2, it occurred to me that something similar could be said of the United States of America.

In 1776 a group of men gathered in Philadelphia to promote the radical and revolutionary idea that all men are created equal and that a government of the people, by the people, and for the people would result in unprecedented prosperity. At the same time, Scottish economist Adam Smith was writing his *magnum opus*—a comprehensive treatise on free market principles called *The Wealth of Nations*. When a man "intends only his own gain," wrote Smith, "he is led by an invisible hand to promote an end which was no part of his intention." As long as cooperation is strictly voluntary—free from coercion, government interference, or restriction of freedom—"a voluntary, informed transaction always benefits both parties."

America's founding fathers embraced these principles—and the resulting convergence of political and economic freedom led to an era of prosperity unmatched in the history of mankind. Though the nation experienced the inevitable growing pains of a young republic—slavery, the Indian Wars, and civil rights issues, for example—America soon became the most powerful nation on earth. Its concepts of freedom, justice, and equality remain so radical that some nations are fanatically convinced America has sold its soul to the devil.

*The Wealth of Nations* was our Paganini. The *Declaration of Independence* our *Il Cannone*—a booming cannon call of freedom and opportunity. That both of these documents were published in the same year is, once again, "true justice of destiny."

★ ★ ★

**THE LAY OF THE LAND** was beginning to look familiar as I crossed the Gallatin River near Bozeman, Montana, where I would meet the Old Man. I approached the town with excitement and nervousness. Would he be up for the ride physically? Would we have a good time together? Would I measure up?

# 39

**B**ELLINGHAM, WASHINGTON.
Bozeman, Montana.

I'd lived a year in each of these college towns and their contrast was remarkable.

In Bellingham a drive to Seattle to protest the World Trade Organization was an affirmative defense for cutting class. In Bozeman the same was true for hunting season. In Bellingham the girls at the Community Food Co-op sprouted facial hair from their latest vegan fad. Bozeman girls killed their own meat.

My year in Bozeman was spent working and auditing business classes at Montana State University—shortly after my aerial adventure in the mountains of Colorado. That following spring, I got to know some Frenchmen from a company called Air Creation. They built a type of aircraft called weight-shift trikes—a certified, open-cockpit airplane that was the closet thing I'd ever seen to a Harley of the air. It was basically a motorized sidecar with a pusher prop, all suspended beneath an oversized hang glider wing. It cruised at about sixty miles per hour and climbed to fourteen thousand feet, though the best vantage point was five hundred feet off the deck.

A genial Frenchman named Gilles suggested his company bring a demonstrator to the Sun 'n Fun Fly-in in Florida, and I fly it home to Montana as part of a joint promotion. They offered the aircraft to me at well below cost—less than a new Harley—so I said yes immediately. There was just one problem: I had no idea how to fly the thing. In a normal aircraft, you push the controls forward to go down and pull back to go up. It's just the opposite in a weight-shift trike.

During spring break I went to Arizona and spent a week at the Ultralight Flight Center north of Phoenix. My fellow students were a mixed lot from all over the world: Canadian Murray Cooper was learning to fly for an upcoming movie called *Fly Away Home*. Charlie O'Connell was a cop from Lexington, Kentucky. Patrick Juin was a Mexican with a wife and young daughter, and Larry Lester was a huge black man who'd come all the way from Guam.

The school's chief instructor, John Kemmeries, was a rakishly handsome fellow who'd been hurt in a paragliding accident several years earlier. He walked with a pronounced limp, but any sign of disability vanished once he took to the air. My instructor was a tall Swede named John Olson—Oley for short.

Each day Oley and I would strap ourselves into the flying machine, lift off the dirt airstrip, and head out over the blossoming Sonoran Desert. My head spun as I tried to take in all the new information Oley patiently tried to feed me. One morning we had just lifted off when I looked down and saw a biker in black leather sitting on a hill just past the end of the runway. He looked like he was shouting.

"Hey, that dude's throwing rocks at us!" yelled Oley.

I looked down again and sure enough, this was one mad biker.

We landed an hour later and Kemmeries asked how it went.

"What gives?" I complained. "It's hard enough flying a new plane without some crazy biker shyin' rocks at me."

"Oh," he said, "sorry about that. That was Charlie Sheen. I guess they're filming a movie called *Terminal Velocity* and you're screwing up the shoot every time you take off. Some lady came up while you were gone and paid us to stop flying for the day."

My aerial excursion from Lakeland, Florida, to Bozeman, Montana—most of it over Lewis and Clark's historic route—had enough adventure to fill a book, but two events stand out.

I'd been flying five hundred feet over the Chattahoochee River all day and finally landed at Eufala, Alabama, to look at my road atlas and refuel. There was enough daylight to fly another hour or two, so on a whim I continued northwest to a town I'd never heard of called Tuskegee.

I parked my odd-looking plane on the tarmac and started poking around the deserted airport. An abandoned redbrick building stood on the outskirts of the field; it looked like a ghost hangar from World War II. I pushed the trike inside to protect it from the oncoming rain.

The next morning, as I prepared to take off, a man came up and introduced himself as Colonel Roosevelt J. Lewis.

"There's a man in my office who'd like to meet you," said Lewis.

"Sure," I replied. "Is he a pilot?"

"I'll let you be the judge of that," he chuckled.

Colonel Lewis went into his office and walked out with an old black man in a blue flannel shirt, gray polyester pants, and loafer shoes.

"My name's Al," he smiled as he extended an aged right hand. "That's some plane you got there, boy."

"It's a kick, that's for sure," I said. "I love flying low and slow. Are you a pilot yourself?"

"Well, yes. Just not so much any more."

Al began to reminisce about his flying days. He told me how, as a boy, no one would teach him how to fly. He told me how he was the first black American to get a commercial pilot's license, and how he took up Eleanor Roosevelt against the strong objections of the Secret Service. As he spoke, I slowly realized I was standing next to a legend.

"See where your little plane's parked," said Al as he pointed to the hangar. "That used to be full of P-40s. I taught a load of boys to fly out of there. They went on to fight in North Africa."

"You flew P-40s?" I gasped.

"Yes sir," Al replied. "We used them as trainers."

"Have you ever heard of a pilot named Scarsdale Jack?"

"Of course," he said. "Everybody knew about him. The Flying Tiger from New York."

As I took off that morning, I circled over Tuskegee's Moton Field and waved my arm in salute to a great American: Chief Al Anderson of the legendary Tuskegee Airmen.

A couple of weeks later, as I meandered up the Missouri, it was becoming clear that at this pace I would miss my friends' graduation. I found a church in Akron, Iowa, that let me store the trike and I bought a round-trip bus ticket from Sioux Falls to Bozeman. After an all-night ride on I-90, I arrived at Montana State University just hours before the ceremony.

A handful of people milled about as custodians set up folding chairs and a podium. I moved out of the way of a chair dolly and accidentally backed into someone. I turned around to say "excuse me" and found myself face-to-face with Jane Fonda.

Among most bikers Jane Fonda is somewhere on the level of the Anti-Christ. It's hard to go to any major bike rally and not find an area dedicated to anti-Jane stickers, patches, or signs. It wasn't the first time I'd blundered into celebrities—but this time, I had an advantage.

Right out of college, I had spent a year working closely with Jane's first cousin. It was clear the apple hadn't fallen too far from the tree. Sarah had strong, prominent Fonda features—dark hair, chiseled jaw, and a predisposition toward the social and political left. She was also one of the most articulate people I'd ever known, and I found myself oddly attracted to her passion and zeal, though it was clear we approached many issues from fundamentally different perspectives.

She'd call me "John Birch" after some right-wing society I had never heard of. I'd call her a variety of nicknames based on the *cause du jour*, and we'd get together after hours to continue our dialogs and chide each other on socio-political issues.

"Sarah," I'd insist, "there's only so long a society can give itself the shirt off someone else's back. It's the old 'give someone a fish and they'll just eat for a day' syndrome. We need to teach them to fish so they can eat for a lifetime."

"That's fine," she'd say, "but the best fishing spots have been taken by a privileged few."

"Not true!" I'd retort. "Opportunity abounds for anyone in this country willing to work for it. To teach otherwise defrauds them of their birthright."

"Which is?"

"The pursuit of happiness!"

Sarah was in the midst of a divorce and had a daughter named Meredith about five years old. One day the three of us met at an outdoor music festival and Meredith started to climb all over me. I carried her on my shoulders and she slid down my arms and legs with complete trust that I wouldn't drop her.

"That's amazing," said Sarah in her sweet, lyrical voice. "I've never seen her so animated around anyone but family. I guess you can't be all bad."

Through the years I watched Meredith grow into a precocious, attractive girl. She looked a little like Bridget, I thought, and she would surely break hearts someday. And though we butted heads on ideology, Sarah and I had an underlying respect that gave more than just lip service to the trendy myth of tolerance—where people offer a perfunctory tip of the hat to open-mindedness but secretly leave a debate hating the other's guts.

We bid goodbye just before I moved to Montana, and I knew I'd miss her.

"Say hello to Jane for me," she said, "—if you ever run into her."

"Right, Sarah," I laughed, "like *that's* ever going to happen."

★ ★ ★

"JANE FONDA!" I exclaimed. "Your cousin Sarah sends greetings from Colorado."

Her cautious expression blossomed into a wide smile. Her voice sounded just as it did in *On Golden Pond* and for some odd reason this surprised me. She offered her hand and I took it, and we spoke about family, friends, and her life on the Flying D Ranch south of town. She said her husband, Ted Turner, was receiving an honorary degree, and she was there to witness it.

I knew my biker bros would consider it high treason for me to consort with the "enemy" like this, but standing face-to-face, I could not bring myself to despise this woman. As we spoke, I sensed a slight contrition in Fonda's demeanor, as though she realized she'd hurt her countrymen deeply and now regretted certain impetuous actions during the turbulent sixties. *Time would tell*, I thought. *And as any biker knows, it takes guts to admit your mistakes.*

Some time later I got word that Meredith, Jane's cousin once removed, had been killed in a car accident in New Zealand. Like the Old Man—and myself, for that matter—Meredith had set out on her own vision quest at age nineteen, first to Costa Rica and then to the Pacific Rim, where she perished on the side of the road forty miles north of Auckland.

Friends and family surrounded Sarah at the funeral. I steadied her arm as she turned to embrace me, and her petite body was wracked with sobs as our tears soaked into my shirt. No words were adequate—or necessary—to express the grief of losing an only child.

Right or left, black or white—we all bleed red. The Fondas and I may never see eye-to-eye, but when the chips are down, it doesn't mean we can't walk arm-in-arm.

★ ★ ★

THAT SUMMER—BETWEEN MOVING, flying, work, and classes—I realized I hadn't been on a bike in over two years. I resolved to get back in the saddle again, but my return to the world of motorcycling was as ignominious as a debutante tripping over her dress.

A "Rent-a-Harley" ad in the *Bozeman Daily Chronicle* caught my eye, and I began to poke around Yellowstone Harley-Davidson a few miles from home. Before long, I'd rented a gorgeous, pearly-white Dyna Glide Low Rider. The Dyna was much larger than my previous bike, so rental agent Kristin Wagner had me putter around their practice lot first. In fifteen minutes I felt comfortable enough to ride back to the office and finalize the paperwork.

A group of bikers bound for Sturgis were parked out front ready to hit the road. They wore full leathers and patches that said "Loud Pipes Save Lives." I was in my sweats, T-shirt, and running shoes, and put on my best James Dean as I came to a stop next to their line of Harleys. I tried to act cool, but I was unfamiliar with the bike and failed to fully extend the kickstand. Six hundred and fifty pounds of metal and leather headed inexorably toward the asphalt. My attempts to save it were hampered by my pinkie finger, which was pinched between the clutch lever and the grip.

"Stupid poser," murmured a biker under his breath.

"Damned RUB," mumbled another.

I grunted and strained to keep the bike from crunching into the pavement.

"Hey, Cherry Bomb!" shouted a greybeard to a blonde in a pert tank top and cutoff jeans, "Think you can help this boy?"

"My pleasure," she cooed, and sauntered over to help me get the bike erect again.

It served me right, of course. While I'd probably been riding as long as any of those bikers, I was a long way from at home with that bike. But more importantly, I'd broken one of the cardinal rules of biker culture: I pretended to be someone I wasn't.

Ten years later, here I was again in Bozeman—my town of a thousand memories.

The Old Man would be here soon, too, and I hoped he would come away with some epic memories of his own.

# 40

THE OLD MAN wasn't scheduled to arrive in Bozeman until the following week, so I used the time to clean up the Harley and take a three-day ride through Yellowstone Park with his 1939 *Motorists Guide to Yellowstone* in my pocket. It was printed in black, green, red, and blue inks and had a stern admonition on the front panel:

FEEDING BEARS IS PROHIBITED

I rode down Highway 191 past Big Sky to the town of West Yellowstone. Tourists were out in force, creating major traffic jams for wildlife as mundane as a single cow elk. Clusters of sightseers walked along the boardwalks of the Norris Geyser Basin and snapped pictures of the countless geothermal pools that dotted the landscape.

Ahead of me on the wooden walkway were a group of Old Order Amish—three young mothers and their children, an older man, and what looked like a Mennonite couple. The women wore plain blue dresses and headscarves, while the men and boys had on wide-brimmed straw hats, long-sleeved shirts, and black pants held up by suspenders. The other tourists gave them about a hundred feet of clearance on either side—as if they were radioactive or something.

I stowed my camera and approached the patriarch.

"*Wie bist?*" I asked. "*Langsam laafe uff 'me scheener Daag is so blessierlich, odder?*"

[How ya doing? Great to take a stroll on such a nice day, isn't it?]

"*Ya, nadierlich,*" he said curiously, "*awwer wu hast du Deitsch glannt, Freind?*"

[Yes, it is. But where'd you learn our language, my friend?]

"*Lancaster—mei Schweschder wunscht in Lancaster. Un du?*"

[Lancaster—my sister lives in Lancaster. How about you?]

"*Mir kumme aus Minnesota. Naame is Bontrager.*"

[We're from Minnesota. My name's Bontrager.]

The women and children stared up politely with wide-eyed smiles as if I were the Yiddish-speaking Indian from *Blazing Saddles*.

★ ★ ★

**A FEW YEARS EARLIER,** my sister had moved to Lancaster, Pennsylvania, with her husband. Their house sat high on a bank overlooking the Conestoga River beside a sprawling Amish farm. The first time I went to visit, I sat on the porch for hours and stared across the river as the Amish family worked their fields behind a team of massive Percheron horses.

"Who are those guys?" I asked my sister. "What's their name?"

"I don't know," Chrissy answered. "We've never met them."

"What?" I exclaimed. "You've been here over a year and haven't met your neighbors?"

"I'm kind of afraid to," she said. "They might think we're heathens or something."

"Well," I resolved, "I'm going over there tomorrow morning and introduce myself. I want to see how they handle those horses."

"Are you sure you should do that? They might get mad."

"They're Amish, for cryin' out loud. I'm pretty sure they won't run me off with a shotgun."

Early the next morning I walked across the bridge and knocked on the door of their milking parlor. An open-framed diesel motor slowly chugged behind the building and a vintage tractor with oversized metal wheels sat outside. I saw no signs of rubber, electricity, or telephones.

"Good morning," said a clean-faced boy of about eighteen.

"Howdy," I said, "I'm from across the river. My sister is your new neighbor and I wondered if I could watch you hitch up those horses. I raise cows myself in Colorado."

"Colorado!" he beamed. "I've never been there."

"It's nice," I said, "but we've got nothing like the dirt you have here. I'll bet you could throw out a nail, come back a day later, and harvest a six-inch spike!"

The boy laughed and introduced himself as Henry Lapp. He invited me to watch the milking operation and said I could help hitch the horses to the plow if I'd stick around for an hour or so.

Two of his sisters, Sarah and Rebekah, breezed into the barn. They looked to be about nineteen and twenty-one. Both smiled politely, disappeared into a stall, and came out with a handsome dark mare that they hitched to their buggy as easily as I might tie a shoe. Lastly, their little brother Samuel came in and emptied the milk buckets into a large vat.

Within a few months we'd become fast friends. Their simple, unpretentious Christian faith was refreshing, and for whatever their bland reputation, the Amish impressed me with their intrepid and adventurous spirits. They were always eager to travel and see new places—though they usually had to hire a Mennonite to get them there. When I invited the Lapps to our family's Lake George camp in New York, Sarah, Rebekah, and Samuel enthusiastically accepted.

As I watched the girls cook, work, clean, and play, I couldn't help but compare them to Paris Hilton and Ivanka Trump. While Sarah and Rebekah Lapp reminded me of the sleek, strong Morgan horses they raised, the hotel heiresses seemed more like French poodles—and there was no question as to whom I'd rather be with.

The Lapps wanted to climb Tongue Mountain to get a view of the lake and see where the Old Man had killed *Crotalus horridus* so long ago. We set out for the summit with the girls clad in their long Amish dresses and headscarves.

The trail up Tongue Mountain contains a section of steep rock that practically amounts to technical climbing. I scrambled up first and reached down to Rebekah, who was struggling to scale the rock in her dress. She looked up and hesitated, as though taking the hand of this English guy—this biker—represented an intimacy she was not yet willing to convey. But then with a resolute smile, she reached out and we locked wrists like two train cars coupling. With a strong heft I pulled her to the top. Our hands remained clasped for slightly longer than necessary, and at that moment a gap was bridged between two cultures hundreds of years apart.

Rebekah and Sarah Lapp stood with me in the wavy grass atop Tongue Mountain. Their long dresses billowed in the summer breeze as we gazed at the boats far below. It looked like Andrew Wyeth's painting *Christina's World*, in which a crippled woman bravely drags herself through her grassy domain.

To the casual observer, the Amish may seem limited by their adherence to a simple life of Christianity, but I found them inspiring. Before long, I'd spent enough time with them to pick up some of their language, which wasn't so different from the German I'd learned in high school.

*Sarah and Rebekah Lapp overlook the Lake George Narrows from the summit of Tongue Mountain.*

★ ★ ★

**I BID GOODBYE** to the Amish family in Yellowstone Park and rode through miles upon miles of skeletonized forest on the way to Fishing Bridge, where the Old Man had camped on the evening of July 9, 1939. His ride had been nearly fifty years before the devastating fires of 1988, and the Park looked much different then. His 1939 *Motorists Guide* warned against feeding the bears, but it ironically went on to point out the public "Bear Feeding Grounds" southwest of the falls.

I stopped at one of the lesser-known Yellowstone campgrounds to stretch my limbs. I was surprised to see a mother black bear with two fuzzy first-year cubs wandering around the picnic grounds. A man with a bag of marshmallows stood nearby, and the mother bear greedily licked the white puffballs off the ground as he tossed them one-by-one in her direction.

"Damn fool," said a man next to me. "Not supposed to feed the wildlife."

"Yeah," I answered. "Think we oughta say something?"

"I dunno," he replied.

But the animal seemed benign enough, and for a time the bear and its benefactor seemed like best friends. The tourist continued feeding the bear as his wife snapped pictures from inside the car. Everything was great—until the man ran out of marshmallows.

He stuffed the empty bag into his back pocket. The bear looked up indignantly and snorted. The man held out his open palms as if to say, "That's all I've got," then turned around and headed for his car. The bear charged and cuffed him on the rear, ripping his jeans as he jumped frantically into the vehicle.

"Holy cow!" shouted the guy next to me. "Did you see that?"

"Yup," I said flatly. "Guess we should've said something."

"You ever seen anything like that?" he asked.

"No," I replied, "but as I sit here, I've never seen a better demonstration of the entitlement mentality, have you?"

"What do you mean?"

"Those bears are certainly capable of thriving on their own—although they might have to work a little harder. Now, along comes some guy who tries to ingratiate himself by handing out freebies."

"Yeah?"

"So what happens when the freebies stop? No appreciation, no thank you, no gratitude whatsoever—just the opposite. They attack him!"

The three bears lumbered off into the woods. The man next to me took a drag from his cigarette and sighed as he exhaled smoke.

"Sounds like our immigration policy," he groused. "I'm from California.

I get attacked whenever I suggest we cut back on free services to illegals—you know—food, education, health care. And now that you mention it, the bear and the marshmallows are a lot like our foreign aid policy too. We've given billions of dollars and thousands of lives to countries in the hope they'd be our friends—only to have them cuff us in the rear when it's over."

"You a biker?" I asked.

"Yeah!" he exclaimed. "I ride a Fat Boy. How'd you know?"

★ ★ ★

**THE OLD MAN** was scheduled to arrive that evening. I rode back to Bozeman and booked a room at the Lewis and Clark Motel and anxiously rode out to the airport to fetch him.

As the plane disgorged its passengers, a familiar figure walked up the passenger ramp with only a small canvas bag. His hesitant gait was testament to nearly ninety years of living. He still had a full head of hair, gray though it was, and he wore a leather biker's vest with an American flag on the front and an oversized patch on the back:

UNITED STATES NAVY
WORLD WAR II VETERAN

He had no Flying Tigers patches on his leathers—he refused to wear them. Not out of disrespect, but because he never wanted anyone to think he was posing as an AVG member. Those were the real heroes, he said. As I watched his aging eyes scan the crowd, I tried to shut out any thought that this might be our last ride together.

"Dad!" I shouted. "Over here!"

"Son," he answered, "you look good. The road treating you OK?"

"You bet," I said. "Wait 'til you hear what I've seen!"

The Old Man and I settled into the motel and spent the next day preparing for our fifteen-hundred-mile ride. I picked up a newspaper and saw that the bluegrass band Alison Krauss and Union Station just happened to be in town. Their banjo player was Ron Block—the man I'd been told about at Columbia Gorge Bluegrass Festival. That evening, we rode over to Montana State University's field house and bought tickets for the concert.

After the show I introduced myself to the band's head of security, a stalwart guy named Nate. He reminded me of Patrick Swayze in *Road House*—respectful, alert, and indefatigably polite, but make a wrong move toward his charges and you'd be kissing the ground faster than you could say *Krav Maga*.

*This guy's a biker,* I thought.

"So Nate," I finally said, "I've been told I simply have to meet your banjo player."

He looked the Old Man and me over as he sized us up. We were still wearing our leathers.

"Come on backstage, boys," he nodded. "The band will be there in a minute or so."

The bass player, Barry Bales, came out, and we began to talk about outdoors and elk hunting. As we spoke, I noticed the band's lead singer was staring at the Old Man's vest. His name was Dan Tyminski—a jovial teddy bear of a fellow who had recently been actor George Clooney's voice-double in the movie *O Brother, Where Art Thou?* Tyminski came over and stood politely beside Bales as we wrapped up our conversation.

"Hey," said Dan, "I wanted to thank that man for his service to our country. We don't see too many World War II vets anymore. Is that your father?"

"Yes," I beamed. "We're riding our Harley to Sturgis together."

"No kidding? I got to ride a Harley in our last music video. I had to give it back, though."

"Bummer," I said. "Kind of grows on you, doesn't it?"

"Yup," Dan agreed. "It belongs to Nate, our head of security."

Ron Block stood with a glass of red wine in his hand beside a man named Jerry Douglas, the band's dobro player. If Tyminski were George Clooney's voice double, then Block could surely be actor Ron Howard's face double—right down to the reddish hair and mustache. The Old Man and I approached Block and thanked him for his performance.

Ever since the 1972 movie *Deliverance*, banjo players have been stereotyped as inbred, hillbilly, idiot savants. Entire books have been written with nothing but banjo jokes. As we conversed with Block, however, it became clear this boyish banjo picker was no idiot. He was eager to hear about our ride, and before long our conversation turned to religion and philosophy.

"Have you ever seen *The Matrix*?" he asked.

"Yeah," I said, "that sci-fi movie about simulated reality?"

"That's right," said Block, "but the film's symbolism actually goes much deeper than that. Neo, you see, is in some ways symbolic of Jesus Christ and in other ways symbolic of us. He's a searcher, seemingly out of place in his world. Agents Brown, Jones, and Smith represent the enemy—demonic forces trying to lull us into complacency and a comfortable illusion of security. Neo is searching for the truth, as we all are, of course, and I think that concept is well described by George MacDonald, who said 'When a man is, with his whole nature, loving and willing the truth, he is then a live truth. But this he has not originated in himself.'"

The Old Man and I stood there amazed.

Nowhere in our riding had we come across a more passionate and articulate apologist for his faith. It was hard to believe this was the same man who only minutes earlier had been pickin' out "Cluck Old Hen" in front of thousands of people.

Block confided that his career path hadn't always been easy. Like Glenn Miller and Aaron Copland, it was strewn with false starts, long hours, and discouragement—but after multiple gold records, ten Grammys, and six International Bluegrass Music Association awards, Ron Block was pretty sure he'd made the right decision.

The Old Man spoke up as we walked out the door.

"Wait a minute," he said, "didn't you want to meet the girl?"

"What girl?" I asked in confusion.

"The girl in the band—Alison Krauss!"

"Wow, Dad," I said, "I was having such a good time with the boys that I didn't even think about it."

The Old Man shook his head.

"Johnny," he grinned, "that's pathetic."

"Isn't it, though?" I laughed as we both threw our legs over the Harley and puttered away under the starry Montana skies.

# 41

THE BIG SKY COUNTRY was sunny and bright as we took off the next morning down U.S. Highway 287 through Ennis, Montana. The bike felt different with the Old Man on the back. Heavy. Solid. Stable. I found myself wishing he'd been with me since San Francisco, but I knew there had been some things I had to face alone.

To the west we could see remnants of old State Highway 1 running high above the Madison River. We pulled off the road and walked a few hundred yards to the disintegrating, weed-choked asphalt of the forgotten highway.

"Do you recognize this, Dad?" I asked. "You rode over this blacktop on July 10, 1939."

"Did I?" he said. "Can't say it looks familiar after all this time."

Farther south, we discovered that old State Highway 1 now lay under millions of tons of rocks, dirt, trees, and water.

On August 17, 1959—twenty years after the Old Man rode through the Madison River Canyon—a massive earthquake hit the area west of Yellowstone Park. The resulting landslide dammed the river, buried the highway, and killed twenty-eight people. It also created Earthquake Lake, a 6-mile-long body of water 190-feet deep. Route 287 now skirts the lake and joins Highway 191 at the park's western boundary.

After just one day's ride, my concern about the Old Man's ability to sit for hours on the Harley seemed unfounded. He was a good passenger and didn't complain, though I could tell he got tired and stiff after an hour with no break. When I felt him dozing off, I'd give him a quick jab with my elbow and pull over at the next convenient spot.

"We can keep going," he would protest, "I'm not tired at all."

"Well, I am," I would fib. "Let's just rest for a while."

Within two minutes he'd be lying face up on the grass sawing logs like Rip Van Winkle. As I watched him sleep, I thought about our role reversal over the years. When I was a child I depended on him for everything. Now—though he was far from helpless—he was growing ever more dependent on me.

In addition to rest, the Old Man was also stubborn about drinking throughout the day.

"Dad," I lectured, "you need to keep hydrated. Riding in the wind all day will dry you out. Here, drink this Gatorade."

"I never did anything like this on my trip," he said as he drank the pale green liquid.

"You were seventy years younger then," I chided.

But he'd made his point—in 1939 he went the entire distance without sports drinks, a modern bike, cameras, laptops, or hotel rooms.

We spent two days in Yellowstone Park revisiting the Raspberry's route. We saw where his spark plug gave out at Yellowstone Falls. We saw where he mailed his postcards from Fishing Bridge, and where he stuffed July 1939 newspapers under his jacket to stay warm.

After a two-day tour of Yellowstone, we left the park through the northeast entrance and stopped in Cooke City for breakfast. This wasn't part of his original route, but I wanted the Old Man to see the breathtaking Beartooth Plateau—a Mecca of motorcycling that bikers come from all over of the world to experience.

As bad luck would have it, a massive mudslide had covered U.S. Highway 212 just a few months earlier. This blocked the route between Cooke City and Red Lodge and prompted the highway department to route traffic around this popular byway. We headed up the road anyway, and to our delight discovered the highway was open for the next twenty miles. The mudslide closure was on the far side of the pass.

To have the incomparable Beartooth Highway all to oneself on a sunny Big Sky morning is practically unheard of. The Old Man and I took full advantage of it and rode leisurely up the twists and turns of the scenic vistas, until we finally climbed off the Harley and gazed toward the rugged Beartooth Peak looming over the Clarks Fork River drainage.

"*Nel cor più non mi sento!*" I shouted with both fists in the air. "*Brillar la gioventù!*"

"What's that mean?" asked the Old Man.

"I have no idea," I replied. "It's just something I say whenever I see something inspiring."

"Then you must be saying it a lot on this trip," he grinned.

We dallied on the Beartooth Plateau until a line of storm clouds chased us away.

"What's the weather forecast, do you know?" he asked.

"No," I said, "but we could probably check it once we get to Cody. I'll walk down Main Street and see if I can piggyback off a Wi-Fi. My laptop's got 802.11g so I can download at 54 megabits—not that their WANs have anywhere near that bandwidth."

"What?" he said. "First you shout in Italian and now you're talking Greek. Guess that expensive college education wasn't all in vain."

"Expensive?" I laughed. "Give me a break—you got off cheap with me."

★ ★ ★

**LIKE HIS FATHER,** Burt, a major incentive for the Old Man to take a professor's job was the tuition break for his family. The University of Denver required faculty kids to pay just 10 percent of normal tuition, so for a family of six on a meager professor's salary, our college choice was a no-brainer.

The sheer number of Middle Eastern students at the university surprised me. I could only speculate that since Denver was a big oil town, their oil-sheik fathers thought an education here would make their kids better businessmen at home. Unfortunately for them, a group of Iranian radicals had just taken fifty-two Americans hostage at the U.S. Embassy in Tehran, and anti-Islamic sentiment was high.

One morning we had a pop quiz in our Fundamentals of Computing class. To my surprise I aced it, and the professor asked me to hand out the graded tests. I could see the Muslim students were struggling—none of them got over 60 percent on the quiz.

"Hey guys," I said, "don't worry about this first one. I'm sure it's just a language-barrier thing. You'll get the hang of it."

They told me they'd have to improve or they'd get sent home.

A few days later a couple of guys in letter jackets started in on me as I sat in the cafeteria.

"So Newkirk, why are you helping out the camel jockeys? They hate us, you know. They'll act like your best friend and then stab you in the back."

"Geez, Matt," I replied, "they don't strike me that way. I'll give 'em a chance."

"Well, I'm not goin' anywhere near those dune coons and neither should you."

"Damn right," said another. "Not if you want to hang with us."

And I suddenly realized I'd heard these voices before.

*Johnny loves Janet! Johnny loves Janet!*
*We saw you helping her! We saw you helping her!*

The next day I walked straight into class and sat down in the middle of the Muslims.

"So," I said, "you guys want some help with this stuff?"

Ali Akbar, Reza, Majid, Suri, and Samira were from Iran. Fadil and Abdul-Aziz came from Saudi Arabia, and Salim was a Kuwaiti. We started an informal study group and met after dinner in an empty lecture hall.

Samira was a stunning Persian beauty of about nineteen—an exotic blend of Disney's Princess Jasmine and the immortal "Afghan Girl" from the cover of *National Geographic*. If the ancient dancer Salome looked anything like Samira, it's easy to see how she so easily bewitched King Herod. It seemed ironic that in her native country, an opaque chadar cloth would smother all of Samira's elegance.

During the Thanksgiving and Easter breaks, I invited these foreigners to our ranch. They all seemed to appreciate it, but there was something feral about Fadil and Majid. I couldn't put my finger on it, but neither of them ever seemed to look me in the eye.

Back in class I occasionally caught Samira sending furtive glances in my direction. I supposed it was the first time in her young life that any man had treated her with respect. In her native country, Samira could be beaten or stoned for the slightest infraction of Islamic law. She would have to live under the absolute authority of her husband and wear the *hijab* nearly everywhere she went.

When it came time to say goodbye, I took Samira aside and gave her a U.S. Peace silver dollar as a memento of her time in America.

Stamped on one side were the words *E Pluribus Unum*.

The other side said *Liberty*.

Samira stared at the coin as she turned it over and over. She was on the verge of tears as she put her soft hand on my face and kissed my cheek.

That fall I transferred to a college in New York and never saw any of them again.

★ ★ ★

**THE OLD MAN** and I returned to his original route at Cody, Wyoming, where U.S. Highway 20 follows much the same path it did in 1939. The road runs alongside Dry Creek until it hits the Bighorn River at Greybull, where we were surprised to see a huge number of civilian and military airplanes parked on the prairie. We had stumbled upon Greybull's famous Museum of Flight and Aerial Firefighting.

The curator was eighty-one-year-old Ralph Reiner, a World War II veteran of the European theater. He said he'd seen Glenn Miller's last performance before the great bandleader vanished over the English Channel. Ralph and the Old Man had a lot to talk about as I poked around the hulks of retired aircraft, which included some of the last PB4Y-2 patrol bombers used against the Japanese in the South Pacific.

We stopped in Worland to pick up groceries and then went east on Highway 16 toward the remote Ten Sleep Canyon, where on the night of July 7, 1939, the Raspberry gave up the ghost west of Hazelton Pyramid. This place was as breathtaking as it was isolated—and I knew it represented a pivotal time in the Old Man's life. Here he had read his father's letter through teary eyes and solved a major mechanical problem with three stones from the creek. Here he had shouted his salutations into the starry, starry night:

*Wilderness of Wyoming! I am a visitor from the World of Tomorrow— courtesy of the 1939 New York World's Fair!*

And now, standing in nearly the exact same spot, I couldn't resist:

"*Nel cor più non mi sento!*" I screamed unblushingly. "*Brillar la gioventù!*"

"There he goes again," quipped the Old Man to the Harley as if it were a horse.

We set up camp, kindled a small fire, and ate a simple supper underneath the stars. He seemed truly grateful to be back here, though I wondered how much he really remembered.

"Dad," I said.

"Yes."

"Do you ever think about that Japanese soldier—the one from Manus Island?"

The Old Man lowered his head and stared into the fire that was crackling beside the north fork of the Powder River.

"Johnny," he finally said. "That was war."

I tried to break the awkward pause that followed.

"Dad, don't think for a minute that—"

"—and war can turn otherwise honorable men into barbarians," he continued.

I added another log to the fire.

"So what would you have done differently?"

"Nothing," he replied. "It was war. But you should never think that I was some kind of hero. The men at Bataan, the First Cavalry, the Flying Tigers, the *Indianapolis*—they were the real heroes. The closest I ever got to combat were those forays into the jungle."

"But your life was at risk—just like anyone else's."

"I suppose," he said. "But to answer your question. Yes, I've thought of that soldier."

"In what way?" I asked.

He poked at the fire with a stick as orange flames reflected in the Harley's chrome.

"Do you remember Fumihiko?" he asked.

I thought back to the early seventies when my father went on an extended business trip to Japan. When he returned he told us about a Japanese colleague in Hiroshima. The man had pointed out exactly where he'd been sitting when the bomb went off. Thirty years later, there they were—former enemies—working together as though nothing had ever happened.

Shortly after the trip, a Japanese student named Fumihiko Kajima came to live with us for a year. My father treated him like a son. Had the Japanese soldier on Manus lived, his own son might have been just about his age.

Just before Fumihiko got on the plane for home, I saw the Old Man give him a shiny piece of metal. I didn't know what it was and I never asked. But thirty years later, in the shadow of Ten Sleep Canyon, I finally understood.

The Old Man had returned the dog tag he'd taken from the solider on Manus Island.

Whether it was guilt, penance, resolution, goodwill, or anything else, one thing was clear: somehow, somewhere—former Lt. John B. Newkirk had made his peace with the Empire that bombed Pearl Harbor and killed Scarsdale Jack.

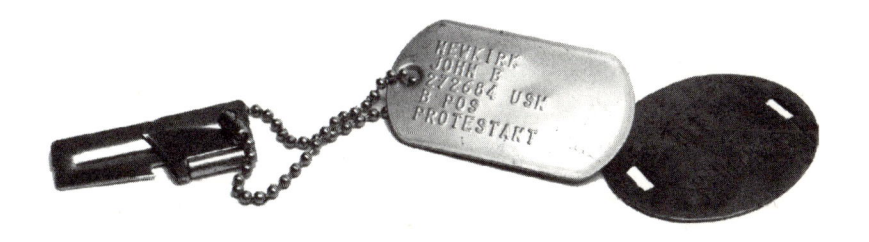

We talked late into the night as the fire subsided to glowing coals. He told me stories of the war, of Scarsdale Jack, Glenn Miller, and of coming back full circle to the place where he had solved the Raspberry's breaker problem with three stones from the creek. As I watched the Old Man fall asleep, I shook my head and tried to visualize him seven decades earlier as a scared, tearful boy confronted with a problem he had no idea how to solve—and how he could never have foreseen that his 1939 trip would ultimately affect thousands of lives.

★ ★ ★

AT AGE THREE, my sister Victoria was diagnosed with hydrocephalus—a disease where abnormal accumulation of cerebrospinal fluid in the skull causes increased pressure on the brain and can lead to convulsions, mental retardation, and death. She was sent to a pediatric neurosurgeon who recommended implanting a device called a hydrocephalus shunt. The shunt failed several months later, and she was forced to undergo a traumatic revision surgery.

I watched as the nurses prepped my little sister for the delicate brain operation. They gave her a sedative before the general anesthesia and she began to drift off.

"Daddy," she whispered to my father, "Daddy?"

"Yes, sweetie," he trembled.

"Can you sing me 'Rock-a-Bye Baby'?"

Her eyes bleared shut and my mother and father were inconsolable as the orderlies wheeled Victoria into the operating room. I'd never seen him cry before.

An hour later the surgeon came out with a device that looked like a string of spaghetti with a bulge near one end.

The shunt system had clogged. There was an obstruction in the line.

He said the next one might clog as well, and could once again threaten Victoria's life.

But beneath my father's tears, a cloudy image began to gel—an image so distant it was no longer even part of his consciousness:

He was once again a teenager in the summer of 1939, and a stranger outside Goshenville, Pennsylvania, had just helped him repair his rickety Harley on the side of the highway. In return Jack promised to *help the next fellow on down the road.* He fulfilled that promise two months later by fixing the Imbergamo brothers' Gar Wood boat on Lake George.

Their fuel system had clogged. There was an obstruction in the line.

My father held the defective shunt in his hands. It wasn't so different from the fuel system on the boat. The shunt body looked like a priming bulb. Its tubing looked like a fuel line. What if—what if the shunt body could be made with no metal, just like the priming bulb, and could be crushed and flushed from the outside instead of having to replace it? It wasn't much different than blowing debris out of a boat's fuel line.

Over the ensuing months he raced to design an improved hydrocephalus shunt in case his daughter should require another operation. The final result was an all-silicone shunt body that could be cleared of obstructions by manipulating it through the scalp.

Within a decade the Denver Shunt was being shipped all over the world. Units with slight cosmetic defects were donated to Third World countries like Ecuador, Sri Lanka, Guatemala, and Viet Nam—saving the lives of thousands of children. Under the astute business management of my mother, the device attracted the attention of some major medical firms. Several years after their retirement—with the children grown, educated, and starting families of their own—a large firm offered to purchase their medical company in a business deal that two children of the Great Depression could only dream of.

On the grand road of life, the wheels of reciprocity roll down casual and circuitous paths. In the case of the Old Man, it took nearly half a century.

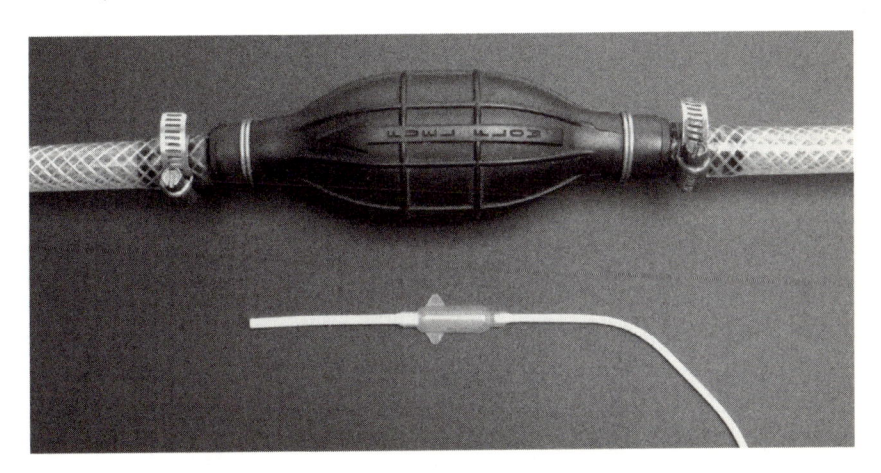

*The Denver Shunt beside a 1939 Gar Wood boat's fuel priming bulb*

★ ★ ★

**WE DAWDLED IN CAMP** the next morning and tried to locate landmarks from his 1939 visit. I wandered over to the creek and stared at the stones.

"So why do you want to go to Sturgis, Dad? I thought crowds weren't your thing."

"I promised I'd go back someday," he said.

After breakfast we rode through the Bighorn National Forest to Buffalo, Wyoming, where modern Interstate 90 now plows through the prairie, across the Powder River, and into Gillette. In 1939, the only route was via U.S. Highway 16, which looks today almost as it did back then. The old route is nearly thirty miles longer than the Interstate, and by mutual consent the Old Man and I decided to ride Route 16 at forty-three miles per hour.

We stopped at the bar in Spotted Horse where a number of leather-clad *hombres* stood outside. It was the first group of bikers we'd seen since Yellowstone. Motorcycles were beginning to come out of the woodwork as we approached the major arteries into Sturgis.

A young man struggled to get a keg of beer into the bar.

"Well, my friend," said the Old Man, "I can't help you lift it, but I can surely help you lighten it!"

The bikers broke into laughter and invited us in for a drink.

Inside the bar, I was touched by the respect the Old Man commanded.

We sat at a table with three men from Reno, Nevada. One of them had his girlfriend with him, and she seemed less than thrilled to be in rural Wyoming with a bunch of road rowdies bound for Sturgis. From the Old Man's body language, I could tell he was looking for a way to draw her into the conversation, but she just sat there sullen and unresponsive.

"So how far is it from Gillette to Sturgis?" I asked the biker next to me.

"I'd have to check the book, but it's about two hours, ain't it?"

"Yeah, somethin' like that," added another. "I think we'll end up with one more gas stop before we get there."

After trading a few stories of the road, we got ready to head out.

"Well, take care," said the Old Man. "Maybe we'll see you there."

"Hope so," replied a large biker with a white handlebar mustache. "My name's John."

"That's my name," said the Old Man.

"Mine too," I said.

The Old Man looked across the table at the sulking woman.

"Well then," he said, "I guess that makes three Jacks and a Queen!"

The bar erupted with laughter. Even the woman cracked a smile.

"Yeah, we got 'em all beat, don't we!"

I went to the cash register to settle up as the laughter continued. Across the bar I could see the woman was now engaged in an animated conversation with the Old Man.

"Who is that guy?" asked the bartender.

"That's my dad!"

★ ★ ★

**HUMAN HABITATION IN** South Dakota's Black Hills began around 7000 BC—a few thousand years after the last Ice Age. By AD 1500 the Arikara Indians had arrived. The Arikara were followed by the Cheyenne, Crow, Kiowa, and Pawnee who occupied the area until the Lakota Sioux drove them out in the 1700s. Territorial disputes continued as the Europeans arrived, culminating in the Wounded Knee Massacre of 1890, which is generally considered to be the last major campaign of the 350-year Indian Wars.

Sturgis, South Dakota, was little more than a dot on the map when the Old Man passed through in July 1939. The first Black Hills Motor Classic was held that previous August, and the Jackpine Gypsies Motorcycle Club anticipated as many as five hundred motorcycles would attend the rally's first anniversary.

Today attendance is more like five hundred thousand—as in half a million. Every bar, restaurant, hotel, nook and cranny within a fifty mile radius is full of bikes, bikers, and vendors of all shapes and sizes. Many locals simply leave town for the week, rent out their homes, and make enough money to cover two months' worth of mortgage payments.

The Old Man and I rejoined Interstate 90 near Spearfish and checked into a local college dormitory. We'd originally planned to set up our tent at Buffalo Chip or Hog Heaven campgrounds, but the dorm opportunity came up, and I told him he'd probably sleep better inside. The truth of the matter was I was embarrassed to expose him to the bawdiness typical of biker campgrounds.

I let this fact slip during lunch.

"What were you worried about, Johnny?" he exclaimed. "I was a navy man. If I were sixty years younger I'd teach those boys a thing or two."

"You mean Buffalo Chip would've been OK with you?"

"Sure," he said. "I'm fine as long as I have my blankets and nine-by-nine shelter cloth."

We went downtown just as the crowd was beginning to thicken. The Old Man took one look at the thousands of bikes along Junction Avenue and Main Street, then sat down and made the mother of all understatements.

"My," he said, "this place has changed."

We walked through the booths and exhibits all along the street. He lagged behind and stopped for anything that caught his interest.

A few blocks later we happened upon a redbrick building with large letters:

## STURGIS MOTORCYCLE MUSEUM & HALL OF FAME

"Hey Dad," I asked, "want to go into the museum?"

"Sure, why not?"

We paid the entrance fee and were greeted by several vintage posters on the museum wall. One was a B-movie promo called *Hell's Angels '69*.

"Hell's Angels?" he exclaimed. "Those don't look like any Hell's Angels I remember."

He was, of course, thinking of the Third Pursuit Squadron of the Flying Tigers.

Just then a muscular man in his sixties walked by and nodded his head with respect as he went into the museum's office. I recognized him immediately. It was Sonny Barger, the "Godfather of the Hell's Angels," who was in town for a book signing.

The museum's director, Pepper Massey, told us that John C. "Pappy" Hoel—the Pappy from the Old Man's 1939 ride—had passed away in

1989 at age eighty-four. The Old Man bowed his head in respect. It was too much to hope that any of the men he'd run across would still be alive.

We headed to the main exhibit area. My back was to the Old Man as I looked over a vintage motorcycle from the 1920s.

"Hey Dad," I said, "here's a single-cylinder—"

I turned around, but he wasn't there. I looked across the room and in the corner—as if she'd been waiting decades for this moment—was a 1930 Harley-Davidson VL Big Twin just like the Raspberry. The Old Man moved inexorably toward the bike. He began to caress her handlebars as if he had just been reunited with a forsaken, long-lost love.

The museum monitor stood up protectively but seemed to realize this was a private moment. She slowly took her seat and watched as my father's eyes turned misty, and I could only imagine the memories flooding through his mind. I could almost hear the strains of the Glenn Miller Orchestra drifting through the air:

*To you, my heart cries out, Perfidia*
*For I found you—the love of my life—in somebody else's arms.*

For a moment the Old Man was back on that dusty street in Moscow, Idaho. Then he was standing under a streetlamp in Bethlehem, Pennsylvania, with six twenty-dollar bills in his hand—blood money for a broken promise. And finally, he was screaming in the rain-soaked jungle of Manus Island holding a Japanese sword over his head.

And for the first time I understood.

The Raspberry had been his "Rosebud."

I left him alone with the VL and stepped around the corner. A group of bikers had seen the whole thing and walked up to me.

"So what's the story behind the old man and the Harley?"

"Brothers," I reflected, "that story could fill a book."

We rode to Crazy Horse Memorial the next day. The Old Man had no idea that it all started in 1939—when Chief Henry Standing Bear learned sculptor Korczak Ziolkowski had won First Prize at the New York World's Fair.

We took a long, dirt road back to Spearfish and stopped at a lush meadow beside a creek to eat a lunch of finger food.

"Is this about where you spent the night at Old Eli's?" I asked.

"Somewhere around here," the Old Man said. "I couldn't say for sure."

"Well, no doubt the Custer Wolf prowled this valley."

"Yes," he said. "Highly likely."

"Good thing we don't have anything like that anymore," I offered between bites.

He looked across the meadow and into the forest.

"But we do, Johnny," he replied pensively, "I'm afraid we do."

"What do you mean?"

"Only it's much worse," he said as he looked into the distance.

"I don't understand."

"The Osama Bin Ladens. The Zarqawis. The Al-Zawahiris. They are our Custer Wolves. They kill out of pure hatred. And we can't catch them—they're too clever—and they still enlist the help of their coyotes. Yes, I'm afraid we still have our Custer Wolves."

★ ★ ★

**WE SPENT SEVERAL** more days visiting places he passed through as a boy. By the end of our time together, we had put fifteen hundred miles on the odometer, and I'd clearly underestimated his ability to ride on the back of the bike. Yes, he was in his eighties, but I was sure now that he could have made it to Milwaukee with me, at least. I felt a twinge of guilt as we headed to Rapid City for his flight home.

The boarding area was full of bikers as the Old Man and I sat in awkward silence waiting for the plane. He looked around at all the commotion, then smiled and stared out the window.

"I've had a good, long ride, son," he sighed.

I clenched my jaws and my eyes began to get moist.

"Tell me something, Pop," I said.

"Yeah?" he asked.

"Are you still proud—"

He looked confused—but I had to know.

"Not of me," I said quickly. "I mean—are you still proud of your country? You saw it then and you've seen it now. Was it worth it—the war and all?"

A group of bikers walked past and saw the World War II and Flying Tigers patches on our leathers. They nodded with respect and the Old Man nodded back.

"Hell, yes," he replied.

★ ★ ★

**THE HARLEY FELT** lighter as I rode down Highway 44 toward Scenic, South Dakota—it felt as if a part of me was missing.

And at that very moment, as the Old Man flew into the clouds, an old Japanese man walked through the gates of the Trinity Test Site near Alamogordo, New Mexico, with the Atomic Flame, which would be extinguished that evening in a global moment of silence.

Both of these old soldiers had come full circle.

And from the bottom of my heart, I wished both of them Godspeed.

# 42

**S**HORTLY BEFORE THE RIDE I had met a Lakota woman named Marilyn Black Elk at a memorial service for her father. Wallace Black Elk was a World War II veteran and a descendant of Nicholas Black Elk, whose tragic story was chronicled in Neihardt's classic book *Black Elk Speaks*.

At Marilyn's suggestion, I rode south on State Highway 44 toward the Pine Ridge Indian Reservation. I remembered this was where the Raspberry's chain had broken and stranded the Old Man in the middle of the Badlands on July 4, 1939. It's also where another, far more sacred, chain had been broken fifty years earlier at Wounded Knee. In the words of Black Elk:

> I did not know then how much was ended. When I look back now from this high hill of my old age, I can still see the butchered women and children lying heaped and scattered all along the crooked gulch as plain as when I saw them with eyes still young. And I can see that something else died there in the bloody mud, and was buried in the blizzard. A people's dream died there. It was a beautiful dream.... The nation's hoop is broken and scattered. There is no center any longer, and the sacred tree is dead.

I turned around and rode back to the small town of Scenic. The Longhorn Saloon looks much as it did in 1939—and the sign out front still says "Indians Allowed." The old post office at Interior, where the Old Man mailed his postcards, is a decrepit green shell with paint flaking off its upper dormer under the relentless Badlands sun. Across the street stands a solid white building with painted letters:

INTERIOR SCHOOL
1939

The sun was well past its peak as I struck out east on Highway 14 toward Midland. The old roadbed was clearly evident to my right as I cruised through countless hills of prairie grass. I pulled off the highway and, lost in thought, rode several miles through the weeds over the same surface the Raspberry once traversed.

I reached Midland, South Dakota, about sundown. To my surprise, John Stroppel's Inn was still in business—complete with the mineral baths he developed in 1939. It's now run by one of his granddaughters, who charged me nineteen dollars for a room and unlimited access to the same mineral baths.

After a long soak at the Stroppel Inn, I walked over to the old redbrick bank building and peered inside its arched sandstone doorway. In the process I flushed a covey of pigeons that had been roosting in the rafters. The bank's interior was straight out of *The Twilight Zone*. The calendar on the teller's desk was frozen in time: Wednesday, May 12, 1976. The chalkboard still contained writing from that day's business, as if the bank's employees and customers had been caught up in some rapture of corporate consolidation.

Like a vital organ deprived of its blood supply, the town of Midland had been choked off from its primary source of revenue. Its major artery, U.S. Highway 14, now bypasses the heart of the downtown district. While still home to a hearty two hundred souls, Midland has certainly seen its better days—which were arguably during that pivotal summer of 1939.

Highway 14 took me through Pierre and past the towering windmills of the South Dakota Wind Energy Center. I stopped in Huron for the night. Heavy clouds loomed over Huron's "World's Largest Pheasant" as I headed east the next morning, and it was raining by the time I crossed the Minnesota border near Lake Benton.

I stopped to wait out the weather and listen to Native American flute music flowing from speakers concealed along the streets. The land was getting greener, and the influence of the Sioux Indians was becoming more evident. The places had earthy names like Split Rock Creek, Pipestone National Monument, and Upper Sioux Agency.

I rode another half-hour in the drizzle and turned south on U.S. Highway 59 toward Lake Shetek, where the Old Man once spent a dismal night under a pounding Minnesota thunderstorm, with the dreaded feeling that something awful had happened there. Thunder boomed in the distance as I rounded a bend in the road, and I could see the grove of trees where the Old Man had camped. A short while later I came upon a tall, gray granite monument perched above the bottomlands:

SLAUGHTER SLOUGH

DEDICATED TO THE MEMORY OF THOSE
WHO WERE SLAIN IN THE LAKE SHETEK
INDIAN MASSACRE OF AUG. 20, 1862

ALMIRA HATCH EVERETT (WIFE OF WILLIAM EVERETT) •
WILLIE EVERETT AGE 5 YRS • CHARLES EVERETT AGE 2 YRS •
SOPHIA WALTERS IRELAND (WIFE OF THOMAS IRELAND) •
SARAH JANE IRELAND AGE 5 • JULIANNE IRELAND AGE 3 •
SOPHIA SMITH (WIFE OF HENRY W. SMITH) • JOHN VOIGT •
ANDREW KOCH • JOHN EASTLICK AGE 29 • FREDERICK
EASTLICK AGE 4 • GILES EASTLICK AGE 2 •
WM. J. DULEY JR. AGE 10 • BELLE DULEY AGE 6

Mrs. Lavina Eastlick, one of the survivors, described the slaughter in her *Personal Narrative of the Indian Massacres of 1862:*

> On the morning of August 20, Charlie Hatch came to our house and told us that the Sioux Indians were close upon us and had already killed a number of neighbors. My husband quickly caught up his two rifles and the baby, and we left the house. I wanted to get my shoes, but my husband said I had no time, so I went barefoot. The two men went to Mr. Everett's house to get a wagon to carry the women and children. I was with Mrs. Koch and Mrs. Wright when Mr. Everett's wagon overtook us.
>
> I saw ten Indians coming after us as swiftly as they could ride. We urged the horses on, but could not get them off a walk. The men thought we had better leave the wagon, and told us to go to a swamp

not far off. Meanwhile the Indians were trying to surround us. While we were running for the swamp, Mrs. Duley's children were both shot through the shoulder. Mrs. Ireland's youngest child was shot through the leg. I received a bullet in the heel, but I kept running.

We concealed ourselves as well as we could in the tall grass, but the Indians had the advantage. Ball and shot were falling around us like hail. I was struck with a ball which passed through my clothes and just grazed my side. Then a shot struck my head, and I shouted to my husband I thought I would die. I heard someone groan twice. I asked my husband if he was shot. "He is dead," shouted Mrs. Koch.

Several times I tried to crawl away from the children to give the Indians less of a target. But as soon as I moved, the children would follow me. The Indians then came closer and shot Mrs. Smith two or three times through the hip. She screamed several times and the Indians laughed about it.

The Indians then told us to come out and said they would not kill any of the women or children. I started for the Indians, but found I could only walk with great difficulty. I looked back to see if the children were coming. My Freddy started, but an old squaw ran and struck him about the head with a club. His face was all streaming with blood. She then raised him as high as she could and threw him to the ground. I then saw my Frank on his knees, with both hands raised. "Mother! Mother!" he called. The blood was running out of his mouth in a stream.

Then an Indian shot me. The ball entered my back and came out my side, passing through my right arm. I fell down, and thought of how brutally my children had been murdered and I could not help them. After the Indians left I crawled into a bunch of weeds and lay there until night.

I could not find the children, but I could hear them screaming and crying. It was a great punishment to me to hear the children crying and moaning as the Indians cruelly tortured them. Finally I heard three guns fired and the children ceased crying. O poor, innocent ones! No one can imagine my feelings, and I wished that I could die.

Lavina Eastlick, 1862

In high school, I'd been taught all about the Sand Creek and Wounded Knee Massacres, where white soldiers brutally cut down hundreds of Native American women and children. For more than twenty years, I carried a burden of culpability for whatever part my forefathers may have played in this. But I'd never been told about the Great Sioux Massacre of 1862, where roving bands of Indians slaughtered more women and children than died at Sand Creek and Wounded Knee combined—where some eight hundred immigrant farmers and their families were tortured and murdered around New Ulm, Lake Shetek, and all along the Minnesota River.

Historians are quick to point out that the Sioux had been grossly mistreated by the U.S. government, which not only took over ancestral lands, but also failed to deliver on promised annuity payments. But as I gazed over Slaughter Slough, I could see no honor in Sioux "braves" snatching babies from their mothers and impaling them on wagons with six-inch spikes simply because they were white. I could see no justification for these "warriors" forcing husbands to watch as they cut open pregnant wives and nailed their gasping fetuses to barn doors.

"Remember Slaughter Slough!" was the rally cry as vengeful citizens used the Minnesota massacre as proof that Indians were no more than treacherous, bloodthirsty savages. And so it was that one atrocity begat another, and another, and another—until the desperate, final days of the Indian Wars at Wounded Knee.

I was glad the Old Man wasn't with me now. I wanted our time together to be positive. He'd seen enough violence in his day and needed no reminder that from Kunming to Hiroshima, Auschwitz to Stalingrad, and Slaughter Slough to Wounded Knee—brutality and hatred know no cultural boundaries.

# 43

THERE ARE STILL a handful of experts who specialize in Harley-Davidson VL Big Twins. Among them are VL Heaven's Steve Slocombe in Kent, England, and Dave "Rat" Scherk of Harbor Vintage in Jonesville, Vermont. I sent both Steve and Rat a color photo of the Raspberry and both quickly identified it as a 1930 VL retrofitted with a single John Brown Motolamp and a nonstandard exhaust. They also noted the toolbox was missing.

I got a call from Rat a few days later.

"You know, I'd stay away from that bike if I were you," he warned.

"What do you mean?" I asked in confusion.

"Looks like she's on her last legs," Rat said. "The tank's dented, cylinders are rusted, frame's probably cracked, the battery box is a mess. She'd probably leave you stranded out in the middle of Wyoming or something. Probably cost a few thousand just to make her reliable. I wouldn't buy it if I were you."

I started laughing over the phone.

"What's so funny?" he barked.

"I'm sorry, Rat," I said. "I wasn't clear. I'm not buying that bike. This picture was taken in 1939—just before the Old Man rode that VL all the way from New York to San Francisco."

"Geez," gasped Rat, "the kid had guts."

"Yep," I said, "but you're absolutely right about one thing."

"What's that?"

"It did leave him stranded in the middle of Wyoming."

A few months later, well into my trip, I discovered that a carefully restored Harley-Davidson VL Big Twin was available from Pete Gagan, the president of the Antique Motorcycle Club of America. The bike had been part of a Canadian museum collection and was just sitting in his garage. After agreeing to some terms, I left my modern Road King at St.

Paul Harley-Davidson in Minnesota and caught a westbound flight out of Minneapolis.

I arrived in Vancouver, British Columbia, and immediately made my way to Pete's garage. The VL was painted a drab, olive green and accented with broad vermillion stripes and maroon edging on the sides of her tanks. The dual Solar Cycle headlamps had been replaced with a flat-lensed John Brown Motolamp, but besides that, she looked exactly as the Raspberry did when Elliot Mills first laid eyes on her.

It took some fancy footwork to get the motorcycle across the Canada–United States border. I pleaded with customs officials that this bike was 390 pounds of Milwaukee's finest—just an old American bike coming home. A no-nonsense U.S. border officer looked over the motorcycle and took down the serial number from the right crankcase:

32VL2070

"I'd like to ride a Harley across the country myself someday," he confided. "Just can't get the time off—after 9/11 and all."

I waited inside for the verdict as customs officials discussed my situation. Finally, a blond in a dark uniform with a badge called me to the counter and said I was good to go.

"Ride safe," she said. "Keep the rubber down and watch out for cagers."

"Are you a biker?" I asked.

"My boyfriend just got me a Sporty."

I spent three days in my former hometown of Bellingham, Washington, preparing the old VL for an eighteen-hundred-mile ride. This distance, I figured, would give me a good taste of what the Old Man had to endure on his beloved but temperamental Raspberry. I tracked down a copy of the Harley-Davidson *Rider's Handbook* before heading east.

Mechanical problems appeared right away. One of the spark plug thumbscrews rattled off and the wire came loose, which caused the engine to fire on only one cylinder. I ran out of gas on State Highway 20 on top of Washington Pass and discovered the line from the bike's reserve tank was hopelessly clogged. Incredibly, I was able to coast nearly fifteen miles through the Cascade Mountains to the town of Mazama where I filled up the main tank. The taillight lens shook off somewhere near Winthrop, and the main drive chain broke just outside of Twisp.

I found a #50 chain at an agriculture supply store and used an old chainbreak tool to cut it down to size. NAPA Auto Parts had a plastic rear reflector that I filed down with a Leatherman, and a local machine shop removed a large blob of solder that was blocking the reserve fuel line. The Schebler carburetor rattled loose near the top of Chief Joseph Pass and I fixed it by dabbing the three hex screws with Loctite.

On my modern Harley, salvation could usually only be found at the nearest dealer, but nearly every problem I encountered on the VL was solved at the local hardware or auto parts store—or by simply using old-fashioned ingenuity on the side of the road.

By the time I hit Montana, I felt comfortable on the vintage bike—and puttering alone through the Big Hole Valley at sunset on that two-wheeled locomotive ranks among the most memorable rides of my life.

*Restored Harley-Davidson VL Big Twin No. 32VL2070*

I checked into a hotel in Bozeman and made plans to spend the next day riding around Yellowstone Park. At breakfast the next morning a tall, dark-haired man sat alone at the table next to me. A girl came by, and I overheard him say he'd been to the park the previous day.

"Hey," I said after she left, "did you say you were in Yellowstone yesterday?"

"Yeah," he replied, "it was beautiful. Are you headed that way?"

"That's the plan," I said. "So how was the traffic?"

"Not too bad. A few small fires are causing some delays, but don't let that discourage you from heading down there."

He looked at the leather patches covering my vest.

"Whoa," he said, "is that your old Harley parked on the grass out front?"

"That it is. I'm retracing a trip my father took in 1939."

"Dude, that's so cool! I was looking over your bike last night. What is it, an old flathead?"

"Yeah, she's a 1930s-era VL Big Twin. You know your Harleys."

"I ride a Road King myself," he said. "Actually, I just told the front desk they should call you. Did you know your bike's parked right on top of the sprinkler? I wasn't sure if you wanted a free bike wash."

I laughed and thanked him for the warning. He said he was from New York City but was in Bozeman for work. It turned out he'd gone to college in Binghamton, only a couple of hours from where the Old Man, Scarsdale, and I went to school at Rensselaer.

"Well," I finally said, "I'm outta here. Thanks for the heads-up."

"No problem," he said. "Have a good ride."

"I'm sure it will be. My name's Johnny, by the way."

"I'm Billy," he said as we shook hands, "Billy Baldwin."

I walked out to the lobby and was immediately approached by a curious group of onlookers.

"Are you with the production?" they asked, "Are you an actor?"

"No—what do you mean?"

"That was William Baldwin you were talking with back there, you know, the movie star? We thought maybe you were going over a scene."

"Nope," I said. "That was just one biker looking out for another. It's our code, you see."

* * *

I LEFT THE VL with some friends in Bozeman and flew back to Minnesota to pick up the Road King. It had been polished shiny and bright as part of the fifteen-thousand-mile scheduled service and its V-twin purred like a tiger as we headed down the Mississippi on Route 61 toward Lake City. The modern Harley felt like a magic carpet compared with the old VL freight train, but there was an almost irresistible minimalism about the vintage bike.

I was intent on learning as much as possible about the Raspberry's history, so I crossed the Mississippi at La Crosse, Wisconsin, and made a beeline for Milwaukee—home of the Harley-Davidson factory and birthplace of the VL in the fall of 1929.

It was dark by the time I hit Madison, so I set up camp at Lake Kengonsa State Park south of the city and looked for a place for supper. As I was scanning a local newspaper, my eyes screeched to a halt on a small ad at the bottom of the page. The Glenn Miller Orchestra—the reincarnation of the most popular dance band of 1939—was scheduled to perform in Milwaukee the very next night. I could hardly believe my luck.

I rode to Milwaukee the next morning and checked in with staff at Wisconsin Lutheran College where the concert was to be held. I bought lunch at the campus cafeteria and watched a lively student body as they dove into their fall semester. A group of kids sat at a table collecting donations for the victims of Hurricane Katrina. A coed named Kristie Frost told me if they reached a certain level, college president Timothy Kriewall had agreed to dye his hair pink.

"Chocolate bar for a dollar?" asked another student. "All proceeds go to Katrina relief."

"Yeah, sure," I said, feeling punchy in my leathers, "I'll take twenty of 'em."

The astonished kid counted out twenty candy bars and I walked around the lunchroom handing them out at random.

"Who's that biker guy?" some of them giggled. "Why's he wearing Panda Bear patches?"

I spent the rest of the afternoon at the Harley-Davidson factory on Juneau Avenue—just four miles down the road from campus. History seeped from each brick of this remarkable building, where the Raspberry was pieced together just as the nation's economy was falling apart. Harley-Davidson's official historian, Marty Rosenbaum, was kind enough to tell me all he knew about the VL series and the history of VL Serial No. 30V8229C.

At seven o'clock that evening, I walked into the college's Schwan Concert Hall and took a seat near the back. I felt bad for the promoters. The auditorium was almost empty—there was no way they'd break even on this gig. While cultural dregs like Eminem and Akon were playing to sold-out arenas, it seemed the Glenn Miller Orchestra—America's #1 Dance Band and inspiration to millions during World War II—could no longer even fill a 370-seat auditorium.

But then—ten minutes before show time—several large buses pulled up and began to unload passengers. Most of them stepped gingerly down the steps and out the door. Some required assistance with their wheelchairs, walkers, and canes. The buses had come from senior centers all over Milwaukee, and within five minutes the auditorium was standing room only.

The Glenn Miller Orchestra opened with "Moonlight Serenade," their signature tune, which had been heard by millions for the first time over NBC radio from the Glen Island Casino in the spring of 1939—while Trylon and Perisphere bore silent witness from the New York World's Fair across Long Island Sound. An elderly woman in front of me stretched a delicate, trembling arm toward the man beside her and placed her hand on top of his. They looked at each other and nodded. This had been their song.

The band followed with a rousing version of "Pennsylvania 6-5000"—and the old-timers gleefully remembered to shout "Pennsylvania six-five-oh-oh-oh" on the final chorus. "Tuxedo Junction" was next, followed by "Perfidia," "Little Brown Jug," and "Elmer's Tune."

Trombonist Larry O'Brien led the orchestra in a haunting version of

"Danny Boy" as an old woman to my right sat alone and dabbed tears from her eyes. It was as plain as day: nearly seven decades earlier, "Danny Boy" had been their song—hers and the young man who never came home from the war—a man like Bert Christman, maybe.

I was prepared for mechanical breakdowns on this ride. I was prepared to sleep in the rain, to go hungry, and to hitch a ride home if necessary. But nothing had prepared me for the sight of these dear, old Americans who had put their lives on the line for my generation and asked for little in return—only our respect, perhaps. It was a sight that would melt the heart of the most hardened biker, and as far as respect goes, they had earned mine in spades.

Surrounded by the Greatest Generation, I suddenly understood the passion that an old barber had tried to pass on to me some twenty-five years earlier.

★ ★ ★

**AN OLD-FASHIONED RED,** white, and blue pole used to sit at the corner of University and Evans near the University of Denver. A painted sign stood beside it:

ELMER'S BARBER SHOP

As a college student I got into the habit of stopping there every six weeks for a haircut and to chat with the proprietor—a fascinating old man named Elmer Wells. Elmer worked alone and was close to ninety. He said he used to be a music teacher in his younger days, and in the 1930s he directed a local swing band.

"Too bad I only play flute," I groused. "Not much room for flute in swing music."

"Oh, baloney!" Elmer scoffed as he worked the clippers. "Plenty of good swing music for flute. In fact, one of the most popular tunes of 1940 was "Frenesi," arranged by William Grant Still and performed by Artie Shaw. It's got a great flute part—and French horns too!"

For two years Elmer Wells cut my hair. He gave an honest haircut, but it was clear that his true passion was music. He knew all about swing and would go on and on about some old bandleader named Miller.

I got one last haircut before taking off for the bicycle trip around England. Elmer seemed keenly interested in this and inquired about my route.

"Are you going anywhere near Bedford?" he asked.

"Well, yes," I thought as I visualized the map. "It's north of London, about thirty miles west of Cambridge. I'll ride right by it."

"Son, could you do an old man a big favor?"

"Sure, you name it."

Elmer disappeared into his office and came out a few minutes later with a piece of faded paper covered in shaky writing:

> *Dreams are the building of life; They often fall apart*
> *We place each block with tender care and feel thrilled at the start*
> *Sometimes we place these blocks for years—Our dreams are coming true*
> *Misfortune strikes. Blocks tumble down. We must start dreams anew*
> *We can't escape these falling blocks no matter how we scheme*
> *It shows the timber in a man to face a broken dream.*
> *And when I reach the end of life I won't go out with fear*
> *For I know I have left some things to show that I was here*

"It'd mean a lot to me," said Elmer, "if you'd stop at an airstrip north of Bedford and pay my respects to an old friend."

"You bet," I agreed. "Just give me his name."

"Glenn Miller," he replied. "That's the last place anyone saw him alive. I wrote this poem for him after he died."

He gave me the paper and asked me to leave it at the old airfield.

"So did you know this guy?" I asked in all innocence. "This Glenn Miller?"

"Yes—" Elmer said pensively. "Yes, I knew him. I was his band teacher.

I taught him to read music. He told me he wanted a band so tight that it would sound like just one musician. That was his dream. It took him almost twenty years—but by God he made it. He didn't forget about me, either. He stopped in for a haircut every time he came back to Colorado."

It was all starting to come together.

"Elmer?" I asked. "As in 'Elmer's Tune'?"

The old man stared out the window.

His lower lip began to quiver and tears welled up in his eyes.

"He used to—" Elmer stammered, "he used to call me 'Boss.'"

# 44

**B**RYAN, OHIO, USED to sit on a major U.S. thoroughfare beside a railroad that serviced a major U.S. city. The road was rerouted in the sixties, and U.S. Highway 6 now runs two miles south of Bryan's city center. It was here that the Old Man gassed up on June 28, 1939, after riding sixty-two miles in the wrong direction.

I rode in on Sunday, September 11.

Nine-eleven is sacrosanct for most bikers. We take off work, go on memorial rides, and pay tribute to the heroes of that infamous attack. The flags at the Harley-Davidson plant fly half-mast, and many of us wear black armbands in solidarity with our fallen brothers. As I rolled out of Bryan, Ohio, I said a silent prayer that I might run into some bikers along the road. On this day in particular, I needed to be with my people.

Fifteen minutes later I spotted a large crowd gathered outside a red-bricked building with a tall white bell tower and a sign out front:

ST. JOHN LUTHERAN CHURCH

Their outdoor service was about to begin, so I cut my motor, coasted off the highway, and rolled onto a grassy parking area behind the congregation. All seats appeared to be full, but an older couple moved their belongings off the chair beside them and motioned for me to sit down.

The St. John Evangelical Lutheran Church of Stryker, Ohio, sits at the corner of the "Devil's Junction"—the spot where U.S. Route 6 crosses State Highway 66. I'd stumbled upon their annual Harvestfest, a celebration and "Feast of Ingathering Harvest" that dates back to the Book of Exodus. The church was founded in 1859.

The service began with the peal of the church's steeple bells: one long toll for each decade and a short one for each agricultural year that God had blessed their parish. I stood with the congregation as we began to sing:

*For the beauty of the earth, for the beauty of the skies.*
*For the love which from our birth, over and around*
   *us lies;*
*Lord of all, to thee we raise, this our hymn of grateful praise.*
*For the joy of human love—brother, sister, parent, child,*
*Friends on earth and friends above, for all gentle thoughts*
   *and mild;*
*Lord of all, to thee we raise, this our hymn of grateful praise.*

The preacher thanked God for their crops. He prayed for peace and understanding, and then announced there would be a special meeting Monday night to coordinate a four-county relief effort for victims of Hurricane Katrina. He called for a moment of silence for the victims of 9/11, and then gave a stirring message entitled "God's Extreme Makeover," which immediately sent my thoughts back to my experience at San Francisco's Pier 33.

A curious throng of parishioners gathered around me after the service. The men wore hats embroidered with patches of John Deere combines, Massey Ferguson tractors, and Parker's Hoosier Hybrid corn seed. They asked about my own patches, and one old-timer clad in overalls stood up and proudly recalled how he'd walked out his front door one day and hitchhiked on U.S. Highway 6 all the way to the 1939 New York World's Fair. They invited me to join them in their sprawling Harvestfest meal, which was followed by the annual Lutheran Youth Fellowship charity auction. Someone challenged Pastor Dale Kern to a $150 race through the inflatable bounce-house maze on the church lawn. The pastor, with perhaps a little divine guidance, won the race handily.

I stayed at the church until midafternoon and listened to stories of the land from the people who worked it. As I got ready leave, a Scripture from one of their bulletins caught my eye:

*I was hungry and you gave me food,*
*I was thirsty and you gave me something to drink,*
*I was a stranger and you welcomed me—*
                                           —MATTHEW 25:35

I'd wanted to spend 9/11 in the company of my people—and as I rode southeast toward Upper Sandusky and Mansfield, I realized this is exactly what had happened.

The Man Upstairs had answered my prayer.

★ ★ ★

**THE OHIO STATE REFORMATORY** in Mansfield—where the Old Man dropped off the hitchhiking prizefighter on June 27, 1939—looked familiar as I rode by in the late afternoon drizzle. One of the locals told me it had been used in the film *The Shawshank Redemption*.

A large, white cargo truck was parked in a field across from the prison. The sign read:

> HURRICANE KATRINA RELIEF TRUCK
> LEAVING FOR GULF 9-16!
> DONATE HERE
> FOOD, MEDS, TOILETRIES, CLEANING SUPPLIES

The clouds parted as the evening wore on. Amber rays of sunset reflected off my chrome as I rode east from Mt. Vernon, Ohio, to Coshocton. A local man told me that old U.S. Highway 36, where the Raspberry once rolled, was now called State Route 715 between Millwood and Nellie. Furthermore, he said, it's common for this portion of the road to be underwater each spring when the Walhonding River overflows its banks.

With the possible exception of Highway 14—west of Midland, South Dakota—Ohio's Route 715 most closely reflected my idealized image of how these roads must have looked in the summer of 1939—a dozen miles that time seemed to have forgotten.

To my amazement the service station where a welder named Pete sealed the Raspberry's gas tank was still standing near the town of Walhonding. The building was in fair condition, though it clearly hadn't seen use in decades. The remnants of three gas pumps stood on top of an oblong slab of raised concrete. Each recessed mounting hole now served as a planter base for a variety of weeds. Faded traces of yellow covered the concrete as white paint flaked off the double doors of the building's expansive service area.

In 1939 this station serviced thousands of cars that chugged along U.S. Route 36, a primary east-west highway that stretched fourteen hundred miles across the country from Uhrichsville, Ohio, to Denver, Colorado. Today it sits forgotten on the side of Route 715—bypassed by modern Highway 36 across the river to the south. The sense of nostalgia was overwhelming as I explored the deserted station and ran my hands over the wood and concrete, as if it might carry me back to when my nineteen-year-old father stood tall, young, and whole.

While the service station was nostalgic, the old steel bridge crossing the Walhonding River was downright spooky. It rose from the mist like a rusty green dragon guarding the entrance to an Emerald City. I climbed over the concrete barriers at the end of the derelict bridge and walked across the ivy-choked metal grating that the Raspberry clattered over just days after traversing the streets of New York City. Thick green paint peeled off the steel rails, giving way to burnt, blistered, and corroded metal. A good-sized tree was stuck in the bridge girders twenty feet overhead. Evidently floodwaters still ran high in this region.

*A Ghost Bridge in the Muskingum Watershed*

I spent the night camped beside the Harley directly below the Mohawk Dam. The smell of hot coffee woke me up in the morning, as two nearby campers named Dave and Phyllis made breakfast and prepared to fish and squirrel hunt in the Muskingum Watershed.

"Is it really worth bagging squirrels?" I asked. "Doesn't seem there'd be much meat on 'em."

"Yes, indeed," Dave replied, "those fox squirrels can get up to two pounds. Plenty of good meat, right babe?"

"You bet," said Phyllis. "You going to be around tonight? You're welcome to have squirrel stew with us if we get any."

An hour later I was in Coshocton eating pancakes at a local café. A couple of guys at the booth next to me were having an animated conversation about the government's response to Hurricane Katrina. It reminded me of my conversations with Jane Fonda's cousin.

"I can't believe the mentality down there," one ranted. "They had fair warning. They were told to evacuate, but they stayed put and now they expect the government to bail them out!"

"Well, that's the government's role, isn't it?" asked the other.

"I beg your pardon?"

"To serve, protect, and take care of the people."

"Well, you're two-thirds right, but the government's role isn't to 'take care of the people.' It's to protect the *rights* of the people, not provide cradle-to-grave support. Where's the self-sufficiency?"

"Yeah, well where's FEMA?" the other asked rhetorically.

"Dodging bullets!" the first man snapped. "Not only is this mob attacking their own people, they're shooting at their rescuers! You don't see that stuff around here, where farmers leave produce and money boxes out in full view on the honor system. But I suppose you'd call me a racist for even mentioning that."

It was a lively debate that only escalated when the bill arrived. Each man insisted on buying the other's breakfast. In true spirit of the biker, these guys could disagree until they were blue in the face, but at the end of the day they were still best friends.

*What a great country,* I thought.

*Nel cor più non mi sento!*

I reminded myself to watch out for anyone who spoke Italian. No luck so far.

* * *

**INTERSTATE 77 NOW** runs due south over old U.S. Route 21 between Newcomerstown, Ohio, and Parkersburg, West Virginia, where the Old Man rode smack through a swarm of bees. This was also the first place he noticed a timing problem that ultimately stranded him in the middle of Wyoming's Bighorn National Forest.

At Parkersburg I took U.S. Highway 50 due east to Clarksburg, where the Old Man had purchased a few nuts and bolts for the Raspberry and gave her a "general going over" at a local Harley-Davidson shop on June 26, 1939.

An hour later I rode into the mountaintop town of Aurora, West Virginia, on the northern edge of the Monongahela National Forest just west of the Maryland state line. It was beginning to feel like Civil War country as I rode by markers commemorating battles 140 years past. It was in Aurora that the Old Man used bailing wire to reattach the Raspberry's chain guard so it wouldn't rattle against the rear sprocket. It's also where he purchased the sardines, pilot biscuits, peanuts, horehound drops, and halazone tablets that sustained him in South Dakota and Wyoming.

An oblong, yellow building stood in the center of town with a General Store sign out front. I went inside and was immediately thrust back in time. Aurora had restored McCrum's General Store! I half-expected to look around the corner and see the Old Man—age nineteen, hands and face covered with grease—carefully counting out his nickels. And I would have given ten years of my life for it to be so.

"This is fantastic!" I gushed to a woman behind the antique register. "What's the story here?"

"We're trying to recreate this store as it might have looked in 1939," she replied.

I stared at the shelves. They were stocked with vintage containers of Boraxo Powdered Hand Soap, Clabber Girl Baking Powder, Ipana Toothpaste, Sal Hepatica, Junket Quick Fudge and Icing Mix, Maxwell House

Coffee, Hershey's Cocoa, Post Toasties Corn Flakes, 1-Minute Quick Mother's Oats, Ivory Soap, candy, flypaper, washboards, mousetraps, and a hundred other items.

A man joined the conversation. He was a historian, an expert in Americana.

"So why 1939?" I asked.

"Well," the man answered, "the world in 1939 was on the brink of an irrevocable transformation, at a 'tipping point' so to speak. There were so many pivotal events that year—from cultural to political to scientific—so much hope wrapped up in one short summer. But it was the calm before the storm. Did you know there were actually two world's fairs in 1939? One in San Francisco and one in New York City. A lucky few were able to see them both."

"That would have been an incredible experience," I said wistfully.

And then it occurred to me that for all his traveling, the Old Man had spent less than a day at each fair—barely enough time to scratch the surface. While the fairs were his destination, truly the most meaningful part of his trip had been the journey.

The historian and I walked outside and stood beside the Harley.

"Think about 1939 for a moment," he continued. "Two world's fairs, *The Wizard of Oz, Gone with the Wind, Of Mice and Men,* Lou Gehrig, *The Grapes of Wrath,* Einstein's letter to Roosevelt—"

*Pensacola, Bert Christman, Tex Hill, Scarsdale Jack, Ten Sleep Canyon, Choctawhatchee, Horace, Burt, the Raspberry, Ron DeMarzio, and Tony Imbergamo—*

I nodded in agreement, "Yes, 1939 is the perfect year for this store."

"And don't forget the music!" he said giddily. "Benny Goodman, Kay Kyser, Glenn Miller, the Dorsey brothers, Louis Armstrong, Billie Holiday. Some great film scores too. Say, have you ever heard of an American composer named Aaron Copland?"

I nodded and smiled slightly, then felt my eyes growing moist as my mind drifted back twenty-five years to a promise I had never kept.

★ ★ ★

MY COUSIN VALERIE was tall, blonde, and drop-dead gorgeous. I was a gawky teenager and knew I could never get a girlfriend as cute as Val. Late one summer afternoon, we were sitting in our swimsuits on the Lake George cabin dock when an announcement came over the radio.

Aaron Copland would be conducting the Philadelphia Orchestra that night in Saratoga Springs, a few miles south of the lake.

"Hey Val," I said, "let's go! We can make it if we shake a leg."

We dashed up to the cabin and pulled out our best clothes. Val wore a light summer dress and I put on a set of slacks with a shirt and tie. We gussied each other up as best we could, jumped into our Fay and Bowen motor launch, and chugged three miles down the lake to where our car was parked.

By the time we got to Saratoga Performing Arts Center a large crowd had gathered, and our seats were somewhere in the nosebleed section. I didn't care. Just to be in the same auditorium with one of my heroes was good enough for me.

Copland conducted portions of *Rodeo, Appalachian Spring, Billy the Kid,* and *El Salón México*. In a chill of déjà vu, the hair stiffened on my neck during "Fanfare for the Common Man" and I felt like standing at attention.

After the concert Valerie and I went to the area behind the outdoor stage where some of the musicians were milling about. In my flute-playing days, I'd memorized the roster of major U.S. orchestras like the Old Man knew the lineup of the New York Yankees. I walked over to one of the musicians and struck up a conversation.

"So which one is Murray Panitz?" I finally asked. "Your principal flute player."

"Panitz?" the man said. "He's the guy standing by the tree over there. Kind of looks like Allen Funt from *Candid Camera*."

"Excellent," I said. "What's your instrument?"

"Cello," he said in a thick Philly accent, "I play the cello."

The seats of the concert hall were almost empty as the audience headed home. The musicians slowly made their way across the grass to Saratoga's Hall of Springs, where there appeared to be some kind of reception.

"Your girlfriend," remarked the cellist, "she's gorgeous. Reminds me of Cheryl Ladd from *Charlie's Angels*."

"Thank you," I said, not particularly eager to confess she was my eighteen-year-old cousin.

"Say," he offered, "we're having a little reception across the way there. Why don't you two join us? I'll get you in if anybody hassles you."

"That'd be great!" I said. "Thanks a lot."

"No problem. What'd you say your name was?"

"Newkirk."

"Oh yeah, like Richard Dawson from *Hogan's Heroes*."

I was beginning to think he did all his practicing in front of the tube.

Valerie and I walked past the bubbling soda fountains of Saratoga Spa State Park to the Hall of Springs. To my dismay a large bouncer in a tuxedo guarded the door and our cellist was nowhere to be seen.

"What do we do now?" I asked Val.

"Don't worry," she said, "I can handle this guy. You sneak in—I'll join you later."

I hid behind one of the tall, white pillars near the door as my "date" began to sweet-talk the bouncer and position her body so he'd have to look away from me. I slipped in at just the right moment and entered the palatial reception hall, which had been decked out with tables covered in food, flowers, and ice sculptures.

Valerie waltzed in a few minutes later and we both giggled in disbelief that we'd actually pulled it off. It was horseracing season in Saratoga, and here we were hobnobbing with royalty. The guest list read like a who's who of New York socialites: Rockefellers, Vanderbilts, Astors, Hiltons, Marylou Whitney, and countless other luminaries. While I wore a tie and could possibly talk the talk, I was still a biker at heart and as out of place at this party as a Connecticut Yankee in King Arthur's court.

"Well," said Val, "when in Rome—"

"Maestro!" I said, extending my hand to conductor Eugene Ormandy. "Good to see you again. The orchestra sounded superb, as usual."

"Why, uh," said the confused conductor, "thank you, young man."

Valerie and I sampled the food and drink and began to explore the building. After a sweep through the hall, we poked our heads into a quiet side room near the rear, and there, sitting in an upholstered wingback chair, was Aaron Copland.

He took a sip from his teacup and set it down on the table beside him. He nodded his head politely, almost as if he were expecting us.

"Come in," said Copland. "Come in. I'm so happy to see young people at these concerts."

He shook our hands, smiled, and told us some of his experiences as a young, struggling musician during the Great Depression. I told him I thought classical music was grossly underappreciated in America, and Copland reluctantly agreed.

"Are you a musician?" Copland asked.

"I play the flute," I replied. "And I'm very fond of your *Duo for Flute and Piano*."

"Ah," he sighed, "the *Duo*. My final composition, you know—"

Copland was about eighty, and over the past few years had been showing increasing signs of senility. To me, he looked poignantly feeble up close. This concert would prove to be one of his last, just as his *Duo for Flute and Piano* was indeed his last extended work.

"Tell me, young man," he said, "have you ever performed my *Duo*?"

"No," I said glibly, "I'm just an amateur. I probably couldn't do justice to your work so I'm not even going to try."

Copland's expression immediately shifted from inquisitiveness to disappointment, as if I had just hurt his feelings. He moved forward in his chair and took both my hands in his.

"Nonsense," he said firmly. "Nonsense, my boy. Play my music. Play it proudly. Play it from your heart. As long as you play it from your heart, I know it will be wonderful."

His hands were soft and warm, though trembling slightly. I looked into his eyes, which were awaiting my response in the prolonged silence that followed.

Valerie looked on as I struggled with what to say.

"I will," I promised. "I *will* play it."

Aaron Copland settled back into his chair.

"Thank you," he sighed. "Thank you."

As Valerie and I motored back across the lake that night, I felt bad about what I'd said. My performing days were over. I'd never have the chance to play Copland's *Duo* and I had no right to promise him I would.

And the Old Man told me never to break my promises.

★ ★ ★

**I CONTINUED EAST** on U.S. Highway 50 to Mt. Storm, West Virginia, and then pointed the Harley south toward Petersburg. I felt compelled to get off the bike and walk back to the junction of Route 42 and Highway 50. As I placed both palms on the pavement, it seemed odd that this was the same highway where, a decade earlier and seventeen hundred miles west, I had landed an airplane in distress and learned a great deal about friendship, honor, loyalty, and integrity.

I stopped in Petersburg that night and inquired about the Fox and Ox Auto Camp where the Old Man first fashioned his shelter cloth cocoon on June 25, 1939. No one had ever heard of the auto camp, but an old timer thought he recalled a Civil War battle site at Petersburg Gap called "Fox and Ox Rocks." By sunrise the Harley and I were chugging over the picturesque Shenandoah Mountains toward Harrisonburg, Virginia.

In one of the more revealing moments of the Old Man's trip, this was where he spent half a day hitchhiking sixty-four miles back and forth from Luray just to save a dollar and a half. A new inner tube would have cost him two bucks—but welding the old one only cost fifty cents. In the Great Depression, every nickel counted.

The Luray Caverns, where the Old Man and Stuart Crossman spent the night of June 24, now boasts half a million visitors per year. The adjoining campground has been covered with a parking lot, but the stonework of the Entrance Building has retained much of its original appearance. I left Luray on U.S. Route 211, part of the original Lee Highway National Auto Trail that connected New York City to San Francisco in the 1920s. Within fifteen minutes I was sitting on the side of Shenandoah National Park's Skyline Drive with a jaw-dropping view of the Blue Ridge Mountains, where the Appalachian Trail has run since 1937. It seemed so incongruous, as I knew the sprawling capital of Washington, D.C., lay just an hour to the east.

The first landmark I saw was the Washington Monument standing in the distance like a watchtower. I soon was on Highway 50 again and crossed the Potomac at Arlington National Cemetery, then rode down Constitution Avenue past the Lincoln Memorial and the U.S. Capitol Building. A group of dignitaries was gathered out front, and "No Parking" signs were everywhere. A Capitol policeman was about to shoo me away, but cut me some slack when I told him I'd come all the way from San Francisco. He rode a Harley, he said.

I couldn't get anywhere near the White House—and the recent security crackdown made the image of the Raspberry coughing, spitting, and backfiring like a rifle beside the South Portico lawn even more amusing. After getting thoroughly lost in Washington's Beltway, I finally hit Baltimore and made a fifty-mile side trip.

The sun was low as I rode into the empty parking lot in the shadow of the huge bar and shield at Harley-Davidson's York, Pennsylvania, plant. Five banners flew half-mast that September evening: the United States flag, the Pennsylvania flag, the Harley-Davidson banner, the POW/MIA flag, and the banner of the International Association of Machinists and Aerospace Workers labor union. It was where my 100th Anniversary FLHRCI Road King Classic No. 1HD1FRW483Y00354 had rolled off the production line several years earlier.

I pulled into Lancaster at sunset and puttered through the countryside searching for my sister's house. The first person I saw was an Amish boy of about seventeen stoically kicking his scooter down Quarry Road.

"*Verzeihen sie!*" I shouted in high German. "*Kennst du die Lapp Familie in der Nähe?*"

[Excuse me! Do you know the Lapp family that lives in this area?]

"Eh?" he replied. "*Welli Lapp Familye? Es gibt doch viele Lapps in der Nochberschaft.*"

[Which Lapp family? There's a bunch of us Lapps around here.]

"Samuel?" I asked. "Is that you? You're all grown up!"

"Johann!" he beamed, recognizing me from years past. "Dot's some scoota you got dair."

# 45

*And the Raven, never flitting, still is sitting, still is sitting
On the pallid bust of Pallas just above my chamber door;
And his eyes have all the seeming of a
demon's that is dreaming,
And the lamplight o'er him streaming throws
his shadow on the floor;*

—Edgar Allen Poe

*Put off, concerning your former manner of living,
the old man which is corrupt*

—Book of Ephesians, Chapter 4, v. 22

A SIGN AT A Mennonite bakery caught my eye as I rode out of Lancaster the next morning:

Pray for the Hurricane Victims

I bought a few baked goods for breakfast and then pointed the Harley east.

New York City—the end of the journey—was only a few hours away.

The number of motorcycles on the road had been like a bell curve across the country. The peak, of course, had been at Sturgis, but there were fewer and fewer bikers as I rode east through Goshenville, around Philadelphia, and on to Trenton, New Jersey, where I stopped for gas.

The attendant walked up to my Harley with a blank, expectant stare.

"Uh, how ya doin'?" I asked after an awkward pause.

"I do OK," he finally said. "So, fill up?"

He was from India—he'd been speaking Hindi with a coworker.

"Sure, I'll fill her up. I'm headed to Manhattan and I don't want to stop for gas again. Do I need to pay first or something?"

"No," he said, "I the one to fill up. Is New Jersey law. No pump your own gas here."

"Say what?" I exclaimed.

"Is stupid law, I know."

"Are you familiar with these bikes?"

"No, but I be careful."

"All right," I mumbled. "But just so you know, most bikers don't like others touching their rides. It's like using their toothbrush or putting a hand on their lady."

"Yeah," he repeated, "is stupid law."

It felt euphoric to ride over the Outerbridge Crossing to Staten Island as I anticipated walking on the grounds of the 1939 New York World's Fair, where the Old Man's journey had begun. Someone said it had been turned into a park, Flushing Meadows Corona Park. Perfect—I'd ride into Queens and get one of those kosher hot dogs from a park vendor. There'd be bicycles and flowers and couples walking hand in hand. Maybe that's where Harry met Sally.

But before I could go to Queens, I had to visit a place where a young man—long since dead—had become the Raspberry's first owner back in the spring of 1930. I took Victory Boulevard northeast and headed down Bay Street toward the Verrazano-Narrows Bridge. As I approached the corner of Baltic and Bay, an old sign appeared above a doorway with plate glass windows on either side:

Frank Lombardi & Sons
Established 1905
Harley-Davidson Motorcycles

Two world wars and a depression had ravaged the nation. Two world's fairs had come and gone. But some things endured—and Frank Lombardi's Harley shop was one of them.

I placed my hands on the wooden window frame and tried to picture the Raspberry peering out with her dual Solar Cycle headlamps during that dreary first winter of the Great Depression. I imagined twenty-one-year-old Elliot Mills gazing back at her.

*Ride me*—she'd said—*if you'll take care of me, I'll take care of you.*

"Can I help you, bro?" said a man from inside.

"You already have," I sighed. "I'm just closing the circle."

I stopped at a Staten Island pizzeria for lunch. An energetic man behind the counter tossed pizza dough into the air like a circus acrobat as he chattered away in a romantic, lyrical language.

"Hey," I asked, "do you speak Italian?"

"Yeah," he smiled.

"You do? Because there's this song, and I've been trying to figure out what it means. It goes *Nel cor più non mi sento*."

"Say it again?" he asked.

"*Nel cor più non mi sento*."

"Oh—*nel corpo non mi sento*? Uh, my body, uh, do no feel, you know, like my body do not feel to do nothin'. You know?"

It didn't make sense—not in the context of what I'd heard in Moscow, Idaho. I thanked him with a handshake and walked perplexed and bewildered out of the restaurant.

Arthur Von Briesen Park sits on the southwest shore of New York's Upper Bay two miles south of Lombardi and Sons. On a clear day the park offers unobstructed views of Manhattan, Brooklyn, the Statue of Liberty, and the Verrazano-Narrows Bridge. I rode south on Bay Street, dismounted, and walked up a winding path to a white oak tree where I looked out on the familiar, stately view of Manhattan's skyline. The absence of the Twin Towers hit me like a gut punch—as if I'd anticipated the welcome smile of a woman, only to discover some thug had knocked out her front teeth while I was away.

I suddenly recalled a scene from my youth, when two boys on shiny mini-bikes had stopped on the path in front of me. They had a freedom I lacked, and for some reason I hated them for it. I was so insanely envious that I sic'd my dog on them. And it was clear to me now that just like that petulant little boy, the terrorists who target us cannot see past their own hatred—their hatred of our freedoms. We live as we choose, come and go as we please, and are free to believe or not believe. They can't stand it, so they sic their dogs on us—then cry foul if we fight back.

A wave of dread swept over me as I sensed the voice of an ancient foe—a foe that had waited for this very moment to launch the attack.

It abruptly reared its head, rattled its tail, and struck.

*Thought you were something, didn't you? Taking those backstabbing Muslims into your home, helping them with their schoolwork, treating them like family. But they played you like the fool you are, then betrayed you with a piece of silver and a kiss—just like Judas!*

"Samira?" I gasped.

My face grew pale and I raised a hand to my cheek and recalled the touch of her rose-petaled lips. Tears welled up in my eyes. My body began to tremble as I stared across the bay toward the former World Trade Center.

"Ali Akbar?" I screamed. "Reza? Fadil? Abdul Aziz? For the love of God, tell me you had nothing to do with this!"

I slouched back down the hill to the Harley and roared across the Verrazano-Narrows Bridge toward Brooklyn and the Grand Central Parkway. I couldn't get the Italian's disturbing words out of my head.

I had to know for sure.

I stopped at a bookstore, found an Italian-English dictionary, and scribbled down the closest translation I could muster beside the words I had shouted so freely across the country:

*Nel cor più non mi sento*
*Brillar la gioventù—*

I shook my head in confusion, crammed the scrap of paper into my pocket, and headed to Flushing Meadows Corona Park. I needed to bask in the glory of Trylon and Perisphere—where my father stood during that gilded summer of 1939—and where my country chose to "look forward in bright hope rather than backward with regret." I should have been elated, jubilant—like that nineteen-year-old as he triumphantly rode over the Golden Gate Bridge.

Instead I was crushed by a nostalgic melancholy.

The park lay deserted beneath a dreary, steel-gray sky. The fountains were bone dry and speckled with trash. The former fairgrounds were empty and desolate. No hot dog vendors. No couples holding hands. No Harry. No Sally. A crusty row of dead trees encircled the decrepit New York State Pavilion and other decomposing artifacts of the previous world's fair.

There was no Roosevelt here. No Mayor LaGuardia. No Mickey Rooney or Judy Garland. No Stuart Crossman—and no Jack Newkirk. The crowds who once flocked to this place had vanished. The hallowed ground of the 1939 New York World's Fair lay fallow—a mirror image of San Francisco's crumbling Treasure Island.

The steely-cold Unisphere loomed in the distance like a sentinel over Trylon and Perisphere's grave, and the old New York City Building bore silent witness as I rode the Harley in feckless circles around the empty fountain. There were no park police, no fairgoers, no biker brothers—no one to share in my uncertain victory. After what seemed like hours, I climbed off the bike and sat down on the cement ring surrounding the Unisphere.

I felt like Charleton Heston in the final scene of *Planet of the Apes*.

Suddenly nothing seemed more important than to hear my father's voice. I desperately punched the familiar sequence into my cell phone and waited—but it just rang and rang like an echo in a primeval cave as a hissing laughter slithered up from the depths.

*And the day is coming when he'll never answer that phone again! Ever! You know that don't you? Don't you?*

I tried desperately to shut it out. I just wanted it to leave me alone.

*Leave you alone? I am Crotalus! I am the Raven! I will always be here— waiting and watching for my moment to strike.*

I buried my head in my hands and tears began to dot the concrete. My mind filled with images of the Old Man and his valiant but futile efforts to ward off the ravages of time. He had asked me why I was taking this trip, and I'd given him some glib answer. But the underlying truth was clear now: my father was passing before my eyes and I had no idea how to deal with it. I thought if I could take one final trip with him—one last journey through time—it would somehow make it easier to say goodbye.

But I had failed. Nothing makes it easier.

I could not escape the inevitable. Someday soon my father and the generation he represents would be gone. My body shook with sobs as I cowered below the Unisphere globe like a fallen statue of Atlas.

*Tears—tears? What kind of a biker are you, you wuss? Your bros would be so ashamed. Real men don't shed tears—not even for their fathers.*

I sat inconsolable as gray skies sprinkled rain onto the concrete and turned the area below me into a uniform patch of wet.

"Yo," said a surly voice to my right. "Why you ridin' a black bike with a yellow helmet?"

I looked up to see two black men standing next to the Harley.

"Because," I growled, "I float like a butterfly and I sting like a bee."

The men paused, looked at each other, and broke into smiles.

"Hey!" they laughed. "You're all right, man! You're cool, brother. So where'd you ride from, anyhow?"

"San Francisco."

"That's one long ride, brother."

★ ★ ★

**I LEFT FLUSHING** Meadows in the rain and rode over the Brooklyn Bridge to Manhattan. Ground Zero at the World Trade Center showed evidence of a memorial some biker brothers had left nearby. My mind swam through a memory-drenched fog as I made my solitary way through the Lower East Side, up FDR Drive, and on toward New Rochelle.

Six million bikers in this country—but I hadn't seen a brother since Baltimore.

Where, oh where, were my people?

I rolled to a stop at Glen Island Park off Pelham Road. The elegant white building that launched the fledgling Glenn Miller Orchestra in the summer of 1939 still stands, but the former Glen Island Casino is no more.

I closed my eyes—for a moment I was back in 1659. The Dutch ship *Moesman* was sailing past Sands Point in the waters of Long Island Sound. My ancestors stood on deck and looked optimistically at their New World as Captain Jacob Staets skillfully piloted the vessel toward the East River.

I lifted my hand to wave, but I sensed that ominous hissing again—and suddenly found myself surrounded by a brood of vipers. They formed a semicircle, reared their heads, and shook their rattles. They had no intention of leaving me alone.

*Slavery, Inequality, Racism*, jeered one.

*Sand Creek, Wounded Knee, My Lai*, taunted another.

They struck from all sides like bullies on the playground.

*Watergate, Lewinsky, Voter Fraud!*

*Terrorism, War, Brutality!*

*Global Warming, Pollution, Nuclear Waste!*

And in the background, one of them whispered a familiar mantra as it swayed to and fro.

*Nel cor più non mi sento, brillar la gioventù—*

I opened my eyes, reached into my chaps, and pulled out the paper scrap from the bookstore: My heart has lost its feeling, and the brilliance of its youth. *So that's been it—all across America. You clever little devils!*

And as surely as my father had vanquished *Crotalus horridus*—as surely as Scarsdale Jack had shouted down the alligators and vultures of the Choctawhatchee—I knew my time had come. It was my turn to face the enemy—an enemy that wanted me to fail, forget, and forsake everything that had brought me here.

I closed my eyes again, and in the spirit of the Flying Tigers, turned to face the adversary head on. I recognized some of them from Pier 33—Anger, Bitterness, Deception, Defeatism, Hatred—but I'd encountered them before and knew how they'd mount their attack.

Anger and Bitterness—having lost the battles in San Francisco and Santa Rosa—had altered their strategy. Instead of celebrating the banquet of freedom I'd just ridden through, they wanted me to fixate on a few spots on the tablecloth—to accentuate the negative—as if any and all of my country's greatness had been eclipsed by a few of her shortcomings.

Deception slithered back and forth like a sidewinder. He wanted me to confuse change with improvement, to embrace hope instead of resolve, and to appease our enemies instead of oppose them. He wanted me to believe that tough times only make us bitter—not better—and that our borders, sovereignty, and common language are somehow tantamount to racism. Deception told me that faith is a sign of weakness—and that I should worship the planet instead of its Creator. And he would have me believe that the heart has gone out of our country, that it has seen its zenith, and that we've squandered the brilliance of our youth.

The largest of them all was Guilt—and I knew that one strike from this monster could paralyze a nation. But Guilt is not the same as repentance. Guilt is an indulgence—a mock penance—and to wallow in it is like nursing those extra few beers at the bar instead of heading back home where we belong. Feeling good is not the same as doing good—and no good ever came from relentlessly revisiting the bad.

And then there was Defeatism. He wanted me to think that only a small percentage of my country—six million screaming bikers—still have faith in freedom's ultimate triumph. But if Defeatism thinks my people can be broken in just one generation, then he has grossly underestimated us.

Because just who are my people, anyway?

He's the farmer from Washington State named Matt Lyons, who feeds four thousand with a crew of four. She's the singer in Idaho named Poeina, who has the guts to belt out opera beside a trash dumpster because it's her passion. He's a New York Jew named Aaron Copland, a black airman from Tuskegee, Alabama, a ninety-year-old barber from Colorado, an Oregon Wal-Mart worker, a Texas billionaire, and a Manhattan fireman. He's the one who faces the foe and says, "Let's roll!"

These are my people—there are three hundred million of us.

And my people don't run from their challenges. They run toward them.

We don't always see eye-to-eye, but when the chips are down, we stand arm-in-arm. We may not always live up to our ideals, but show me a people who have ever set higher ones.

The heart has not gone out of my country. The brilliance of its youth is reborn with each generation that values freedom, honor, and respect—and I believe our Greatest Generation is yet to come.

Ours is not a time for surrender. It is a time for choosing.

And if I truly have to bid the Old Man goodbye, then I can also say goodbye to the old man within me—the old man that is corrupt—the one that listens to the voices of Fear, Hatred, Guilt, Apathy, Defeatism, and Bitterness. Because after a ten-thousand-mile ride through the promised land, that man is no longer who I am.

When I opened my eyes again, the sun had broken through the clouds and the snakes had scurried back to hell where they came from.

I walked back to the Harley, crumpled up the paper scrap, and tossed it into the trash.

I had one more promise to keep.

★ ★ ★

**THE CHURCH OF** St. James the Less sits a few blocks north of Popham Road in Scarsdale, New York. My V-twin shuddered to a stop beside the churchyard as I dismounted the Harley and took the flute out of my saddlebag—the flute I'd carried all across America. I meandered slowly through a garden of stone until I came upon an old, gray granite slab covered with ivy:

And in the stillness of the graveyard, surrounded by the birds and the trees, I brought the flute to my lips and played Aaron Copland's *Duo*.

I played it proudly.

I played it from the heart.

And I played it in hope that the notes of a twenty-five-year-old promise would float over the trees and up the Hudson to Peekskill, where the composer spent the last years of his life.

The Mexicans working on the church roof laid down their tools. They stood up, removed their hats, and faced my direction. They seemed to understand that in a biker's world, it's all about respect—and what a world it would be if this were true for everyone.

I drew my knife and cut the Panda Bear squadron patch off my leather jacket. I thrust the wooden shaft of an American flag into the ground through a hole in the patch, then faced the Panda eastward so my fallen brother could once again face the Rising Sun.

I removed a stone from my vest pocket—the stone I'd picked up a decade earlier on Highway 50 beside my broken airplane. *It's so smooth*, I thought, *as though it's made a ten-thousand-mile journey down a river.* I dug a small hole in the grave and buried it over Scarsdale's heart.

And I suppose, in a sense, that I am that stone.

I am a biker.

I stand by my opinions. I stand by my convictions. I stand by my people.

But like that stone, a ten-thousand-mile journey has softened my rough edges. It's rolled me over ten thousand other stones of all colors and sizes—and I have respect for them all.

But don't tread on me—or any of my people—because I will defend them to my last breath.

I've made my mistakes. But I've learned from them.

I am not an American. I am *the* American.

★ ★ ★

THE HARLEY-DAVIDSON V-TWIN chugged up Route 9N toward Bolton Landing, New York. There was a touch of fall in the air—a time of year that some people call Indian summer. A blue Morris canoe lay upside down on the dock near a place they used to call Bell Point. Lake George was calm across Northwest Bay and into the Narrows, and it was a fine day for a ride.

I parked the Harley under an oak tree and lowered the canoe into the lake. My paddle dipped into the water five hundred times before I reached the tip of Tongue Mountain, where small wavelets broke gently against the rocks as they'd done for centuries.

High on the mountainside, *Crotalus horridus* cowered deep within the rocks—and he dared not come out today. I paddled out of the Narrows and let the canoe glide into the bay.

I'd ridden all the way from San Francisco.

Now I'm in New York—and once again, I see ghosts.

Horace is doing handstand pushups from the gunwales of his green canoe. Scarsdale stands on the porch discussing aeronautics with Burt, as both of them make fluid motions with their hands like Tai Chi. My nineteen-year-old father bounds up the stone path with a snapping turtle he's just caught for his mother.

A broad smile spreads over my face. I thrust my right hand high with fingers outstretched. My salute is returned as Burt, Horace, Scarsdale, and Jack turn to me and reach toward the sky. Their message is as clear as the water beneath my canoe:

*Behold your country—which we now pass on to you. Travel her with pride. Treat her with respect. Defend her with your life. And leave the place a little better than when you found it.*

My eyes blink in the morning sun. When I open them again, all the men have disappeared—all but the Old Man, who lies asleep on the porch hammock.

His body is spent, his hearing is gone—a sacrifice to the guns of war—and he is not long for this earth. He has begun "the journey that will lead to the sunset of his life."

Ride safe, Old Man. *Vaya con Dios.*

We'll do our best to make you proud.

But remember, you promised you'd all wait up for us at the Golden Gate.

# *Epilogue*

IN JULY 1991—fifty years after their formation—the AVG Flying Tigers were officially recognized as legitimate veterans of World War II. Scarsdale Jack Newkirk was posthumously awarded the Distinguished Flying Cross by the Secretary of the Air Force. In April 2007 Scarsdale Jack's medal was presented to former Lt. John B. Newkirk—the Old Man—by Panda Bear pilot Pete Wright at the Flying Tigers' sixty-fifth annual reunion with the following citation:

> John V. Newkirk distinguished himself by extraordinary achievement while participating in aerial flight in the South China and Southeast Asia theater, from 7 December 1941 to 24 March 1942 . . . this extraordinary performance in the face of seemingly overwhelming odds was a major factor in defeating the enemy's invasion of South China. The professional competence, aerial skill, and devotion to duty displayed by "Scarsdale Jack" reflect great credit upon himself and the Armed Forces of the United States.

Over a dozen AVG veterans were in attendance, including Tex Hill, Buster Keeton, Dick Rossi, Frank Losonsky, Joe Poshefko, Red Foster, and Chuck Baisden. Pete Wright died five weeks later. Tex Hill passed away on October 11, 2007, and Dick Rossi died April 17, 2008. As of this writing, fewer than twenty Flying Tigers remain.

Virginia Jane Dunham, Scarsdale Jack's widow, eventually remarried. Her husband was U.S. diplomat Charles Dudley Withers, the United States Ambassador to Rwanda. She died in Naples, Florida, on July 16, 1982, and left no children.

The airfield west of Ft. Collins, Colorado, was named in honor of that town's first World War II casualty—AVG Flight Leader Bert Christman. Greg "Pappy" Boyington went on to lead the Black Sheep Squadron in the Pacific, where he was ultimately awarded the Medal of Honor.

Throughout this book, I have used *crotalus horridus*—the eastern timber rattlesnake—as a metaphor for the lesser angels of our nature. In actuality, *crotalus* is a vital part of our ecosystem and national heritage, and since 1983 has been a protected species under New York Environmental Conservation Law. The seasonal residents of Tongue Mountain—including the Newkirk family—no longer kill this animal and have learned to coexist in an environment of mutual respect. Should the reader be fortunate enough to encounter this rare creature, please treat it with the same respect you would the American Bald Eagle.

John J. Newkirk
Denver, Colorado

# Acknowledgments

**M**Y GRANDMOTHER Louise Leavenworth Newkirk (1885–1964) deserves credit for preserving the numerous postcards, World War II clippings, letters, and telegrams central to this book. For sixty years these artifacts sat in a dusty corner in Upstate New York—and it was largely through her foresight that this story came to light.

Greg Johnson, my agent, provided the extra push I needed to climb that long, winding, writer's road. I also owe a debt of gratitude to my literary mentors: Lyn Cryderman, Joe Wheeler, Paul Dinas, James C. Humes, Philip Yancey, Corinna Fales, and the fine folks at Thomas Nelson, where I was blessed to work with crackerjack editors Joel Miller and Thom Chittom, as well as my longsuffering rubber-solemates, Kristen Parrish and Kristen Vasgaard.

Special thanks to Yvonne Newkirk Johnson, Judy Avery, Gordon White, Pamela Pond, Rod Chisholm, and Janis Bunchman for their genealogical information.

My sincere appreciation goes to the close-knit AVG Flying Tigers family, including Charlie Bond, Tex Hill, Bus Keeton, and Pete Wright for sharing their recollections of Scarsdale Jack. Frank Losonsky, Dick and Lydia Rossi, Chuck Baisden, Tom Pandolfi, and Dick Peacher helped with AVG research, and David Lee Miller made the Flying Tigers patches on my leathers.

John Dojka and Amy Rupert, archivists at Rensselaer Polytechnic Institute, provided invaluable historical information, as did Michael Barnes of the Authentic History Center. Steve Slocombe, Dave "Rat" Scherk, Pete Gagan, and Scott Collignon helped me with the ins and outs of the Harley-Davidson 1930–1936 VL Big Twin, and Michael Paquette of Worsham Castle Cycle Leather supplied my vintage saddlebags.

Thanks also go to my German teacher Eric Lassner, my flute teacher Maralyn Prestia, and of course Aaron Copland, who showed me that it's still OK to meet your heroes.

And here's to my biker bro's Jazda and Nico, who lost their fathers during the writing of this book, to Wreckerman who lost his wife—to Bear and BadBikerKitty (RIP), Atch, Wide, SchimDog, Ozbiker, Hellswraith, Tony, Drebbin, Thorsblood, HighNWide, Julie, Whodatt, FallenHarleyAngel, BlackDog—you were the bridge beneath my wheels.

And to my wife, Melissa, for her forbearance—as she is the antithesis of biker culture.

# Selected Bibliography

Appelbaum, Stanley. *The New York World's Fair 1939/1940*. New York: Dover Publications, 1977.

Bond, Charles R. and Terry H. Anderson. *A Flying Tiger's Diary*. Texas A&M University Press, 1984.

Caras, Roger. *The Custer Wolf: Biography of a Renegade*. New York: Puffin Books, 1971.

Center of Military History. *The Admiralties*. Washington, D.C.: U.S. Government Printing Office, 1946.

Clements, Terrill. *American Volunteer Group Colours and Markings*. New York: Osprey Publishing, 2001.

Cornelius, Wanda and Thayne Short. *Ding Hao: America's Air War in China, 1937–1945*. Pelican Publishing Company, 1980.

Cummins, D. Duane and William Gee White. *Contrasting Decades: The 1920s and the 1930s*. New York: Benziger, 1972.

Drimmer, Frederick. *Captured by the Indians: 15 Firsthand Accounts*. New York: Dover Publications, 1985.

Ford, Daniel. *Flying Tigers: Claire Chennault and the American Volunteer Group*. Smithsonian Institution Press, 1991.

Friedman, Milton and Rose. *Free to Choose: A Personal Statement*. New York: Harcourt, 1980.

Gelernter, David. *1939: The Lost World of the Fair*. New York: Avon, 1995.

Greenlaw, Olga. *The Lady and the Tigers*. New York: Dutton, 1943.

Hill, David Lee and Maj. Reagan Schaupp, USAF. *"Tex" Hill: Flying Tiger*. San Antonio: Universal Bookbindery, 2003.

Losonsky, Frank S. and Terry Losonsky. *Flying Tiger: A Crew Chief's Story*. Schiffer Publishing Ltd., 1996.

Murray, Presbrey, & Van Dyke, Boy Scouts of America Editorial Board. *Third Edition of the Handbook for Boys*. New York: 1927–1940.

Oehler, C. M. *The Great Sioux Uprising*. New York: Oxford University Press, 1959.

Pistole, Larry M. *The Pictorial History of the Flying Tigers*. Publisher's Press, 1981.

Pollack, Howard. *Aaron Copland: The Life and Work of an Uncommon Man*. New York: Henry Holt and Company, 1999.

Schultz, Duane. *Over the Earth I Come: The Great Sioux Uprising of 1862*. New York: St. Martin's Press, 1992.

Schultz, Duane. *The Maverick War: Chennault and the Flying Tigers*. New York: St. Martin's Press, 1987.

Simon, George. *Glenn Miller and his Orchestra*. New York: T.Y. Crowell Co., 1974.

Slocombe, Steve. *Harley-Davidson 1930–36 Big Twins: Buying, restoring, and riding a VL*. Folkestone, England: VL Heaven Publications, 2005.

Wagner, Herbert. *Harley-Davidson, 1930–1941: Revolutionary Motorcycles and Those Who Rode Them*. Atglen, PA: Schiffer Publishing, Ltd., 1996.

Wells, Elmer. *Patterns of Life*. Denver: Private Collection, 1980.